Evidence Textbook

6th edition

William Bojczuk
LLB, MA, Barrister

Revised and updated by D G Cracknell
LLB, Barrister

Yegappan Muthupalaniyappan, Bar Finals

HLT Publications

HLT PUBLICATIONS
200 Greyhound Road, London W14 9RY

First published 1989
6th edition 1994
© The HLT Group Ltd 1994

Acknowledgement
The publishers and author would like to thank the Incorporated Council of Law Reporting for England and Wales for kind permission to reproduce extracts from the Weekly Law Reports.

ISBN 0 7510 0285 2

British Library Cataloguing-in-Publication.
A CIP Catalogue record for this book is available from the British Library.

Printed and bound in Great Britain

Contents

Preface

HLT Textbooks are written specifically for students. Whatever their course, they will find our books clear and precise, providing comprehensive and up-to-date coverage. Written by specialists in their field, our textbooks are reviewed and updated on an annual basis.

Many changes have been made in this edition. While most of them reflect recent judicial decisions, note is made of the Sexual Offences Act 1993 and of relevant provisions of the Criminal Justice Act 1993.

Cases covered in the text include *R* v *McLeod* (1994) The Times 14 April (cross-examination of defendant on previous convictions), *R* v *Jefferson* [1994] 1 All ER 270 ('appropriate adult') and *C (a minor)* v *Director of Public Prosecutions* (1994) The Times 30 March. The decision of the Court of Appeal in *R* v *Smurthwaite* [1994] 1 All ER 898 (discretion as to evidence of undercover police officers) is also of particular significance.

Developments up to 1 May 1994 have been taken into account.

Table of Cases

Table of Statutes

1

Introduction

1.1 Relevance

Relevance and admissibility

The purpose of calling evidence in court is to try to prove certain facts to be true. Evidence which assists in this process is relevant and that which does not assist is irrelevant. It is the first rule of evidence, and one to which there are no exceptions, that irrelevant evidence is never admissible in court. This does not mean that relevant evidence is always allowed, because sometimes the court disallows it despite its relevance. The greater proportion of this book is about rules which limit the extent to which relevant evidence may be used. It is necessary first to consider exactly what is meant by relevance.

The issues in every case can be divided into two types. First, there are those which are directly relevant to the decision the court has to make. For example, on a theft charge the Crown must prove that: (a) the accused acted dishonestly; (b) in appropriating property; (c) which belonged to another; and (d) that he intended to deprive that other person of his property permanently. In order for the defendant to be convicted the Crown must prove each of these facts. They are known as the facts in issue. It is possible for an accused person to make binding admissions so as to narrow the field of investigation. For example, he might accept that he acted

1

dishonestly in appropriating property and that he intended to keep it, thereby leaving only the question whether it belonged to another. If this were done the only fact in dispute would be issue (c), but the Crown would still have to prove the other issues by telling the court of the admissions which had been made.

Proof of facts in issue can be achieved by witnesses or documents which show directly that that fact is true, or by evidence from which the only proper inference is that the fact is true. For example, in a negligence case arising out of a motor accident, failure to take reasonable care when driving a car could be proved by a passenger saying that the driver did not have his hands on the steering wheel at the relevant time, or by evidence that the car went out of control but was mechanically fit. The passenger's evidence is direct evidence of failure to take reasonable care when driving. The other evidence does not directly show lack of care, but from the circumstances it is clear that the driver must have been negligent because there is no other explanation for what happened. In other words, from the circumstances which are proved, the court can infer that there was negligence. Evidence which proves a case in this way is known as circumstantial evidence and, contrary to popular opinion, can be sufficient to prove both civil and criminal cases.

The second type of issue relates to the evidence which is called in order to prove the facts in issue. If the only evidence the prosecution calls on the disputed issue is that of someone who says he was the owner of the goods in question but who appears to be thoroughly dishonest in the witness box and can produce no evidence to substantiate his claim of ownership, the accused may be acquitted. This is not because there is no evidence on issue (c), but because the evidence is insufficient to prove that issue. The truthfulness of the witness is not directly relevant on the question of whether the defendant committed the offence, but it is indirectly relevant in that it is around his truthfulness or lack of truthfulness that the trial will revolve.

Therefore evidence about the reliability and honesty of witnesses is relevant, even though it does not of itself tell the judge or jury anything about the defendant. And it follows from this that the court is not entitled to prevent a party from calling evidence about the reliability of witnesses, although as we will see there are limitations on the right to call evidence about that matter.

Many cases involve the calling of a number of witnesses, none of whom is able to give the court the full picture of what happened, but who can do so when they are all considered together. It is often said to the jury in Crown Court trials that they should look at the evidence as the pieces of a jigsaw, putting the pieces together to form the whole picture. If they do not feel that they are able to form a clear picture at all, the prosecution will not have proved its case. But it is clear that each piece of evidence need not be self-sufficient. It need not be directly relevant, and it is enough if it becomes relevant by comparison with the other evidence called.

1.2 Advance notice

Civil proceedings

Where there is a dispute of fact in civil proceedings the parties exchange pleadings in which each sets out the facts which he claims to be true. Any allegation made in evidence which is not made in the pleadings will be treated with scepticism, although the judge may allow amendment even during the course of the trial.

There is no advantage to be gained by keeping one's case secret and any delay caused by late amendment of pleadings is likely to result in the defaulter having to pay the costs incurred by delay, even if he wins the case at the end of the day.

In all civil disputes where documents may be of relevance, each side should allow each other party to examine relevant documents. This is the stage of civil litigation known as discovery.

In the High Court discovery occurs as provided by RSC Ord 24. Detailed discussion of Ord 24 is outside the scope of this book: see, however, 8.1 'Disclosure of documents'. The general principle is that each party must disclose all relevant documents once all pleadings have been served. The test of relevance is not the documents' probative value but whether they might or could reasonably be expected to provoke a line of enquiry which would be of assistance to a party to the proceedings: *The Captain Gregos* (1990) The Times 21 December. Discovery has two stages, first, the exchange of lists in which relevant documents are described, and secondly the inspection of documents on the list.

Each list must be divided into two schedules of which the first is in two parts. Schedule 1 lists those documents which are in the party's possession, custody or control. Part 1 of Schedule 1 lists those documents which the party is content to allow his opponent to see. Part 2 lists those documents for which privilege is claimed, in other words, which the party serving the list claims to be entitled to withhold from his opponent. Schedule 2 lists those documents which were once within the possession custody or control of the party but are not any longer. The inspection of documents is usually effected by a request for copies which are sent by post.

Expert evidence may only be called in civil courts if the expert's report has been disclosed in advance. This is usually done without any need for the court to order it: see also 10.3 'Rules of court'.

As the modern approach to the conduct of litigation requires the earliest possible identification of both the real issues and the relative strengths of the parties, the exchange of witness statements prior to trial under RSC Ord 38, r2A is an important and appropriate procedure, the normal rule being for simultaneous exchange. No exception applies to jury trials in general or as a class to jury trials involving claims for wrongful arrest and false imprisonment. It is wrong to make a general order that all witness statements so served should stand as examination-in-chief at trial. Regard should be had to the circumstances of the case, in particular to the type of evidence and witness, the degree of controversy and credibility involved and the mode of trial: *Mercer* v *Chief Constable of Lancashire* [1991] 2 All ER 504.

Since 16 November 1992 parties have been required to exchange statements of all oral evidence which they intend to adduce on any issues of fact to be decided at the trial. Such an exchange has to take place within 14 weeks (High Court) or 10 weeks (county court) of close of pleadings. The parties can call no other witnesses nor add to the evidence of those whose statements have been disclosed without the leave of the court.

For procedure when a trial judge directs that a witness statement do stand as the evidence-in-chief of the witness and directs that such statement be certified as open to inspection, see *Practice Direction* [1992] 4 All ER 679.

As to the compulsory exchange of witness statements in county court proceedings, see CCR Ord 20, r12A, as substituted.

See also s5 of the Courts and Legal Services Act 1990 (power to make rules requiring any party to civil proceedings to serve on the other parties a written statement of the oral evidence which he intends to adduce). This provision does not prejudice any other power to make rules of court: ibid, s5(3). A power to make rules regarding evidence given in arbitrations on small claims in county courts is contained in s6 of the 1990 Act.

Advance information

A person accused of an offence which could be tried either in the magistrates' court or the Crown Court is entitled to receive from the prosecution advance notice of the nature of the case he has to face. Section 144 of the Magistrates' Courts Act 1980 allows the Lord Chancellor to make regulations providing for advance information to be given to the defence. The relevant rules are the Magistrates' Courts (Advance Information) Rules 1985, as amended.

The rules apply to 'either way' offences only (r2). As soon as is practicable after the accused is charged or a summons issued he should be given a notice informing him of his right to advance information (r3). If he makes no request he is not entitled to receive anything, although as a matter of practice the Crown Prosecution Service often prepares information and gives it to an accused person whether he asks for it or not.

The information to which he is entitled is a copy of those parts of every statement which contains information about the facts the prosecution proposes to use in court, or a summary of those facts (r4). Whether he gets copies of statements or a summary of the allegations is a matter for the prosecution. Photocopiers make it easier for copies of statements to be given and do not require anyone at the Crown Prosecution Service to compile a summary, so it is normally copies of statements which are given.

Magistrates' courts may not decide in which court the case should be heard until they are satisfied that the accused has received advance information. In some

London courts stipendiary magistrates have adopted the practice of inviting the prosecutor to allow defence advocates to see the original statements in his file where advance information has not been prepared. This saves costs but is only appropriate where there are few statements because of the difficulty of considering all aspects of the papers when in court.

Preparatory hearings

Where a Crown Court judge believes that he is confronted by a case of fraud of such seriousness and complexity that substantial benefits are likely to accrue from a preparatory hearing, he may order that such a hearing be held: s7(1) of the Criminal Justice Act 1987. This procedure is quite distinct from an informal pre-trial review: *R* v *Gunawardena* [1990] 2 All ER 477.

If a judge orders a preparatory hearing, he may also order the prosecution to prepare and serve any documents that appear to him to be relevant and whose service could be ordered at the preparatory hearing by virtue of Part I of the 1987 Act or Crown Court Rules: s7(3) of the 1987 Act. Where a judge has made an order under subsection (3) above and the prosecution have complied with it, the judge may order the person indicated or, if the indictment charges a number of persons, any of them to prepare and serve any documents that appear to him to be relevant and whose service could be so ordered at the preparatory hearing: ibid, s7(4).

At the preparatory hearing the judge may determine any question as to the admissibility of evidence: s9(3)(b) of the 1987 Act. He may also order the prosecution to supply the court and the defendant or, if there is more than one, each of them with a statement (a 'case statement') of the principal facts of the prosecution case, the witness who will speak to those facts, and any exhibits relevant to those facts: ibid, s9(4)(a). Where the prosecution has complied with such an order, the judge may order each defendant to give the court and the prosecution a statement in writing setting out in general terms the nature of his defence and indicating the principal matters on which he takes issue with the prosecution: s9(5) of the 1987 Act. After a defence statement has been served, the Serious Fraud Office may re-interview witnesses for further statements on matters arising from the defence statement: *R* v *Nadir* [1993] 4 All ER 513.

The court has no power to direct a defendant to serve a copy of his statement on the other defendants: *Re Tariq* [1991] 1 All ER 744.

An order or ruling made at or for the purpose of a preparatory hearing has effect during the trial, unless it appears to the judge, on application made to him during the trial, that the interests of justice require him to vary or discharge it: s9(10) of the 1987 Act. Where there has been a preparatory hearing, any party may depart from the case which he disclosed at the hearing but, in the event of such a departure or of failure to comply with a requirement imposed at the hearing, the judge or, with the leave of the judge, any other party may make such comment as appears to him to be appropriate and the jury may draw such inference as appears proper: ibid, s10(1).

Committal statements

All criminal cases start in the magistrates' courts. Those which go to the Crown Court for trial are sent there by the magistrates who commit the accused for trial. Committal for trial is the result of a court hearing which is often a formality because the defence does not challenge the evidence in any way. Nevertheless, evidence must be produced to the court to show that there is a case to answer, that is, that the case against the defendant is sufficiently strong that a jury could convict him. This evidence will either be given by witnesses on oath or, more commonly, be in the form of written statements.

These statements must be in the form prescribed by s102 of the Magistrates' Courts Act 1980, which requires them to be signed by their maker and to contain a declaration that they are made knowing that if they are false the maker is liable to prosecution. Written statements taken from witnesses living outside the jurisdiction may be tendered in evidence in commital proceedings but it is not permissible to read them at any subsequent trial: *R* v *Bateman* (1991) The Times 9 October.

If objection is made to the admission of evidence in the form of a written statement, that evidence must be given orally by the witness under oath: *R* v *Barnet Justices, ex parte Wood* [1992] Crim LR 312.

In cases where either the prosecution or the defence wishes to test the strength of the Crown's case, there will be a hearing of oral evidence or a consideration of the witness statements to see whether they disclose a prima facie case: s6(1) Magistrates' Courts Act 1980. The vast majority of committal hearings, however, do not require the magistrates to consider any evidence because the defence concedes that there is a case to answer. In such cases the witness statements are handed into court but not read and no oral evidence is given. A committal for trial without consideration of the evidence is known as a 'new-style committal' or a 's6(2) committal', the power to commit cases in this way being derived from s6(2) of the Magistrates' Courts Act 1980. Committals where evidence is heard are, not surprisingly, known as 'old-style committals' or 's6(1) committals'.

From the point of view of the defence the greatest use of committal hearings is that they give an opportunity to assess the evidence which the accused faces. Advance information frequently does not disclose every statement, the gaps being filled at committal. At trial in the Crown Court the defence has the advantage of the statements which are served at committal, those statements being the proofs of evidence of prosecution witnesses. With three exceptions the Crown does not have any opportunity to test the defence case before trial. The three exceptions are where:

1. the defendant has been interviewed by the police and given his version of events;
2. the defence is one of alibi; and
3. The defence relies on expert evidence.

The second and third of these require separate discussion.

Alibi defences

An alibi defence is a defence in which the accused says that, at the time the offence is alleged to have been committed, he was not at the scene of the crime but was elsewhere, so he could not have committed it: Criminal Justice Act 1967 s11(8); see *R v Johnson* (1994) The Times 22 March (evidence must be that defendant was at some other place). Evidence in support of such a defence may only be given at the Crown Court with the leave of the court unless the defence served a notice on the prosecution within seven days from the date of the committal hearing giving details of the facts upon which the alibi defence is based: Criminal Justice Act 1967, s11(1) and (2). There is no need to serve an alibi notice unless the case is tried in the Crown Court.

At the committal hearing in the magistrates' court the defence and prosecution are asked whether the 'alibi warning' should be given. This is a warning to the accused of the effect of s11(1) and (2) of the Criminal Justice Act 1967. The failure to give the alibi warning prevents the Crown Court from refusing leave to allow alibi evidence: Criminal Justice Act 1967 s11(3).

The requirement in the 1967 Act that the defence gives notice of the details of any alibi it may wish to rely on, is not as strict as may appear at first sight. The prosecution can always ask for the case to be adjourned to allow the alibi to be investigated. Indeed, if the alibi raises questions of fact which will take a long time to investigate, the jury can be discharged and the case listed for hearing at a later date once the police have finished their investigations. In *Sullivan* [1971] 1 QB 253 the Court of Appeal held that failure by a Crown Court judge to allow evidence of an alibi will be a good ground of appeal. If the defence has given notice of alibi very late, or if the police's investigations of the alibi have shown that it is spurious, these are matters which can be given in evidence by the Crown. The jury can then consider the alibi and the prosecution's evidence and can reach whatever conclusion is appropriate.

The burden is on the Crown to disprove an alibi defence and the jury should acquit if they think evidence in support of an alibi might be true: *R v Anderson* [1991] Crim LR 361. There is no general rule of law that a direction to the jury as to the burden of proof in relation to alibi evidence has to be given in all cases where alibi is raised as a defence, but it is good practice to do so: *R v Preece* (1993) 96 Cr App R 264.

Expert evidence

Apart from alibi evidence, the only instance in which the defence in a criminal case must disclose its evidence is where it wishes to rely upon expert evidence. This applies to the prosecution as well. Section 81 of the Police and Criminal Evidence Act 1984 allows rules to be made about this. Rule 3 of the Crown Court (Advance Notice of Expert Evidence) Rules 1987 requires the service of a notice as soon as possible before trial if either the prosecution or defence wishes to adduce expert evidence. The notice must not just say that a particular expert is to be called, but must state the substance of the evidence he is to give.

Rule 5 provides that expert evidence may not be relied on if no notice is served. It is likely that the Court of Appeal would apply the reasoning in *Sullivan* to any appeal which argues that the trial judge was wrong to refuse to allow the defence to rely on expert evidence where no notice has been served. Where no notice is served the court should adjourn the case or stand it out to be heard once the Crown has had a chance to instruct its own expert.

1.3 Functions of judge and jury

Questions of fact

With a few exceptions it is for the jury to decide questions of fact and for the judge to decide questions of law. The only exceptions to this general rule are instances where the judge decides questions of fact. There are no times when the jury must decide a matter of law.

The distinction between questions of fact and law is not always clear. A particular difficulty comes with the construction of statutes because words in statutes can have special meanings which may not be appreciated by a jury unless the judge tells them of the special meaning. It is not possible to give an exhaustive list of statutes which use ordinary words as technical terms. In *Brutus* v *Cozens* [1973] AC 854 the House of Lords held that the words 'insulting behaviour' in s5 of the Public Order Act 1936 were not used in a technical sense and therefore the judge should leave the jury to assess whether they feel the defendant exercised such behaviour. Where words are used in a technical sense it is for the judge to explain their special meaning to the jury.

Two questions of fact are for the judge and not the jury. The first arises where there is a question whether evidence is admissible, and its admissibility depends upon the proof of certain facts. For example, if it is alleged that a question need not be answered because the answer would disclose information which is privileged, the judge will have to decide whether there is a true claim to privilege. This may require evidence to be given and it will be for the judge to assess that evidence and decide whether the facts from which privilege arises are proved.

The second time when the judge decides questions of fact arises where foreign law is relevant. In English courts, the state of foreign law is a question of fact and is tried by the judge hearing evidence from experts in the field. Questions of foreign law are questions of fact in all jury trials, no matter the court in which the trial takes place: High Court: s69(5) Supreme Court Act 1981; county court: s68 County Courts Act 1984; Crown Court: *R* v *Hammer* [1923] 2 KB 786.

Where there is the slightest doubt as to which issues should be left to the jury, the judge should raise the matter with counsel, at the latest before the commencement of the final speeches, in order that the matter may then be resolved: *R* v *Wren* (1993) The Times 13 July.

In *Berry* v *R* [1992] 3 All ER 881 it appeared that the jury in the circuit court in Kingston, Jamaica, had returned after an hour's deliberation and indicated that they had a problem with the evidence. The judge reminded the jury, inter alia, that they were the sole judges of the facts, but he did not find out what was the problem. In giving the Privy Council's decision on the appeal, Lord Lowry said:

> 'Their Lordships have already met this difficulty in some other recent cases. The jury has sought assistance and, once it appears that the problem is one of fact, the judge has not inquired further but has merely given general guidance, as in the present case. The jury are entitled at any stage to the judge's help on the facts as well as on the law. To withhold that assistance constitutes an irregularity which may be material depending on the circumstances, since, if the jury return a guilty verdict, one cannot tell whether some misconception or irrelevance has played a part. If the judge fears that the foreman may unwittingly say something harmful, he should obtain the query from him in writing, read it, let counsel see it and then give openly such direction as he sees fit. If he has decided not to read out the query as it was written, he must ensure that it becomes part of the record. Failure to clear up a problem which is or may be legal will usually be fatal, unless the facts admit of only one answer, because it will mean that the jury may not have understood their legal duty. The effect of failure to resolve a factual problem will vary with the circumstances ...'

Where a person is charged with importuning for an immoral purpose, contrary to s32 of the Sexual Offences Act 1956, it is for the judge to rule, in the light of earlier decisions, whether a particular purpose is capable of being immoral and for the jury to decide whether it was: *R* v *Kirkup* [1993] 2 All ER 802.

Questions of law

Legal argument is not subject to rules of evidence in that evidence is not called to establish what the law is. Rather, there is argument in which law reports and textbooks are cited. Arguments on points of law take place in the absence of the jury but in the presence of the parties, including the accused in criminal trials.

The admissibility of evidence is a question of law. If evidence is required in order for the judge to decide whether a particular piece of evidence is admissible or inadmissible, that evidence is given at a trial within a trial. This is often known as a trial on the voir dire or, for short, a voir dire.

In all cases, whether or not there is a jury, there may be a submission that there is no case to answer. This happens most frequently in criminal trials in the Crown Court. We will see in Chapter 3 that in general the prosecution must prove every element of the offence charged. At the close of the Crown's case the judge will be entitled to withdraw the case from the jury and direct them to acquit the accused if so little evidence is called that one or more of the elements cannot be proved. It is not for the judge to decide whether the case is proved. But he may rule that a conviction is impossible on the evidence which has been called because it is wholly inadequate. For example on a charge of handling stolen goods the prosecution must call evidence that the goods in question were stolen goods. If there is no evidence at all on this issue, there is no possibility of the jury returning a verdict of guilty, so the judge may direct an acquittal.

The Court of Appeal laid down the proper approach to submissions of no case to answer in *Galbraith* [1981] 1 WLR 1039. The relevant rules are three. First, if there is no evidence that the accused committed the offence charged, the judge must direct an acquittal. Secondly, if there is some evidence but it is so poor that no jury could properly convict upon it, he must direct an acquittal. And thirdly, if there is evidence against the accused which may or may not be sufficient to justify conviction depending upon the weight which is given to it, the judge must leave the case to the jury: see also *Daley* v *R* [1993] 4 All ER 86. The same principles apply in magistrates' courts: *Practice Direction* [1962] 1 All ER 448.

In civil trials the principles in *Galbraith* also apply. But in trial by judge alone the defence must be wary of making a submission because no evidence may be called if the submission is unsuccessful: *Alexander* v *Rayson* [1936] 1 KB 169.

Where a submission of no case is wrongly rejected in criminal proceedings the accused will succeed on appeal, because the result of the judge's error is that he was not acquitted whereas he should have been. In *Abbott* [1955] 2 QB 497 it was held that the appellate court may not consider both the evidence called by the Crown and that called by the defence in order to assess whether the accused was rightly convicted. This went contrary to the earlier case of *Power* [1919] 1 KB 572 in which it was held that the defence evidence is relevant on appeal and that the court would only allow an appeal if the conviction was not merited on the whole of the evidence. The Court of Appeal in *Cockley* (1984) 79 Cr App R 181 upheld *Abbott*. It is therefore the law that the wrongful rejection of a submission of no case is a good ground of appeal no matter how strong the evidence against the accused at the end of his case.

After the judge has ruled that there is a case to answer, the prosecution cannot be discontinued, or a plea to a lesser charge accepted, without his consent: see *R* v *Grafton* [1992] 4 All ER 609.

The wrongful rejection of a submission of no case in a civil jury trial will not necessarily be a good ground of appeal. In *Payne* v *Harrison* [1961] 2 QB 403 the Court of Appeal held that a party to civil litigation who makes a submission of no case to answer is free to call evidence when that submission is rejected. If he does so, but that evidence strengthens his opponent's case, he cannot properly complain about the jury's verdict because, as Holroyd Pearce LJ said: 'Truth has superseded hypothesis'.

The difference between the principles applicable on wrongful rejection of a submission of no case in criminal and civil cases is explainable by the different functions of the Court of Appeal when sitting in its Criminal and Civil Divisions. The Criminal Division must allow an appeal where, because of an error of law by the judge, the defendant has been convicted rather than acquitted. The Civil

Division, however, is not bound by such a rule and may decide the case according to the whole of the evidence.

1.4 Oaths

Oaths of witnesses

With the exception of some evidence given by children in criminal proceedings, no oral evidence may be given unless the witness has promised to tell the truth. The promise normally takes the form of an oath. Section 1(1) of the Oaths Act 1978 provides that the witness should take the New Testament, or if Jewish the Old Testament, in his uplifted hand and say 'I swear by Almighty God that ...' followed by the words of the relevant oath. By s1(3) any person who is neither Christian nor Jewish may take an oath in any lawful manner.

The normal form of oath for a witness is: 'I swear by Almighty God that the evidence I give shall be the truth, the whole truth, and nothing but the truth.' Muslims normally hold the Koran rather than the Old or New Testament and say 'Allah' in place of 'Almighty God'. Appropriate adjustments are made for witnesses of other religions.

Someone who objects to taking an oath may affirm: Oaths Act 1978, s5(1). The form of affirmations is: 'I [name] do solemnly, sincerely and truly declare and affirm that the evidence I shall give will be the truth, the whole truth, and nothing but the truth.' Where a witness wishes to swear on a religious book but the court does not have a copy of that book and it is not reasonably practicable to obtain one without inconvenience or delay, he should affirm: Oaths Act 1978, s5(2).

Witnesses' oaths are the same in civil and criminal courts, with the exception of any oath in the youth court and the oath taken by those of 14 to 17 years of age. In these instances the oath is 'I promise before Almighty God' etc, rather than 'I swear ...': Children and Young Persons Act 1963, s28(1), as amended.

Whether administration of an oath to a witness was lawful within s1 of the Oaths Act 1978 does not depend on what might be the considerable intricacies of the particular religion adhered to by the witness, but on whether it was an oath which appeared to the court to be binding on the witness's conscience and, if so, whether it was an oath which the witness himself considered to be binding on his conscience: *R* v *Kemble* [1990] 1 WLR 111.

Other oaths

There are special forms of oath for jurors. Jurors in the Crown Court swear that they will 'faithfully try the defendant and give a true verdict according to the evidence', the obvious adjustment being made where there is more than one defendant to ensure that the juror is sworn to try the defendants and reach true verdicts. In civil courts jurors swear that they 'will well and truly try the issues joined between the parties and give a true verdict according to the evidence'.

Interpreters swear that they will 'well and truly interpret and explanation make [to the court] [to the witness] [to the defendant] of all such matters and things as shall be required of me to the best of my skill and understanding'.

A person who makes an affidavit must swear that its contents are true to the best of his knowledge and belief. By virtue of s113 of the Courts and Legal Services Act 1990, the right to administer oaths and take affidavits (and to use the title 'Commissioner for Oaths') was extended, inter alia, to authorised advocates and authorised litigators (as defined by s119(1) of the 1990 Act) as well as to practising solicitors and public notaries who are members of the Incorporated Company of Scriveners.

1.5 Competence and compellability

Introduction

A witness is competent if the law recognises him as fit to give evidence if he wishes to do so. He is compellable if he can be required to give evidence against his will. The general rule is that all persons are competent save for one or two categories of persons who are clearly unreliable. At common law there were many categories of incompetent witnesses such as the mentally unsound, children, defendants in criminal trials, accomplices, persons who had been convicted of a felony and the accused's husband or wife.

Over the years the strictness of the common law has steadily abated, the view being taken that unreliability or potential bias in a witness is something which should go to the strength of his or her evidence and not to whether he or she is allowed to give it. Nevertheless, some of the strict common law rules still apply.

There is a similarity between a law which says a witness may not give evidence and one which says that a witness who is competent may not give evidence about particular matters. All witnesses are subject to the law on privilege, which disallows them from giving evidence about certain facts. However, privilege only affects what someone may say in evidence, not his status as a competent witness.

All witnesses who are competent are also compellable subject to any limited exceptions. These will be considered along with the rules on competence.

Children

Criminal proceedings

In criminal proceedings, by virtue of s33A(1) of the Criminal Justice Act 1988 (as inserted by s52(1) of the Criminal Justice Act 1991) the evidence of a child (ie, a person under 14 years of age) is given unsworn. A deposition of a child's unsworn evidence may be taken for the purposes of such proceedings as if that evidence had been given on oath: ibid, s33A(2). Accordingly, the power of the court to determine that a particular person is not competent to give evidence applies to children of tender years as it applies to other persons: s52(2) of the 1991 Act.

There is no age limit below which a child cannot be competent. In *Wallwork* (1958) 42 Cr App R 153 the Court of Appeal said, obiter, that a child of five should not give evidence. In *R* v *B* [1990] Crim LR 511 the Court of Appeal affirmed that it could, very rarely, be that a child aged five would satisfy the requirements of s38(1) of the Children and Young Persons Act 1933, as amended but now repealed, but it was for the judge to exercise his discretion judicially in the light of established criteria. In *R* v *Z* [1990] 3 WLR 940 the Court of Appeal upheld the trial judge's decision to allow a girl then aged six to give unsworn evidence, by means of a video link, of events when she was five years of age.

The judge's investigation into the competence of a child witness must, it seems, be conducted in the presence of the parties and also in the presence of the jury, if there is one. In *Dunne* (1929) 21 Cr App 176 the trial judge took a seven-year-old child into his room and when they emerged ruled that she could give evidence. The Court of Criminal Appeal allowed the defendant's appeal, holding that investigation into the competence of a child witness should be conducted in court. The trial judge in *Reynolds* [1950] 1 KB 606 conducted the enquiry in court but in the absence of the jury. In this case also the accused's appeal was allowed, it being held that the jury should have been present because they must assess the child's evidence and their assessment may be affected by what they see and hear when competence is tested.

Screens. In a trial involving sexual abuse, a screen was erected to hide young children from the defendants: this arrangement was approved by the Court of Appeal in *R* v *X* (1989) The Times 3 November. Screens have been used with increasing frequency, but generally only where the witness is a child. Although screens have been used with adults, this should happen only in the most exceptional cases and by no means always in cases of rape and other sexual offences: *R* v *Schaub* (1993) The Times 3 December.

The guidelines set out in the *Report of the Enquiry into Child Abuse in Cleveland* should be regarded as expert advice as to what would normally be the best practice to adopt in seeking to ensure that a child's evidence is reliable: *R* v *Dunphy* (1993) The Times 2 June.

Television links. Children under the age of 14, when not the accused, may give evidence through a live television link on a trial on indictment for certain offences, including offences under s1 of the Children and Young Persons Act 1933 (cruelty to persons under 16) and the Sexual Offences Act 1956: s32(1)(b), (2) of the Criminal Justice Act 1988. In proceedings before a magistrates' court inquiring into like offences, a child is not to be called as a witness for the prosecution but any statement – which may include a transcript of a video tape of a child's interview with the police: *R* v *H* (1991) 155 JPR 561 – made by or taken from the child is admissible in evidence of any matter of which his oral evidence would be admissible: s103 of the Magistrates' Courts Act 1980, as inserted by s33 of the 1988 Act. However, there are exceptions to this rule, for example, where the prosecution requires the attendance of the child for the purpose of establishing the identity of any person.

Certain amendments were made to s32 of the 1988 Act by s55 of the Criminal Justice Act 1991. In particular, the use of live television links was extended to include:

1. Proceedings in youth (formerly juvenile) courts and appeals therefrom to the Crown Court, and youth courts are empowered to hear evidence by this means at any place appointed by the justices.
2. The case of sexual offences, to child witnesses up to the age of 17.
3. Cases where the witness is to be cross-examined following the admission of a video recording of testimony under s32A of the 1988 Act: see below.

Where a person is charged with certain offences involving children (ie, those to which s32(2) of the 1988 Act apply – sexual offences and offences involving violence or cruelty), in certain circumstances, and before the magistrates' court has begun to enquire into the case as examining justices, the Director of Public Prosecutions may by notice have the proceedings transferred to the Crown Court: s53 of the Criminal Justice Act 1991. By virtue of *Practice Note* [1992] 3 All ER 922, the transfer is to be made to a Crown Court centre equipped with live television link facilities.

Video recordings. Section 54 of the 1991 Act inserted s32A of the 1988 Act and so enables video recordings of testimony from child witnesses regarding sexual offences and offences involving violence or cruelty to be used in youth courts, Crown Courts and the Criminal Division of the Court of Appeal as the children's evidence-in-chief: s32A(1), (2) of the 1988 Act. The leave of the court is required, but the court must (subject to the exercise of any power of the court to exclude evidence which is otherwise admissible) give leave unless:

1. It appears that the child witness will not be available for cross-examination.
2. Any rules of court requiring disclosure of the circumstances in which the recording was made have not been complied with to the satisfaction of the court.
3. The court is of the opinion, having regard to all the circumstances of the case, that in the interests of justice the recording ought not to be admitted.

Where the court gives leave it may, if it is of the opinion that in the interests of justice any part of the recording ought not to be admitted, direct that that part shall be excluded: s32A(3) of the 1988 Act.

In considering whether any part of a recording ought to be so excluded, the court has to consider whether any prejudice to the accused, or one of the accused, which might result from the admission of that part is outweighed by the desirability of showing the whole, or substantially the whole, of the recorded interview: ibid, s32A(4).

Where a video recording is admitted under s32A, the child witness must be called by the party who tendered it in evidence and that witness must not be examined in chief on any matter which, in the opinion of the court, has been dealt with in his recorded testimony: ibid, s32A(5). Where a video recording is given in evidence under s32A, any statement made by the child witness which is disclosed by the recording is to be treated as if given by that witness in direct oral testimony. Accordingly, any such statement is admissible evidence of any fact of which such testimony from him would be admissible and no such statement is capable of corroborating any other evidence given by him. In estimating the weight, if any, to be attached to such a statement, regard is had to all the circumstances from which any inference can reasonably be drawn (as to its accuracy or otherwise): ibid, s32A(6).

In s32A 'child' means a person who, in the case of an offence involving assault or cruelty, is under 14 years of age or, if he was under that age when the video recording was made, is under 15 years of age; or in the case of sexual offence, is under 17 years of age or, if he was under that age when the video recording was made, is under 18 years of age; ibid, s32A(7).

These offences here include offences which consist of attempting or conspiring to commit, or of aiding, abetting, counselling, procuring or inciting the commission of, those offences: ibid, s32A(8).

A magistrates' court inquiring into an offence as examining justices under s6 of the Magistrates' Courts Act 1980 may consider any video recording as respects which leave under s32A of the 1988 Act is to be sought at the trial, notwithstanding that the child witness is not called at the committal proceedings (ibid, s32A(10)), although s53 of the 1988 Act (see above) enables such proceedings to be bypassed in certain cases. Nothing in s32A prejudices the admissibility of any video recording which would be admissible apart from that section: ibid, s32A(12).

Section 55(7) of the 1991 Act inserted s34A of the 1988 Act which provides that no person who is charged with a sexual offence or an offence involving cruelty or violence may cross-examine in person any witness who is a child or is to be cross-examined following the admission under s32A of the 1988 Act of a video recording of testimony from him.

For these purposes s32A(7) of the 1988 Act applies (see above), but with the omission of the references to a person being, in the cases there mentioned, under the age of 15 years or under the age of 18 years: ibid, s34A(2).

The procedure for making application for leave to adduce a video recording of testimony from a child witness under s32A of the 1988 Act is laid down in r23c of the Crown Court Rules 1982, as inserted by the Crown Court (Amendment) Rules 1992. Further detail is given in *Practice Note* [1992] 3 All ER 909.

Where a court grants leave to admit a video recording in evidence and directs that a part of the recording be excluded, the party who made the application to admit the video recording must edit the recording in accordance with the judge's directions and send a copy of the edited recording to the appropriate officer of the Crown Court and to every other party to the proceedings. Where a video recording is to be adduced during proceedings before the Crown Court, it should be produced and proved by the interviewer, or any other person who was present at the interview with the child at which the recording was made. The applicant should ensure that such a person will be available for this purpose, unless the parties have agreed to accept a written statement in lieu of attendance by that person. It is for the party adducing the video recording to make arrangements for the operation of the video playing equipment in court during the trial. Once a trial has begun, if by reason of faulty or inadequate preparations or for some other case these procedures have not been properly complied with, and an application is made to edit the video recording, thereby making necessary an adjournment for the work to be carried out, the court may make at its discretion an appropriate award of costs.

For the recommended approach to video interviews, see 'Memorandum of good practice on video-recorded interviews with child witnesses for criminal proceedings' published by HMSO.

Civil proceedings

Section 96(1), (2) of the Children Act 1989 provides that where a child who is called as a witness in any civil proceedings does not, in the opinion of the court, understand the nature of an oath, the child's evidence may be heard by the court if, in its opinion, he understands that it is his duty to speak the truth and he has sufficient understanding to justify his evidence being heard.

In this context a child is a person under the age of 18: ibid, s105(1). As to the order made under s96 regarding the admissibility of hearsay evidence, see 5.4, below.

The *mentally unsound*

In any proceedings a person who is unable to give coherent evidence because he suffers from mental illness is not a competent witness. In *Hill* (1851) 2 Den CC 254 the witness suffered from delusions but they did not affect his ability to recall the events about which he was called to give evidence, therefore he was competent.

If the judge is satisfied that a witness is competent, but during the course of his evidence it appears that he is no longer able to give coherent evidence, he becomes incompetent and the judge should prevent him from continuing and the judge or, if there is one, the jury must disregard any evidence given after he became incompetent: *Whitehead* (1866) LR 1 CCR 33. As with child witnesses, the judge should test the competence of a person of suspect mental soundness in open court in the presence of the jury.

Deafness and dumbness are not bars to competence, although for obvious reasons it is necessary for an interpreter to be sworn to use sign language if possible. In theory, a witness who is dumb and knows no sign language, may write down his answers to the questions put to him.

The *defendant in criminal proceedings*

Subject to the possibility of the defendant being an incompetent child, he is always competent to give evidence in his own favour: Criminal Evidence Act 1898, s1. There may be tactical reasons why he chooses not to give evidence, for example if he does not wish the jury to know that he has previous convictions or if he is aware of his guilt and is simply putting the Crown to proof, but these do not affect his ability to give evidence if he so chooses.

Section 1 of the 1898 Act gives defendants the right to give evidence from the witness box, as opposed to the dock, unless otherwise ordered, a right to be denied only in exceptional circumstances: *R* v *Farnham Justices, ex parte Gibson* [1991] RTR 309.

In *R* v *Everitt* (1989) The Times 29 December, the Court of Appeal said that the words of s1(b) of the Criminal Evidence Act 1898, that a defendant's failure to give evidence 'shall not be made the subject of any comment by the prosecution', meant that there should be no comment whatsoever by the prosecution, whether favourable or unfavourable. In the event of a breach of this rule, the court should consider whether it had been put right by the summing up: here, it had.

A defendant who exercises his right to silence by not answering questions when interviewed by the police after his arrest and declining to give evidence at his trial does not thereby in any way add credibility or weight to the evidence of an accomplice or any other prosecution witness: *R* v *Hubbard* [1991] Crim LR 449. Where a defendant decides not to give evidence, the judge should remind the jury in summary form of anything that the defendant may have said about the matter prior to the trial, but it is no part of the judge's duty to build up his defence: *R* v *Hillier* (1992) The Times 31 December.

Where counsel decides not to call a defendant to give evidence, either in defiance of or without proper instructions, or when all promptings of reason and good sense have pointed the other way, in an exceptional case any conviction could be set aside on the basis that it was unsafe and unsatisfactory: *R* v *Clinton* [1993] 2 All ER 998. See also 7.2, below.

One defendant (C) is not competent to give evidence for the Crown against another defendant (D): *Sharrock* (1948) 32 Cr App R 124. However, once C ceases to be a co-defendant he is competent for the prosecution against D. A co-defendant is someone who is charged in the same proceedings. He may be jointly charged, that is, he and D face a charge which accuses them of having acted together. But C is also a co-defendant if he and D face identical charges, albeit as separate counts on the indictment. Indeed, C and D will also be co-defendants if they are not charged on the same indictment or with the same offence, provided that they are tried at the same time. In short, those who sit in the dock together are co-defendants.

C will cease to be D's co-defendant once he is no longer being tried with D. This can happen in four ways: first, where C had pleaded guilty, secondly where the Attorney-General has entered a nolle prosequi, thirdly where the trial of C and D are heard separately and fourthly where C has been acquitted by the prosecution offering no evidence against him. C could be acquitted by making a successful submission that there is no case to answer, but this can only happen at the end of the prosecution case. In theory the Crown could apply to reopen their case by calling C to give evidence against D, but such an application is highly unlikely to be successful.

If C gives evidence in his own favour, anything he says which goes against D must be considered by the jury. In this way he can be a prosecution witness, albeit not one who is called by the prosecution. Although it only rarely happens, C may call D to give evidence: Criminal Evidence Act 1898, s1. In this event D is not compellable (Criminal Evidence Act 1898, s1(a)), but if he chooses to give evidence he may be cross-examined by the Crown with a view to proving his own guilt.

In *R* v *Palmer* (1993) The Times 5 October the Court of Appeal held that an alleged accomplice, who had been separately committed for trial and had pleaded guilty, could be called to give evidence against a defendant in committal proceedings before he had been sentenced. Russell LJ added that if two people were charged and it was sought to commit them together as co-defendants it would be an irregularity to bring down from the dock one man to give evidence against the other.

Parties' spouses

A defendant's husband or wife in criminal proceedings is competent to give evidence for the prosecution against any defendant including his or her spouse: Police and Criminal Evidence Act 1984, s80(1)(a). The only exception to this general rule is where husband and wife are jointly charged with an offence and jointly tried: s80(4). If they are tried separately each is competent for the Crown at the trial of the other, and if no evidence is offered against one, he or she is then competent at the trial of the other. A husband and wife are not 'jointly charged' if they are charged on separate counts in the same indictment: *R* v *Woolgar* [1991] Crim LR 545.

Spouses who are jointly tried are in the same position as all other defendants. We have seen that at common law one defendant is competent to give evidence for another, and s80(1)(b) of the 1984 Act provides that this is also the case between spouses. A defendant's spouse is also a competent witness to be called on behalf of any other defendant: s80(1)(b). In civil cases the only limit to the competence of spouses is that they must be sane.

The Police and Criminal Evidence Act 1984 provides rules for the compellability of the defendant's spouse, as well as for his or her competence. By s80(2) the spouse is compellable on behalf of the defendant, save that he or she is not compellable where the spouses are jointly charged: s80(4).

The defendant's spouse is only compellable for the Crown in a limited number of cases. They are defined in s80(3) of the 1984 Act, and are as follows. First, if the accused is charged with an offence which involves an assault on, or injury to, or threat of injury to, the spouse or a child under the age of 16. The child does not have to be a child of the defendant or his spouse. Secondly, where the accused is charged with having committed a sexual offence in respect of a child under 16. The sexual offence need not involve an assault on the child and the Act specifically refers to 'a sexual offence alleged to have been committed in respect of a person under 16'. This wording is very wide and catches any sexual offence which may involve a child. The third category of cases where the spouse is compellable is where the charge is one of attempting or conspiring or aiding and abetting or counselling and procuring or inciting the commission of one of the offences set out in the first two categories.

Former spouses of the defendant do not count as spouses for these purposes, so they are not subject to the limitations on competence and compellability set out in s80 (s80(5)). A divorced wife or husband is a competent and compellable witness in any proceedings after s80(5) came into force (1 January 1986), regardless of whether the events in question occurred before that date: *R* v *Cruttenden* [1991] 3 All ER 242.

In civil proceedings there remains a rule making former spouses of a party incompetent. Spouses were made competent to give evidence for any party by s1 of the Evidence Amendment Act 1853. But this Act did not extend to former spouses, with the result that the common law applies to them. According to *Monroe* v *Twistleton* (1802) Peake Add Cas, the former spouse of a party to civil proceedings is not competent to give evidence about matters which occurred during the course of the marriage. That case has never been overruled, so the position is that spouses may give evidence for or against each other, but a former spouse is wholly incompetent to testify about matters occurring during the marriage.

Compelling attendance

A compellable witness may decide quite voluntarily to attend court and give evidence without anybody having to apply any pressure. But if he is reluctant he may be ordered to attend by the court. The method of ordering someone to attend is essentially the same in all courts, namely, either a judge or an authorised officer of the court issues an order requiring attendance.

In the High Court the order made is known as a sub poena (RSC Ord 38 rr14-19). It can require the witness to attend and give evidence (sub poena ad testificandum) or can require him to produce a document to the court with or without him having to give oral evidence as well (sub poena duces tecum). In the county courts the order is known as a witness order (CCR Ord 20 r12), as it is in the magistrates' courts when they order someone to attend the Crown Court on the defendant's trial: Criminal Procedure (Attendance of Witnesses) Act 1965 s1(1). In both the Crown Court and the magistrates' courts, when sitting as trial courts, it is a witness summons: Criminal Procedure (Attendance of Witnesses) Act 1965 s2(1) and

Magistrates' Courts Act 1980 s97(1), respectively. A witness summons issued under s2 of the 1965 Act must relate to evidence that is not only material but also admissible: *R* v *Clowes* [1992] 3 All ER 440.

A witness who does not attend court when ordered or summoned to do so is liable to have a warrant issued for his arrest: see *R* v *Bradford Justices, ex parte Wilkinson* [1990] RTR 59. Failure to attend, without just excuse, is a contempt of court (s3(1) of the 1965 Act) and culpable forgetfulness is not such an excuse: *R* v *Lennock* (1993) The Times 16 March.

Until the coming into force of the Children Act 1989, a witness summons could be issued under s97 of the Magistrates' Courts Act 1980 to secure the presence of a child party in care proceedings. However, in the exercise of his discretion, a magistrate would not make such an order where it would be oppressive to do so, or where he was satisfied that the summons would be so inimical to the child's welfare that it outweighed the legitimate interest of the person seeking it or that in any event the child would not be permitted to give evidence at the oral hearing: *R* v *B County Council* [1991] 1 WLR 221; see now the Family Proceedings Courts (Children Act 1989) Rules 1991.

1.6 Examination of witnesses *popular area in exam.*

Definitions and general rules

The party who calls a witness is entitled to examine him by asking questions with a view to adducing from the witness evidence favourable to his case. This process is called examination in chief. In some circumstances the prosecution does not wish to examine its witness in chief, calling him simply to allow the defence to cross-examine him. But apart from this instance, all witnesses are examined in chief. Cross-examination is the process by which one party may ask questions of his opponent's witnesses in order to undermine their evidence or support that of his own witnesses. After witnesses are cross-examined they may be re-examined by the party who called them.

There are limits to the sorts of questions one may ask when examining a witness in chief. These will be discussed in more detail below, but in outline they are that leading questions may not be asked and one may not contradict one's witness either by evidence of his bad character or by evidence that he has previously made a statement inconsistent with what he says in the witness box.

In criminal trials, pre-trial discussions of evidence between potential witnesses, the rehearsal of evidence and the coaching of witnesses are strongly discouraged because of the risk of abuse: *R* v *Arif* (1993) The Times 17 June.

By virtue of RSC Ord 38, r3, (or CCR Ord 20, r8), in civil proceedings the court may order that evidence may be given by a witness in a foreign jurisdiction by means of a live television link with the court: *Garcin* v *Amerindo Investment Advisors*

Ltd [1991] 1 WLR 1140; see also *Arab Monetary Fund* v *Hashim (No 7)* [1993] 4 All ER 114 (evidence may be given by a video link). Similarly, a person other than the accused may give evidence through a live television link on, inter alia, a trial on indictment, if the witness is outside the United Kingdom: s32(1)(a) of the Criminal Justice Act 1988.

Leading questions

A party may not ask his witness leading questions. This rule is often misunderstood because it is not an absolute rule. It is common practice to lead a witness through certain parts of his evidence where it is known that these parts are not in dispute. The obvious example of this is the witness's name – one may quite properly say 'Are you Joe Bloggs and is your address 1 Acacia Avenue?' A witness may also be asked a leading question where the questions ask him to reply to evidence which has already been given. For example, the defendant may be asked 'The police officers said that they are able to identify you as the driver of the car which ran over Mrs Smith, what do you have to say about that?'

Leading questions come in two forms. One is a question which indicates to the witness the answer which is required, that is, a question which puts words into the witness's mouth. For example, if evidence is given that someone was run over by a car with registration number A123 BCD and the question for the court is whether the defendant was driving the car, a prosecution witness who says he saw the defendant on the same day should not be asked 'Was the defendant driving car number A123 BCD?', he should be asked 'What was the registration number of the defendant's car?'

The other sort of leading question is one which assumes something to be true when it has not been established. To adapt the example given above, before the witness has said whether he saw the defendant on the day in question he should not be asked 'What was the number of the car the defendant was driving when you saw him that day?' The asking of leading questions does not nullify proceedings, but the judge will stop an advocate from asking questions in the prohibited form. Furthermore, evidence given in answer to leading questions is not inadmissible. Clearly, however, where a witness has been led by the form of questioning to say things he might otherwise not have said, he may find that his evidence is given little weight by the judge or jury.

Hostile witnesses

As well as not being allowed to ask leading questions, subject to the exceptions mentioned above, a party may not usually contradict his witness or challenge his credibility by calling evidence of his bad character. Contradiction is allowed to the extent that one's witness may not give the evidence which is expected of him with the result that a later witness contradicts him. But he may not be contradicted by the questions he is asked during examination in chief. On occasions it is good tactics to ask one's witness to disclose his criminal record in order to avoid the element of surprise which accompanies one's opponent asking him about it, but in general this may not be done in order to discredit one's own witness.

In limited circumstances a party may contradict his own witness. What is required is that the witness is a hostile witness. A hostile witness is one who is deliberately giving evidence contrary to the statement he previously gave to the solicitors of the party calling him – his proof of evidence. Many witnesses 'fail to come up to proof' but this does not make them hostile if they try to recall matters as accurately as possible but, inevitably, forget certain details. Such a witness is said to be 'unfavourable' but the only way in which he may be contradicted is by calling other witnesses of fact whose testimony is different.

A hostile witness may be asked leading questions: *Bastin* v *Carew* (1824) Ry & M 127. He may also be asked about his character and any previous statement he has made. These last two matters are governed by s3 of the Criminal Procedure Act 1865, which applies in civil as well as criminal trials, and reads as follows:

> 'A party producing a witness shall not be allowed to impeach his credit by general evidence of bad character, but he may, in case the witness shall, in the option of the judge, prove adverse, contradict him by other evidence, or, by leave of the judge, prove that he has made at other times a statement inconsistent with his present testimony; but before such last-mentioned proof can be given the circumstances of the supposed statement, sufficient to designate the particular occasion, must be mentioned to the witness, and he must be asked whether or not he has made such statement.'

The effect of s3 is that a hostile witness may be attacked in two ways, first, by evidence being called about his character, including his criminal record; and secondly by proving that he has made a statement which is inconsistent with his evidence. Either of these methods of attack requires the leave of the trial judge, who will refuse it unless he feels the witness is being deliberately obstructive. In theory a witness who refuses to answer questions at all could not be asked about his previous statement, because s3 requires the witness's previous statement to be 'inconsistent with his present testimony'. But in *Thompson* (1976) 64 Cr App R 96 the Court of Appeal held that a witness whose hostility takes the form of a refusal to answer questions, may be asked about his previous statement. Section 3 makes no difference to the right of a party to contradict an unfavourable witness by calling witnesses who are favourable.

In criminal cases the previous statement of a hostile witness is not evidence of anything other than the fact that the witness has been inconsistent: *Golder* [1960] 1 WLR 1169. But in civil cases in the county court and High Court, it is evidence which the court can take into account: Civil Evidence Act 1968, s3(1)(a). What this means, in practical terms, can be illustrated as follows. The witness says in evidence that he saw a car which was blue, but in his statement said that it was red. In a criminal case the only evidence about colour is that it was blue, although the court may be sceptical about the truth of this in view of the witness's inconsistency;

whereas in the civil case there will be evidence both that it was blue and that it was red, and the court may take its pick.

Refreshing memory

A witness who is unable to remember the things he is asked to give evidence about may refresh his memory from any contemporaneous document of his. Such a document must have been made by the witness, or made by another and verified by him. Verification can occur by the witness, while matters are fresh in his mind, seeing what is written by another and accepting it as correct: *Whalley* (1852) 3 Car & Kir 54. He may have it read out to him and accept it as correct (*Langton* (1876) 2 QBD 296), but in such a case the writer should be called to state that what he read out is what the document said.

In *Kelsey* (1982) 74 Cr App R 213 the Court of Appeal reviewed the authorities in this area and held that the principle in *Langton* was correct, stressing that it is important that the maker of the document which was read to the witness and verified by him should confirm it was read accurately. The witness in *Kelsey* dictated a car registration number to a police officer who wrote it down and read it back to him. The officer's note was held to be a document from which the witness could refresh his memory because it had been read to him and accepted as accurate. Had it been read to the witness at some later time when matters were not fresh in his mind, he could not have relied on it. Although the person who wrote down what the witness said was a police officer, there is no need for him to be a policeman; the note of anyone who writes down what an eye-witness tells him may be used by that witness as a memory-refreshing document provided it is verified. The need for the witness to have verified the police officer's note was made clear in *Jones* v *Metcalfe* [1967] 3 All ER 205 where the witness did not verify the note and the Divisional Court held that the policeman could not give evidence of what he was told. The Court of Appeal on facts which were in all relevant respects indistinguishable from those in *Jones* v *Metcalfe*, upheld that case in *McLean* (1968) 52 Cr App R 80.

Refreshing memory can take one of two forms. Either the witness sees his note and this sparks his recollection, or he has no independent recollection at all and is simply able to say that his note was correct when he wrote it. There is nothing wrong with this second method of refreshing memory, although in reality the witness's memory is not really refreshed at all: *Maugham* v *Hubbard* (1828) 8 B & C 14, *Simmonds* (1967) 51 Cr App R 316.

A note may be used to refresh memory provided it was compiled at the first reasonable opportunity while events were still fresh in the mind of the witness: *Attorney-General's Reference (No 3 of 1979)* (1979) 69 Cr App R 411. It is sometimes said that the note must be contemporaneous, but this is wrong in so far as it suggests that the note must be written at the same time as the event it describes. The test for contemporaneity is in two parts; first, the note must have been made at the first reasonable opportunity, and secondly events must have been fresh in the mind of the witness. The purpose of the test is to ensure, so far as possible, that the note is accurate. By insisting that it should be compiled at the first reasonable opportunity, the court will prevent a witness from having the opportunity to sit back and think about events because that process often leads to witnesses reading a lot more into events than they actually saw. And insistence on it being made while events were fresh in the witness's mind reduces the risk of details being forgotten.

It is impossible to give a time limit within which a note must be made in order for it to have been made at the first reasonable opportunity. In most cases police officers write their notes within an hour or so of returning to the station after an incident, but this cannot be taken as a guideline to what is and what is not proper practice. Indeed in many cases the police officers involved wait until they are all able to meet to pool their recollections. Although this can lead to someone writing in his notebook that he witnessed something which he was told about at the station but did not in fact see, it also allows memories to be assisted. For example an officer who witnessed a particular piece of action may be reminded of it by another, thereby allowing the first officer's note to be a more accurate record of what he saw than it would otherwise be. The practice of pooling recollections was approved by the Court of Appeal in *Bass* [1953] 1 QB 680, in which it was recognised that the accuracy of the officer's recollection can be tested in cross-examination.

Cases on what is and what is not the first reasonable opportunity should be treated with caution because they are only examples and do not lay down time limits. In *Simmonds* Customs and Excise officers visited and interviewed the defendant without taking notes and then compiled notes about the interviews when they returned to their offices. This was held to be the first reasonable opportunity even though they could have taken notes during the interviews. The case establishes that the court must always bear in mind the practical considerations, such as the fact that it would extend the length of interviews if everything was written down as it was said, and much of what was said might be of no relevance at all. Similarly in *Richardson* [1971] 2 QB 484 the Court of Appeal said that the test is a flexible one. The point was further emphasised in *Attorney-General Reference (No 3 for 1979)* where a police officer wrote a full record of interview after the interview was over by referring to very brief notes made during the interview. The Court of Appeal held that the trial judge was wrong to rule that the officer could not refresh his memory from the full note. There is no definition of 'fresh in the mind of the witness'. It is taken to mean that the witness must still have had a clear memory of events undistorted by reflection and unclouded by the passage of time.

Normally a witness will refresh his memory by referring to the original note which he made or verified. If this is not possible he may use a copy provided it is proved that the copy is an accurate copy of a document which itself was compiled at the first reasonable opportunity when events were fresh in the witness's mind. For example, in *Cheng* (1976) 63 Cr App R 20 a police officer lost his notebook but was allowed to refresh his memory by reference to a statement which he made by copying parts of his notes. It is rare for witnesses to use photocopies of their original note, although this is permissible if the court is satisfied that it is a true copy of a document which could properly be used. Old authorities indicate that a witness who is only able to say that he knows his note was accurate but who has no independent recollection of events may only refresh his memory from the original note and not from a copy: see for example, *Doe d Church* v *Perkins* (1790) 3 Term Rep 749, *Harvey* (1869) 11 Cox CC 346. These cases were decided when copies were all written by hand and must be of doubtful authority in modern conditions where accurate photocopies of the original can be made.

During cross-examination a party may call for the memory-refreshing note to be handed to him so that he can see for himself what the witness is relying on. Normally the judge and jury do not see the note, but they will be allowed to do so in some circumstances. The rules are simple. If one party asks to see the memory-refreshing note of his opponent's witness, that of itself does not allow the court to see the note. If he asks questions about those parts which the witness has refreshed his memory from, the court also may not see the note. But if in cross-examination he asks about other parts of the note, the party calling the witness may require the note to be made an exhibit in the case, and the court may then look at it: *Senat* v *Senat* [1965] P 172. In civil cases in the High Court and county court the contents of the note are then evidence which the court may take into account: Civil Evidence Act 1968, s3(2). But in criminal hearings the note is only evidence of the consistency or inconsistency of the witness. Judges must be careful to avoid telling the jury in the Crown Court that memory-refreshing notes are anything other than evidence of the consistency of the witness. In *Virgo* (1978) 67 Cr App R 323 the judge said the note was the most important document in the case. The Court of Appeal allowed an appeal against conviction because that direction suggested that the note was evidence in the same way that what was said in the witness box was evidence.

To a degree, the strictness of the rule that memory may only be refreshed from a document compiled at the first reasonable opportunity while events were fresh in the witness's mind can be overcome by the witness looking at a document outside court before he is called to give evidence. That he may look at any document before he gives evidence, regardless of whether it could be used in court, was made clear in *Westwell* [1976] 2 All ER 812. It was also said, obiter, in that case that the Crown should inform the defence where this has been done in order to allow a challenge to the witness's powers of recollection, although no similar obligation is placed on the defence to inform the prosecution of what its witnesses have read. Until recently it was unclear whether in cross-examination a note used outside court for the refreshing of memory can be called for and inspected. In *Owen* v *Edwards* (1983) 77 Cr App R 191, however, the Divisional Court held that a document referred to out of court may be inspected and used as the basis for cross-examination in exactly the same way as can a document used in court.

Subject to certain conditions, it is open to the judge, in the exercise of his discretion and in the interests of justice, to permit a witness who has begun to give evidence to refresh his memory from a statement, such as a witness statement, made near to the time of the events in question, even though it does not come within the definition of contemporaneous: see *R* v *Da Silva* [1990] 1 WLR 31.

Cross-examination to credit

When one party opposes the case put forward by the other, he can call evidence himself and may also challenge his opponent's evidence by cross-examining his witnesses. Cross-examination can consist of a challenge to the evidence of the witness, perhaps by suggesting that he was mistaken, or a challenge to the witness's truthfulness. Whether it is appropriate to attack one's opponent's witnesses depends upon many factors, and the proper way of approaching each case is something which is learned by experience. But if it is decided to challenge the truthfulness of a witness the law limits the extent to which this can be done. In general one may question a witness about his truthfulness but may not call evidence to contradict his answers. The explanation given in the authorities is that to allow such evidence to be called would have the effect of raising unnecessary side-issues.

It is important to note that there is no limit to one's right to call evidence in support of one's case provided that evidence is relevant to the issues in dispute between the parties. The limit imposed by the rule under discussion here is a limit to the right to call evidence on collateral issues. A collateral issue is one which is only relevant to the credibility of the witness. One can test whether an issue is or is not collateral by asking whether it would be relevant if the witness had not given evidence. For example, if W gives evidence about what he saw, his account may be challenged by evidence from X that he saw something different, or by evidence from Y that W's eye-sight is defective. X would be allowed to give evidence even if W did not, because his evidence is directly relevant. But Y's evidence about W's eye-sight is only relevant because W has given evidence; had he not given evidence it would have been of no interest to the court at all.

The general rule preventing one from calling evidence on collateral issues emanates from *Attorney-General* v *Hitchcock* (1847) 2 Camp 637. To this rule there are five exceptions. They are that evidence may be given to show that a witness is biased, has previous convictions, has a reputation for untruthfulness, is unreliable because of some physical or mental disability or illness, or has made a statement inconsistent with what he has said in the witness box. Some of the older textbooks treat the third and fourth of these exceptions as special cases and not exceptions to the rule in *Attorney-General* v *Hitchcock*, presumably because they clearly pre-date that case.

In *R* v *Edwards* [1991] 2 All ER 266 the Court of Appeal affirmed that where cross-examination was directed at collateral issues, such as the credibility of the witness, as a rule the answers of the witness were final and evidence to contradict them would not be permitted. The rule was necessary to confine the ambit of a trial within proper limits and to prevent the true issue from becoming submerged in a welter of detail. However, there were exceptions to the rule of which bias was the most important. The court decided that, while it would be rare for a trial judge in his discretion to allow cross-examination on the activities of a witness in another case, where a police officer who had allegedly fabricated an admission, had also given evidence in an earlier case of an admission which the jury by its acquittal had manifestly disbelieved, it was proper for the jury in the later case to be made aware of that fact.

The potential for bias may arise in several ways, the most obvious of which is by the acceptance of a bribe. In *Attorney-General* v *Hitchcock* a witness was asked if he had been offered a bribe to give evidence against the defendant. He denied this and evidence was not allowed to contradict his answer because the mere offer of a bribe does not show possible bias, whereas the receipt of a bribe would. By contrast, in *Phillips* (1936) 26 Cr App R 17 children gave evidence against their father who faced charges of incest. They denied that they had been told by their mother what to say in court. The defence was not allowed to call evidence that they had been schooled in their evidence and the defendant was convicted. The Court of Criminal Appeal held this ruling to have been wrong because if the children had been schooled they could have been biased by reason of what their mother told them. In *Shaw* (1888) 16 Cox CC 503 it was held that evidence could be called to contradict a witness who denied having expressed animosity towards the defendant. In *Thomas* v *David* (1836) 7 C & P 350 evidence was allowed to contradict the evidence of a defence witness that she was not the defendant's mistress. Although *Thomas* v *David* was a civil case, the same principle applies in criminal trials, so the prosecution and defence have equal rights to call evidence to show potential bias in the other's witnesses. This was the position in *Mendy* (1976) 64 Cr App R 4 in which evidence was held admissible to show that the defendant's husband, who waited outside court until he gave evidence, had been spoken to by someone who had heard the evidence given by prosecution witnesses. There was a risk that the husband had been told what earlier witnesses had said, thereby giving rise to a risk that he was manipulating his evidence to suit his own ends and those of his wife.

A witness who is asked whether he has a criminal record may be contradicted if he denies it by proof from the Criminal Record Office's records: Criminal Procedure Act 1865 s6, as amended. This rule applies in both civil and criminal proceedings: Criminal Procedure Act 1865 s1. The defendant's criminal record, however, may only be disclosed in a criminal trial in limited circumstances which are discussed in Chapter 7.

Evidence may be given of a witness's bad reputation for truthfulness. This has been allowed at common law since before the general rule against calling evidence on collateral issues was established. These days it is extremely rare for anyone in any type of case to call evidence to show that his opponent's witness is a notorious liar, but that it may still be done despite the rule in the *Hitchcock* case was established by the Court of Criminal Appeal in *Gunawardena* [1951] 2 All ER 290 which was approved by the House of Lords on this point in *Toohey* v *Metropolitan Police Commissioner* [1965] AC 595. In *Watson* (1817) 2 Stark 16 it was held that the only evidence which may be given on this issue is evidence of general reputation, so evidence that on a particular occasion the witness was not truthful is not admissible under this principle, although it may be admissible if it is evidence of bias. This rule was repeated in *Brown & Hedley* (1867) LR 1 CCR 70 and *Richardson* [1969] 1 QB 299.

In *Toohey* v *MPC*, above, the House of Lords held that evidence is admissible to prove that a witness is suffering from some physical or mental defect, disability or instability which affects the reliability of his evidence. This might include such matters as short-sightedness which would undermine the reliability of eye-witness evidence.

The fifth instance in which evidence may be given on a collateral issue arises where a witness has made a statement which is inconsistent with his evidence. As has been noted above, all witnesses make a statement before they give evidence. The prosecution must usually disclose its witnesses' statements to the defence. This, of course, allows the defence to detect inconsistencies. The right to challenge a witness as to his consistency is not limited to any previous written statement of his, however. If he is to be challenged about his consistency he must be given an opportunity to answer the allegation. He must be told when and in what circumstances he is alleged to have made the previous statement, for example that it was in a written statement given to the police or an oral statement made to a particular person. If he does not admit that he made the previous statement, evidence may be given to show that he did: Criminal Procedure Act 1865 s4:, and see for example *R* v *Funderburk* [1990] 1 WLR 587. Normally it is not necessary to call evidence on this because the previous statement is in writing and the witness accepts that the document is his statement. Where the statement is in writing he should be shown the document in question and his attention drawn to those parts which it is said are inconsistent with his evidence: Criminal Procedure Act 1865 s5. These rules apply to civil as well as criminal cases, although in civil cases the earlier statement is admissible as evidence of what it states, whereas in criminal proceedings it is only evidence of the witness's inconsistency.

The rules described above do not prevent a party from asking his opponent's witnesses about any matter which, if accepted by the witness, will undermine his evidence; they merely prevent such questions being followed-up by evidence where the witness's answer does not suit the cross-examiner. In one special case, however, a witness may not be asked about certain aspects of her character. By s2(1) of the Sexual Offences (Amendment) Act 1976 the complainant in a trial of a man for rape, attempted rape, incitement to rape, and aiding and abetting or counselling and procuring rape or attempted rape, may not be asked about her sexual experience with men other than the defendant, nor may evidence be called about this matter. The purpose of this provision is to prevent the complainant from having her evidence attacked by general accusations of promiscuity. It should be noted that there is no limitation on the right to cross-examine her about her sexual experience with the defendant, nor is there any embargo on examining her in chief about her experience with other men.

The trial judge may, under s2(1), give the defence leave to cross-examine the complainant or call evidence about her sexual experience, but s2(2) provides that leave shall be given 'if and only if he is satisfied that it would be unfair' to refuse it. In *Viola* [1982] 3 All ER 73 the Court of Appeal held that where the complainant's sexual habits or experience is relevant to an issue in the case the judge should give leave for her to be asked about them. It was pointed out by Lord Lane CJ, doubtless correctly, that few juries these days would consider the sexual habits of the complainant to be relevant to her credibility as a witness. This repeats what the Court of Appeal decided in *Mills* (1978) 68 Cr App R 327, namely that the purpose of s2 is to protect the complainant from irrelevant but distressing cross-examination. In practice leave is usually given where consent is in issue.

At common law it has long been permissible to ask the complainant whether she is a prostitute and to call evidence on the matter if it is denied: *Holmes* (1891) LR 1 CCR 334, *Bashir* (1969) 54 Cr App R 1. In *Krausz* (1973) 57 Cr App R 466 the defence to a charge of rape was that the complainant freely consented to sexual intercourse and then demanded money, and that when the defendant did not pay her she alleged rape. It was held that evidence was admissible from another man who said that she had done the same to him, although he paid in order to avoid any unpleasantness. These cases do not involve any departure from the principle in *Attorney-General* v *Hitchcock* because the evidence which was called and the questions which were asked were held to be relevant to the issue of consent, not to the credibility of the complainant. Section 2 of the 1976 Act now governs the position in such cases, although it is clear from *Mills* and *Viola* that the effect of s2 is to prevent questions and evidence unless it goes to an issue. It can therefore be said with some conviction that *Holmes, Bashir* and *Krausz* would be decided the same way today.

Although the limits on cross-examination as to credit imposed by s2 of the 1976 Act do not apply in, say, a trial for unlawful sexual intercourse with a girl aged 13, the court will be alert to see, in such a case, that the cross-examination is not abused or extended unnecessarily: *R* v *Funderburk* [1990] 1 WLR 587.

In *R* v *Sharp* [1993] 3 All ER 225 Stuart-Smith LJ said that, in general, when a cross-examination is being conducted by competent counsel a judge should not intervene, save to clarify matters he does not understand or thinks the jury may not understand. If he wishes to ask questions about matters that have not been touched upon it is generally better to wait until the end of examination or cross-examination. While a judge should not be criticised for occasional transgressions, there could come a time, depending on the nature and frequency of the interruptions, that a reviewing court concludes that defence counsel was so hampered in the way he properly wished to conduct the cross-examination that the judge's conduct amounted to a material irregularity. The Court of Appeal subsequently explained (*R* v *Marsh*

(1993) The Times 6 July) that the whole purpose of the adversarial process is that the judge sits and holds the ring. It is for counsel on each side to conduct examination and cross-examination and for the judge to see that they do it fairly. It is most undesirable for the judge to anticipate cross-examination or to interrupt the flow of evidence-in-chief, particularly that of the defendant. Nevertheless, judges should intervene to curb prolixity and repetition and to exclude irrelevance, discursiveness and oppression of witnesses: *R* v *Whybrow* (1994) The Times 14 February.

Re-examination

Once a witness has been cross-examined, the party calling him is entitled to re-examine. Leading questions are not allowed and questioning must be restricted to those matters upon which there was cross-examination.

It sometimes happens that a question should have been asked during examination in chief but was overlooked. Judges normally allow the question to be asked during re-examination, giving the other party the opportunity to cross-examine about it.

Further evidence

This whole question was considered by the Court of Appeal in *R* v *Francis* [1991] 1 All ER 225 where Lloyd LJ affirmed, in the light of the authorities, that it is the general rule that the prosecution must call the whole of their evidence before closing their case.

However, to this general rule there are two well established exceptions. First, the prosecution may call evidence in rebuttal to deal with matters which have arisen ex improviso: *R* v *Pilcher* (1974) 60 Cr App R1. Second, further evidence may be called where what has been omitted is a mere formality as distinct from a central issue in the case: *Royal* v *Prescott-Clarke* [1966] 2 All ER 366.

Lloyd LJ identified a third and wider exception, the essence of which is its flexibility, which should only be exercised 'on the rarest of occasions'. His Lordship refrained from defining precisely the limit of this discretion, but in the case which was then before him it allowed the recall of a police inspector to say who it was had been standing in a particular position in a group identification. The evidence had not been adduced originally because of a misunderstanding between counsel.

In *Ladd* v *Marshall* [1954] 3 All ER 745, Denning LJ said that, in a civil matter, in order to justify the reception of fresh evidence or a new trial, three conditions must be fulfilled: first, it must be shown that the evidence could not have been obtained with reasonable diligence for use at the trial: second, the evidence must be such that, if given, it would probably have an important influence on the result of the case, although it need not be decisive: third, the evidence must be such as is presumably to be believed, or in other words, it must be apparently credible, although it need not be incontrovertible.

Although it is a power which is sparingly exercised, new evidence may be admitted on the hearing of an appeal, but it must be direct evidence: see *Sutcliff* v *Pressdram Ltd* [1990] 2 WLR 271.

In *Merritt* v *Merritt* [1992] 2 All ER 504 Bracewell J explained that, where the purpose of an appeal is to adduce new evidence, the restrictions on admitting fresh evidence under RSC Ord 59, r10(2) apply and therefore the discretion to admit new evidence should be exercised sparingly, bearing in mind the importance that there should be an end to litigation, and it must be shown that the new evidence strikes at or falsifies the basis of the judgment or order under appeal.

In criminal matters, the approach is rather less strict insofar as s23(1) of the Criminal Appeal Act 1968 allows the Court of Appeal, 'if they think it necessary or expedient in the interests of justice', inter alia to receive the evidence, if tendered, of any competent but not compellable witness or to order any compellable witness to attend for examination, whether or not he was called at the trial. This approach will be adopted on the hearing of an appeal against a finding of contempt of court in civil proceedings: *Irtelli* v *Squatriti* [1992] 3 All ER 294. The s23(1) power was exercised in *R* v *Ahluwalia* [1992] 4 All ER 889 to admit fresh evidence of the appellant's alleged endogenous depression. Such evidence was not put forward at the trial and it could have provided an arguable defence to the charge of murder. See also *R* v *Guppy* (1994) The Times 8 March (appellant invited to give oral evidence).

1.7 The presentation of evidence

Crown Court trials

After the indictment has been put to the defendant and he has entered his pleas, there must be a trial of all counts to which he pleaded not guilty, save for those, if any, with which the Crown is content not to proceed. The jury is therefore sworn and the case proceeds in the following manner. Counsel for the Crown opens the case, summarising to the jury the evidence which the prosecution says proves the case. Each prosecution witness is called, examined, cross-examined and re-examined. The prosecution case is then closed.

The defence may make a submission of no case but if none is made or if such a submission is unsuccessful, the defence then calls its evidence. Its witnesses are called and examined in the same way as those of the Crown. If the defendant is to give evidence he must be called first unless the judge exercises his discretion and allows other witnesses to be called before him: Police and Criminal Evidence Act 1984 s79. In principle the defence may make an opening speech before calling its evidence, but if it does so it may not make a closing speech without leave. In practice opening speeches are very rare. Once all defence evidence has been heard, the defence closes its case. The Crown may then call evidence in rebuttal if this is permitted by the circumstances of the case. It will only be permitted where something has arisen during the defence case which the prosecution could not reasonably have been expected to deal with in advance. The trial judge always has a discretion to allow rebuttal evidence, but he should exercise it in favour of the defence unless the prosecution was taken by surprise and could not reasonably have been expected to anticipate the line of defence which was adopted: *Milliken* (1969) 53 Cr App R 330.

Once all evidence has been heard the prosecution may make a closing speech, which is followed by the defence closing speech. In very short cases the prosecution often waives its right to a final speech. The final stage of proceedings prior to the verdict is the judge's summing-up. The verdict is given by the foreman of the jury and, if the accused is convicted, his counsel then argues in mitigation of sentence. Finally the judge passes sentence. Where the accused is acquitted he will be discharged by the judge.

Majority verdicts are permissible if the jury is unable to reach a unanimous decision. All jury trials start with a jury of 12 members. However, it is not uncommon for one or more jury members to be taken ill during the course of a trial, especially in extremely long cases. The permitted majorities are 11:1 and 10:2 where there are 12 jury members, 10:1 if only 11 jurors remain and 9:1 if the number is reduced to ten. A smaller jury than ten members must be unanimous: Juries Act 1974 s17. Majority verdicts may only be returned once the judge has directed the jury that they may do so, and he must not give such a direction until at least two hours and ten minutes have passed since they retired to the jury room to consider their verdicts: Juries Act 1974 s17(4), *Practice Direction* [1970] 1 WLR 916.

A jury which is unable to reach even a majority decision is known as a 'hung jury' and may be discharged once stalemate has been reached. On the jury being discharged no verdict is entered, so the accused is neither convicted nor acquitted. Normal practice is for there to be a re-trial if the first jury to hear the case is hung. On a second jury being hung the Crown will normally ask for the indictment to be put again and on the defendant pleading not guilty no evidence will be offered and a formal verdict of not guilty entered.

Arguments of law may arise at any stage in the trial. Disputes about the admissibility of evidence are aired in the absence of the jury, and normally take place shortly before the disputed evidence is to be called. Prior to the judge summing-up he may invite counsel to make legal submissions if he feels in difficulty about how the jury should be directed about a particular principle of law. There is no obligation on the defence to help him, although the prosecution must do so and as a matter of courtesy the defence often also does so.

Summary trials

The course of evidence in summary trials is the same as in the Crown Court, save that it is extremely rare for the Crown to make a closing speech. Points of law are argued between the parties' legal representatives, who may be solicitors or barristers, and the clerk of the court who is legally qualified. The clerk directs the justices on the law and they should follow his direction, although it is for the magistrates alone to decide questions of fact. Stipendiary magistrates decide the law themselves, although they often discuss the law with the clerk on the principle that two heads are better than one.

Lay magistrates do not give reasoned decisions, they merely say whether or not the case is proved. Usually, but not always, stipendiary magistrates give judgment by explaining what evidence they accept and what evidence they do not.

County court and High Court

Trials by judge alone in civil courts are opened by the party who bears the general burden of proof, usually the plaintiff: see Chapter 3, paragraph 3.1. He then calls his evidence. Once his case is closed the other party, usually the defendant, calls his evidence. Opening speeches by the defence are not uncommon, although leave is required to make a closing speech if there is an opening address by the defence. Unlike in criminal trials, the party who opens the case in the county court or High Court also closes it by making the final speech. Usually, therefore, the defendant makes his speech before the plaintiff.

There is great flexibility in civil trials in that it is common practice for the judge to allow the plaintiff to call extra evidence during the defence case and for him to call upon counsel to make additional submissions even after they have made their final speeches if he feels he needs assistance.

No set pattern exists for the raising of legal points. They may be dealt with at the beginning of the trial where this assists the judge and advocates in deciding what evidence to require to be called. Alternatively they may be left to the end once the evidence has been given and the factual issues in dispute are clear.

As to written statements of oral evidence, see 1.2, above.

Translation

An accused who does not understand the conduct of proceedings against him cannot, in the absence of express consent, be said to have a fair trial and the judge, by virtue of his duty to ensure that the accused has a fair trial, is bound to ensure that effective use is made of an interpreter. When a foreign accused is defended by counsel the evidence should be interpreted to the accused, except when he or counsel on his behalf express a wish to dispense with the translation and the judge thinks fit to permit the omission. The judge should not permit a translation to be dispensed with unless he considers that because of what has passed before the trial, eg at a preliminary hearing, the accused substantially understands the evidence and the case against him: see *Kunnath* v *The State* [1993] 4 All ER 30.

Letters of request

In civil matters, the court has inherent jurisdiction to issue a letter of request (only a request – not an order) to the judicial authorities of a foreign country seeking their aid in the production of documents which would constitute material evidence in the matter before it: *Panayiotou* v *Sony Music Entertainment (UK) Ltd* (1993) The Times 2 August. As to letters of request in relation to criminal proceedings and investigations, see s3 of the Criminal Justice (International Co-operation) Act 1990.

1.8 Types of evidence

The standard classifications

There are several categories of evidence. They are not rigid and many types of evidence fall into more than one category. Nevertheless, it is important that the classifications are known.

The terms primary and secondary evidence are used to describe a number of different principles. The most common use is in relation to documents. As we will see in Chapter 12 the court should be shown the original of any document which is in dispute. The original document is primary evidence, copies of it or oral evidence about its contents being secondary evidence.

Oral evidence given by a witness from the witness box is known simply as oral evidence. But the evidence he gives will be either direct or indirect. It will be direct if he repeats something he has seen or otherwise perceived, it will be indirect (otherwise known as hearsay) if he repeats what someone else has told him in order to prove that what that other person said is true, and it will be opinion evidence if he gives his opinion.

Real evidence is evidence other than oral evidence. It comprises things known as exhibits which are put before the court to illustrate or explain oral evidence. Thus in a murder trial the Crown will produce perhaps a gun or knife which is alleged to be the murder weapon; and in a contract case the court must see the written contract if there is one. Documents are real evidence, although they form a special sort of real evidence known, not surprisingly, as documentary evidence.

Many types of evidence are known as original evidence. It is a term used most commonly to describe two principles. First, evidence from a witness who repeats what he saw or heard is known as original evidence, as well as being known as direct evidence. It is original because he actually perceived the events which he recounts and does not have to rely on what others have told him about those events. The other common usage is to describe a principle of great importance in the field of hearsay evidence. We will see in Chapter 4 that hearsay evidence is generally not allowed. We will also see that hearsay evidence comprises the repetition of a statement in order to prove that the statement is true. But not all repetition of statements is hearsay. For example in a libel case a witness may say: 'The defendant said that the plaintiff is a thief.' This is not hearsay because the purpose of repeating the statement is to show simply that it was made, not to prove that it was true. A witness who repeats a statement in order to prove that it was made is said to give original evidence. In this context 'original' is used in contrast to 'hearsay'.

The use of the classifications

The classifications given above are not set by law and therefore they are flexible. For instance, some judges and commentators will call non-hearsay evidence 'direct' whereas others prefer 'original'. The importance of the classifications is that they illustrate principles which are explained in more detail later in this book.

The categories of evidence described above define evidence without saying anything about whether it is admissible or inadmissible, and without stating anything about the strength of the evidence. There are classifications which relate specifically to the weight of evidence. For example, prima facie evidence is evidence which is admissible and may prove a fact in issue between the parties. Prima facie evidence can be contrasted with conclusive evidence which, as its name suggests, is conclusive so that the issue is proved once such evidence is adduced.

2

Corroboration

2.1 Introduction

2.2 Corroboration required by law

2.3 Corroboration required by practice

2.4 Corroboration required by caution

2.5 Problem areas

2.1 Introduction

Reasons for corroboration

English law does not normally prescribe that any particular number of witnesses be called or any particular type of evidence be adduced before a case can be proved. It is usually for the parties to call as much or as little evidence as they wish and the court will decide what has been proved by hearing, comparing and weighing all of the evidence.

Some types of evidence have been shown by experience to be unreliable, and so for limited classes of witnesses and cases the law prescribes that evidence in support is required. That supporting evidence is known as corroboration. In civil trials there are no common law rules prescribing a need for corroboration, although some statutes require it. There are neither common law nor statutory provisions requiring the accused to provide corroboration in support of his defence. In a great many cases it would be hard for him to provide any, because often the only witness called by the defence is the defendant himself.

It is quite rare for the Crown to rely on the oral evidence of one witness only but there is no reason why it should not if that is all that is available. The cases in which corroboration is required are set out in the following parts of this chapter. Lying behind them all is the need to protect the defendant from potentially unreliable evidence unless other evidence shows it to be true.

The law has set two different rules on corroboration. In some cases the jury is not allowed to convict in the absence of corroboration. In these cases it is said that corroboration is required as a matter of law and they are all provided for by statute, although one of the statutes, the Perjury Act 1911, merely codifies the common law.

But in others the jury may convict on uncorroborated evidence provided the judge has directed them to look for corroboration; here corroboration is needed as a matter of practice. In addition there are a few instances where the judge directs the jury to approach the evidence with caution even though there is no strict need for corroboration.

What must be corroborated

There is some confusion in the cases and statutes about whether it is the witness or his evidence which must be corroborated. In principle, the difference between corroboration of a witness and corroboration of his evidence is that evidence which supports the credibility of the witness would corroborate him, whereas evidence which supports the story he has told corroborates his evidence. At common law the correct approach is to ask whether there is corroboration of the evidence given by the witness, but one or two of the statutes in this area have a more relaxed requirement of corroboration and avoid some of the more technical aspects of the common law.

The common law definition of corroboration which is explained below requires other evidence which implicates the accused. Evidence that a witness is generally truthful will not amount to corroboration, although it may in some circumstances be called and can be extremely important: see paragraph 1.6, above.

Statutes which require corroboration are not all drafted in the same way and this can lead to confusion. For example ss2, 3, 4, 22 and 23 of the Sexual Offences Act 1956 all say that a person cannot be convicted of certain offences on the evidence of one witness only, 'unless the witness is corroborated in some material particular by evidence implicating the accused'. Whereas s13 of the Perjury Act 1911 says that the accused may not be convicted of certain offences 'upon the evidence of one witness'. In some instances, the different wording is used in these statutes to express different requirements for corroboration. But the courts are jealous of their own definition and wherever possible construe Acts of Parliament as defining a need for corroboration as defined at common law. Without doubt, some of the statutes relax the normal rules and are construed accordingly. For this reason a dictum in *Baskerville* [1916] 2 KB 658 that the test for corroboration is the same whether it arises by statute or common law is not correct.

Because the essence of corroboration is that evidence of suspect reliability is supported by other evidence, it is important not to assume that simply because two witnesses say the same thing they must be believed. Yet this assumption may be drawn where the judge directs the jury to look for corroboration, because their minds may be concentrated on the need for supporting evidence without sufficient emphasis being placed on the need for that evidence to prove the case against the accused. Dicta of Lord Hailsham in *DPP* v *Kilbourne* [1973] AC 729 and Lord Morris in *DPP* v *Hester* [1973] AC 296 expressed the need to assess not only whether one witness says the same as another but also whether that evidence should be believed. Lord Hailsham said:

'Corroboration can only be afforded to or by a witness who is otherwise to be believed. If a witness's testimony falls of its own inanation, the question of his needing, or being capable of giving, corroboration does not arise.'

In a similar vein, Lord Morris asserted:

'The essence of corroborative evidence is that one creditworthy witness confirms what another creditworthy witness has said ... The purpose of corroboration is not to give validity or credence to evidence which is deficient or suspect or incredible but only to confirm and support that which as evidence is sufficient and satisfactory and credible; and corroborative evidence will only fill its role if it is completely credible evidence.'

One criticism of these passages is that they suggest the jury should look at witnesses in isolation, decide whether they are telling the truth, and then look to see whether there is evidence which corroborates what they say. Lord Hailsham made clear in his speech in *Kilbourne* that this is not what he meant. The Privy Council took up the criticism in *AG of Hong Kong* v *Wong Muk Ping* [1987] AC 501, explaining that one cannot look at witnesses in isolation, because usually the only way to decide whether a witness is telling the truth is by comparing his evidence with what others have said. It was said that Lord Morris's speech in *Hester* did not make this clear and it was disapproved in that respect. It is, of course, true that where someone is obviously untruthful or unreliable, the jury need not waste time looking around to see if his evidence can be rescued when it is obvious that it cannot.

The legal definition

The legal definition of corroboration is very simple in principle but unnecessarily technical in application. It follows from the reason why corroboration is needed, that the essence of corroborative evidence is that it supports evidence which may be unreliable. But it is not enough in law for the judge to direct the jury to ask whether the suspect evidence is supported by other evidence.

The definition of corroboration is a common law definition. It comes from *Baskerville* and has three elements: it must be independent of the witness whose evidence needs corroboration, confirm what that witness has said, and implicate the accused in a material particular.

The requirement of independence is that the source of the corroborative evidence should be independent. If witness A's evidence needs corroborating, corroboration cannot come from other evidence given by A, nor from witness B testifying about something which A said or did, nor from a document written by A. The court tests the independence primarily by asking whether there is a real risk of witnesses having colluded: see paragraph 2.5, below. It is for a judge, not a jury, to decide whether a real risk exists that potentially corroborative evidence is contaminated (ie, that it is not truly independent), since in carrying out that task he is deciding a question of admissibility. If he finds such a risk exists, he has no discretion to let the evidence go to the jury as corroboration: *R* v *Ananthanarayanan* (1994) 98 Cr App R1.

In *R* v *H (evidence: corroboration)* (1994) The Times 2 March the Court of Appeal said that in *Ananthanarayanan*, once the risk of contamination arose, admissibility of evidence had not been the problem: instead, contamination went to weight and probative value, matters properly left to the jury. However, in the later case their Lordships granted leave to appeal to the House of Lords, the question being: 'How should the trial judge deal with a similar fact case (*Director of Public Prosecutions* v *P* [1991] 2 AC 447) where the Crown proposes to call more than one complainant and to rely on each as corroborating the evidence of the other or others, and the defence demonstrates that there is a risk that the evidence is contaminated by collusion or by other factors?'

The second and third elements overlap. It is not necessary for corroborative evidence to confirm the witness in every part of his or her evidence, provided it confirms at least part of what he or she has said. The need to implicate the accused in a material particular is connected to the need for evidence to be confirmatory. Since it need not be confirmatory in every aspect, the law draws a balance and requires it to implicate the accused in at least one way that the suspect witness implicates him. Various problems have been encountered in applying this definition and these problems will be discussed as it arises in the context of the substantive law.

The common law definition does not apply to all cases in which corroboration is needed by statute. The definition applicable to each statutory instance will be discussed as the instance in question is explained. Perhaps surprisingly, the common law definition of corroboration is the same in all cases where the common law requires corroboration, although the reasons for it being required are not always the same. This aspect of the subject will also be discussed as each example is explained.

See also s62(10) of the Police and Criminal Evidence Act 1984 (refusal of intimate sample capable of amounting to corroboration).

2.2 Corroboration required by law

Perjury

Where it is in issue whether evidence given by a witness was false, he may not be convicted of the offence of perjury on the evidence of one witness alone as to the falsity of what he said: Perjury Act 1911, s13. This provision applies not just to the offence of perjury but also to that of subornation of perjury, which means inciting someone to commit perjury by offering some sort of bribe.

The need for corroboration only arises on the issue of the falsity of the evidence which was given. So if the accused admits that what he said was untrue, but, for example, says that he did not know or believe it to be untrue or alleges that it was not on a material issue in the case, s13 will not apply: *Rider* (1986) 83 Cr App R 207.

Whether what the defendant said on oath was true or false can be proved without calling evidence which directly implicates him, so the common law definition of corroboration does not apply. Instead, all that is needed is evidence from two sources which establishes that what the defendant said on oath was false. The statute does not place any limits on the sorts of evidence which may be called as corroboration. A second witness will suffice and in both *Mayhew* (1834) 6 C & P 315 and *Threlfall* (1914) 10 Cr App R 112, letters written by the defendant were admitted as corroboration. There is no reason in principle why any evidence of the falsity of what the accused said should not be used.

In *R* v *Peach* [1990] 1 WLR 976 the Court of Appeal accepted that evidence to the effect that the defendant had confessed that his sworn statement was false, may be evidence of the statement's falsity. The court also decided that the requirements of s13 of the 1911 Act are satisfied if two witnesses testify to having heard the defendant's confession on the same occasion.

Sexual Offences Act offences

Certain offences created by the Sexual Offences Act 1956 specifically provide that the accused cannot be convicted unless there is corroboration of the evidence which has been given against him. The offences concerned are procuring a woman by threats or intimidation to have unlawful sexual intercourse (s2), procuring a woman by false pretences to have unlawful sexual intercourse (s3), administering a drug to a woman so as to induce her to have unlawful sexual intercourse (s4), procuring a woman to engage in prostitution (s22), and procuring a girl under the age of 21 to have unlawful sexual intercourse with someone other than the procurer (s23). None of these offences is often encountered in practice in England.

The Act does not say that the evidence of the woman who was procured into unlawful sexual intercourse must be corroborated. It does say, however, that the accused cannot be convicted on the evidence of one witness alone unless that evidence is corroborated in some material by evidence which implicates the accused. Therefore, whoever is the first witness called by the Crown, his or her evidence must be corroborated. Any admissible evidence may corroborate; it need not be a second witness, and a document will suffice. Each section specifically refers to corroboration which implicates the accused in a material particular; this equates to the common law definition which therefore applies.

Speeding

Someone accused of driving in excess of a speed limit is not liable to be convicted if the only evidence that he was speeding is the opinion of one witness: Road Traffic (Regulation) Act 1984 s89(2). It is widely appreciated that people's judgment of speed is not generally reliable and this is the sole and very simple reason why s89(2) says what it does.

There is no requirement that evidence of opinion of speed be given at all, indeed a great many speeding cases today are proved not by opinion evidence but by a policeman saying that he used a radar gun to test the speed of the vehicle or that he followed behind it at a steady speed and that his speedometer registered a speed in excess of the legal limit. As to the admissibility of evidence obtained by using radar, photographic equipment or other approved devices, see s20 of the Road Traffic Offenders Act 1988, as substituted. So, the need for corroboration arises only in a limited number of cases where the prosecution tries to prove the offence by opinion evidence alone. In *Russell* v *Beesley* [1937] 1 All ER 527 the Divisional Court said, without holding this as a point of law, that s2 of the Road Traffic Act 1932, which laid down a similar requirement for corroboration, simply did not apply where the evidence called by the prosecution was not opinion evidence. In that case the evidence called was of a police inspector who followed the accused at a steady speed and gave evidence that his speedometer read between 5 and 12 mph in excess of the limit. On the face of it the court was absolutely right, the evidence was not opinion evidence but was evidence of what the inspector saw on his speedometer. If the inspector had said that in his opinion the defendant exceeded the limit and that his speedometer gave a reading in excess of the limit, the section would apply, because his opinion would have been put forward and was something the court should consider. This was the position in *Nicholas* v *Penny* [1950] 2 KB 466, where the Divisional Court held that evidence of the speedometer reading corroborated the opinion of the police officer. It should be noted that *Nicholas* v *Penny* is authority that the common law definition does not apply to s89(2). The evidence about the reading on the speedometer did not implicate the accused in any way, all it did was support the opinion.

If there is to be corroboration of an opinion of speed there is no limit to what sort of evidence that corroboration must be, provided it is admissible evidence and does in fact corroborate. In *Brighty* v *Pearson* [1938] 4 All ER 127 the opinion of one witness that the accused was speeding at one place on a road was not corroborated by the opinion of another that he was speeding further along the same road. Lord Hewart CJ, who also gave the leading judgment in *Nicholas* v *Penny*, stressed the need for the evidence of both witnesses to show that the accused committed a single offence. The witnesses in that case gave evidence of two separate offences, committed at two separate places on the road. Section 89(2) would require each to be corroborated, but they could not corroborate each other because neither implicates the accused in the offence alleged by the other.

Affiliation

The Affiliation Proceedings Act 1957 was repealed by s17 of the Family Law Reform Act 1987 with effect from 1 April 1989: it was replaced by proceedings under the Guardianship of Minors Act 1971, as amended by the 1987 Act, and the 1971 Act was, in turn, repealed by the Children Act 1989.

The magistrates court may order that blood be taken and tested (Family Law Reform Act 1969 s20, as amended by s89 of the Children Act 1989 and Schedule

16, para 3, to the Courts and Legal Services Act 1990), and whether this is taken as the result of such an order or by agreement the result is admissible and may corroborate the mother's evidence: *Turner* v *Blunden* [1986] Fam 120. Blood tests can prove conclusively that a particular man is not the father of a child, but cannot prove conclusively that he is. They show the statistical probability of the defendant being the father, and if the probability is high the court may infer from this that the case is proved. By statutory instrument the application of s20 has been extended so that genetic fingerprint tests may be ordered. These are more probative than blood tests, in fact they are so probative that they are for all practical purposes conclusive because the chance of the result being wrong is minimal.

For an example of the exercise of the court's discretion under s20(1) of the 1969 Act, see *Re F (a minor) (blood tests: parental rights)* [1993] 3 All ER 596 (tests refused principally because not in child's interests that they should be taken because could disturb present family situation).

From a day to be appointed, the provisions of s20(1), (2) of the Family Law Reform Act 1969 will be substituted by new provisions enabling scientific tests on bodily fluids as opposed simply to blood: s23 of the Family Law Reform Act 1987.

2.3 Corroboration required by practice

Accomplices

The definition of accomplice for the purposes of corroboration is restrictive and specific. There are three types of accomplice. The first is a person who participated in the actual offence alleged and the second is a handler of stolen goods who gives evidence against the alleged thief of those goods. In some circumstances it is permissible to prove that the accused has committed other offences in order to prove that he committed the offence with which he is now charged. In chapter 7 we will see the extent to which this is allowed. The third type of accomplice is someone who was a party to one or more of the other offences. These three categories were finally established in *Davies* v *DPP* [1954] AC 378 where the House of Lords held that no new categories may be formed.

The limits of each category must be appreciated. Participants in the crime alleged means exactly what it says. Someone who was involved in the incident which gave rise to the charge against the accused is not an accomplice unless he is liable to be convicted of the exactly the same offence. In *Davies* v *DPP* the defendant was charged with murder by stabbing someone during a fight between two gangs of youths. One of the prosecution witnesses was a member of the same gang as Davies, and had previously been tried for and acquitted of the same murder. He was held not to be an accomplice because there was no evidence that he knew anything about Davies having a knife. In any event, his acquittal of the same charge is conclusive evidence that he did not commit it, so on this basis as well he was not an accomplice. The facts of *Davies* v *DPP* were clear on the question whether the witness was an accomplice, but other cases are not so simple. It was said, obiter, in *Davies* v *DPP* that where it is clear that someone is an accomplice the judge should direct the jury accordingly. But where it is not clear, the jury must be directed to investigate whether he was an accomplice and then treat his evidence with the requisite degree of caution. This may involve the jury in an interesting exercise in mental gymnastics: if they decide that the witness is not an accomplice they need not look for corroboration. If they find that he is an accomplice they must look for corroboration, but may still convict in the absence of corroboration if they are sure that he is telling the truth. It is doubtful whether it is realistic for a jury to have to undertake such a complex exercise.

Where there are two or more defendants charged with the same offence and they give evidence against each other the jury's task could be even more complicated, because each would be an accomplice only if the jury was satisfied that he committed the offence charged. They would have to ask themselves whether defendant X was guilty before knowing whether corroboration of his evidence against defendant Y was required, yet in deciding X's guilt they may have to consider evidence given by Y. Y's evidence will have to be corroborated if they are satisfied that he is guilty. So, in deciding whether X is guilty or innocent they must decide Y's guilt or innocence in order to know whether to look for corroboration of his testimony, and in deciding Y's guilt or innocence they will have to decide whether X is guilty or innocent in order to know whether to look for corroboration of his testimony. The task of the jury is circular. The answer to the problem lies in the decision in *Prater* [1960] 2 QB 464 in which the Court of Criminal Appeal held that a corroboration warning should be given where a witness has an interest of his own to serve. In other words, the judge should direct the jury to look for corroboration of the co-defendant's evidence without confusing matters by requiring them to investigate whether he is an accomplice. The defence can have no complaint if this course is taken, because the defendant is given extra protection by the trial judge. This approach was approved by Lord Hailsham in *DPP* v *Kilbourne* [1973] AC 729. In any event, of course, in order for the case to proceed past the end of the prosecution case there must have been evidence against each defendant, so it can be safely assumed that there will be corroborative evidence before the court. A judge who fails to give such a warning where it is clear that either X or Y but not both committed the offence, will have acted correctly because neither could be a participant in the commission of the offence if the other is guilty of it: *Whitaker* (1977) 63 Cr App R 193.

Furthermore, it is only if one defendant clearly implicates the other that the need for a corroboration direction arises. In *Barnes* [1940] 2 All ER 229 five defendants were charged with murder. Two of them, A and B, gave evidence which to a small degree implicated two others, C and D. The trial judge directed the jury that that evidence was relevant to the guilt or innocence of A and B only. He gave no corroboration warning and the prosecution did not rely on anything which was said by A and B against C and D. The Court of Criminal Appeal held that this was not a case where the corroboration warning was needed because A and B were not called as prosecution witnesses and the jury was not asked to rely on anything they said against C and D. It was implicit in this decision that had the jury been invited by the prosecution to rely on the evidence of one defendant against another, a corroboration warning should have been given, despite the fact that the witness in question would not have been called by the Crown.

There is some authority that some witnesses who are clearly accomplices within the definition set out in *Davies* v *DPP*, do not need to be corroborated. Police officers who deliberately provoked the commission of an offence were said not to count as accomplices in *Sneddon* v *Stevenson* [1967] 2 All ER 1277. Strictly speaking, the officers were not accomplices within the *Davies* v *DPP* definition, but the Divisional Court said that even if they were, they would not be treated as accomplices provided they were acting under orders. Also, accomplices whose evidence does not go against the defendant need not be corroborated: *Royce-Bentley* [1974] 1 WLR 535.

Receivers of stolen goods are accomplices at the trial of the alleged thief, whether or not the receiver has any interest of his own to protect. If he has been tried for and convicted of receiving the goods he will not be in danger of a second trial for theft and therefore will not be in danger from the law if he testifies against the thief. But the need for the corroboration warning remains: *Jennings* (1912) 7 Cr App R 242. The rules does not apply to thieves who give evidence against someone alleged of receiving stolen goods from them, although a conviction for receiving stolen goods was quashed in *Vernon* [1962] Crim LR 35 because no corroboration warning was given in relation to the thief who gave evidence for the prosecution. The proper explanation of that decision is that the witness was a participant in the reception of the goods by Vernon and that a warning was required under the first category in *Davies* v *DPP*.

Davies v *DPP* specifically refers to 'receivers' of stolen goods being accomplices of the thieves from whom they received them. There is no authority that the need for a corroboration warning applies to other types of handlers, such as retainers of goods, or those who dispose of such goods. The cases which establish the rule requiring corroboration for receivers are cases of receivers who received the goods directly from the defendant, so there is little scope for the rule applying to handlers unless they were directly connected to the accused.

The third category in *Davies* v *DPP* will be considered in greater detail in Chapter 7.

Complainants of sexual offences

No matter what the sexual offence which is alleged, a corroboration warning must be given about the evidence of the complainant. Not only is it irrelevant what the sexual offence is, it is also irrelevant what issues arise in the case and whether the complainant is male or female: *Burgess* (1956) 40 Cr App R 144.

In *Trigg* [1963] 1 WLR 305 the charge was rape and the only issue was whether the defendant was the rapist. The Court of Criminal Appeal allowed the appeal against conviction because no corroboration warning was given. This should be compared with *Turnbull* [1977] QB 224 in which the need for a careful direction about the danger of convicting on identification evidence was stressed. As we shall see, the sort of direction which has to be given to the jury in a case revolving around identification evidence is different from the corroboration warning. There is nothing about the facts of *Trigg* which makes it anything other than an 'identification case', yet it is not governed by the *Turnbull* rule because the evidence of complainants is treated, quite artificially, as requiring a warning to look for corroboration, and all the technicalities of the law on corroboration come into play.

The warning

Where a corroboration warning must be given there is no definitive form of words which must be used (*DPP* v *Kilbourne*), although the following dictum from Lord Hewart CJ in *Freebody* (1935) 25 Cr App R 69 is often followed:

> 'The proper direction ... is that it is not safe to convict upon the uncorroborated evidence of the [witness], but that the jury if they are satisfied of the truth of the evidence, may, after paying attention to that warning, nevertheless convict.'

The judge must make two things clear: first, that there is a danger in convicting on the uncorroborated evidence of the witness in question, and secondly that the jury should look for other evidence which both supports it and implicates the accused. He should also identify that evidence which can corroborate and that which cannot. In this context the definition of corroboration laid down in *Baskerville*, which was an accomplice case, is important, because the judge must apply that test when deciding what can and what cannot corroborate the evidence which needs corroboration. In *Zielinski* [1950] 2 All ER 1114 the Court of Criminal Appeal held that provided the judge gave the jury a corroboration warning and explained what corroboration was, it was not necessary to go further and identify the evidence which could corroborate. But this was disapproved in *Goddard* (1962) 46 Cr App R 456, where Lord Parker CJ said that the judge need not refer to every piece of evidence which could corroborate, but he should give a broad indication of what can and cannot corroborate. The point was taken further in *Charles* (1976) 68 Cr App R 334 where the Court of Appeal stressed the need for the judge to assist the jury by identifying that evidence which could corroborate. This was upheld as the correct approach in *Reeves* (1979) 68 CR App R 331, and *Cullinane* [1984] Crim LR 420 holds that where there is more than one witness who needs corroborating, the judge should indicate what evidence can corroborate each of them.

There is always a risk in the judge directing the jury in detail about what can and cannot corroborate, because he could leave himself open to an allegation that he usurped the function of the jury by giving too firm a direction about the facts. This problem is most easily overcome by inviting submissions from counsel on what can and cannot amount to corroboration. Even this is not fail-safe, because the defence is not debarred from appealing simply because they were invited to make submissions or, indeed, because the judge followed the submissions they made.

Where there is no corroboration the judge need not waste time explaining what corroboration is and it is good practice for him to say specifically that there is no corroboration, emphasising the need to approach the uncorroborated evidence with caution: *Spencer* [1987] AC 128.

As to the warning to be given in respect of co-defendant's evidence, see *Need for review*, below.

Each direction must be tailored to fit the circumstances of the case, which necessarily means that the judge will give a different emphasis to different aspects of the evidence which has been called. In all cases he should avoid using the word 'corroboration' because it is not a word in ordinary usage, but he may use the word provided he explains what it means: *DPP* v *Kilbourne*.

Effect of failure to give warning

In *Davies* v *DPP* the House of Lords held that failure to give a warning in an accomplice case will lead to any conviction being quashed on appeal unless the proviso to s2(1) of the Criminal Appeal Act 1968 can be applied. The proviso allows the Court of Appeal to dismiss an appeal despite an irregularity at trial where no miscarriage of justice has occurred. In *Jenkins* (1981) 72 Cr App R 354 the Court of Appeal said that where there is 'enough other convincing evidence to make the conviction safe and satisfactory' the proviso should be applied. The same principle applies, of course, where the judge gives a warning which is defective, perhaps by not identifying what could corroborate: see, eg, *R* v *L (corroboration directions)* (1994) The Times 16 March (direction incomplete, appeal dismissed).

In sexual offence cases the Court of Appeal has taken a stricter view. In *Trigg* [1963] 1 WLR 305 it was held that, although there was corroboration of the evidence of the three complainants, the failure of the judge to direct the jury properly was fatal to the conviction because the proviso should only be applied in exceptional cases. The reason for not upholding the conviction in *Trigg* was that the court was not able to say that the jury would have convicted had they been properly directed. The fact there there was evidence which corroborated the complainants did not mean that the jury would have been satisfied that the case was proved. This is an important point, because it does not follow that the accused is guilty simply because more than one witness gives evidence that he committed the offence charged. In exceptional cases the appellate court will be able to say that a conviction would have followed from a proper direction but it would have to be clear that the evidence against the accused was overwhelming. Such a case was *O'Reilly* [1967] 2 QB 727 where there was no corroboration warning, but the judge directed the jury to ignore the evidence of the complainant and to concentrate on scientific evidence which was extremely strong.

Need for Review

In *R* v *Cheema* [1994] 1 All ER 639 the Court of Appeal affirmed (a) that English law does not recognise a rule requiring a full corroboration direction in respect of a co-defendant's evidence (all that is required is simply a warning to the jury that the defendant witness may have had a purpose of his own to serve) and (b) that there is no absolute rule that one accomplice cannot corroborate another. Beyond this, their Lordships said that the rules regarding corroboration had become arcane, highly technical and difficult to convey to juries. They noted that the Law Commission in its Working Paper No 115, *Corroboration of Evidence in Criminal Trials* (1990), recommended the abolition of the present rule in favour of a simpler form of judicial warning. Their Lordships added their support to recommendations for a review of this area of the law.

2.4 Corroboration required by caution

Witnesses of unreliable character

The categories of case in which a corroboration warning must be given by law are closed, and the only categories are those discussed already, namely accomplices and complainants of sexual offences. There is authority that trial judges should warn the jury to approach evidence with caution where the witness who gave it is unreliable because either he has an interest of his own to serve by testifying against the accused or his character shows him to be unreliable. In these cases there is no rule of law that a warning must be given, but in order to be fair to the accused the judge ought to give one and his failure to do so may lead to a conviction being quashed as being unsafe or unsatisfactory. To date three sorts of witness have been identified as falling within this principle – witnesses of unsound mind, witnesses who have an interest of their own to serve by giving evidence against the defendant, and witnesses whose character is very bad, which in general terms means people who have shown in the past that their word cannot be relied on.

In *Bagshaw* [1984] 1 WLR 477 the Court of Appeal said that witnesses who were in-patients in mental hospitals were likely to be so unreliable that nothing short of a full corroboration warning would be appropriate in relation to their evidence. In effect the court created a new category of witnesses for whom a corroboration warning had to be given, but it was a category which only lasted for two years because the House of Lords overruled *Bagshaw* in *Spencer* [1987] AC 128. Nevertheless, the House held that in order to ensure that the trial was fair to the accused, where the prosecution relies wholly on evidence from witnesses whose mental capacity is questionable, a warning should be given of the danger of convicting where there is no corroboration.

A similar principle was stated by the Court of Appeal in *Beck* [1982] 1 WLR 461 where prosecution witnesses were not accomplices but had their own interests to serve by giving evidence against the accused because they had made false insurance claims and their evidence helped to deflect blame for this onto the defendant. The Court of Appeal applied *Prater*, in which, as we have seen, it was held to be good practice to give a corroboration warning even though there was no need in law because the witness in question had an interest of his own to serve by giving evidence against the defendant.

In *DPP* v *Kilbourne* Lord Hailsham referred to witnesses 'of admittedly bad character' as a category about whom the jury should be given a corroboration warning. He qualified this dictum in *Spencer*, saying that a warning of the danger of convicting on the evidence of a witness who was clearly unreliable was always necessary in order to ensure that the accused was treated fairly. It is difficult to generalise about the characteristics which are necessary before someone falls into this category, but it would include people with such serious criminal records or such long records of lying on oath that as a matter of common sense a jury would not consider them to be believable.

There is a very thin line between requiring a corroboration warning to be given and saying that a conviction may be unsafe unless the jury is directed to approach the evidence of a witness with caution because he may be unreliable. In *Spencer* Lord Ackner explained that the difference between the cases where a corroboration warning is required by law and those where it is good practice to give one, is that in the former it would not normally be apparent to a jury that caution is required whereas in the latter it would.

Evidence of children

In *R* v *Pryce* [1991] Crim LR 379 the Court of Appeal affirmed that, in passing s34(2) of the Criminal Justice Act 1988, Parliament had intended to place children on the same footing as adults so far as their evidence was concerned. It is sufficient for the judge to tell the jury that they should take into account the fact that the witnesses were children, but where a warning would have to be given in the case of an adult so it must still be given in relation to a child.

A child's unsworn evidence may corroborate evidence (sworn or unsworn) given by any other person: s34(3) of the 1988 Act, as amended.

Identification evidence

Where the prosecution relies wholly or substantially on identification evidence the jury must be directed to approach that evidence with caution.

This principle was first stated in *Turnbull* [1977] QB 224 and has been expanded and explained in a number of authorities since. We will discuss these in detail in Chapter 11.

2.5 Problem areas

Mutual corroboration

As a general rule any two witnesses can corroborate each other's evidence provided they are independent and confirmatory of each other and implicate the accused in a material particular: *Baskerville*. The need to ensure that the evidence of each witness is independent of the other is not satisfied if they have put their heads together and come up with the same story. It sometimes needs a careful investigation of the relationship between two prosecution witnesses in order to determine whether they are truly independent of each other. According to Lord Reid in *Kilbourne*, what must be asked is whether there is any 'real chance' of collusion. This test, however, only dictates whether the witnesses are corroborative and not the admissibility of what they say. Where corroboration is required by law, failure by the prosecution to satisfy the judge beyond reasonable doubt that there was no real chance of collusion will lead to the accused being acquitted at the direction of the judge unless there is other corroborative evidence.

The function of the judge where corroboration is needed as a matter of practice rather than law, is similar. He must direct the jury what evidence is capable of amounting to corroboration, so he must decide whether there is a real chance of collusion. The decision whether to believe witnesses is, of course, one for the jury, which means that they will also have to investigate the possibility of collusion. The proper way for the judge to direct them depends upon the view he takes of the chance of collusion. If he decides that the witnesses do not corroborate each other he should direct the jury accordingly; such a direction helps the defence because it automatically casts doubt upon the prosecution case and for this reason it can give the defence no cause for complaint. Where, however, he decides that there is no real chance of collusion he should leave the final decision on that issue to the jury, directing them to investigate whether there is a real chance of collusion and to treat each witness as being uncorroborated unless they are sure that there was no real chance of collusion. On one view of things this is a complicated and rather futile exercise because in the event that the jury feels prosecution witnesses may have put their heads together they will treat the evidence of one or more of them with suspicion. On the other hand, for as long as the common law applies the existing test of corroboration it is necessary for the jury to look for corroboration with that test in mind and the judge must direct them carefully about it.

There is some authority that certain witnesses may not corroborate each other even if there is no possibility of them having colluded. In *DPP* v *Hester* the House of Lords held that children who give unsworn evidence cannot corroborate each other's evidence. Since there is now no need for corroboration of such evidence, there is nothing to prevent the jury from attaching what weight they think appropriate to the unsworn evidence of children. This rule in *Hester* was limited in scope because it only applied to unsworn evidence and it was expressly held that evidence given on oath by one child can corroborate that which is given by another unsworn. This repeated the law as stated by Lord Goddard CJ in *Campbell* [1956] 2 QB 432.

There is no absolute rule of law that accomplices to the same offence cannot corroborate each other: *R* v *Cheema* [1994] 1 All ER 639.

Cumulative corroboration

Until recently there was no clear authority whether a number of pieces of evidence could be added together to provide corroboration where each piece by itself did not fulfil all parts of the definition of corroboration. In *Baskerville* it was said that corroborative evidence need not be direct evidence that the accused committed the crime, but could be circumstantial evidence that he was connected with it. The Court of Appeal held in *Thomas* v *Jones* [1921] 1 KB 22 that evidence which had been heard by a magistrates' court did not amount to corroboration because it did not implicate the accused, Atkin LJ saying that items of evidence could not be added together to make corroboration where each item taken separately did not satisfy every element of the *Baskerville* test. On the facts of that case the items of evidence did not overlap so as to provide corroboration when looked at as a whole and neither of the other two judges expressed a general view on the possibility of an accumulation of evidence giving corroboration.

There is now no doubt that in some circumstances a jury can treat an accumulation of evidence as providing corroboration. In *Hills* (1988) 86 Cr App R 26 the Court of Appeal allowed the defendant's appeal against conviction because the direction about corroboration was defective. But in the course of its judgment the court accepted that a number of pieces of evidence could properly be combined to provide corroboration where that accumulation of evidence implicates the accused. An example was given by Lord Lane CJ. He said:

> '... in a rape case, where the defendant denies he ever had sexual intercourse with the complainant, it may be possible to prove (1) by medical evidence that she had had sexual intercourse within an hour or so prior to the medical examination, (2) by other independent evidence that the defendant and no other man had been with her during that time, (3) that her underclothing was torn and that she had injuries to her private parts. None of those items of evidence on their own would be sufficient to provide the necessary corroboration, but the judge would be entitled to direct the jury that if they were satisfied so as to feel sure that each of those three items had been proved, the combined effect of the three items would be capable of corroborating the girl's evidence.'

This case does no more than uphold the right of the jury to apply common sense to their deliberations. The combining of evidence to implicate the defendant can be illustrated further by an example in which corroboration is irrelevant:

D is accused of the murder of his wife. There are two prosecution witnesses. Witness A says that he was looking into D's bedroom at 2pm on 1 January and saw a carving knife fly through the air and hit D's wife in the heart, but he only saw one half of the room – the half in which D's wife was standing. Witness B says that he also was looking into the room at 2pm on 1 January, that he could see only the other half of the room and that he saw D throw a knife which he describes in a similar way. From the questions which are asked of A and B it is clear that the direction in which D threw the knife was the direction from which the knife which hit his wife came.

The jury would be acting contrary to common sense if they did not conclude that the knife which D threw was the knife which hit his wife. A's evidence, taken by itself, does not implicate D because he did not see D. But in fact his evidence does implicate D because it does not stand by itself; it must be looked at in connection with all other evidence, and when B's testimony is also taken into account it is obvious that A does implicate D. Similarly B's evidence does not disclose an offence unless it is combined with A's.

What is shown by the above examples is not unique to any particular sort of case. Even where corroboration is not required the analysis of evidence by the jury will follow the same pattern; they will examine each item of evidence in the light of the other evidence called. The more the prosecution case is confirmed by each successive witness, the more likely the accused is to be convicted. What cannot be done is to dispense altogether with the need for independent evidence implicating the accused. In *Nicholas* v *Penny* the evidence of the reading on the speedometer only implicated the accused when combined with the evidence of the police officer that the car he was following was that of the defendant. There was, therefore, nothing which directly implicated the accused other than the evidence of that officer.

Indeed, even if corroboration is required as a matter of practice but it is not possible to find either direct or cumulative corroboration, the jury may still be satisfied of the defendant's guilt because the total effect of the evidence is that the case is proved. In the example of the rape case given by Lord Lane in *Hills*, the absence of item (2) would not necessarily be fatal to a conviction if the jury is sure that the girl is correct in saying that the man involved was the defendant. Items (1) and (3) support her evidence in that they go to prove that there was a rape and the jury may feel that they can rely on the complainants' evidence of the identity of the rapist.

Distress

In cases involving an allegation of a sexual offence the evidence of the complainant can sometimes be corroborated by evidence that she was seen to be distressed at the time of the alleged offence. The problem which arises is often that there is nothing to link the apparent distress to the accused other than the evidence of the complainant that it was he who caused it by his assault on her, in other words that it is not independent evidence. For example, in *Dowley* [1983] Crim LR 169 the defendant's wife went to a house and complained to its occupant that her husband had attempted to rape her. She appeared to be distressed and the householder gave evidence about this. That witness did not see the defendant and the only thing to link his wife's distressed condition with him was her own evidence. The Court of Appeal held that the evidence of the householder could corroborate that of the complainant. In this respect the case appears to be wrongly decided because the element of independence was missing. In the end it made no difference, however, because the appeal was allowed on other grounds.

The need for independence was stressed by the Court of Criminal Appeal in the leading case in this area, *Redpath* (1962) 46 Cr App R 319. The defendant was accused of indecent assault. He was seen entering an area of moorland with the complainant and soon afterwards the same witness saw her run out of the moor looking distressed. This was held to be corroboration because the complainant did not know she was being observed and therefore the chance of her pretending to be distressed was minimal. In addition the accused was implicated because of the observation of him with the complainant. As well as showing the importance of the *Baskerville* test being applied in full to evidence of distressed condition, this case also illustrates the meaning of independence of corroborative evidence. It was said above that for evidence to be independent it must have originated from a source other than the person whose evidence requires to be corroborated. On the face of things this is not the case where distressed condition is put before the jury because what the court hears is that the complainant looked distressed, in other words the corroborative evidence is about the person whose evidence needs corroborating.

The emphasis in *Redpath* on distress being corroboration where the risk of pretence can be discounted is the key to understanding how it can be independent of the complainant. If she has not fabricated her distress, it must be real. And if it is real, she will have no physical control over showing her distress. Therefore her distress is independent of her because she has no control over whether or not she shows it.

This does not mean that the jury should not be told of the complainant's distress unless the judge is satisfied that it was genuine, because they may feel it to be of some significance even if they cannot be sure that it was genuine. In *Knight* [1966] 1 WLR 230 Lord Parker CJ, who gave the judgment in *Redpath*, said that the tendency was for judges to leave evidence of distress to the jury with a direction that little weight should be given to it except in special circumstances. It is now common practice for this to be done, but where the *Redpath* test is satisfied the judge may go further and direct the jury that there is evidence which is capable of being corroboration.

In *Chauhan* (1981) 73 Cr App R 232 the Court of Appeal reviewed the authorities, concluding that the position adopted by Lord Parker CJ in *Knight* was still correct. *Chauhan* is a difficult case because it contains dicta which suggest that distress can corroborate in every case and the risk of the complainant having deliberately pretended to be upset was something which affected the degree to which it corroborated her evidence. Such dicta are not to be followed because it is clear from the report that the court was not attempting to redefine the extent to which evidence of distress can corroborate a complainant.

Admissions

The defendant's admissions can have two effects on the matter of corroboration. Clearly they can amount to corroboration, because there is no better evidence of guilt than a confession voluntarily given by someone of sound mind. For example in *Dossi* (1918) 13 Cr App R 158 the accused admitted fondling a girl but denied that it was indecent. This was held to be capable of corroborating her evidence because it supported her assertion that she had been touched by the defendant. It is not necessary for corroborative evidence to implicate the accused in every material respect. It did not matter that Dossi's admissions in the witness box went only to the issue whether the girl was correct in saying that she had been touched but did not go to the question whether the touching was indecent. That question is a matter of inference from the facts which are proved because once the jury is satisfied that there was an assault which could have been innocent or could have been indecent, there is little that the girl could say one way or the other on the question of indecency, because she could not give evidence of the defendant's intention. What he said in evidence was independent of the girl, supported her evidence in part, and also implicated him in that it showed that he committed the act alleged by the girl.

But admissions can also have the effect of dispensing with the need for corroboration at all: *Rider* (1986) 83 Cr App R 207. Another way of explaining the decision in *Dossi* is by saying that the only issue in dispute between prosecution and defence was whether the assault upon the girl was accompanied by an indecent intention. It would not have been open to the jury to decide that there was no touching of the girl because that much was accepted by the defence. On this analysis there was no need for corroboration at all because the truth of the evidence of the girl was not in issue. It goes without saying that the jury need not look for corroboration of a witness whose evidence is accepted by all parties as being true.

Lies

It is not uncommon for persons arrested for an offence to tell a story to the police which is not true in an attempt to divert attention from themselves or to hide the fact that they were doing something which they do not want disclosed at the time the offence was committed. For example a man accused of rape may say that at the time in question he was having a drink at his local public house when in fact he was in bed with his mistress. The motive for telling the lie is not to hide guilt of rape but to prevent his wife hearing that he was having an affair. Similarly someone with a long record for sexual offences may give a false alibi in order to deflect attention from him, out of a fear of the police not believing a simple denial of involvement.

Indeed one can go further; a person charged with one offence may tell a pack of lies because the truth is that at the time in question he was committing some other offence. It is quite understandable in these cases why the defendant would lie to the police, but the jury should not consider his lies to corroborate the prosecution evidence because they do not.

These practical points have led to a very strict definition of the occasions when lies told by the accused may corroborate. Four features must be present. First, the lie told must be deliberate and not just a slip of the tongue. Secondly, it must relate to a material issue on the offence charged. Thirdly, the motive for lying must be a realisation of guilt and a fear of the truth being known. Fourthly, the fact that the defendant is lying must be clearly proved by evidence other than that which needs to be corroborated: *Lucas* [1981] QB 720. To an extent the third element of this test is only satisfied if the jury are sure of guilt, yet if they are sure of guilt from other evidence they do not need to look for corroboration of an unreliable witness's testimony. But in reality all that was meant was that the jury should investigate all of the circumstances in which the lie was told to see whether they can construe it as an admission of guilt, and in particular they should bear in mind that it may have been made because the defendant wished to hide something else.

In *R v Goodway* [1993] 4 All ER 894 Lord Taylor of Gosforth CJ said that it is well established that where lies told by the defendant are relied on by the Crown, or may be relied upon by the jury as corroboration, where that is required, or as support for identification evidence, the judge should give a direction along the lines indicated in *R v Lucas* [1981] 2 All ER 1008. The jury must therefore be told that the lie must be deliberate and must relate to a material issue and that they must be satisfied that there is no innocent motive for the lie. As to the last, the jury should be reminded that people sometimes lie, eg, in an attempt to bolster up a just cause, or out of shame, or out of a wish to conceal disgraceful behaviour. In regard to corroboration, the lie must be established by evidence other than that of the witness who is to be corroborated. In *Goodway* the appellant's lies were relied upon by the Crown as support of identification evidence and the summing up encouraged the jury so to regard them. Accordingly, it was a case in which a *Lucas* direction was required. The court concluded that the omission of such a direction was a material misdirection and that it would not, in all the circumstances, be appropriate to apply the proviso. The appeal was therefore allowed and a retrial ordered.

In *R v Richens* [1993] 4 All ER 877 the Court of Appeal held that the trial judge's failure to direct the jury to consider whether there was any explanation for the appellant's lies other than guilt of the offence charged, and his indication that the jury might regard the appellant's lies as probative of murder rather than manslaughter, amounted to a material misdirection.

A trial judge must direct the jury to consider whether there might be an innocent explanation for the defendant's lies where lies could amount to (a) corroboration or (b) evidence supporting identification. Beyond these situations, the trial judge has a discretion, but not a duty, whenever fairness demands, to direct the jury that the mere fact that the defendant had told a lie was not of itself evidence of guilt and that the burden remained on the Crown to prove the defendant's guilt. The greater the importance of the lies in the case, the stronger would be the case for giving such a direction: *R* v *Bey* [1993] 3 All ER 253. Where such a direction does not have to be given, and is not given, the judge must be careful not to suggest that dishonesty either to the police or in court is tantamount to establishing any element of dishonesty which has to be proved: *R* v *Sharp* [1993] 3 All ER 225.

3

Burden and Standard of Proof

3.1 Introduction

Meaning of burden of proof

Most people are familiar with the concept that the prosecutor or plaintiff must prove the allegations he brings against a defendant. But the complexity of issues in criminal and civil trials prevents there being any such absolute rule. This not to say that there is no such general rule, because there is – he who asserts must prove. We must investigate the matter in greater detail however in order to see both what this phrase means and when there are exceptions to it.

The term 'burden of proof' covers three different onuses which a party to litigation may bear. The first two are correct uses of the phrase, the third is not. The first use is to describe the duty to prove that on consideration of the whole of the evidence, the party wins the case. The second is to describe the duty to prove a particular fact in issue. The third, inaccurate, use is to describe the burden of calling enough evidence to require the court to ask itself who has won.

The burden on a party of proving that he wins the case is often called the ultimate burden, the general burden, the persuasive burden or the legal burden. The burden to prove that a particular fact in issue should be decided in his favour is also commonly known as the legal burden. In the discussion which follows we will refer to the first burden as the general burden and the second as the legal burden; the third will be called the evidential burden.

It is doubtful whether it is correct to distinguish between the general and the legal burdens, because whether a party proves the whole of his case depends upon

56

whether the evidence on the relevant individual issues is in his favour. For example, in a theft case the prosecution will have to prove all elements of the offence, namely, that the defendant dishonestly appropriated property belonging to another with the intention of permanently depriving that other of it. If they cannot prove any one element they will not gain a conviction, even if every other is proved. To this extent it is meaningless to talk of a general burden, because what the court must investigate is whether the legal burden on each individual issue is satisfied; if it is, then the general burden is satisfied, if it is not the general burden is not satisfied.

Nevertheless, the concept of the general burden has its uses, the most important of which is in defining a general rule. We will see below that in criminal cases the general rule is that the prosecution must prove the defendant's guilt. This applies, subject to specific exceptions, in every case and it is legally accurate to say that the Crown bears a general burden in criminal cases. But this does not help the magistrates, judge or jury to conclude how each case must be decided, because that requires an investigation of the evidence called in order to see whether the elements of the offence are made out. It does, though, help the court where no evidence at all is called, because the party with the general burden will lose.

The evidential burden

The evidential burden is the burden of putting sufficient evidence before the court to make out a prima facie case. It is best explained with reference to criminal cases. If the prosecution in a trial for theft fails to call any evidence that the goods allegedly stolen did not belong to the defendant, it is impossible for a conviction to result and therefore the defence may submit to the judge that there is no case to answer and the judge will direct the jury to acquit. Because there is no evidence on one of the vital issues there is no need for the defendant to call any evidence; he is not in danger of conviction unless the prosecution calls evidence to make every issue a live issue. This does not mean that the judge will direct an acquittal unless he is satisfied that the defendant is guilty. Rather he will direct an acquittal if he is satisfied that on one or more issues that there is no case to answer. One way in which the evidential burden has been described is as the burden of passing the judge.

We will see below the amount of evidence which must be called in order to get past the judge and have the case left to the jury. It is important that the evidential burden is not called a burden of proof because in order to satisfy it nothing has to be proved; all that must happen is that evidence is called. The evidential burden does not always lie on the party who bears the legal burden on an issue. Whether it does lie on him or on his opponent depends entirely upon what evidence has been called. For example, in a criminal case where assault is alleged, the victim may give evidence that he started a fight with the accused but that the accused over-reacted and used an unreasonable amount of force in self-defence. In such a case the prosecution itself has called evidence which makes self-defence an issue, and the jury will have to be directed to consider self-defence even if the accused calls no evidence at all. In contrast, if the victim says he was set upon for no reason at all and denies that the accused acted in self-defence, there will be no evidence of self-defence before the court. In that case the defendant will have the burden of making self-defence a live issue by calling evidence. But in either case the prosecution will have to prove the absence of self-defence if it is to earn a conviction. The evidential burden will be on the defendant, but the legal burden remains on the prosecution. We will investigate this aspect of the evidential burden in greater detail below.

The tactical burden

Stone ((1944) LQR 379) described what we have called the evidential burden as the 'tactical burden'. These days, however, that term is used in the way suggested by Cross, namely to refer to cases where practical considerations impose a burden on a party to call evidence even though the law does not.

The legal burden arises as a matter of law, because if no evidence is called on an issue the party whom the law requires to prove that issue before he may receive judgment must lose – the tribunal of fact has no option but to decide the case against him. The position is the same with the evidential burden; if no evidence is called so as to make a potential issue a live issue, the tribunal of fact is not entitled to decide that that issue is proved.

But there is more to every trial than what the law says about the need to call evidence. In the example of the assault case given above, where the prosecution witness gave evidence that he was attacked for no reason at all, the defendant is entitled to sit back, call no evidence and invite the jury to disbelieve that witness. The law does not say he will lose unless he calls evidence, indeed it specifically provides that he is not obliged to give evidence. However, as a practical matter, if the prosecution witness gave clear evidence and sounded as though he might well have told the truth, the defendant is likely to be convicted unless he calls evidence. He would be well advised to give evidence in order to stand some chance of acquittal. It is this practical need to give evidence where a strong case has been made against a party which is the tactical burden. As a matter of tactics in the trial he must call evidence to stand any chance of winning.

In fact the tactical burden has both positive and negative aspects. The positive aspect is what has been mentioned already, that a party who will lose if no further evidence is called in his favour has the burden of calling evidence. But the negative aspect is no less important; it is that a party who is likely to win if no further evidence is called must decide whether to call another witness and run the risk of him doing more harm than good. In the abstract it is easy to answer this question; the answer is that you should not call any further evidence once you have called enough to win. This assumes that it is easy to tell who will win, but it is not; how the judge or jury will assess a particular witness is a matter for them. In addition the lay client may insist that a witness is called when the advocate's instinct and experience tell him that it would be unwise.

Shifting burdens

The suggestion is made occasionally that burdens can shift from one party to another during the course of a trial. Any such suggestion is wrong save insofar as it refers to the tactical burden. The legal burden cannot shift because it is provided by law which party must prove an issue. There is only one stage at which that burden arises, and that is at the end of the case when all the evidence has been heard and the court must decide what has been proved. Of course it will be in the mind of the party who bears the legal burden that throughout the case he has to call evidence and challenge his opponent's evidence, otherwise he will lose. But the court will hear all evidence regardless of who bears the legal burden and will only consider whether it has been satisfied at the very end. The evidential burden cannot shift from one party to another, because that burden decides who must call evidence in order to make an issue a live issue. Once evidence has been called to raise the issue, that is the end of the evidential burden. It has been satisfied.

The tactical burden lies at any time on the party who is likely to lose unless further evidence is called. It follows from the very nature of the tactical burden that it can shift from party to party as the case proceeds. Before any evidence is called the general and tactical burdens are identical in effect. If no evidence is called the party with the general burden will lose and so, as a matter of tactics, he should call evidence. But once evidence is called the general and legal burdens are placed on ice to be resurrected at the end of the trial, and it is the tactical burden which will dictate what evidence is called and what questions are asked of witnesses.

3.2 Burden of proof – criminal cases

The general burden

Lord Sankey LC, in *Woolmington* v *DPP* [1935] AC 462, said:

> 'Throughout the web of the English criminal law one golden thread is always to be seen, that is the duty of the prosecution to prove the prisoner's guilt ... No matter what the charge or where the trial the principle that the prosecution must prove the guilt of the prisoner is part of the common law of England and no attempt to whittle it down can be entertained.'

The charge in *Woolmington* was murder, the accused having admitted that he shot his wife. The trial judge had directed the jury that it was for the defendant to establish that the shooting was an accident, but the House of Lords ruled this to be incorrect. The House re-affirmed the old rule that a plea of not guilty puts every allegation in issue. Only two exceptions were recognised by Lord Sankey, first, the defence of insanity on which the defendant must prove his defence, and secondly defences the proof of which lie on the defendant because statute says so. The 'golden thread' speaks of the burden on the prosecution as being a single burden, what we have called the general burden. Lord Sankey did not differentiate between the legal and general burdens and his speech has been taken as meaning that the legal burden on every issue in every case is on the prosecution save for the two exceptions mentioned above.

No serious challenge has been made to the correctness of Lord Sankey's golden thread, but its limitations as a comprehensive exposition of English law on the burden of proof have been exposed in a number of decisions. What Lord Sankey did not specifically address was the question of the evidential burden, which is hardly surprising since the defence of accident does not raise any issue which is not already before the jury. After all, one element of the actus reus of murder is that the accused committed a voluntary act which caused the death of another. But this does not diminish the correctness of what he said on the general burden.

The evidential burden

If the law held rigidly to the principle that a plea of not guilty puts in issue every allegation which might be made against the accused, the prosecution would have to call evidence to establish lack of duress, provocation, non-insane automatism, drunkenness and self-defence in every case where such a defence might be raised. This would simply waste time if the defendant has no intention of raising the defence. So the law places an evidential burden on the accused in each of these cases. It is not possible to give a comprehensive list of defences which might be raised first by evidence from the defence. Those which have just been mentioned are examples, but as we shall see there are others.

The test of when the prosecution must anticipate a defence has never been stated clearly by the courts. Necessarily the Crown must call evidence on every element of the offence alleged; the example of a theft case was used above to illustrate this. The Crown must lead evidence about both the actus reus and the mens rea. If at the end of the prosecution case any element has not been dealt with, the defence may submit that there is no case to answer. It is only if there is a case to answer all elements of both the actus reus and the mens rea that the defence may have to call evidence at all. This much is clear from the passage from *Woolmington* cited above.

Where the defence wishes to suggest that the evidence which, prima facie, shows guilt, in fact does not prove guilt, it may do so by arguing that the prosecution's evidence simply should not be believed. But this is not always possible, either because that evidence is very strong, or because the accused accepts what the prosecution witnesses say but puts forward an explanation for what happened. This is the test for whether the accused may bear an evidential burden – is he raising an explanation which is not raised by the prosecution evidence? One must assume that the prosecution evidence is accepted, even if it is not, and ask whether the case is proved in the absence of an explanation for the defendant's conduct. If a possible explanation has come from the prosecution witnesses themselves, the accused would not be raising a new issue by giving evidence which attempts to reinforce what the court has already heard about that explanation. But if the prosecution evidence could not be construed as giving him a defence, then the onus will be on the defendant to raise his explanation.

It is important to distinguish between cases where the accused is raising an explanation for what he is alleged to have done, and cases where he is saying that he did not do it. The latter type of case imposes no burden on him other than a tactical burden. It is also important to remember that in cases where the accused does have the burden of raising an issue which has not already been raised, that does not mean that he must give evidence himself. He may call witnesses or may use any other form of admissible evidence.

Room was left in Lord Sankey's speech for an evidential burden to be placed on the accused, because he said:

'When evidence of death and malice has been given ... the accused is entitled to show, by evidence or by examination of the circumstances adduced by the Crown, that the act on his part which caused death was either unintentional or provoked.'

This passage shows that he felt that the accused might raise the issue of provocation without it expressly having been dealt with by the prosecution. But, of course, what was said was obiter.

In *Mancini* v *DPP* [1942] AC 1 the House of Lords (which included Lord Sankey) held that a trial judge does not have to leave the defence of provocation to the jury unless there is evidence from which the possibility of provocation arises. It was not said that that evidence had to come from the accused, but it was implied that it is not necessary for the prosecution to deal with the possibility of provocation unless either their own witnesses gave evidence from which provocation might be found, or the defence gives such evidence. The same was said more clearly in *Chan Kau* v *R* [1955] AC 206 where the accused gave evidence from which provocation might have been inferred. The Privy Council held that the judge should have left the question of provocation to the jury.

Chan Kau v *R* recognised that self-defence should be treated in the same way and did not suggest that the prosecution should call evidence of lack of self-defence in every case. This was made part of English law by *Lobell* [1957] 1 QB 547 in which the trial judge directed the jury that it was for the accused to prove self-defence. The Court of Criminal Appeal disagreed, applying *Woolmington*. It was said, as was said in *Mancini*, that the jury must always decide a case upon the whole of the evidence and if evidence of a possible defence comes from the accused, it must be considered. It was also said that when the possible defence is self-defence that evidence would ordinarily come from the accused himself, although that does not mean that it must come from him. No change in the law on the burden of proof was made by s3 of the Criminal Law Act 1967 which altered the legal definition of self-defence.

That the accused will also bear an evidential burden if he alleges non-insane automatism is clear from *Bratty* v *A-G for Northern Ireland* [1963] AC 386. The facts in that case did not raise the issue of non-insane automatism, but a dictum of

Devlin J in *Hill* v *Baxter* [1958] 1 QB 277 in which he said that the defence will have to lay the foundation for non-insane automatism to be considered, was followed. The defendant also bears an evidential burden on the issues of drunkenness (*DPP* v *Beard* [1920] AC 479) and duress (*Gill* [1963] 1 WLR 841). If he argues that he is not guilty of a charge of reckless or careless driving because his car was mechanically defective, the Crown will be entitled to rely on the presumption that mechanical things work properly and so will not have to prove in every case that the car was not defective. But if the defendant raises this issue, the burden will be on the Crown to prove by evidence that the car was not defective. The authority for this is *Spurge* [1961] 2 QB 205, in which the charge was the now defunct one of dangerous driving. We will return to this presumption in paragraph 3.6.

The cases in which the defendant bears the burden of proving a defence also impose on him an evidential burden. For example, if the defence alleges insanity, that defence will not be left to the jury at all unless enough evidence is called to make it a live issue. Little evidence is needed to satisfy a defendant's evidential burden, and this matter will be discussed in more detail in 3.4 below.

Insanity

Ever since *M'Naghten* (1843) 10 Cl & Fin 200 it has been beyond dispute that an accused who raises the defence of insanity must prove that defence. This onus is not just to raise the issue but to prove it. *Woolmington* accepted this rule as the only common law exception to the golden thread.

Difficult cases can sometimes arise where the evidence called by either the Crown or the defence is ambiguous and may be evidence of insanity or of non-insane automatism. In such cases the accused does not have to prove non-insane automatism any more than he had to prove it where it was the only possible defence. This has the result that the trial judge must direct the jury that the defendant must prove insanity but the Crown must prove the lack of non-insane automatism. Inevitably any direction like this may confuse the jury, but that is no reason to alter the normal rules on burden of proof and *Hill* v *Baxter* makes clear that those rules are not changed.

Insanity is relevant to the question whether the defendant is fit to plead as well as to whether he has a defence to the crime alleged. Whenever it is alleged that he is not fit to plead, whichever party raises the issue will have to prove it. In *Podola* [1960] 1 QB 325 the Court of Criminal Appeal held that where the prosecution asserts that the defendant is not fit to plead, it must prove it, and likewise where the defence makes the assertion, it must prove it.

In *Dickie* [1984] 1 WLR 1031 the Court of Appeal held that the trial judge may raise the issue of the defendant's sanity, even if neither prosecution nor defence raises it. Clearly the judge cannot have to prove anything, so he cannot bear a burden of proof. Nor can he require either party to prove insanity. The question therefore arises, where the judge has raised the issue, what evidence is necessary before he can find the accused insane. We shall see below that the effect of a legal burden on any issue being on the Crown is that it must prove the issue beyond reasonable doubt, whereas a legal burden on the defence is satisfied if it makes out its case on the balance of probabilities. Where the judge raises the issue of insanity he must give both prosecution and defence the opportunity to call what evidence they wish, and he probably has to decide whether on the balance of the whole evidence before him insanity is more likely than not.

Statutory exceptions

It is a matter of statutory construction whether an Act of Parliament imposes a burden of proof on the accused. But it is not necessary for the Act to do so expressly. The authorities are not the same in the Crown Court and the magistrates' courts, because there is a general statutory rule in s101 of the Magistrates' Courts Act 1980, the effect of which is to place a legal burden on the accused to prove certain types of defence.

It will be seen from the wording of the s101 that it is concerned with cases in which the defendant is accused of doing something which may be done by some people but not by others, or which may be done in some circumstances but not in others. Its main application is to regulatory offences for which a licence or permission is required. It will be for the defendant to prove that he possessed the necessary licence or permission. There will be two stages to the trial of an offence which falls within s101. First, the prosecution must call evidence that the accused did the act which he may or may not have been allowed to do, and then the defendant will have to call evidence to prove that he was allowed to do it.

The first stage requires the prosecution to call evidence in the same way that it must in cases where it bears the legal burden on every issue. However, there are problems defining when s101 comes into play. For example, if the accused is charged with obstructing the highway without lawful excuse, the absence of lawful excuse could be seen to be something which the Crown has to prove, or it could be seen as an excuse or qualification, proof of which, by virtue of s101, lies on the defence.

The House of Lords had an opportunity to give general guidance on this matter in the Scottish appeal of *Nimmo* v *Alexander Cowan & Sons Ltd* [1968] AC 107, where the dispute was civil. An employee fell during the course of his work and alleged that his place of work was not safe. In order for the employee to succeed it would have to be decided that the employer had committed an offence, because the alleged breach of the Factories Act in question was only actionable as a civil wrong if it was also a criminal wrong. The Act laying down the duty said that working places 'shall so far as is reasonably practicable, be made and kept safe for any person working there'. All members of the House said that the placing of the burden of proving reasonable practicability was the same in civil and criminal cases arising from the Act, so the decision is relevant to criminal cases.

The employee did not allege what should have been done to make and keep safe the workplace, arguing that by virtue of an enactment in practically identical terms to s101 of the Magistrates' Court Act 1980, the employer was relying upon an excuse or qualification if he said he had taken all reasonably practicable steps to make and keep it safe. It was held that the burden lay on the employer to prove that he had taken all reasonably practicable steps. All five Law Lords said that it is a matter for the construction of the statute in question in each case whether qualifying words such as 'so far as is reasonably practicable' impose a burden on prosecutor or defendant.

One of the Scottish judges in a lower court had said:

'The words "so far as is reasonably practicable" ... become, in my view, an integral part of the duty imposed and define the ambit of what is obligatory.'

Lords Reid and Wilberforce agreed with him, holding that it was for the employee to prove that the employer had done an unauthorised act, that act being the failure to provide a safe place of work so far as was reasonably practicable.

Lords Guest, Upjohn and Pearson disagreed, holding that the prohibited act was the act of providing a place of work which was not safe. They said that if the employer proved that he had taken all reasonably practicable steps to make the place safe he would be excused from liability.

This difference of view in the House of Lords does little to assist in the construction of other statutes. All five Law Lords held that every Act must be construed so as to determine the scope of the prohibited act. In other words, was it unlawful to provide an unsafe workplace or was it only unlawful to fail to take all reasonably practicable steps to make it safe? Normal rules of statutory construction had to be applied to determine what was prohibited. One final important point is that the question who would have the easier task in satisfying a burden of proof is only a relevant circumstance if the proper construction of the Act in question leaves it unclear who bears the burden.

There are other cases in which the incidence of the burden of proof in criminal cases has been discussed, but none gives any further help than *Nimmo*. In *Gatland* v *Metropolitan Police Commissioner* [1968] 2 QB 279 the defendant was charged that without lawful authority or excuse he deposited a thing on the highway endangering a user of the highway. The Divisional Court held that this offence required the prosecution to prove first, that the defendant deposited a thing on the highway and secondly that it caused a user of the highway to be endangered. Only if sufficient evidence was called to satisfy the evidential burden on those issues was there any need for the defendant to call evidence with a view to establishing that he had lawful authority or excuse. It was argued that the defendant had to prove the lack of danger to a user of the highway, but the court disagreed, holding that the only exception, exemption, proviso, excuse or qualification in the section creating the offence was the question of lawful authority or excuse.

Some offences obviously make conduct unlawful unless the defence establishes an excuse, for example driving without insurance (*Machin* v *Ash* [1950] WN 478) or without a licence (*John* v *Humphreys* [1955] 1 WLR 325) or serving alcohol without a licence (*Edwards* [1975] QB 27); in all these cases the accused can easily prove his right to do the act in question by producing evidence of his insurance or licence. It cannot be doubted that in these cases the section creating the offence says that certain things may not be done unless the defendant has a licence or otherwise qualifies to do them. But other cases are more difficult.

To return to an example cited above, if the accused is charged that without lawful excuse he wilfully obstructed the highway, is the absence of lawful excuse part of the offence, or is obstruction an offence unless the defendant can prove lawful excuse? *Gatland* v *MPC* holds that in the offence of depositing a thing on the highway the accused must prove lawful authority or excuse, but in *Hirst* v *Chief Constable of West Yorkshire* [1987] Crim LR 330 the Divisional Court held that where the obstruction is by a person's body rather than by a thing, the Crown must prove the lack of lawful excuse for obstruction. The difference between these cases is that in *Gatland* the act of depositing a thing on the highway was seen to be prima facie unlawful so that the defendant had to prove that he was authorised to deposit it, whereas in *Hirst* it was said that being on the highway was prima facie lawful and the Crown had to prove that the accused should not have been there.

Necessarily the courts must construe each offence separately to see whether the act complained of is one which you may not do without permission, or one which you may do unless there is some special feature of the case making that conduct unlawful. All of the circumstances are relevant, such as, the extent to which the offence would limit personal freedom of movement, whether it would be difficult for the prosecution to prove that the defendant did not have permission to do the act, and whether it would be easy for the defendant to prove the permission. But the question is one of statutory construction and if the Act is clear, the practical difficulties which the party bearing the burden may have are irrelevant.

Some statutes which create offences triable only in magistrates' courts make clear where the burden lies by saying that the defendant must prove his defence. For example, s1(1) of the Prevention of Crime Act 1953 says that a person who has an offensive weapon in a public place must prove that he had either authority or a reasonable excuse for carrying it. By s15(3) of the Road Traffic Offenders Act 1988, as substituted, someone charged with driving with excess alcohol has a defence if he proves that he consumed alcohol after he drove and that when he drove he was not over the limit.

Strictly speaking s101 is not needed in such cases because the Act creating the offence makes clear that the defendant bears a legal burden. But these examples do come within the scope of s101 because the defendant would be relying upon an exception, exemption, proviso, excuse or qualification.

In the Crown Court s101 has no direct application, but the defendant may still bear a legal burden if the Act creating the offence expressly or impliedly imposes such a burden. Some Acts are explicit, like those cited above. For example, s2(2) of the Homicide Act 1957 says that the defence must prove diminished responsibility, and s2 of the Prevention of Corruption Act 1916 says that a defendant who has received money from a certain type of person must prove that it was not a bribe. This last example is of an either way offence, that is an offence which can be tried either by the magistrates' court or the Crown Court. If the Act does not expressly say that the accused must prove an issue, it may do so impliedly. In *Edwards* [1975] QB 27 the Court of Appeal held that the defendant will bear a legal burden where he is charged under an Act which prohibits the doing of an act subject to certain exceptions, excuses or qualifications. In effect the court held that there was a common law rule which was the same as s101 of the Magistrates' Courts Act 1980, although it did not go so far as to say so in so many words.

However, the House of Lords reviewed the position in *Hunt* [1987] AC 352. Lord Griffiths said:

> 'The law would have developed on absurd lines if in respect of the same offence the burden of proof today differs according to whether the case was heard by the magistrates or on indictment.'

This was a questionable conclusion on the authorities, but there is now no doubt that the rule is the same in the Crown Court as in the magistrates' court, so s101 of the 1980 Act can be applied in all cases.

As the passage above states, the position which Lord Griffiths wanted to avoid was that the rule should be different depending upon the court in which the accused was tried. If each offence was triable in the magistrates' court only or in the Crown Court only, it might make sense to have different rules in different courts. But many offences are triable in either court depending upon whether the magistrates are prepared to hear it and where the defendant wishes to be tried. The charge in *Hunt* was triable either way and this was undoubtedly a strong factor in favour of the view taken by the House that the rules in both courts should be the same.

The picture which emerges from *Hunt* is as follows. First, if the words of the Act creating the offence are clear in imposing a legal burden on the defendant, then they must be applied and he must try to satisfy that burden. Secondly, if they are unclear all of the circumstances of the case must be considered in deciding whether Parliament has impliedly placed a legal burden on the accused. Finally, the most important consideration is whether the placing of a burden on the accused would be onerous.

The admissibility of evidence

There is little authority on whether there is a burden of proving the admissibility of evidence. Challenges are often made to admissibility, and trial judges are asked to rule whether a particular piece of evidence may be used. Often admissibility is simply a matter of law. Both prosecutor and defendant know what the evidence is and the judges must decide whether the law allows that sort of evidence to be given. Necessarily there may be argument about exactly what the law says and there is never any suggestion of either party having a burden of proving that what he says about the law is right. The judge will simply hear the arguments and decide what he feels is right.

But where the admissibility of evidence depends upon whether certain facts are in existence, the judge does have to ask himself whether there is proof of those facts and whether there is proof of admissibility. In *Yacoob* (1981) 72 Cr App R 313 the question arose whether a potential prosecution witness was married to the accused. If she was, she would not have been competent to give evidence against him. The trial judge ruled that the burden was on the defendant to establish the lack of competence, but the Court of Appeal held that whenever there is a challenge to the competence of a prosecution witness, competence must be proved by the prosecution.

We will see in chapter 6 that the prosecution must prove that a confession made by the defendant was properly obtained before it may be used against him. This is now specifically provided for by s76 of the Police and Criminal Evidence Act 1984, but even before the law about confessions was put into statutory form by that Act the common law required the Crown to prove admissibility where it was challenged: *Thompson* [1893] 2 QB 12.

Where the accused wishes to rely on a witness whose competence is in issue it has been suggested that he would have to prove competence. Nothing was said in *Yacoob* about what the position would have been if the defence had tendered the suspect witness. But a passage from *Cross on Evidence* (5th edition) was cited which suggests that whichever party wishes to rely on a piece of evidence must prove its admissibility. *Woolmington* and *Hunt* seem to go against this in that they make clear that the defendant only ever had to prove his defence in the cases of insanity and where statute requires it. Yet is is one thing to say that a defendant need not normally prove his defence, and another to say that he need not prove the admissibility of evidence upon which he intends to rely. The common law rules on admissibility of evidence are the same for prosecution and defence. For example, in *Sparks* v *R* [1964] AC 964 it was held that the defendant is not allowed to rely on hearsay evidence any more than the prosecution is allowed to rely on it. Nevertheless, it would cause no great hardship to require the Crown to prove the inadmissibility of defence evidence, and it would certainly be consistent with *Woolmington* for the burden of proving admissibility to lie on the Crown in all cases and at all times. In the absence of authority specifically dealing with this point it should be taken that the accused bears no burden of proving that evidence upon which he intends to rely is admissible.

3.3 Burden of proof – civil cases

Pleadings

The great majority of civil disputes only get to court after the issues are defined in writing in documents called pleadings. Cases can be heard without pleadings but such cases are comparatively rare. In most actions pleadings comprise a document from the plaintiff setting out his claim and a document from the defendant answering the allegations. The plaintiff's pleading is known as the statement of claim in the High Court or particulars of claim in the county court, and the defendant's pleading is known as the defence. There can be other additional pleadings, such as a counterclaim which is a claim made against the plaintiff by the defendant. For almost all purposes a counterclaim is treated as though it were a separate statement or particulars of claim, so the plaintiff can put in a defence to counterclaim.

The purpose of pleadings is to set out each party's allegations and part of this process is the agreement of those matters which are not in issue. Most cases revolve around issues of fact, so pleadings are mainly concerned with setting out allegations of fact. But the facts are not argued about in a vacuum, they must be related to the law which is applicable to the case.

The legal burden

Who bears the legal burden on any issue in a civil case depends primarily upon who is claiming a remedy from the court. In some circumstances the legal and evidential burdens are on different parties, but the general rule is 'He who asserts must prove'. This maxim applies so as to require the party who would lose if no evidence were called not just to start the ball rolling by calling evidence to make something a live issue, but also to prove that that issue should be decided in his favour. This does not automatically mean that the party who would lose if no evidence is called has the right to begin, because RSC Ord 35, r7, which applies in both the High Court and the county courts, allows the trial judge to make a ruling that a party shall start even if the burden of proof on any issue does not lie on that party. This rule is not often used, however, and the general principle is that the party who would lose if no evidence was called is entitled to begin the case, and whether this is the plaintiff or defendant in any case depends upon the issues which arise on the pleadings.

The phrase 'He who asserts must prove' can be misleading, because there are cases where on the pleadings one party is stating an affirmative and the other a negative, but it is the party who is stating a negative who bears the legal and evidential burden. For example, in a breach of contract case, the plaintiff may argue that the defendant did not do what he should have done and the defendant may argue that he did do it. On the face of things the defendant is pleading the affirmative in that he is saying he did perform his obligations. But if no evidence at all were called the law would not presume that the defendant breached the contract, in fact it would presume the contrary. Unless the plaintiff calls evidence he cannot possibly get a remedy from the court, so he will have to begin and will bear the legal burden. This was the position in *Soward* v *Leggatt* (1836) 7 C & P 613 where a landlord claimed that his tenant had failed to make repairs to the demised property. It was held to be for the landlord to begin because the substance of the case was that an allegation was being made by him and so he should have to substantiate it. A similar case is *Amos* v *Hughes* (1835) 1 M & R 464 where the plaintiff alleged that the defendant did not carry out printing work to a proper standard and the defendant argued that his work was adequate. The plaintiff was held to bear the legal burden of proving the alleged breach of contract because the law presumes that people do not break contracts. In *Abrath* v *North Eastern Railway* (1883) 11 QBD 440 the plaintiff claimed damages for malicious prosecution. The Court of Appeal held that he had to prove not only that the defendant instituted a prosecution when no crime had been committed, but also that he had no reasonable cause for doing so. Although this second element of the plaintiff's claim involved proving a negative, namely the absence of reasonable cause for prosecuting, the law does not presume that a prosecution is malicious simply because it turns out that no crime has been committed. If the plaintiff did not prove malice he would fail and so he bore the legal burden on that issue.

In order to know who would lose if no evidence were called it is necessary to know what presumptions the law makes. Everyone is familiar with the idea that someone is presumed to be innocent until his guilt is proved and we have seen that in *Woolmington* v *DPP* this was said to be the 'golden thread' running through English criminal law. There is a similar presumption in the civil law. But because there are so many different types of civil wrong, whereas, at least so far as the burden of proof is concerned, all crimes are the same, so the civil presumption of innocence differs in its application to different types of case.

We will investigate certain specific presumptions in detail in paragraph 3.6 of this chapter, but there are some generally applicable presumptions to which reference can usefully be made here. We have already seen that the party who wishes to claim a remedy from the court normally has to prove his entitlement to that remedy; we have also seen that this will usually be the plaintiff. It does not matter whether he is alleging that the defendant has done a positive wrong, such as an assault, or has failed to do something which he should have done, for example has failed to perform a contractual duty. If there is no court hearing the plaintiff will have no remedy apart from self-help which is not always lawful, so he must prove his entitlement to a remedy.

In *Joseph Constantine Steamship Line Ltd* v *Imperial Smelting Corporation Ltd* [1942] AC 154 the House of Lords held that where frustration is raised as a defence to a claim in contract the defendant must prove the occurrence of the frustrating event and it is for the plaintiff to prove that that event was caused by the fault of the defendant if he wishes to argue that the frustration was self-induced. All members of the House said that the party who alleges that the other has done something wrong will normally have to prove it. In other words it is presumed that someone has not done wrong. A similar presumption was applied many years earlier in *Williams* v *East India Company* (1802) 3 East 192 where the plaintiff alleged that the defendants had put dangerous material on board ship without the consent of the captain. The plaintiff was required to prove the defendant's wrongdoing.

Many further examples can be given. In *Wakelin* v *London & South Western Railway* (1886) 12 App Cas 41 it was held that it is for the plaintiff in a negligence action to prove the existence of a duty of care, its breach and that loss was occasioned by the breach. A plaintiff in an assault and battery action must prove that there was physical contact and that that contact was accompanied by a hostile intent on the part of the defendant: *Wilson* v *Pringle* [1986] 2 All ER 440. A person arguing that a company acted outside the powers given to it by its memorandum of association must prove his claim: *Rolled Steel Products (Holdings) Ltd* v *British Steel Corporation* [1986] Ch 246. A landlord must prove the tenant's breach of the terms of a lease if he is to establish a right to possession because of breach: *Wisbech St Mary Parish Council* v *Lilley* [1956] 1 All ER 301, Rent Act 1977 s98(1), Housing Act 1988 s7(3). A plaintiff who argues that his ship was lost at sea must prove that the loss was caused by a peril against which he was insured before he will be able to recover: *The Gloria* (1936) 54 Ll L Rep 35.

These cases illustrate two points, first, that the party who claims a remedy must normally prove his entitlement, and secondly that this normally means that there is a legal burden on the plaintiff to prove all elements of his claim.

The presumption of innocence does not always apply so as to require the party claiming a remedy to prove that the defendant has no defence. Everything depends upon the sort of defence which is raised. Necessarily, the plaintiff must prove the facts which form the foundation of his claim, for example he must prove that the defendant did not perform contractual obligations or that the defendant breached a duty of care and caused loss.

Any assertion by the defendant that he did perform the contract or that he was negligent would be taken into account when the court decides whether the plaintiff has proved his case. But defences which arise by way of excuse are normally for the defendant to prove. In *The Glendarroch* [1894] P 226, the plaintiff had the burden of proving that he made a contract by which the defendant was to deliver goods and that they were not delivered; but it was for the defendant to prove that he was entitled to rely on an exception in the contract which excused him from having to deliver where the goods were lost because of a 'peril of the sea'. The defence was not something the plaintiff had to rebut as part of his main case, because the only essential elements of a breach of contract action are that there was a contractual duty which was not performed. Any excuse for non-performance must therefore be proved by the party relying on it, namely the defendant. A similar point can be made about the *Joseph Constantine* case because, although it was for the plaintiff to prove that the ship did not arrive in time, it was for the defendant to prove that this was because of a frustrating event. By contrast, the plaintiff was required to prove that the defendant could not rely on an excuse in *Hurst* v *Evans* [1917] 1 KB 352. The plaintiff claimed under an insurance policy for the loss of certain property. The policy provided that the plaintiff was not insured for losses caused by theft by his employees. The onus was held to be on the plaintiff to prove that the loss was not caused by such a theft. Although it has not been expressly overruled, this case was disapproved in *Munro Brice & Co* v *War Risks Association* [1918] 2 KB 78 in which the decision in *The Glendarroch* was preferred.

Proving excuses is sometimes necessary in non-contractual cases. For example, it is for the defendant to prove contributory negligence: *Wakelin* v *London & South Western Railway, Esso Petroleum Co Ltd* v *Southport Corp* [1956] AC 218. But by far the most common instances of the defendant bearing a legal burden in a civil action are where he must prove an excuse for non-performance of a contract.

In some cases practical considerations are cited as the reason for the legal burden being placed on the defendant rather than the plaintiff. Of particular significance is the difficulty which the plaintiff may have of proving something which is only within the knowledge of the defendant. In the *Joseph Constantine* case it was held that proof of a frustrating event was for the defendant. The plaintiff was unable to say why the ship had not arrived, so the defendant who was in control of the vessel at all material times had the burden of proving both the occurrence of the fire and that it was sufficiently serious to frustrate the contract. This does not mean that in all cases where it is easier for one party to prove something than it is for the other to disprove it, the party with the easier task bears a legal burden. If it is easier for the plaintiff to prove that the defendant had no excuse than for the latter to prove that he did, the court may be inclined to draw an adverse inference from a failure by the plaintiff to call strong evidence on the issue; but this will not place a legal burden on him.

There is, however, a special rule in insurance cases where it is alleged that the plaintiff has 'scuttled' a ship. If he claims under a policy of marine insurance he will have to prove what caused the loss of the ship: *The Gloria*. This is so whether or not the defendant insurance company pleads that the plaintiff acted fraudulently by deliberately causing the ship to sink in order to be able to claim under the policy: *The Popi M* [1985] 1 WLR 948. The rule is clearly based on the need to protect insurance companies where the evidence about the cause of the ship sinking may be at the bottom of the seas and therefore unavailable to the defendant.

Parties may make provision in a contract for the legal burden on certain issues to lie on one or other of them. At common law such clauses are perfectly valid but will have to be clearly expressed if they are to put a legal burden on the party who would not normally bear it. As we have seen from *The Glendarroch*, contracts will normally be construed so as to impose strict duties on the defendant and unless he can prove a good reason for not performing them he will be liable for any failures which the plaintiff can prove. A contract term which alters the normal rules on burden of proof counts as an exemption clause for the purpose of the Unfair Contract Terms Act 1977: see s13(1)(c).

The evidential burden

We saw in paragraph 3.1 of this chapter that evidential burdens can be of importance at two stages of a criminal trial, first, when the defendant submits that there is no case to answer and secondly when the jury is directed by the judge about what the issues are in the case.

In civil actions tried by judge alone submissions that there is no case to answer are rarely made. The reason for this is the procedural rule in *Alexander* v *Rayson* [1936] 1 KB 169 which prevents a party from calling evidence in an action tried by judge alone if he has made a submission of no case. This does not mean that submissions of no case are never made, simply that they are reserved for cases where the evidence called by the party who started calling evidence was weak and that to be called by the other party may be equally weak or weaker.

Nevertheless, the trial judge will often make clear to the defendant that he does not consider the evidence called by the plaintiff to be enough to prove a particular issue. In this way he shows that a submission of no case on that issue would have been successful if made and that the defendant need not trouble him with unnecessary evidence. Not all judges do this, however; some will hear all the evidence which is called and only make their decision on considering the whole of it.

The second stage at which evidential burdens arise in criminal proceedings is of less significance in civil trials because the danger of confusing a jury with unnecessary issues does not often arise.

There is a second use of evidential burdens in civil actions. It arises because of the way in which legal burdens may be distributed between the parties. The classic example is the *Joseph Constantine* case where the plaintiff had the legal burden of proving the non-arrival of the ship. The defendant bore the legal burden of proving the happening of the frustrating event and then the plaintiff had to prove that the frustrating event was caused by the fault of the defendant. The burden on the defendant was only relevant if the plaintiff called sufficient evidence to require the court to consider whether the ship had not arrived. Therefore his evidential burden on that issue had to be satisfied before the defendant's legal burden arose at all. And the defendant had to satisfy his evidential burden on the issue of the happening of the explosion and its effect on the ship before the plaintiff had to call evidence about the cause of that explosion. The issues were inter-linked in that the second was irrelevant unless the first was proved, and the third was irrelevant unless the second was proved.

Accordingly, a judge who gives indications about what he thinks of the evidence before the end of the case might say to the defendant that he need not call evidence about the explosion because he is not satisfied that the ship failed to arrive.

It must be stressed however that in most cases judges leave it to the parties to decide what evidence they wish to call. It is a very brave advocate, or one who has no faith at all in the evidence at his disposal, who will gamble by calling no evidence and saying that the evidence called by his opponent does not amount to proof.

There is a degree of artificiality about analysing the task of calling evidence in civil trials into legal and evidential burdens because practical necessity requires each party to call evidence if it is available, leaving the judge to sort it all out at the end of the day with the legal burdens only in his mind. Indeed, a judge in a case like *Joseph Constantine* may cause great trouble and expense if he hears all the evidence and decides, for example, that there was an explosion but it was not so serious as to frustrate the whole contract. He may then, because of this decision, refuse to decide whether the explosion was caused by the fault of the defendant. If he is overturned by the Court of Appeal and that court holds that the explosion was a frustrating event, the case will have to be remitted to the judge for a decision whether the defendant was at fault. Undoubtedly judges bear this practical problem in mind and make findings of fact on all issues which the parties have chosen to argue.

The shifting of burdens

The *Joseph Constantine* case lends some support to the theory that the legal burden on an issue can pass from one party to another during the course of the trial.

On the face of things, therefore, it could be said that the legal burden shifted from party to party during the case once an evidential burden was satisfied. But this is misleading because what the House of Lords was considering was where the legal burden lay on certain issues. It was on the plaintiff to prove that the ship did not arrive, and the burden on the defendant to prove the frustrating event was a different burden because that was a different issue. There was no question of the defendant having to prove that the ship did arrive because whether it arrived was an issue raised by the plaintiff, to be proved by the plaintiff. The legal burden on the defendant to prove that the explosion was sufficiently serious as to amount to a frustrating event was, therefore, the burden of proving a new issue.

It is arguable that the proper way of analysing that case is that there was one issue only, namely was the plaintiff entitled to the damages he claimed? On this analysis the need of different parties to prove particular facts could be seen to involve the shifting of the legal burden from plaintiff to defendant and then back again. It aids the understanding of the substantive law to look at cases in terms of a number of issues, because this emphasises that a piece of evidence may be relevant to part only of the case. Similarly it aids the understanding of the task of a party in court to analyse the case on one issue from the evidence on another. Accordingly it is better to talk of there being a separate legal burden of proof on each issue, that burden remaining on the same party throughout.

Magistrates' courts

A few civil cases are heard in magistrates' courts, but no special rules about the burden of proof apply to the magistrates' court, apart from s101 of the Magistrates' Courts Act 1980, although there are some special statutory rules applicable to certain types of proceedings.

Hearings of civil disputes before justices are often relatively informal in terms of the way the courtroom is laid out and with witnesses and lawyers being seated at all times, but submissions of no case are frequently made.

Discretion

There is no proper authority on the question of the burden of proof in cases where the court has to exercise a discretion. For example, if the landlord wishes to obtain possession of premises because of rent arrears from a tenant whose tenancy is protected because of the Rent Act 1977, the court is only entitled to give possession if it is reasonable to do so: Rent Act 1977 s98(1). The landlord must prove the terms of the tenancy and that there are arrears, but does he have to prove that the discretion should be exercised in his favour?

3.4 Standard of proof – criminal cases

Legal burden on prosecution

Whenever the Crown has to prove an issue in a criminal court, be it the Crown Court or a magistrates' court, proof is required to a very high standard. The trial court will not incur the disapproval of the Court of Appeal if it asks itself either whether the case is proved beyond reasonable doubt or whether it is satisfied so that it is sure. Both formulae have been upheld on many occasions as being a proper way for a judge to direct a jury about the standard of proof.

Failure of the judge to direct the jury properly is fatal to a conviction; there is no power to remit the case for retrial. Where magistrates have misdirected themselves however, the Divisional Court will remit the case with a direction about how they should approach it.

Many judges have fallen into error by trying to define what is meant by a reasonable doubt. Denning J described it as follows in *Miller* v *Minister of Pensions* [1947] 2 All ER 372:

> 'It need not reach certainty, but it must carry a high degree of probability. Proof beyond reasonable doubt does not mean proof beyond the shadow of a doubt … If the evidence is so strong against a man as to leave only a remote possibility in his favour which can be dismissed with the sentence "of course it is possible, but not in the least probable," the case is proved beyond reasonable doubt.'

This was said in the course of a civil action, but it tells us nothing of what is required before a jury will consider something to be 'not in the least probable'. Undoubtedly many jurors will be more easily satisfied of an accused's guilt than others and the judges cannot, of course, change the character of the jurors, they can only give them general guidance and trust to decide whether the case is proved.

It used to be common practice for judges to direct the jury to pool their thoughts and reach a collective decision, indeed it was mandatory for him to do so if they were unable to reach a unanimous verdict: *Walhein* (1952) 36 Cr App R 167. The power to accept a majority decision which was introduced in 1967 has removed the need for him to apply any sort of pressure on the jury to be unanimous: see *Watson* [1988] 1 All ER 897. It is therefore less common to find judges directing juries to reach a collective decision. This increases the problems which arise from 12 people each having to be satisfied when some may be more easily satisfied than others. No change has been made in the law about the directions on the standard of proof which are proper and those which are improper. See also *R* v *Berry* [1992] 3 WLR 153.

The Court of Appeal has stressed the importance of judges not trying to define what is meant by a reasonable doubt. Denning J's formula should not be repeated. Nor should they be told that a reasonable doubt is a doubt which might affect someone in his everyday affairs (*Gray* (1973) 58 Cr App R 177) nor that a reasonable doubt is one for which reasons could be given (*Stafford and Luvaglio* (1968) 53 Cr App R 1) nor simply that they should be satisfied (*Attfield* [1961] 1 WLR 1135) nor that they should give the defendant the benefit of the doubt (*Onufrejczyk* [1955] 1 QB 388). From time to time a jury will ask the judge to define a reasonable doubt. Such a question indicates that the jury have decided that it may be right to convict or it may be right to acquit depending upon what is meant by a reasonable doubt. In *Yap Chuan Ching* (1976) 63 Cr App R 7 the judge answered such a question by saying that a reasonable doubt is not a fanciful doubt but is one for which reasons could be given. The direction he gave was similar to Denning J's definition in *Miller* v *Minister of Pensions*. The Court of Appeal upheld the conviction feeling that, because the judge had said it was the sort of doubt which might influence a person in an important matter such as a mortgage for his house, the judge had if anything been generous to the accused.

Lord Goddard CJ expressed concern about judges directing the jury that the case had to be proved beyond reasonable doubt, because that formula often prompts the jury to ask what is a reasonable doubt. In *Summers* (1953) 36 Cr App R 14 he said that the better direction is that the jury should be satisfied so that they are sure. He had in mind that in ordinary life people may ask themselves whether they are sure of something, but will not ask themselves whether they entertain a reasonable doubt, so a direction that they had to be sure had the benefit of using language with which they were already familiar. The suggestion in *Summers* that it was obligatory to use the 'satisfied so that you are sure' formula was put to rest in *Hepworth and Fearnley* [1955] 2 QB 600 where Lord Goddard said that it was perfectly correct for a judge to say that the case had to be proved beyond reasonable doubt, provided he did not try to define what a reasonable doubt is.

These days most judges combine the two approved formulae by using words to the effect, 'the case must be proved beyond reasonable doubt which means that you must be satisfied so that you are sure before you may convict'. This adopts a dictum from Lord Scarman in *Ferguson* v *R* [1979] 1 WLR 94.

Although the cases cited so far have all been addressed to the standard of proof required before there can be a conviction, the same standard is required every time the prosecution must prove something. In *Ewing* [1983] QB 1039 the Crown wished to compare handwriting on a disputed document with a sample of handwriting alleged to be that of the defendant. The Court of Appeal held that it had to be proved beyond reasonable doubt that the sample was a sample of the defendant's writing. Statute could provide that the prosecution has to prove certain facts to a lesser standard than is required by the common law. But no statute does so provide. In s76 of the Police and Criminal Evidence Act 1984 it is expressly provided that the Crown must prove beyond reasonable doubt that a confession made by the defendant is admissible, but this does not mean that any statute which simply imposes a burden of proof on the Crown impliedly allows a lower standard.

The ordinary criminal burden and standard of proof applies on a charge of theft of treasure trove and the jury should only convict, therefore, if they are sure that the articles in question were treasure trove: *R* v *Hancock* [1990] 2 WLR 640.

Similarly, a coroner's jury should be satisfied beyond all reasonable doubt, or satisfied so that they are sure, before bringing in a verdict of unlawful killing: *R* v *Wolverhampton Coroner, ex parte McCurbin* [1990] 1 WLR 719.

Legal burden on the accused

A defendant never has to prove any issue to the same exacting standard that is required of the prosecution. He only has to satisfy the jury on the balance of probabilities. We will see below that to prove something on the balance of probability means to prove that it is more likely than not.

In *Sodeman* v *R* [1936] 2 All ER 1138 the burden on the accused to prove insanity was said by the Privy Council to be not 'higher than the burden which rests upon a plaintiff or defendant in civil proceedings'. The same was said by the Court of Criminal Appeal in *Carr Briant* [1943] KB 607, where by statute the accused had to prove that a payment given by him was not given corruptly, and in *Dunbar* [1958] 1 QB 1 where the accused had to prove diminished responsibility. *Carr Briant* contains a dictum that every occasion on which the accused bears a legal burden of proof, he must prove the issue on the balance of probabilities. Burdens imposed by s101 of the Magistrates' Courts Act 1980 are in the same position: *Islington Borough Council* v *Panico* [1973] 1 WLR 1166.

Evidential burden on the prosecution

There is no point in the court considering whether an issue has been proved if the evidence on that issue is so weak that it obviously is not proved. Another way of saying this is that the court need only consider an issue if evidence has been called which would amount to proof if it is believed and not contradicted.

Where the Crown has to make something a live issue it has been established for some time that the evidential burden is satisfied if evidence is called which might amount to proof beyond reasonable doubt. A good example of this is that on a charge of handling a stolen car the accused has no case to answer unless there is evidence that the car in question was stolen. If the evidence on that issue comprises its owner who says it was taken without his permission and never returned, it is a question for the jury whether or not they believe him. If they do not believe him, the accused must be acquitted, but that is a matter for the jury and not for the judge. All the judge has to decide when considering whether an evidential burden has been satisfied by the Crown is whether there is evidence from which a reasonable jury could decide that issue in favour of the Crown. He is not concerned with whether he believes the evidence which has been called, merely with whether a reasonable jury could believe it: *Jayasena* v *R* [1970] AC 618.

Whether the prosecution has satisfied is evidential burden on each issue has to be decided if the defence makes a submission that there is no case to answer. Such submissions are frequently made at the close of the prosecution case, but there is nothing to prevent the defence from making such a submission at any time before the jury retires. In *Galbraith* [1981] 1 WLR 1039 the Court of Appeal held that a submission of no case should be upheld if:

> 'the judge comes to the conclusion that the prosecution evidence, taken at its highest, is such that a jury properly directed could not properly convict upon it.'

Evidential burden on the accused

A similar principle applies to the defence as to the prosecution. An issue on which the prosecution bears a legal burden is brought to life by calling evidence from which it could be found that that issue is proved, and the defendant raises an issue in the same way. The only difference is that the prosecution must call evidence from which the issue in question could be proved beyond reasonable doubt, whereas the defence must call evidence from which the issue could be proved on the balance of probabilities. If such evidence is not called the judge should not leave the issue to the jury. Not surprisingly judges rarely refuse to allow any point taken by the defence to be left to the jury, but by a clear direction about the burden of proof no harm will be done by allowing the accused to argue any defence he wishes.

The same test applies where the accused wishes to raise a defence on which he bears an evidential burden only. It is important, however, to remember that all he has to do is raise the issue – it is for the prosecution to prove beyond reasonable doubt that the defence raised does not apply. The defendant will be entitled to be acquitted if he can raise a reasonable doubt, and consequently he will satisfy his evidential burden if he raises evidence from which a reasonable jury could conclude that there was a reasonable doubt. This point was made by Lord Morris in *Bratty* v *A-G for Northern Ireland* [1963] AC 386 where he spoke of evidence 'which might leave a jury in reasonable doubt'.

The position where the defendant bears neither an evidential nor a legal burden but does bear a tactical burden is in some ways similar because if he does not raise a doubt he will lose the case. But there is a real difference between his positions where he bears a tactical rather than an evidential burden. If he has an evidential burden to raise a point of defence, a failure to call evidence will allow the judge to direct the jury that they need not consider that defence at all. If he has a tactical burden and yet calls no evidence the jury must consider all issues, although they will decide the case against him.

3.5 Standard of proof – civil cases

The legal burden

There are two ways of expressing the extent to which the court must agree with the case put forward by the party with the legal burden on an issue before it can decide that issue in his favour. The most commonly used of the two it that the court must be satisfied on the balance of probabilities, the other is that the court must be satisfied on a preponderance of probability. They both mean the same thing. Denning J in *Miller* v *Minister of Pensions* [1947] 2 All ER 372 said of the evidence which will satisfy a legal burden in a civil case:

> 'It must carry a reasonable degree of probability, but not so high as is required to discharge a burden in a criminal case. If the evidence is such that the tribunal can say: "We think it more probable than not," the burden is discharged, but, if the probabilities are equal, it is not.'

The standard of proof is the same whether it falls on plaintiff or defendant. The task of the trial judge is not to decide whether the case put by the plaintiff is more likely to be true than the case put by the defendant. Rather his task is to decide whether the party who bears the legal burden on each issue has proved that issue. His opponent may have raised a feeble defence or no defence, but the judge may still feel that the necessary facts are not proved. This was illustrated in *The Popi M* [1985] 1 WLR 948.

Jury trials are subject to the same principle, but there is an important practical difference. Trial by jury inevitably requires arguments to be put to people who may not be used to deciding between conflicting versions of events. It is therefore important that it is made clear to the jury exactly what each party is saying. Unlike the trial judge, the jury does not have the right to interrupt an advocate and ask him to make himself clearer, so the onus is on the judge to ensure that arguments are clearly put. It is common practice in the Crown Court for the prosecution to leave to the jury only the arguments which were raised by counsel's opening speech, and the same practice prevails in civil jury trials. The cry is often heard from the defence during the trial that the Crown or the plaintiff is asking questions which are not relevant because they go to an issue which was not opened to the jury. Therefore there is great emphasis on ensuring that what each side has said is considered by the jury. This can and does lead to juries being asked to decide which party's version of events is true. In most cases, where it is clear that either the plaintiff's or the defendant's witnesses are telling the truth, a straight comparison of the parties' evidence is all that is required. But there can be instances of the jury being invited to consider which party has called the better evidence, without it being made clear that if on any issue they are unable to decide that one case is stronger than the other they must decide the case against the party bearing the legal burden.

The assessment of whether a party's case is more likely than not involves weighing the evidence called by each party. But weight is not determined by the number of witnesses, because ten people who are lying have no right to be believed in comparison to one who is telling the truth. The trier of fact, be it judge or jury, must consider all the circumstances in deciding who to believe. The demeanour of the witnesses is often extremely important. Some give the appearance of being uncomfortable in the witness box, contradicting themselves in the course of their evidence and generally appearing to be obviously untruthful. Others, of course, are equally clearly telling the truth. The difficulty for the court comes where there is little to choose between the witnesses called by each side. If it is not possible to choose between them, the party with the legal burden must lose. One thing which the judge must always bear in mind is the inherent likelihood or unlikelihood of what is argued. For example, if the plaintiff claims that he was assaulted by the defendant for no reason at all as he was walking along the road, he will have an easier job of proving his case if the defendant has a long criminal record for assaults than he will if he is the Archbishop of Canterbury. Similarly, a judge may treat with considerable scepticism a claim that a contract for the sale of goods was frustrated by the goods being carried away by little green men from outer space. No matter how many witnesses are called and no matter how truthful they may appear, the very nature of the claim militates against it being proved.

A sliding scale?

There are three types of case in which civil courts normally require to be satisfied by strong evidence before they will find the claim proved. The first, as we have seen, is where an unusual allegation is made. This is one aspect of the court having to take into account the inherent likelihood in the claim. The second is cases where the claimant alleges that a serious wrong has been done or claims a severe remedy. The third is divorce cases.

Enough has been said already about the first of these three types of case, but the second is something on which the authorities are numerous. The starting point in analysing why strong evidence is required is *Hornal* v *Neuberger Products Ltd* [1957] 1 QB 247. The plaintiff claimed damages for breach of contract and, in the alternative, fraud. It was alleged that an agent of the defendant company had deliberately made a false statement about goods which were sold to the plaintiff. The claim for fraud inevitably required the plaintiff to prove a criminal offence. The trial judge held that he was satisfied on the balance of probabilities that the statement was made but was not satisfied beyond reasonable doubt. The Court of Appeal held that he was right to find the plaintiff's claim proved because the action was a civil case and so the civil standard of proof applied.

But all three members of the Court of Appeal (Denning, Hodson and Morris LJJ) cited with approval the judgment of Denning LJ in *Bater* v *Bater* [1951] P 35, in which he said,

> 'A civil court, when considering a charge of fraud, will naturally require a higher degree of probability than that which it would require if considering whether negligence were established. It does not adopt so high a degree as a criminal court, even when it is considering a charge of a criminal nature, but still it does require a degree of probability which is commensurate with the occasion. Likewise, a divorce court should require a degree of probability which is proportionate to the subject-matter.'

Undoubtedly this means that is is harder to prove a serious allegation than a trivial one. Whether this is fair to the plaintiff is open to debate, because if he has suffered at the hands of the defendant he should have a remedy which, arguably, should be equally available in all cases. Nevertheless, Ungoed-Thomas J applied *Hornal* v *Neuberger Products Ltd* in *Re Dellow's Will Trusts* [1964] 1 WLR 451 and Lord Denning repeated his view in *Blyth* v *Blyth* [1966] AC 643 saying:

> 'The case, like any civil case, may be proved by a preponderance of probability, but the degree of probability depends on the subject-matter. In proportion as the offence is grave, so ought the proof to be clear.'

Morris LJ in *Hornal* v *Neuberger Products Ltd* adopted a different analysis in that he said that the more serious the allegation and the more severe the effect of the plaintiff's remedy on the defendant, the less likely it is that the defendant has committed the act alleged. This is probably not correct. The most serious remedy which can be granted in civil courts is a prison sentence which can be imposed for breach of an injunction, but an allegation that there has been a breach is not necessarily inherently unlikely. For example, if an injunction has been granted against a husband because he has assaulted his wife many times it is by no means inherently unlikely that he will breach the injunction. Consequently, the judge will not necessarily approach with scepticism the wife's application to have her spouse committed to prison for breach of the injunction. As a matter of policy, however, the law requires judges to think carefully before finding someone to be in breach of an injunction because such a finding may lead to the defendant being sent to prison for up to two years. The explanation for this is what Lord Denning said in *Blyth* v *Blyth*, 'as the offence is grave, so ought the proof to be clear'.

In *Khawaja* v *Secretary of State for the Home Department* [1984] AC 74 Lord Scarman considered the standard of proof required on an application for judicial review. In substance he repeated what Denning LJ said in *Bater* v *Bater*, emphasising that it is the gravity of the issues in the case and not the ease or difficulty with which they may be proved which determines the weight of evidence which is required before the court will be satisfied that they are proved. Lord Scarman said:

> 'The flexibility of the civil standard of proof suffices to ensure that the court will require the high probability which is appropriate to what is at stake.'

In the 1940s and 1950s it was common to find judges saying that the right to a divorce had to be proved beyond reasonable doubt – see for example *Ginesi* v *Ginesi* [1948] P179. The importance of marriage and of questions of legitimacy led the courts to make strong presumptions upholding both. Section 26 of the Family Law Reform Act 1969 provides that proof of legitimacy need be on the balance of probabilities only. This, coupled with the emphasis placed in *Blyth* v *Blyth* and *Khawaja* on the flexibility of the civil standard of proof, gives little scope for any civil court to decide a case otherwise than on the balance of probabilities.

However, in a civil action for damages for murder, the standard of proof is the criminal one: *Halford* v *Brookes* (1991) The Times 3 October. As Rougier J explained in that case, no one, whether in a civil or criminal court, should be declared guilty of murder unless the tribunal is sure that there is no other sensible conclusion.

The type of proceedings

From what has been said above it can seen that it is the type of proceedings which determines the standard of proof. Criminal proceedings require proof beyond reasonable doubt, whereas in a civil action proof on the balance of probabilities normally suffices. In most cases it is obvious whether the proceedings are civil or criminal, but there are some borderline cases.

In *R* v *Police Complaints Board ex p Madden* [1983] 1 WLR 447 McNeill J held that disciplinary proceedings taken against a police officer were criminal proceedings. This case must now be doubted because disciplinary proceedings against a fireman were held by the Court of Appeal to be civil proceedings in *R* v *Hampshire County Council ex p Ellerton* [1985] 1 WLR 749 and *ex p Madden* was disapproved. *Ex p Ellerton* is to be preferred because the penalty which could be imposed by a disciplinary tribunal can never involve a loss of liberty and findings made are generally not looked upon by the public like criminal convictions.

Re Bramblevale Ltd [1970] Ch 128 holds that proceedings for contempt of court are quasi-criminal because a prison sentence could be imposed if the allegation is proved. Therefore proof beyond reasonable doubt is required.

In *H* v *H and C (Kent County Council intervening) (child abuse: evidence)* [1989] 2 FLR 333 the Court of Appeal decided that, in custody, access and wardship applications, the civil standard of proof had to be applied. In *Re W (minors) (sexual abuse: standard of proof)* (1993) The Times 1 December the Court of Appeal affirmed that the burden of proving an allegation of sexual abuse of a child is on the party making the allegation and that the standard of proof is of probabilities. While it was possible that some lesser degree of probability is required if a court merely has to be satisfied that a child has been a victim of sexual abuse, any such lower standard is not applicable if there is only one possible candidate for the role of perpetrator.

The criminal standard of proof is required before a court can be satisfied that a defendant has benefited from drug trafficking so as to assess the value of his proceeds from that trafficking under s2(2) of the Drug Trafficking Offences Act 1986: *R* v *Enwezor* [1991] Crim LR 483. However, the civil standard of proof applies to a defendant when he is seeking to rebut, under s2(2), assumptions made under s2(3) of the 1986 Act. If he fails to rebut an assumption it stands as a fact: *R* v *Redbourne* [1993] 2 All ER 753. Such an assumption has to be made on the basis of prima facie evidence that property has been held by or transferred to the defendant as a payment or reward in connection with his drug trafficking, and not merely because the court has some reason to suspect that the defendant has benefited from drug trafficking: *R* v *Rose* [1993] 2 All ER 761. When s7 of the Criminal Justice Act 1993 is brought into force, the civil standard of proof will be required to determine whether a person has benefited from drug trafficking for the purposes of the 1986 Act and the amount to be recovered under a confiscation order made under s1 of that Act.

The standard of proof to be applied by a tribunal considering whether to strike off a solicitor should, where what amounts to a criminal offence is alleged, be that required for criminal conviction: *Re a Solicitor* [1991] 2 All ER 335. Lord Lane CJ recalled that the Code of Conduct of the Bar provides that in proceedings before a disciplinary tribunal the criminal standard should be applied and his Lordship felt that it would be anomalous if the two branches of the profession were to adopt different approaches in this regard.

The evidential burden

Because an evidential burden places a duty on a party to call enough evidence to require the court to consider whether the issue in question is proved, the standard of the evidential burden is that evidence must be called which could be considered to be proof on the balance of probabilities.

The rule in *Alexander* v *Rayson* means that on a submission of no case the judge only need ask himself whether the legal burdens are satisfied, because it would be pointless asking first whether the evidence could amount to proof when no further evidence may be called.

3.6 Presumptions

Categories of presumptions

The law presumes that no wrong has been done unless it is proved to the appropriate standard. No evidence need be called before innocence is presumed because the presumption is imposed as a ground-rule by which litigation is conducted. This sort of presumption is in reality a rule of law. It defines who will lose if no evidence is called. And if the judge in a negligence action is satisfied that the plaintiff has proved negligence on the part of the defendant, the law presumes the plaintiff to have been without fault unless the defendant proves fault.

These rules are examples of random points of law which determine who bears a legal burden on certain issues. As we have seen above there are some general rules, the most important of which is that he who asserts must prove. General rules which impose a legal burden on a party to prove an issue are often referred to as presumptions. Those discussed already are the following: it is presumed that there is no negligence unless the plaintiff proves it; it is presumed that there was no contributory negligence unless the defendant proves it; it is presumed that a party has performed his contractual duties unless the contrary is proved; it is presumed that failure to perform a contract is because of breach unless it is proved that there was a good reason for non–performance.

These presumptions all fall into the same pattern. On proof of one fact (fact A) the court will draw a conclusion, and presume that another fact (fact B) is true. Fact A is known as the basic fact and fact B as the presumed fact. In every case a presumption will only be drawn if fact A is proved. If sufficient evidence is called to prevent fact A from being proved, there is no scope for the presumption to arise.

Every court is entitled to draw reasonable inferences from the evidence which is called before it. The proper way to analyse the drawing of inferences is to say that the court must find what facts are directly proved by the evidence and then ask itself what conclusions can properly be reached from those facts. For example, if it is proved that the plaintiff was hit by a golf ball while walking past a golf course and there is no evidence of where that ball came from, the court may conclude that it came from the course. The facts which are proved directly are that the plaintiff was hit by a golf ball and that this happened while he was walking past a golf course. Of course, there is no direct evidence that the ball came from the golf course, but from the primary facts it can be inferred that it did.

Presumptions work in much the same way. Fact A, the basic fact, is a primary fact, and from it the inference is drawn that the presumed fact, fact B, is true. As we will see, not all presumptions have exactly the same effect, and five different varieties exist. There is an important difference between how they apply in civil and criminal trials, which will be examined in due course. What follows applies only to civil cases unless the contrary is indicated.

The first type of presumption is what we have seen already. On proof of fact A the court must presume fact B to be true but the presumption can be rebutted by proof that fact B is not true. Here the party which tries to rebut the presumption faces a legal burden. These are known as persuasive or compelling presumptions. The courts occasionally say that strong evidence is required in rebuttal and sometimes that less strong evidence will suffice, but in either case the evidence must prove that the presumed fact is not true.

The second variety also requires the court to conclude that fact B is true once fact A is proved, but the presumption can be rebutted by evidence which shows that fact B is not proved. If the rebutter can show that fact B is equally likely to be false as it is to be true, he will have successfully rebutted the presumption. On one proving fact A, the other party does not have to call sufficient evidence to prove that fact B is not true, but he does have to call enough to balance the probabilities of fact B being true or false. The legal burden of proving fact B will remain on the first party, yet he will not have satisfied that burden because he will not have proved that fact B was more likely than not to be true.

These presumptions are known as evidential presumptions because they place an evidential burden on the rebutter. It is not always strictly true to say that the rebutter bears an evidential burden, because on proof of fact A, fact B is sometimes already in issue. In such cases there can be no burden on the rebutter to call any evidence about fact B before the court will be entitled to conclude that fact B is true, but he does have to question fact B by calling sufficient evidence to balance the probabilities of its truth and falsity.

Thirdly come presumptions which cannot be rebutted. There are few examples of these and they are all provided for by statute. It has been argued that statutes which make proof of fact A conclusive proof of fact B do not lay down a presumption at all, but rather that they state rules of law. This is really a matter of semantics, but in so far as they fall into the same pattern as the first two types (on proof of fact A the court will presume fact B to be true) they are presumptions and they do not lose that characteristic simply because they cannot be rebutted. A foundation still has to be laid for them by proving fact A, and it is only when that foundation is laid that fact B will be held to be true. These presumptions are generally referred to as irrebuttable presumptions of law.

The fourth type is also a creature of statute. It arises where an Act of Parliament provides that on certain evidence being called the court must conclude that an evidential burden has been satisfied. Such provisions are not numerous and they are designed to prevent submissions of no case in certain criminal trials. The purpose of these rules is to ensure that there is no doubt about the admissibility of evidence which at common law may be inadmissible or of no weight. They are referred to by Carter only of the major commentators on the law of evidence, and he labels them permissive presumptions, because their effect is that proof of fact A permits the court to find fact B proved, but does not require it to find it proved.

The final sort are known as presumptions of fact. These are inferences which must be drawn because everyday experience of life dictates that if fact A is true, fact B is true. There are many examples, one of which is that if Mr X was alive and aged 20 on a particular day, he is likely to be alive a year later, and so should be presumed to have been alive then.

Presumptions of fact are designed to ensure that on certain matters all courts will draw the same inference from the same primary facts. In all cases where it has been held that a presumption of fact applied, the presumed fact was one which would have been inferred by any reasonable court anyway. The greatest significance of these presumptions is that they allow a judge to direct the jury about how they should approach certain evidence without risk of an allegation that he was usurping their function. In addition, they ensure that judges and juries approach certain questions of fact in a sensible and consistent way.

To a great extent presumptions of fact and evidential presumptions are the same because neither affect, the placing of legal burdens and both require particular conclusions to be drawn once certain facts are proved. One difference between them is that evidential presumptions may require a conclusion to be drawn from the primary facts which would not be drawn as a matter of common sense, whereas presumptions of fact arise because as a matter of logic fact B is normally true if fact A is true. Another way of saying the same thing is to say that evidential presumptions place an evidential burden on the rebutter whereas presumptions of fact place a tactical burden on him.

What has been said above about presumptions states general principles. A number of examples are given below to show how those principles apply to actual cases. These examples are not exhaustive of the presumptions known to English law.

Presumptions in criminal cases

1. The rules set out above about the weight of evidence required to rebut different types of presumption are applicable to civil cases only. In criminal trials the defendant cannot have a burden of proving anything imposed on him unless he argues insanity or a statute expressly or impliedly places a burden of proof on him: see paragraph 3.2 above. If the Crown relies on a presumption in order to prove its case the accused will not have to prove that the presumed fact is not true unless the case falls within the special rules set out in paragraph 3.2.
2. The defendant may, however, bear an evidential burden by reason of a presumption which goes against him. For example, in *Spurge* [1961] 2 QB 205 the defendant had the burden of raising the issue of mechanical defect because the law presumed that his car was not mechanically defective. Once he raises some evidence, however, the issue is alive and the prosecution must disprove his defence beyond reasonable doubt.
3. If the defendant himself relies on a presumption, the Crown will always have to rebut it beyond reasonable doubt. This must be remembered in the discussion of specific presumptions which follows.

The presumption of validity of marriage

In order for two people to be validly married it is necessary for two conditions to be fulfilled; first, each must have had capacity to marry, and secondly they must have gone through a ceremony of marriage which the law recognises. The capacity of the parties to marry affects what is known as the essential validity of the marriage and the ceremonial requirement affects its formal validity.

The law draws two presumptions about validity of marriage, one for each sort of validity. It is presumed that a ceremony of marriage which has been celebrated was valid. In other words it is presumed that the person who conducted the ceremony was authorised to do so and that the requisite licence had been obtained. In *Piers* v *Piers* (1848) 2 HL Cas 331 the House of Lords held that a marriage was valid where there was no evidence that any licence had been obtained. It was held that the presumption of formal validity places the burden of proving invalidity on the party who asserts invalidity, proof of the basic fact of the ceremony having taken place being on the party who alleges validity.

The speeches contain dicta to the effect that strong evidence is required to rebut the presumption. These dicta were adopted as correct in *Mahadervan* v *Mahadervan* [1964] P 233 where the High Court held that the presumption of formal validity could only be rebutted by proof beyond reasonable doubt that the marriage ceremony was not effective. This case must be read in the light of *Blyth* v *Blyth* which holds that in civil disputes the party bearing the burden of proving an issue must prove it on the balance of probabilities. The flexibility of that term has been discussed above in paragraph 3.5, and that discussion should be referred to here.

In *Piers* v *Piers* there was no question of the parties not having capacity to marry. But in *Re Peete* [1952] 2 All ER 599 the question arose whether the 'wife' was already married at the time she went through a marriage ceremony in 1919. Had she been married already she would not have had capacity to marry again unless her previous marriage had ended. There was clear proof that she had previously gone through a ceremony of marriage, and poor evidence that her first husband was killed in 1916. The judge held that the presumption of essential validity was rebutted by proof that the wife was married before, because the evidence in support of the argument that the former marriage had ended was weak. This case is authority for the proposition that the presumption of essential validity imposes a legal burden on the rebutter, but that the amount of evidence required to rebut the presumption is less than that required to rebut the presumption of formal validity.

The difference between the weight of evidence required to rebut the two presumptions of validity of marriage lies in the difficulty of proving that an apparently valid ceremony was in fact invalid, compared to the relative ease with which one can prove that someone does not have the capacity to marry.

There is a further presumption relating to marriage, namely that it is presumed two people are married if they cohabit as man and wife and are reputed to be married. The presumption imposes a legal burden on the rebutter and strong evidence in rebuttal is needed: *Re Taylor* [1961] 1 WLR 9. These days this presumption is of minimal importance because of the efficient system of registration of marriages. People who live together but do not pretend to be married are not presumed to be married because one basic fact which must be proved before the presumption arises is that they are reputed to be married, not just that they cohabit.

The presumption of legitimacy

It is presumed that a child which is born or conceived while its mother was married is legitimate: *The Banbury Peerage Case* (1811) 1 Sim & St 153. The basic facts which need to be proved are either that the mother was married at the time of conception or that she was married at the time of birth; the law will presume that the woman's husband is the father of the child. In *Re Overbury* [1955] Ch 122 the mother gave birth two months after she married for a second time, her first husband having died six months before her remarriage. The Chancery Division held that because the child was conceived approximately nine months before birth, the presumption which was to be applied was that the father of the child was the man, if any, that the mother was married to at the time of conception, namely her first husband. The subsequent remarriage of the mother did not affect that presumption.

The separation of husband and wife prior to conception pursuant to an order of judicial separation will prevent the presumption arising: *Ettenfield* v *Ettenfield* [1940] P 96. It is important to note that in such a case there is no presumption of legitimacy; it is not the case that there is a presumption but it is rebutted by evidence of judicial separation.

Divorce proceedings have two stages. First, a decree nisi is pronounced, followed not less than six weeks later by that decree being made absolute.

The purpose of the two stages is to allow the parties to think again once the decree nisi is issued, and in many cases each year they do think again and no decree absolute follows. The marriage is not dissolved until the decree of divorce is made absolute. In *Knowles* v *Knowles* [1962] P 161 the child was conceived after the decree nisi but before it was made absolute. It was held in the High Court that the presumption of legitimacy arose because the mother was still married at the time of conception. The case is authority not just that the presumption arises until the decree is made absolute but also that judicial notice is taken of the fact that a child is conceived approximately nine months before its birth, although expert medical evidence is admissible to prove more precisely the period during which it was conceived.

The presumption can be rebutted by evidence which proves on the balance of probabilities that the husband is (or was) not the father: Family Law Reform Act 1969, s26. Until the 1969 Act came into force the common law stated that the presumption of legitimacy must be rebutted by proof that intercourse did not take place between husband and wife at any time when conception could have occurred: *Bowen* v *Norman* [1938] 1 KB 689. Section 26 does not limit the rebutter in this way, it provides that the presumption of legitimacy may be rebutted by proof that the child is more likely to be illegitimate than legitimate.

Such proof may come about in a number of ways, for example by proving that no intercourse took place between the mother and her husband at the time of conception, or that he was impotent, or that blood group or DNA tests show that he is not the father. Evidence that contraception was used will not always suffice; it depends upon what evidence there is about the effectiveness of the type of contraception used. These days DNA tests ('genetic fingerprints') are the best method of testing paternity, and their availability will undoubtedly lessen the number of cases in which issues of paternity fall to be decided on hearing oral evidence only. If such a test cannot be carried out, perhaps because the alleged father is dead or has disappeared, the presumption will remain in force and must be rebutted by other evidence.

Until quite recently the parties to a marriage were not entitled to give evidence in court to the effect that intercourse had not taken place between them: *Russell* v *Russell* [1924] AC 687. Section 48(1) of the Matrimonial Causes Act 1973, however, allows husband and wife to give evidence that intercourse did not take place between them.

Illegitimacy

The presumption of legitimacy arises in all cases where the mother was married at the time of conception or at the time of birth. Where she was not married at either of those times there is said to be a presumption of illegitimacy: *Ettenfield* v *Ettenfield*. In the vast majority of cases this is a meaningless presumption, because if the mother was not married at the time of conception or birth the child could not be legitimate. There are two situations in which the presumption of illegitimacy can arise.

The first is that recognised in *Ettenfield* v *Ettenfield*, namely where the parties are separated by reason of a decree of judicial separation. Although the child will be presumed to be illegitimate, the mother and her husband are still married. Therefore, if there is proof on the balance of probabilities that the husband is the father despite his separation from his wife, the presumption of illegitimacy will be rebutted: Family Law Reform Act 1969, s26(1).

The second instance in which the presumption can arise is where the mother is unmarried at the time of conception and birth but later marries. Marriage of the parents of a child after it is born serves to legitimate the child, but this depends, of course, upon the child being the child of the man and woman who marry. The presumption of illegitimacy serves to place a legal burden on the rebutter, and the mere fact that the woman marries after birth is not proof that that man is the father.

In *S* v *McC* [1972] AC 24 Lord Reid considered the effect of s26 of the Family Law Reform Act 1969. That section provides, as we have seen, that the presumptions of legitimacy and illegitimacy can be rebutted by proof of illegitimacy or legitimacy on the balance of probability. He held that the effect of this provision was to place a burden of proof on the rebutter, but that the presumption itself had no weight as evidence. In other words the court must weigh the evidence called by the parties and only if that evidence shows equal probabilities of legitimacy or illegitimacy will the presumption be applied.

This approach was adopted by Rees J in *T(H)* v *T(E)* [1971] 1 WLR 429, who held that the mother's husband was the father of her child on the basis of the oral evidence of the parties and blood test evidence. The judge expressly refused to apply any presumption because he was able to reach a conclusion on the facts before him.

Lord Reid's analysis of s26 is difficult to understand because the result of saying that the presumption only applies where the judge cannot reach a decision one way or the other on the evidence called before him, is that the presumption becomes not a presumption at all but a rule of law about the burden of proof. If it is not possible to decide on the evidence who is the father, there can be no possibility of the presumption being rebutted. It is doubtful whether Parliament intended to dispose of the presumptions of legitimacy and illegitimacy in a statutory provision which expressly only refers to the amount of proof required to rebut the presumptions.

In *Re F (a minor) (blood tests: parental rights)* [1993] 3 All ER 596 it appeared that, at the time of her child's conception, a mother had been having sexual relations with both her husband and the man who claimed to be the child's putative father and that her relationship with that man had ended as soon as she had discovered that she was pregnant. Now, though, he applied for the taking and use of blood tests for DNA profiling, but the Court of Appeal dismissed his application on the ground that it was not in the child's best interests for the presumption of legitimacy to be disturbed. However, in *T* v *T* (1992) The Times 31 July the Court of Appeal ordered the taking of blood tests at the husband's request and with the wife's consent as it was perceived to be in the child's best interests that her paternity should be so clarified.

Death

As a matter of common sense it is possible to infer in certain circumstances that someone is dead. For example, if it is proved that in 1980 a man was aged 110 years, it is a safe inference to draw that he is not still alive in 1989. But no such inference can be drawn where the man was, say, 30 years old in 1980, unless there are additional factors such as evidence that in 1980 he was suffering from a terminal illness which was likely to have proved fatal within nine years.

The law allows inference about the likelihood of death to be drawn in all case, but also applies a persuasive presumption about death in the event of certain basic facts being proved. Once it is proved that:

1. someone has not been heard of for at least seven years;
2. by people who would have been expected to have heard of him; and
3. that all due enquiries have been made to discover whether he is alive but those enquiries have not been fruitful,

the law will presume that he is dead (*Chard* v *Chard* [1956] P 259).

The first and second of these basic facts are really part of one basic fact, namely that there are people who would have expected to hear of him but they have not, from which it is presumed that the reason for this is his death. The third basic fact requires enquiries to have been made among those people who would have been expected to hear from him: *Doe d France* v *Andrews* (1850) 15 QB 756. This means that the third basic fact is closely connected to the first and second and it could be said that they are all really one basic fact.

It is a question of fact whether in any case there are people who would have expected to hear of the person. They may, but need not, have expected to have heard from him personally, or they could have expected to have heard of him from others: see, eg, *Prudential Assurance Co* v *Edmonds* (1877) 2 App Cas 487.

Because the enquiries which are 'due enquiries' must be made of those people who would be expected to have heard from the person whose death is in issue, the presumption of death is capable of rebuttal by proof that others have heard of him.

In cases where the presumption of death cannot be drawn because one or more of the basic facts is not proved, the court may infer as a matter of fact that someone is dead. For example, in *Re Watkins* [1953] 1 WLR 1323, a man aged 34 when last heard of by his wife, father and sister was presumed to be dead 26 years later because none of those people had heard of him. The presumption of law did not arise because there was no proof that all due enquiries had been made, for example, no enquiries were made of the man's brother and his other two sisters. Nonetheless, the facts were held to be sufficiently strong to give rise to an inference that the man was dead. A similar decision was reached in *Bullock* v *Bullock* [1960] 1 WLR 975 where the husband had been absent for 14 years by the time of the wife's remarriage. In addition he was not heard of in the 16 years between the remarriage and the date of trial and a warrant for his arrest had not been executed because the police were unable to trace him.

Time of death

Where death is presumed, either by reason of the persuasive presumption or by reason of an inference being drawn as a matter of fact, the law does not have any hard-and-fast rule about when death occurred. In *Re Phene's Trust* (1870) LR 5 Ch 139 Giffard LJ in the Chancery Appeals Court said, obiter, that the effect of the persuasive presumption of death is that at the date of trial it can be presumed that someone is dead, but it cannot be said exactly when he died. This dictum was described as unusual in *Chard* v *Chard* and was disapproved in *Chipchase* v *Chipchase* [1939] P 391, where it was held in the High Court that death can be presumed once seven years have elapsed. Like *Re Watkins* and *Bullock* v *Bullock, Chipchase* v *Chipchase* was a case where a woman remarried many years after her first husband was last heard of. Unlike those two cases, the basic facts of the presumption of death were proved. It was held that the first husband was presumed dead once seven years had elapsed after he was last heard of.

But, where two or more people have died in circumstances where it is uncertain which died first, the law will presume that they died in order of age, the oldest first and the youngest last. This rule, which is made by s184 of the Law of Property Act 1925, only applies in cases where questions of title to property are relevant. The House of Lords held in *Hickman* v *Peacey* [1945] AC 304 that s184 applied where a bomb fell on a house and several members of a family died. Viscount Simon LC and Lord Wright dissented because they considered the evidence to show that the people in question died absolutely simultaneously. The majority, however, held that the section applies in every case where it cannot be proved whether one person survived another. Therefore, if the deaths might have been simultaneous but might have been consecutive, the section applies and the eldest of the deceased will be presumed to have died first.

The presumption which arises from s184 of the 1925 Act is a conclusive presumption, in other words it is incapable of being rebutted. This is because, if it is possible to tell who died first, the presumption never arises. The basic fact which must be proved before the presumption is drawn is that it is not possible to tell whether one person survived another. The presumed fact is that the deceased died in order of seniority. Any evidence which suggests that one person died before another must be considered when deciding whether the basic fact is proved. It therefore cannot be held that the basic fact is proved but also that the presumption is rebutted by evidence that one person died before another: *Re Bate* [1947] 2 All ER 418.

Continuance of life

There is a presumption of fact that people live for a reasonable time: see, eg, *Chard* v *Chard* above. Indeed, all of the cases cited above under 'Illegitimacy' involve application of the presumption of continuance of life, because in the absence of such a presumption there would be no need to consider whether someone was still alive many years after he was last heard of. In particular, the whole basis of *Re Watkins* and *Bullock* v *Bullock* is that the court will presume that someone lives for a reasonable time unless it can be inferred from the evidence that that person has probably died.

The case which is always cited as the leading authority for the presumption of fact that life continues for a reasonable time is *Lumley* (1869) LR 1 CCR 196. However, the Court for Crown Cases Reserved stressed that the presumption of continuance of life was a presumption of fact only, not a presumption of law. It expressly stated that a jury may infer that someone is alive from his state of good health or may fail to draw that inference if he was in poor health.

The presumption being one of fact, no court must infer that someone was alive at any particular time after he was last seen or heard of, but it will look at all the circumstances. No clear rules can be laid down, although it is beyond doubt that the court will consider all the circumstances and draw reasonable inferences.

Res ipsa loquitur

Where something happens which in the ordinary way of things would only happen if someone was at fault, the law presumes that such fault was the cause of the event. The basic principle was stated in *Scott* v *London and St Katherine Docks Co* (1865) 34 LJ Ex 220. For detailed consideration of the circumstances in which the basic facts are proved, reference must be made to textbooks on the law of tort.

It is not clear on the authorities whether res ipsa loquitur is a persuasive presumption, an evidential presumption or a mere presumption of fact. Many cases contain judgments in which it is simply not considered whether the defendant bore a legal, evidential or tactical burden once the basic facts of the presumption were proved. From those in which the nature of the presumption was considered, the prevailing view seems to be that the presumption is persuasive.

In *The Kite* [1933] P 154 Langton J said that the presumption is evidential. His view was repeated by Bucknill LJ in *Barkway* v *South Wales Transport Co Ltd* [1949] 1 KB 54, in *Colvilles Ltd* v *Devine* [1969] 1 WLR 475 by Lords Guest and Donovan in the House of Lords, by Lord Pearson in *Henderson* v *Henry E Jenkins & Sons* [1970] AC 232 and by Lawton and Megaw LJJ in *Ward* v *Tesco Stores Ltd* [1976] 1 WLR 810. No full explanation was made in any of these dicta why the burden on the defendant is evidential only, it was simply asserted to be the case.

There is, however, a greater weight of dicta in favour of the burden on the defendant being legal. In particular Langton J's dictum in *The Kite* was expressly disapproved by Sir Raymond Evershed MR in *Moore* v *R Fox & Sons* [1956] 1 QB 596 because it was inconsistent with the views expressed by Asquith LJ in *Barkway* v *South Wales Transport Co Ltd* and Lord Radcliffe in *Esso Petroleum Co Ltd* v *Southport Corporation* [1956] AC 218.

On one view of *Woods* v *Duncan* [1946] AC 401 it is authority for the burden being legal. A submarine sank because one of its torpedo tubes was left open when it submerged, preventing it from surfacing again. The plaintiff, the widow of one of the drowned officers, claimed that the death of her husband was caused by negligence and argued res ipsa loquitur. Evidence was given on behalf of the defendant which established that there was no negligence. Therefore, the plaintiff's claim failed. It was argued by the plaintiff that it is for the defendant to prove exactly how the accident happened and thereby to prove that he was not negligent. The House of Lords disagreed, holding that the defendant successfully rebuts the presumption by proving that he took all reasonable care, because once he has proved that he was not negligent it is irrelevant that he is unable to prove who, if anyone, was negligent. It was implicit in all of the speeches that the burden on the defendant was to prove that he was not negligent. It must, however, be noted that the nature of the burden on the defendant was irrelevant to the outcome of the case because the evidence clearly established that he was not negligent. It therefore did not make any difference to the decision whether he bore a legal or an evidential burden because he satisfied both. Nonetheless, it was necessary to the decision to consider in broad terms the nature of the duty on the defendant, and in this way it is arguable that the case is authority for the presumption being persuasive. The Privy Council followed *Woods* v *Duncan*, holding that the presumption was persuasive, in *Swan* v *Salisbury Construction Co Ltd* [1966] 1 WLR 204.

The third view, that res ipsa loquitur is a presumption of fact only placing a tactical burden on the defendant appears only in a few dicta. Megaw LJ in *Lloyde* v *West Midlands Gas Board* [1971] 1 WLR 749, for example, said that res ipsa loquitur is a way of expressing a common sense approach to the assessment of evidence. He said that the reason why negligence is presumed once the basic facts are proved is that the only proper conclusion to draw from the basic facts is that there was negligence. He suggested that this is no more than a matter of drawing a reasonable inference from primary facts.

There is no obvious answer to the question whether res ipsa loquitur should impose a legal, evidential or tactical burden on the defendant. One view is that the burden should be legal because in cases where the presumption arises only the defendant can be in a position to explain what he did. It must be borne in mind at all times when considering the presumption that the defendant does not have to prove exactly what caused the incident which led to the plaintiff suffering loss. All he has to show is that he was not negligent: *Woods* v *Duncan*. This being the case, it is probably no great hardship to him to have to prove his lack of negligence. But it will be a hardship if he does not have special knowledge. For example, in *Woods* v *Duncan* the defendant may not have been in any better position than the plaintiff to prove exactly what happened, so it is arguable that he should be treated like any other defendant and should succeed if he can establish either that he was not negligent or that the probability of him being negligent was only 50 per cent.

If he only bears an evidential burden, by calling evidence which shows that the probability of him being negligent is 50 per cent, the plaintiff will lose the case. Where the defendant has special knowledge it seems only right that he should bear a legal burden, otherwise the plaintiff may have an impossible task in trying to prove his case.

In practical terms it makes little difference whether the presumption is persuasive or evidential because there are hardly any cases where the judge finds on the facts that the evidence is equally balanced on the issue whether the defendant took reasonable care. Where the defendant has special knowledge the judge may be inclined to find negligence in the absence of a good explanation by him of what happened. On the other hand, where he does not have special knowledge the court might hold that his explanation is sufficient to rebut any inference of negligence. In order to allow flexibility in the presumption so that the question whether the defendant has special knowledge can be taken fully into account, it may be preferable for the presumption to be factual only. This, however, is not a view with any great support in the authorities, although *Swan* v *Salisbury Constructions Co Ltd* and *Barkway* v *South Wales Transport Co Ltd* both contain dicta which can be construed in this way.

Recent possession

A person who is found in possession of goods very soon after they were stolen runs the risk of magistrates or a jury finding that he came by them dishonestly. Such a finding is no more than an inference which is drawn from all of the circumstances of the case. In *Hepworth & Fearnley* [1955] 2 QB 600 the Court of Criminal Appeal held that the burden of proving that the defendant came by stolen goods dishonestly lies on the prosecution, but that the jury should be directed that they are entitled to find dishonesty in the absence of an explanation from the accused of how he came by them. This was a repetition of a principle established in *Langmead* (1864) 9 Cox CC 464 and *Garth* (1949) 33 Cr App R 100.

These authorities indicate that the presumption that possession of goods which were stolen recently imposes an evidential burden on the accused, such that he must raise a doubt or he will lose the case. However, in *Aves* [1950] 2 All ER 330 and *Williams* [1962] Crim LR 54 the Court of Criminal Appeal expressly stated that no jury is bound to find guilt in the absence of an explanation from the defendant. This was recently repeated in *Ball* [1983] 2 All ER 1089. There can therefore be no doubt that the presumption is one of fact only which the jury may or may not draw depending upon their view of the whole of the evidence, including any explanation given by the accused.

Intention

As a matter of common sense someone who acts in a particular way normally intends to bring about the consequences of his actions. Conduct which appears to be deliberate rather than accidental or spontaneous will normally have been the result of a conscious decision to cause the result of that conduct. An obvious example would be where someone is seen to pick up a stone, take aim and throw it at another. One can infer from this that he intended to do harm to that other person. On the other hand, if he picked up a pebble on the beach and lobbed it into the sea, it would be difficult to infer that he meant to do harm to anyone who was underwater. Whether in any case it can properly be inferred that someone did intend the natural and probable result of his actions, can only be decided by looking at all of the facts which are proved and drawing inferences from them.

There is no rule of law that in either civil or criminal proceedings a person must be presumed to have intended the natural and probable consequences of his acts, although such an inference may be drawn.

In *Steane* [1947] KB 997 the Court of Criminal Appeal held that the trial judge was wrong in directing the jury that the accused, who had broadcast radio messages for Germany during the Second World War, must have intended to assist Germany by his actions. It was held that it is a matter for the jury whether or not he intended to assist the enemy. Some doubt was cast on whether this presumption of intention is one of fact or law in *DPP v Smith* [1961] AC 290, but s8 of the Criminal Justice Act 1967 now provides that whether someone intended or foresaw the natural and probable consequences of his actions is a question of fact. The jury may infer that he did or they may choose not to draw that inference.

There is little direct authority in civil cases, but in a number of cases culminating in *Kaslefsky* v *Kaslefsky* [1951] P 38, Denning LJ said that there is no presumption of law that someone did intend the natural and probable consequences of his acts. In *Gollins* v *Gollins* [1964] AC 644 and *Williams* v *Williams* [1964] AC 698 the view was expressed in the House of Lords that there is a persuasive presumption of law that everyone intends the natural and probable consequences of his acts. But these cases were concerned with proof of cruelty as a ground for divorce, and cannot be taken to lay down a general rule. Indeed, Lord Reid who sat in both appeals expressed the view clearly in both of his speeches that the presumption is one of fact only – it may be drawn or not depending upon the state of the whole of the evidence.

Regularity

The Latin phrase omni praesumuntur rite esse acta is often used to express the evidential presumption of regularity. The presumption is that on proof that something happened which required a person to be qualified in a particular way, or to be appointed to a particular position, or which required the obtaining of a licence, it will be presumed that the person was properly qualified or appointed so to act or that the appropriate licence was obtained. In general the presumption applies in both civil and criminal cases.

In *Cresswell* (1876) 1 QBD 446 it was presumed that the church in which a marriage ceremony took place was properly licensed for the purpose and in *Rodwell* v *Redge* (1824) 1 C&P 220 the fact that a building was operated as a theatre gave rise to a presumption that it was licensed for such use. Similarly, in *Berryman* v *Wise* (1791) 4 Term Rep 366 a person who acted as a solicitor was presumed to have been properly qualified as a solicitor. In *Gordon* (1789) Leach 515 a person who acted as a police officer was presumed to have been appointed to that office. In *Roberts* (1878) 14 Cox CC 101 it was presumed that someone who sat as a deputy county court judge was both properly qualified for the job and properly appointed and in *Campbell* v *Wallsend Slipway & Engineering Co Ltd* [1977] Crim LR 351 it was presumed that a person who acted as a health and safety inspector was appointed to that position.

The presumption applies to people acting in a public capacity or to licences which are issued in order to enable activities which are accessible by the public to be carried on, but does not always apply to private appointments. For example, in *Short* v *Lee* (1821) 2 Jac & W 464 a person who had collected tithes over many years was not presumed to be properly appointed because the appointment of tithe-collectors was a private appointment and not an appointment to a public office. On the other hand, there are examples of presumptions of appointment to private positions, such as the presumption in *Fordingbridge* (1858) EB & E 678 that a person who acted as a man's apprentice was in fact his apprentice. The presumption of marriage arising from cohabitation of man and woman as husband and wife and reputation that they are married is explainable as an example of the presumption of regularity.

There is little authority on the nature of the presumption. *Verelst* (1813) 3 Camp 432 suggests that it is a persuasive presumption, but being a criminal case it is not possible to draw from that decision any clear rule about the burden which would lie on the rebutter in a civil court. That it is a presumption of law is established by

Campbell v *Wallsend Slipway & Engineering Co Ltd* in which it was held that the presumption required the court to find that the person in question was a properly appointed health and safety inspector unless the defendant called evidence from which the appointment could be doubted.

In *Lewisham Metropolitan Borough and Town Clerk* v *Roberts* [1949] 2 KB 608 the Court of Appeal held that the presumption in favour of someone having been properly authorised to act on behalf of the Minister of Health could only be rebutted by proof that he was not properly authorised. Although that case revolved to a certain extent around the wording on the statutory instruments which enabled the appointment to be made, it was approved by the Court of Appeal in *Woolett* v *Minister of Agriculture and Fisheries* [1955] 1 QB 103, and must be taken as correct.

Mechanical regularity

A similar principle to that just discussed is the presumption that mechanical things work properly. We have already seen examples of it in the cases of *Spurge* and *Nicholas* v *Penny*. It was also applied in *Tingle Jacobs & Co* v *Kennedy* [1964] 1 WLR 638 where it was presumed that traffic lights were in proper working order. Most recently, in *Castle* v *Cross* [1984] 1 WLR 1372, the Divisional Court held that magistrates were correct in presuming that a breath-testing device worked properly in the absence of evidence to the contrary. However, in *R* v *Shepherd* [1993] 1 All ER 225 the House of Lords said that the duty to show that a department store's central computer, to which its tills were linked, was working properly could not be discharged without evidence by the application of the presumption expressed in the maxim omnia praesumuntur rite esse acta.

Spurge is clear authority that in a criminal case the presumption imposes an evidential burden only on the accused, which he may rebut by his own evidence or by calling one or more witnesses. There is no authority whether it is a persuasive or evidential presumption in civil proceedings. In principle it should be treated in the same way as the presumption of regularity, which, as we have seen, is a persuasive presumption in civil trials: *Lewisham Metropolitan Borough and Town Clerk* v *Roberts*.

Innocence

Woolmington v *DPP* is the clearest possible authority for the presumption that every person is presumed to be innocent until the contrary is proved. This is not really a presumption because no basic facts have to be proved before the court will presume the accused innocent. Rather it is a rule of law defining where the general burden lies in criminal cases.

A special presumption of innocence applies to the young in so far as no person under the age of 10 may be guilty of an offence, the irrebuttable presumption being that a child so young cannot form the mens rea of any offence: Children and Young Persons Act 1933, s50. There was also a rebuttable presumption that a child between the ages of 10 and 14 could not commit any offence, but in *C (a minor)* v *Director of Public Prosecutions* (1994) The Times 30 March the Divisional Court declared that such a presumption no longer existed in English law.

The presumption of criminal law that a boy under the age of 14 is incapable of sexual intercourse (whether natural or unnatural) was abolished by s1 of the Sexual Offences Act 1993. It follows that boys aged 10-13 may be convicted of any offences involving penetration, including attempts to commit those crimes.

The presumption of innocence arises in civil as well as criminal cases: *Williams* v *East India Co* (1802) 3 East 192. As in criminal trials, the presumption defines who bears the general burden and the cases in paragraph 3.2, above, must be referred to for full details of where the burden on particular issues lies.

Sanity

The presumption that all people are sane is rebuttable by proof to the contrary. As we have seen it is the only instance in which the common law imposes a duty on the defendant of proving anything: paragraph 3.1, above, *M'Naghten's Case*.

There is authority that in civil cases the presumption is one of fact only (*Sutton* v *Sadler* (1857) 3 CB NS 87), but this was impliedly overruled by the House of Lords in *Williams* v *Williams*. It can safely be said that the presumption is persuasive and can only be rebutted by proof of insanity.

Conflicting presumptions

In many cases presumptions can conflict. For example, in three of the cases cited above on the presumption of death a woman married once and then married again, the question for the court being whether her first husband was still alive at the time of the second ceremony. The presumptions which apply in such cases could not conflict more starkly. On the one hand it is presumed that the first marriage was valid, and on the other hand it is presumed that the second marriage was valid.

But cases on the presumption of death also illustrate another conflict of presumptions. If a man of 20 is not heard of for seven years by persons who would have expected to have heard of him and all due enquiries are made, he will be presumed dead. That is a conclusion which must be reached even though he might normally be expected to have lived to more than the age of 27. The presumption of death therefore overrules the presumption of continuance of life.

Unlike the example just given, most cases in which presumptions conflict do not involve a presumption of law which specifically goes contrary to a presumption of fact. The method of sorting out the difficulty which was adopted in the cases cited above on the presumption of death was to take matters in chronological order. We can use *Chipchase* v *Chipchase* as an example. The first relevant event was the woman's first marriage in 1914. Her husband left her in 1916 and in 1928 she married for a second time. The first marriage was presumed to be both formally and essentially valid. Therefore in 1914 she was properly married. She was still married in 1916 when her husband left. She was able to establish the basic facts from which the presumption of death was drawn. Therefore in 1923 (seven years after he was last heard of) he was dead and the first marriage was over. And therefore, in 1928 she was free to marry and the second marriage was presumed valid.

Were the facts of *Chipchase* v *Chipchase* different and the woman married for a second time in, say, 1917, there would be a clear conflict of presumptions because the first marriage would be presumed valid, the husband could not be presumed dead and the second marriage would also be presumed valid. In such cases a chronological approach is again appropriate, such that the first marriage would be presumed valid and the presumption of essential validity applicable to the second would be rebutted by the presumption that the wife was properly married in 1914.

The position in *Willshire* (1881) 6 QBD 366 was rather more complicated than in the example just given, but illustrates the principles of conflicting presumptions very well. Willshire married A in 1864. In 1868 he was convicted of bigamy because he married B while A was still alive. In 1879 he married C and in 1880 he married D. He was charged with bigamy, the charge being that he married D while married to C. The charge specifically cited C as the lawful wife, not A. Willshire argued that A was still alive because of the presumption of continuance of life. The Court of Queen's Bench held that it was a question of fact for the jury whether A was still alive when Willshire married C. If she was alive at that time he was not guilty because he would not then have been validly married to C, whereas if she was not alive he was guilty; provided, of course, the jury was satisfied that C was still alive when he married D. In *Willshire* the presumption of validity of marriage did not automatically have precedence over the presumption of continuance of life because the presumptions deal with different matters.

It is sometimes said that *Willshire* is authority that where presumptions conflict they are to be ignored and the case decided according to the facts. This is rather misleading because no jury can be expected to ignore completely the presumption of continuance of life. But if one adopts the chronological approach suggested above, the analysis becomes easier. Willshire's marriage to A was valid. As a matter of law she could not be presumed dead when he married B, and nor could such an inference properly be drawn. Therefore the marriage to B was bigamous. It was a matter for inference whether A was still alive when he married C, because there was insufficient evidence from which it could be presumed in law that A was dead at that time. If the jury was satisfied that A was dead or if it felt that she might have been dead, Willshire would have been guilty because his marriage to C would have been valid. The presumption of essential validity of the marriage to C could have been rebutted by the inference that A was still alive. It was then a matter for inference whether C was still alive when he married D.

It would be artificial to say that the presumption of validity of marriage means that one must presume that earlier spouses of the defendant are deceased at the time of his remarriage. Presumptions are meant to assist in the resolution of factual disputes, not to add to the problems. The jury must approach the matter using common sense. Presumptions assist to fill in gaps which it would waste time to fill by formal proof.

Thus in a case like *Willshire* there was no need for proof of the validity of the ceremonies he went through with his various 'wives', the presumption of formal validity prevented such proof being necessary. But the essential question was whether there was essential validity and the presumption in favour of such validity could not prevail over reasonable inferences which rebutted it.

4

Hearsay

4.1 Definition

4.2 The common law in criminal cases

4.3 The common law in civil cases

4.4 The doctrine of res gestae

4.1 Definition

The principles

The courts must decide cases by ascertaining what the relevant facts are, ascertaining what the relevant law is and then marrying the law to the facts so as to reach a decision. Facts are proved primarily by witnesses on oath. Each witness must give evidence only of matters within his own knowledge. If we take a murder trial as an example, it is not generally permissible for a witness to say 'X told me that the defendant killed the deceased', because the witness does not know whether the defendant did commit the crime, all he can say is that X told him so. X may know whether the defendant did commit the killing, but the court cannot assume that he had this knowledge. It may be that X could only say 'Y told me that the defendant killed the deceased'. Again, unless Y gives evidence the court will not know whether he knew the truth of what he told X; it may be that he was told it by Z. The longer the chain of people between the person who actually knows whether a statement is true and the person who gives evidence, the more difficult it is for the court to assess whether it is true. It also is more difficult for the court to be satisfied that the statement has been repeated accurately from one person to the next.

Various explanations can be given for the reluctance of the courts to allow repetitions of statements. The most important, and most sensible, objection to allowing repetitions, is that the truth of the statement cannot be tested by cross-examining the witness, because in most cases all he can say is 'I do not know whether what X told me is true, but I have repeated it accurately.' Cross-examination can test the second part of this – whether X's statement has been accurately repeated. But it cannot test the first part. The first reported case setting out this objection was *Paine* (1695) 5 Mod 163 and it has been repeated many times, most recently and most authoritatively in *Andrews* [1987] AC 281.

Other objections have less merit as general rules, although they may be applicable to particular cases. It has been said that evidence which comes otherwise than from someone who knows whether it is true is not allowed because it can lead to a waste of the court's time in investigating the reliability of the chain down which the information has passed. It has been said that such evidence is irrelevant and that there is too much scope for the information having been invented. It is said that things said otherwise than on oath are unreliable. All of these points may be applicable to individual cases, but the overall picture is that it is the inability to test the evidence by cross-examination which leads to its exclusion.

Repetition and hearsay

What has been said above has not used the word 'hearsay' to describe evidence which comprises a repetition of that which someone other than the witness has said. The reason for this is that not all such evidence is hearsay. Evidence is hearsay evidence if it consists of the repetition of a statement in order to prove that the facts asserted in the statement are true. There is considerable difficulty in defining precisely what amounts to a statement for these purposes and this difficulty will be examined below.

In a slander action a witness for the plaintiff may give evidence as follows: 'The defendant told me that the plaintiff stole his car.' The witness repeats the defendant's statement in that he tells the court what the defendant said. He does not, however, give that evidence in order to prove the truth of what the defendant said, because if what he said was true the plaintiff would not have been defamed. The purpose of the witness giving this evidence is in order to prove that something was said. It is not hearsay evidence.

In a criminal trial for offering a bribe, a witness for the prosecution may give evidence as follows: 'The defendant said to me that he would pay me £100 if I awarded a building contract to him rather than to any of his competitors.' Again, the witness repeats what the defendant told him, but he also does not do so in order to prove the truth of what the defendant said. The defendant said that he would give the witness £100. The charge being one of offering a bribe, it does not matter whether he really would hand over the money; all that is relevant is that the offer was made. Unlike the slander case in the previous paragraph, the party calling the witness does not care whether the statement of the defendant was true or false. Yet, like that example, the evidence given is not hearsay, it is evidence that something was said. It can be tested in cross-examination because the witness can be questioned about the only relevant matter, which is whether the statement was made by the defendant.

In contrast, the following would be hearsay evidence: 'Mr Smith told me that the defendant told him the plaintiff stole his car' or 'my secretary said that the defendant had telephoned offering me £100 if I awarded him the contract'. In *Subramaniam* v *Public Prosecutor* [1956] 1 WLR 965, the Privy Council said:

'Evidence of a statement made to a witness by a person who is not himself called as a witness may or may not be hearsay. It is hearsay and inadmissible when the object of the evidence is to establish the truth of what is contained in the statement. It is not hearsay and is admissible when it is proposed to establish by the evidence, not the truth of the statement, but the fact that it was made.'

The defendant in *Subramaniam* v *Public Prosecutor* was charged with possession of ammunition. He admitted having ammunition in his possession but said that he acted under duress. In order to show duress he wished to repeat threats which he said were made to him and which he was told would be carried out if he did not help terrorists by carrying ammunition for them. The Privy Council held that the trial judge was wrong in disallowing this evidence because the only purpose of the defendant repeating the statements in evidence was to prove that they were made. It did not matter whether the terrorists would carry out the threats, what was relevant was that threats were made which the defendant believed would be carried out. Therefore the repetition of the statements by the accused was not hearsay.

Similarly, in *Woodhouse* v *Hall* (1980) 72 Cr App R 39 (which was distinguished in *R* v *Kearley* [1992] 2 All ER 345: see below), evidence that girls at a massage parlour had offered sexual services to customers was admissible on a charge against the manager of the parlour of managing a brothel. It was not hearsay because it was the fact that sexual services were offered which was relevant and not whether the particular offer of which evidence was given, would have been carried out.

A more difficult case is *Mawaz Kahn* v *R* [1967] 1 AC 454. The two defendants who were charged with murder gave statements to the police in which they said that they were at a place called the Ocean Club at the time of the killing. It was clear from other evidence that they were not at that club at the relevant time. Neither defendant gave evidence at trial. As we will see, a statement made to the police by one defendant is not usually evidence against any other because if it says, for example, 'I did not do it, it was my co-defendant' it is hearsay evidence against that co-defendant. The trial judge directed the jury that the statements of each accused was not evidence against the other, but he went on to say that if they were satisfied that the defendants were not at the Ocean Club they were entitled to ask themselves whether they had conspired together to put up false alibis. The Privy Council held this to be a correct direction. In other words the jury could use the fact that the statements were not true as something from which they could infer that the defendants had agreed between themselves that they would tell the police a false story, and from that conclusion they could infer that the reason for telling a false story was that they did not want the truth to be known.

In *Ratten* v *R* [1972] AC 378 the defendant was charged with his wife's murder. Evidence was given by the operator at Ratten's local telephone exchange that at about 1.15 pm on the day of the murder she received a telephone call from Ratten's house. The call was made by a sobbing woman who said 'Get me the police please'. Ratten gave evidence that he was in the house at that time and that no call was made. The Privy Council held that the operator's evidence was admissible in order to show that a call was made. But, somewhat surprisingly, it was held that the operator was able to repeat what the woman said without breaching the hearsay rule. As we will see later in this chapter, it was held that even if the operator's evidence was hearsay it was admissible. That part of the decision is clearly correct. But in order to rebut the defendant's assertion that no call was made at 1.15 pm all that was necessary was for the operator to say that she received a call. Once she gave evidence of the contents of the call there was a risk of the jury drawing inferences from what the caller said. Therefore to allow repetition of those words was to allow hearsay evidence to be given. This decision was distinguished in *R v Kearley* [1992] 2 All ER 345: see below.

In cases like the examples of slander and bribery given above it is clear that the statement is repeated in order to prove not its truth but the fact that it was made. It is impossible to give examples to cover all possible situations in which the repetition of statements is not hearsay. The issues in the case must be worked out and the question asked whether it makes any difference whether the statement is true or false.

In the slander example, the plaintiff had to establish that the defendant had said he was a thief. Once the making of such a statement was proved, slander was proved unless the defendant proved that it was true. Therefore on the issue whether the alleged statement was made, it mattered not whether that statement was true or false. Of course, at the end of the case when all evidence is being weighed the truth or falsity of the allegation of theft is relevant because if in fact the plaintiff did steal the car he would not have been slandered. But the truth or falsity of the statement is a separate issue from whether it was made. This is seen most clearly by the burden of proof in the trial. Whether it was made is something which the plaintiff would have to prove. On the issue whether it was true or false the burden is on the defendant.

In the bribery example, it is the making of the offer which constitutes the offence. If the defence shows that the money would not have been paid in any event, no defence to the charge of making the offer is established. The only issue which arises is whether an offer was made and the witness gives direct evidence that it was.

The examples given above both involve the repetition of statements made by the defendant. In fact statements made by anyone, whether or not a party to the case, may be repeated if they are relevant and are proved for the purpose of proving that they were made and not that they were true. Indeed, statements made by the witness himself may be repeated, such as would happen where the party to an oral contract gave evidence about what he and the other party agreed about the terms of the contract.

In *R v McCay* [1990] Crim LR 338 the Court of Appeal held admissible evidence by a police officer as to the number of the accused in an identification parade as told to him by a witness. It was either original evidence or within an exception to the hearsay rule.

Documents

For the purposes of the hearsay rule the law treats documents like witnesses. It will allow documents to be used in evidence provided that assertions made in them are not relied on as evidence of their truth. To adapt the examples used earlier, a letter which contains a libel about the plaintiff is admissible as original evidence rather than hearsay. As we will see in chapter 12, it will be necessary for someone to prove formally that the document emanated from the defendant, but that is not something which alters the effect and application of the hearsay rule. A document could also prove the making of a contractual offer without being hearsay.

The most common use of documents as non-hearsay arises when contracts, wills and the like are proved. Unless the parties agree that a particular document is the contract they made it will be necessary for evidence to be given that it is. But the document is not hearsay, rather it is the very thing which is the subject matter of the litigation. The position is different if a contract was formed orally and then reduced to writing for convenience. Strictly speaking the document is hearsay evidence of the terms of the contract, although parties rarely take issue with use of the document itself as the contract.

In chapter 1 we saw that witnesses may refresh their memory by reference to documents written or approved by them at the first reasonable opportunity while the matters recorded were still fresh in their minds. In many cases the witness has no independent recollection of the facts recorded in his memory-refreshing note and simply reads it out to the court. This is not, however, treated as hearsay evidence because the law treats what is said from the witness box as having been spoken from memory (*Maugham* v *Hubbard* (1828) 8 B & C 14).

In chapter 12 we will examine the special rules of evidence which apply to documents. The only special rule of any significance is that the court requires the original of a document to be produced in evidence if possible. For the purposes of that rule, commonly referred to as the best evidence rule, photographs, films, video recordings and audio recordings are treated as documents. To an extent the same can be said about the hearsay rule. But there is an important principle which is applied every day in the criminal courts. Tape recordings, films and photographs are not hearsay unless they contain hearsay. A photograph of the victim of an assault, for example, is not hearsay evidence of his injuries but direct evidence because the photograph does not interpret the injuries. It has no mind of its own, it simply records what it sees. It is admissible as original evidence in the same way that a witness who saw the injuries would be entitled to give evidence of what he saw. This was recognised as long ago as 1864 in *Tolson* (1864) 4 F & F 103 and recently re-affirmed by the Court of Appeal in *Dodson* [1984] 1 WLR 971.

Both *Dodson* and *Kajala* v *Noble* (1982) 75 Cr App R 749 recognise that video recordings are to be treated in the same way; and two first instance decisions, *Stevenson* (1971) 55 Cr App R 171 and *Robson* [1972] 2 All ER 699 hold that audio recordings are also direct evidence and not hearsay. It must always be borne in mind, however, that evidence which is hearsay does not become admissible simply because it is contained in a recording or photograph. So, a photograph of a document is not original evidence and a tape recording of a conversation is hearsay if the truth or falsity of statements made in the document or conversation is in issue.

The definition of assertions

If A says to B 'I saw X hit Y' it is obvious that B would give hearsay evidence if he repeated that statement in a trial where it is in issue whether X hit Y. Similarly, if B overheard A saying to C 'I saw X hit Y', B's repetition of this would be hearsay. It makes no difference that A was not speaking to B when he made his statement, because he was clearly intending to assert a fact and B is repeating that assertion.

But what if B gives evidence and says 'I saw a fight and heard X, one of the combatants, say "please don't hit me Y", he was then hit by the man he spoke to'? This evidence goes to the issue of the identity of the person who hit X. Were Y to say that X was not hit at all by anyone, the last 10 words of B's evidence would not be hearsay because he would be giving direct evidence of what he saw. However, were Y to accept that X was hit but deny that he was the assailant, B's evidence could be hearsay. It would not be hearsay if he were able to identify Y from his appearance so that he does not have to rely on what X said about his identity. But it would be hearsay if he could not remember what the assailant looked like and, therefore, repeated what X said in order to prove that the assailant was Y.

This is an example of an implied assertion: X did not intend to assert that his assailant's name was Y, but from what he said it is possible to infer that he was Y and therefore X impliedly asserted this fact. There is no doubt on the authorities that implied assertions come within the hearsay rule: see, eg, *Teper* v *R* [1952] AC 480.

At common law implied assertions are hearsay in civil cases in the same way that they are in criminal cases. In *Wright* v *Doe d Tatham* (1837) 7 Ad & El 313 one question for the court was whether the man who made a will was sane at the time he made it. It was sought to put in evidence letters which were written to him on the ground that the content of the letters was such that they would only have been sent to a sane man. They were held to be inadmissible for two reasons. First, the use which was sought to be made of them involved the court receiving the opinions of the writers, yet opinion evidence was not admissible on the question of sanity unless the person giving it was an expert such as a psychiatrist: see chapter 10 for the present state of the law on opinion evidence. Secondly, and more importantly for present purposes, the court was being asked to infer from the letters that the writers were saying that the testator was sane. This made the letters hearsay, just as they would be hearsay if they contained the statement 'Dear Tatham, I am writing to you while you are still sane because ...'. Of course there was no such direct assertion of the writers' opinions that he was sane, but it was an inference which could be drawn from the contents of the letters.

The difficulty of defining implied assertions can be illustrated as follows. If a witness had given evidence that he was on an aeroplane and that the man sitting next to him had opened his briefcase in which there were letters the envelopes of which were addressed to 'Mr Smith', is this hearsay? Clearly the jury would be asked to infer from the fact that the man had these letters in his possession that his name was Smith. In the ordinary course of things it is highly unlikely that he opened his case deliberately in order to give someone the impression that he was Smith; the likelihood is that he gave no thought to the possibility of someone looking over his shoulder. The proper view of this scenario is that the evidence is not hearsay. The witness gives evidence of certain facts and from those facts the jury would be entitled to draw a conclusion. But it is not realistic to say that the jury is being invited to rely on any assertion made by the man or the envelopes, because the envelopes do not say 'The person in possession of this letter is called Smith', all they say is that 'We are addressed to someone called Smith'. That is a statement which cannot be challenged, it is clearly correct; the question for the jury is what conclusion they draw from it.

In *R* v *Kearley* [1992] 2 All ER 345 the House of Lords decided that evidence tendered by police officers that they had received, while searching the appellant's flat, ten telephone calls and seven personal visits, with the implied assertion in the callers' and visitors' requests for drugs that the appellant was a supplier of drugs, was inadmissible as hearsay. In reaching this conclusion their Lordships applied *Wright* v *Doe d Tatham*, above, *Myers* v *DPP* [1965] AC 1001 and *R* v *Blastland* [1986] AC 41, but *Kearley* was distinguished in *R* v *Warner* (1993) 96 Cr App R 324: see 13.4, below.

Assertive conduct

In *Chandarasekera* v *R* [1937] AC 220 a woman who had had her throat cut was asked whether Alisandiri (the defendant's name) had done it. She nodded assent. In answer to other questions she made signs which referred to the defendant, such as pointing to a policeman and slapping her face – it was well known in the district at the time that the Chandarasekera had slapped a constable around the face. Whether evidence of her gestures was admissible depended upon the Ceylon Evidence Ordinance, No 14 of 1895 s32 which made the evidence admissible if it amounted to a written or verbal statement. The Privy Council held that it was a verbal statement. The reasoning was that, because the woman was incapable of speaking, she was in the same position as someone who was dumb to whom sign language would be verbal communication. Although it was not specifically held that the evidence of her gestures was hearsay, it is clear that the Privy Council did consider it to be hearsay, otherwise they would not have had to ask whether it came within the terms of the Ordinance.

The assertions made by the woman in *Chandarasekera* v *R* were intended to assert facts which she would in all probability have stated in words had she not had her throat cut. In principle there is no reason why evidence of conduct which implies something is not also hearsay. Indeed, it is possible to analyse writing in this way. For example, a note written by X which reads 'Y phoned 11 am, offered to buy car' could not be produced as evidence that X made the offer because it is hearsay. But it is likely that X did not mean to do anything other than record the fact of the call and its contents for his own reference. Nevertheless, he makes two assertions in the note, that Y called and that he made an offer. There is no distinction between X stating these facts to someone orally, writing them down on a piece of paper and nodding if someone asks him whether they occurred. All three ways of stating the facts are uses by him of his physical faculties to convey a message.

Evidence about certain conduct, however, is not hearsay. We can take an illustration *Redpath* (1962) 46 Cr App R 319: see 2.5 *Distress*.

4.2 The common law in criminal cases

The general rule

The hearsay rule as we know it today was first stated as a general principle in *R v Eriswell (Inhabitants)* (1790) 3 Term Rep 707. Evidence was given at a court hearing by a child. Five years later in the course of a different case a different court relied upon the evidence given at the first hearing, although the child did not give evidence before them. Grose J said that the relevant question for the Court of King's Bench was whether the evidence of what the child said at the first hearing was admissible. He said:

'It is what is commonly called hearsay evidence of a fact. Now it is a general rule that such evidence is not admissible.'

The four judges were divided upon the admissibility of the evidence in question in the *Eriswell* case. All four said that it was hearsay but Grose J and Lord Kenyon CJ said that it did not come within any exception to the rule whereas Buller and Ashhurst JJ said that it was admissible because the child was on oath when testifying before the first court. Eleven years later in *Ferry Frystone* (1801) 2 East 54 it was made clear that hearsay evidence is not admissible simply because what is repeated was originally said on oath.

The stringency of the hearsay rule in the nineteenth century is shown by *R v Rishworth (Inhabitants)* (1842) 2 QB 476 in which it was held that no one may give evidence of the time and place of his birth because he necessarily relies on others having told him these facts.

The first recognition that the repetition of acts is hearsay as well as the repetition of words came in *Gibson* (1887) 18 QBD 537. The defendant was charged with malicious wounding, the allegation being that he had thrown a stone at the victim. The victim gave evidence that immediately after he was hit by the stone he saw a woman point to a door and say 'The person who threw the stone went in there.' The door in question was the door to Gibson's home and he was found to be there. The woman who had told the victim where his assailant had gone did not give evidence. Gibson's conviction was overturned on appeal because the evidence of what the woman did and said was inadmissible.

In *Myers* v *DPP* [1965] AC 1001 the House of Lords reviewed the authorities and laid down authoritatively that hearsay evidence is inadmissible unless it is made admissible by statute or it falls within an exception recognised at common law. New common law exceptions may not be created. *Myers* v *DPP* did not define hearsay evidence by reference to a formula, save that all members of the House said that the repetition by a witness of a statement made by another is hearsay.

Indirect introduction of hearsay

Various devices have been used from time to time to try to get hearsay evidence before the court in an indirect way. For example in *Saunders* [1899] 1 QB 490 it was relevant to the case whether the defendant had had dealings with certain tradesmen. A police officer gave evidence that he had made enquiries and had been unable to find that any trade had been conducted by the defendant. He was not asked directly to repeat what people had told him, but by telling the court the result of his enquiries he had made known what others had told him. Therefore his evidence was hearsay and inadmissible. The position was effectively the same in *Howarth* (1926) 19 Cr App R 102 in which a witness was not allowed to say that he had ascertained that the defendant was in the vicinity where a crime had been committed at the time it was committed. Again, the witness was informing the court of what others had told him, despite not repeating their words.

An assertion by a prosecution witness that someone receiving a package is a heroin addict is inadmissible in evidence unless the witness has first-hand knowledge of the fact or it is based on that person's conviction for possession of the specified drug: *R* v *Rothwell* (1993) The Times 27 April.

In *Glinski* v *McIver* [1962] AC 726 Lord Devlin criticised attempts to introduce hearsay by asking a witness what he did as a result of what he was told because the only purpose of such evidence is to allow the jury to infer what was said to him. The Court of Appeal Criminal Division expressly approved this criticism in *Turner* [1975] QB 834. It is now clearly the law that no indirect introduction of hearsay is permissible.

Statements in documents

If a witness were asked to prove his identity he is likely to try to do so by producing a document such as a passport which bears his photograph. It flies in the face of common sense to refuse to allow such a document in evidence, subject to the right of counsel to cross-examine the witness about its genuineness. But the passport would be put in evidence in order to prove the truth of what it asserts, namely the identity of the person whose photograph it contains. In principle, therefore, it is hearsay.

In *Rice* [1963] 1 QB 857 the Court of Criminal Appeal said, obiter, that a passport is not hearsay evidence because of the high degree of likelihood that what it says is correct. The issue for the Court of Criminal Appeal was the admissibility of an air ticket which bore the names Rice and Moore. Rice and Moore were convicted of conspiracy to steal cars. One issue at their trial was whether Rice was in Manchester on 10 May 1961. The ticket, which was proved to have been used, was held to have been rightly admitted in evidence on this issue. Winn J said that once it is proved that the ticket was used, the jury would be entitled to draw an inference from the fact that it contained the names Rice and Moore that one of the people who used the ticket was called Rice.

Rice is a difficult case because what the court held was that it was not permissible for the jury to approach the ticket as saying 'I was issued to Y', but from the fact that it was used they could infer that it was used by a person whose name it bore. As Winn J said, correctly:

'The balance of probability recognised by common sense and common knowledge that an air ticket which has been used on a flight and which has a name on it has more likely than not been used by a man of that name or by one of two men whose names are on it.'

Common sense and common knowledge would also suggest that if a Manchester hotel's record showed that someone booked in on 10 May 1961 giving the name Rice, the likelihood is that someone of that name booked into the hotel. But this does not prevent the book or the air ticket from being hearsay evidence, it simply means that it is probative hearsay evidence.

It is submitted that *Rice* was wrongly decided and that the airline ticket was hearsay evidence. It contained on its face an assertion, namely that it had been booked in order to allow someone called Rice to travel on a flight to Manchester. Without that assertion it was of no use to the jury at all. It is irrelevant whether the assertion was relied on directly by the jury or was something from which they drew the conclusion that someone called Rice flew to Manchester, because the importance of the ticket was the assertion on it. In some ways the use of the ticket which was approved by the Court of Criminal Appeal is similar to the indirect introduction of hearsay by asking a witness what he did as a result of what he was told. In both cases the purpose of putting the evidence before the jury is to allow them to draw an inference from what was said.

One way of testing whether a piece of evidence is hearsay is to ask whether the truth of the assertion which is repeated to the court makes any difference to the outcome of the case. If a witness gave evidence that a passenger on the flight had introduced himself as Mr Rice, this only assists the jury if what the passenger said was true. Similarly the ticket was only of assistance if the jury believed what it said to be true. As we have seen, it is the inability to test the truth of hearsay evidence which renders it inadmissible. Where there is no need to test its truth, it is not hearsay, as was the case with the evidence of threats in *Subramaniam* v *Public Prosecutor*. But the truth of the assertion on the face of the ticket in *Rice* was relevant and therefore the ticket was hearsay.

Rice was cited only by Lord Pearce in *Myers* v *DPP*. He dissented from the majority on the question whether the microfilm records were admissible at common law and it was in this context that he approved and relied on *Rice*. The majority decision in *Myers*, however, suggests that *Rice* is wrong. In *Patel* v *Comptroller of Customs* [1966] AC 356 the Privy Council distinguished *Rice* holding that evidence that a bag of seed had 'produce of Morocco' printed on it was hearsay evidence about the origin of the bag.

In *Cook* [1987] QB 417 the Court of Appeal held that a photofit picture is the same as a photograph and is not hearsay. It is hard to see what justification there was for this decision. There can be no doubt that a written statement by a witness that the defendant had blue eyes and brown hair is not admissible because it is hearsay, although the witness could, of course, use it to refresh his memory if the test in *Kelsey* (1982) 74 Cr App R 213 is satisfied. A photofit is a picture which is built up from the description given by the witness. It is exactly the same as the written document. No doubt the witness could say 'I am unable to put into words the identity of the offender, but I have made this photofit picture', thereby producing the photofit as part of his oral evidence. But *Cook* suggests that the photofit is admissible whether or not the witness gives evidence. Indeed the court approved *Percy Smith* [1976] Crim LR 511 in which it was held, again by the Court of Appeal, that a sketch made by a police officer who was a skilled artist was in the same category as a photograph. Yet, there is a difference between a photograph and a sketch or photofit in that the photograph records what the camera sees whereas the photofit and sketch record what the witness says he saw. In *R* v *Constantinou* [1989] Crim LR 571 the Court of Appeal affirmed that photofit pictures, together with photographs and sketches, are in a class of their own to which neither the hearsay rule nor the rule against admissibility of an earlier consistent statement applied.

Absence of statements in documents

Myers v *DPP* holds that a witness may not repeat what a document says in order to prove the truth of statements in it. But nothing in *Myers* deals with the case of a witness who gives evidence that a document does not contain a relevant statement. In *Patel* (1981) 73 Cr App R 117 the accused was charged with assisting an illegal immigrant, Ashraf, to gain entry into the United Kingdom. It was, of course, necessary to prove that Ashraf was an illegal immigrant. The Court of Appeal allowed the appeal because the Home Office records which were used in evidence were inadmissible hearsay. It was said, obiter, that if an officer of the Home Office who was responsible for keeping records of legal entrants gave evidence that he had inspected the records and they did not contain Ashraf's name, no hearsay evidence would have been given and the jury would have been entitled to infer that Ashraf did not enter this country legally.

This dictum from *Patel* was applied in *Shore* (1983) 76 Cr App R 72 where the accused was charged with dishonestly handling three car springs. It was necessary for the Crown to prove that the springs in question had been stolen from a particular firm. Two employees of that firm gave evidence that the way the system operated was that when goods were received a card was completed and then an entry was made on the same card when goods were sold. They said that there was no entry indicating that any of the three springs in question had been sold. The Court of Appeal held this evidence not to be hearsay but was direct evidence of facts which the witnesses perceived and from which an inference could be drawn.

These cases are not inconsistent with *Myers* v *DPP*. It is clearly impermissible for someone to say 'I have consulted the company records and they tell me that spring number 1 was sold on 1 January.' And it seems to follow from this that it is equally impermissible for him to say 'I have consulted the company records and they tell me that spring number 1 has not been sold.'

There is, however, a difference between the two statements. In the first the witness is putting before the jury the statement of the person who compiled the records and is asking them to accept that what he said is true. Whereas in the second case he is not repeating anyone's statement, he is asking the jury to infer from his own evidence of how the records are compiled that they would contain a statement if the spring had been sold. It could be said that he is asking the jury to believe the records' own assertion that the spring was not sold, but the reality is that the records do not make assertions, they merely store assertions made by others. For a witness to say that the records do not contain a particular statement is not to repeat anyone else's assertion and does not fall within the hearsay rule as defined in *Myers* v *DPP*.

This matter was taken further by the Court of Appeal in *Abadom* [1983] 1 WLR 126 where Kerr LJ said about *Myers* v *DPP*:

> 'The bounds of that decision appear to be still unsettled in cases of systematically compiled records where evidence about the conclusions to be drawn from such records is adduced from witnesses who were themselves concerned in their compilation in the ordinary course of their duties.'

In order for the court to be able to draw correct inferences from such records it is necessary for someone who is responsible for them to give evidence. He will be in a position to explain the procedures by which they are compiled and can be cross-examined about such matters as whether it is possible for the records to have failed to store an entry.

Mechanical and computer printouts

Repetition by a witness of what a mechanical instrument says is also not hearsay in most cases. The policeman's reading of the speedometer in *Nicholas* v *Penny* [1950]

2 KB 466 was not hearsay. Unlike a human being who can invent something before speaking about it, the only way in which the reading on a speedometer could be wrong is if there is some mechanical failure. The law presumes that mechanical things work properly. Therefore to state what a speedometer says is to repeat something which the law presumes to be accurate and not to repeat a statement which may or may not be true. If thus falls outside the hearsay rule. The witness can be cross-examined about whether he read the speedometer accurately and the device itself can be tested for accuracy.

Whether a reading taken from a machine is hearsay depends, therefore, upon what the machine does. If it records what it perceives it is not hearsay. This point was addressed in *The Statue of Liberty* [1968] 1 WLR 739 which concerned the admissibility of a film recorded by radar equipment.

Sir Jocelyn Simon P held that the film was not hearsay. He illustrated the law on readings from machines by saying that a witness could give evidence of readings from a barometer where weather conditions were relevant, and that a print-out produced by the barometer would be equally admissible.

In *Wood* (1982) 76 Cr App R 23 metal samples were analysed by computer to assess what metals were contained in them. The result of this analysis was admissible without infringing the hearsay rule. Samples of glass were analysed by computer in *Abadom* to find their refractive index. The Court of Appeal did not question the admissibility of the result of the computer's analysis. Further, in *Castle* v *Cross* [1984] 1 WLR 1372 the Divisional Court held that a print-out from a breath testing machine was admissible to prove the proportion of alcohol in the defendant's breath. In all these cases the evidence of what the machine said was only admissible because direct evidence was given of what was fed into it.

See also 5.1 *Computer printouts*, below

Hearsay for the defence

Hearsay evidence is no more admissible at common law for the defence than it is for the prosecution. In *Thomson* [1912] 3 KB 19 the defendant was charged with performing an abortion. He wished to call evidence that several weeks before the girl had an abortion she had stated that she would perform it herself. This was held to be hearsay and inadmissible to prove that she did perform the operation. In *Sparks* v *R* [1964] AC 964 the defendant, a white man, was charged with indecently assaulting a young girl. The trial judge refused to allow him to call the girl's mother to say that shortly after the assault her daughter had said of her attacker, 'it was a coloured boy'. Had the girl given evidence she could have been questioned about this, but she did not and her mother's evidence would have been hearsay. The Privy Council upheld the trial judge's ruling.

More recently, in *Blastland* [1986] AC 41 the defendant, who was charged with buggery and murder, was not allowed to give evidence that someone else (Mark) had expressed knowledge of the offences at a time when only the offender would know of them. The House of Lords held that this evidence would have been hearsay and inadmissible. Indeed, Mark had gone further than just to exhibit knowledge of the offences, during interviews with the police he had admitted committing them but had later withdrawn those admissions. The admissions were not admissible in Blastland's favour either.

Most recently, in *Harry* (1988) 86 Cr App R 105 Harry and another were charged with possession and supply of drugs. The Crown's case was that both defendants had been dealing in cocaine from a particular flat. Harry wanted to put in evidence that telephone calls were made to that flat asking for his co-defendant and not for him. The Court of Appeal upheld the trial judge's ruling that this evidence was hearsay because the purpose of calling it was to establish the truth of what the callers implied, namely that it was the co-defendant and not Harry who was the dealer: see also *R* v *Kearley* [1992] 2 All ER 345.

4.3 The common law in civil cases

The authorities

Some of the leading authorities on the inadmissibility of hearsay at common law are civil cases. In *Myers* v *DPP* Lord Reid relied on two previous House of Lords decisions (*Sturla* v *Freccia* (1880) 5 App Cas 623 and *Woodward* v *Goulstone* (1886) 11 App Cas 469) as authority for the hearsay rule not being subject to further relaxation by the courts. Both of these cases are still good authority that hearsay evidence is generally inadmissible in civil courts.

There are no common law exceptions to the hearsay rule applicable only in civil cases. In fact the common law is virtually redundant in the county courts and the High Court because the Civil Evidence Act 1968 governs the admissibility of hearsay in those courts. Section 9 of the Act expressly preserves the common law as it applies to some exceptions to the hearsay rule. These will be discussed in paragraph 5.2 below.

The magistrates' courts

The magistrates' courts hear a small number of civil disputes, such as applications for a child to be placed into the care of a local authority. Because the 1968 Act does not apply in the magistrates' courts, the common law applies as defined most clearly in criminal appeals.

The Evidence Act 1938, which allows certain documentary hearsay to be used, applies in civil magistrates' courts hearings. This is discussed in paragraph 5.3

4.4 The doctrine of res gestae

Definition

'Res gestae' means things done or, less accurately, the transaction. The so-called doctrine of res gestae allows evidence to be given so as to show the transaction in issue in the case in its full context. Some evidence which falls within the res gestae is hearsay and some is not. That which is not hearsay is admissible because it is relevant. That which is hearsay is admissible because the authorities say so. One thing which is not known is why the admissibility of evidence which is part of the res gestae is said to be a doctrine.

Evidence which is part of the res gestae is admissible regardless of whether it is hearsay or, indeed, is subject to any other rule of exclusion. We will see in later chapters that for various reasons certain types of evidence are not normally allowed to be called. At this stage those rules will not be discussed, but the examples of evidence admitted as part of the res gestae which follow should be borne in mind when chapters 7 and 10 are read. It should also be remembered when paragraph 5.2 is considered that hearsay evidence in the county courts and the High Court is only admissible under the provisions of the Civil Evidence Act 1968 and that hearsay evidence which is part of the res gestae is only admissible if it falls within ss2, 4 or 9 of that Act.

It is not always easy to divide evidence admissible as part of the res gestae into that which is hearsay and that which is not. As we have seen, whether evidence about what someone said or did is hearsay depends upon whether assertions made by that person are put forward as evidence of their truth. It is only in reference to the issues in the case that this can be assessed. How difficult this assessment can be will be shown as the cases are discussed.

Statements about one's health

Evidence may be given of statements made by a person about his state of health: see, eg, *Aveson* v *Kinnaird* (1805) 6 East 1258.

In order to be admissible the statements must be contemporaneous with the state of health they describe and thus must not relate to symptoms which no longer exist: *Gloster* (1888) 16 Cox 471. They must also be oral statements and not statements in letters because the recipient of the letter will not be able to give evidence of the conduct of the writer and it is necessary for the court to be able to place the statements in their full context: *Witt* v *Witt* (1862) 3 S & T 143.

Further, they are admissible only as evidence of the person's state of health and not as evidence of the cause of that state of health. For example in *Gilbey* v *Great Western Railway* (1910) 102 LT 202 a man returned home after suffering an accident at work. His wife's evidence of the description given to her by her husband as to how the accident was caused was held to be inadmissible.

Where what is in issue is someone's mental health evidence may be given of the way he behaved, including what he said, although expert evidence will be required about the conclusions which may be drawn from that conduct: see chapter 10.

Why is evidence of what one says about one's health not hearsay? Lawrence J's explanation in *Aveson* v *Kinnaird*, namely that it is not hearsay because evidence of this type if always allowed, is hardly compelling. The answer to the question lies in the way the court should treat the evidence. What the court must investigate where someone's state of health at a particular time is in issue, is whether that person appeared to be suffering from any illness. It can judge that from evidence of what people who saw the person perceived. It is beyond doubt that a witness can say 'I saw her, she was covered in a nasty rash', without infringing the hearsay rule. The witness could also say, for example, 'She was asleep, I tried to wake her by shaking her and shouting in her ear, but it had no effect.' This does not infringe the hearsay rule because the witness can be cross-examined about the genuineness of the sleep. In other words he could be asked how loudly he shouted, whether the person in bed responded in any way, and so on. The court then relies on what the witness perceived and not on anything asserted to the witness by the person in bed. If it appears that the person in bed was only pretending to be asleep, the court will not rely on the evidence of the witness and, indeed, may infer that there was no illness.

Words that are spoken by the patient are to be treated in the same way as his or her conduct. It is not the words themselves which are relied on as evidence, but the circumstances in which they are spoken. The court investigates whether those words reflect a particular state of mind. It asks this question: in all the circumstances of the case, does the fact that the words in question were spoken indicate anything about whether the speaker was ill? The witness can be asked about the overall appearance of the patient, whether he or she spoke clearly, and so on. It is thus not the words which are put forward as evidence, but the state of mind behind them.

We saw in chapter 3 that evidence can be given about the distressed condition of a woman where it is alleged that she was indecently assaulted. Whether that distress amounts to corroboration of her evidence depends upon the *Baskerville* definition of corroboration. But the evidence can be given because it is relevant to show how she felt at the time. She can be questioned about her apparent distress, as can anyone who testifies to it. The court can therefore judge for itself whether it was genuine. But it does this not by relying on assertions made by the woman when she was, for example, screaming. Rather it relies on the circumstances in which the screams came to be made.

Statements showing motive

Evidence may be given of statements which accompany conduct in order to define the motive behind that conduct. In *Rawson* v *Haigh* (1824) 2 Bing 99 a man left the country and the question arose whether he did so in order to avoid his creditors. The Court of Common Pleas held that letters written by him while he was away and which showed that he did leave intending to avoid his creditors were admissible. The letters were not admitted as hearsay evidence of the truth of the statements made in them. Rather they were admitted because the act of leaving the country was equivocal. It could have been done with intention to avoid creditors or it could have been done out of some other motive; the letters defined the motive.

See also *Rouch* v *Great Western Railway* (1841) 1 QB 51.

Statements of intention

A person's statement that he intends to do something in the future is not admissible as evidence that he did that thing. As we have seen, statements which accompany acts may be admitted to prove the motive behind those acts. Statements which are not contemporaneous with an act cannot define the motive with which it was done because the declarant may change his mind between the declaration and the act. This is merely a restatement of the matters discussed under the immediately preceding heading.

There is an authority which causes some difficulty here. In *Buckley* (1873) 13 Cox CC 293 a police officer left the station and told the duty sergeant that he intended to visit Buckley later in the day. The officer was found dead the same evening and Buckley was charged with his murder. The trial judge allowed evidence to be given of what the sergeant had been told because the officer was acting in the course of his duty when he made the statement. The decision was not appealed. *Buckley* was a different sort of case from *Rawson* v *Haigh* and *Rouch* v *Great Western Railway* because the officer's state of mind when he left the station was not directly in issue, whereas the state of mind of the writers of the letters in the latter cases was.

What someone says, where his intention is in issue, is a very different matter to investigating what someone says he is going to do in order to decide whether he carried out his stated intention. Preferable decisions about statements of intention are *Wainwright* (1875) 13 Cox CC 171 and *Thomson* [1912] 3 KB 19. In the former case a girl left her home, telling her mother that she was going to visit Wainwright. In the latter, a girl said that she intended to perform an abortion on herself. Both statements were held to be inadmissible because the declarant's intention was not directly relevant. The issues were, respectively, whether there was a meeting with Wainwright and whether the pregnant girl performed the abortion herself. The statements of intention may or may not have been carried out, in either event they did not accompany and define the facts in issue.

It is arguable that the decision in *Buckley* is sustainable because the likelihood is that a police officer who says he is going to meet someone in the course of his duties later in the evening will do just that, whereas the intentions asserted by the girls in *Wainwright* and *Thomson* may or may not have been carried out. As is clear from *Myers* v *DPP*, however, hearsay is inadmissible unless it falls within an exception to the normal rule of exclusion, and statements of intention which are likely to be carried out do not form a recognised hearsay exception. Furthermore, *Wainwright* was expressly approved by the House of Lords in *Christie* [1914] AC 545.

It follows from what has already been said under this heading, that where it is in issue whether someone held a particular intention, evidence of his words or conduct is admissible if it discloses whether he held that intention. For example in *Lloyd* v *Powell Duffryn Steam Coal Co* [1914] AC 733 a man was killed at work and a woman who was pregnant at the time of his death claimed compensation on the ground that the child was his and he would have maintained it. Under legislation in force at the time, she was able to claim compensation provided she could prove that the deceased would have maintained the child had he lived. At trial evidence of statements he made to the woman in which he declared that he was the father and that he intended to marry her was held to be inadmissible. The House of Lords overturned that decision. It was held that from the fact that the man said that he would marry the child's mother, it could be inferred that he probably would have done so, otherwise he would not have said what he did.

Lord Atkinson said that to treat the words spoken by the deceased as hearsay was to mistake their true character and significance, because it was the fact that they were spoken which was significant. Lord Moulton treated the speaking of the words as an act, saying that evidence can always be given of acts in order to determine the state of mind of the actor. Earl Loreburn and Lord Shaw held that the issue in the case was the status of the child: would it have been illegitimate if the deceased had lived? The evidence showed that it would not because of the agreement between its father and mother that before its birth they would marry. Their agreement, as evidence by what the deceased said to the mother, could be proved in the same way that any contract can be proved, by repeating the words used and inferring from it an agreement to marry.

It is arguable that *Buckley* was correctly decided because it falls within the same factual pattern as *Lloyd* v *Powell Duffryn Steam Coal Co* This is not correct. Although in both cases evidence was given of what the deceased said, the context in which each statement was made was different. In the *Lloyd* case the question was whether the child would have been maintained by the deceased. Whether this would have happened depended upon the relationship between the deceased and the mother. That he had agreed to marry her was a fact from which it could properly be inferred that he would have provided financial support; there was a continuing relationship from which this inference could be drawn. But in *Buckley* the statement of the police officer was nothing but a bare statement of intention. It did not form part of any relationship between him and Buckley, and one cannot properly say that because the officer said he was going to visit Buckley, it can be inferred that he did visit him.

In fact there were two issues in *Lloyd* v *Powell Duffryn Steam Coal Co*: whether the deceased was the father of the child, and whether he would have maintained it had he lived. The woman's evidence of his agreement to marry her and to support the child were relevant to and admissible to prove the second issue. On the first issue it was the evidence of the woman herself which was accepted by the trial judge and the assertions by the deceased that he accepted paternity were not directly relied on.

Spontaneous declarations

The cases discussed above concern statements made either by a party to the proceedings or by someone whose health or state of mind is in issue. Statements made by observers of events may be admissible as part of the res gestae if they were a spontaneous consequence of the event. Statements admissible under this principle are hearsay because the state of mind or intention of the observer is never in issue. It is a recognised exception to the hearsay rule that they are allowed provided they are sufficiently spontaneous.

In *Thompson* v *Trevanion* Holt CJ held that what the victim of an assault said about it immediately after she was assaulted was admissible because she did not have time to contrive a false statement. A similar principle was stated in *Bedingfield* (1879) 14 Cox CC 341, although the evidence was held to be inadmissible. Bedingfield was charged with murder. Evidence that the victim had come out of a room with her throat cut and said something which implicated *Bedingfield* was inadmissible because the transaction it described had already finished by the time she spoke. Evidence of what the victim said was, therefore, hearsay.

The strict contemporaneity required by *Bedingfield* was not present in *Gibson* because the woman who pointed to the door and said that the person who threw the stone had gone through it, spoke after the event was over. There was ample opportunity for her to consider the position and decide to blame an innocent person if she so chose.

Teper v *R*, to which reference has already been made, also failed the contemporaneity test because the person who shouted from the crowd did so at least 26 minutes after the fire started at Teper's shop. But it also suggests, obiter, that it will be no bar to evidence being admitted as part of the res gestae that the person whose statement is repeated cannot be identified. Lord Normand approved *Gibson*, saying of the statement in that case: 'They were not words spontaneously forced from the woman by the sight of the assault.' This dictum states accurately the common law's requirement. In recent years the *Bedingfield* definition of spontaneity has been relaxed.

In *Ratten* v *R* the evidence showed that Mrs Ratten had died between 1.12 pm and 1.20 pm. Evidence was given by the operator from the local telephone exchange that at about 1.15 pm she received a call from Ratten's house and that the caller, a woman, was hysterical and said, 'Get me the police please.' We have already seen that the Privy Council held this evidence not to be hearsay. But it went on to discuss the position if it had been hearsay. Lord Wilberforce said that it fell within the res gestae and after reviewing both English, Scottish, Australian and American authorities, stated the principle as follows:

'Hearsay evidence may be admitted of the statement providing it is made in such conditions (always being those of approximate but not exact contemporaneity) of involvement or pressure as to exclude the possibility of concoction or distortion to the advantage of the maker or the disadvantage of the accused.'

This being a decision of the Privy Council it could not overrule *Bedingfield*, but Lord Wilberforce stated clearly that in his view the decision on the facts of that case was not correct.

The significance of *Ratten* v *R* was that it put aside the idea of asking whether the statement made was part of the transaction which it described. Instead, what must be asked is whether the statement was a spontaneous statement forced out of the speaker by the event he or she has witnessed. This is to restate what Lord Norman said in *Teper* v *R*.

In *Nye and Loan* (1977) 66 Cr App R 252 the Court of Appeal applied *Ratten* v *R* in preference to *Bedingfield*. There was a collision between a car driven by a man called Lucas and a car in which Nye and Loan were travelling. Either Nye or Loan got out of the car and assaulted Lucas. Lucas stayed in his car for a few minutes until the police arrived, at which time he told a police officer that it was the passenger who assaulted him and he identified Loan as the passenger. At trial he could not remember whether it was Nye or Loan who was his assailant. The Court of Appeal upheld the trial judge's decision allowing the police officer to whom the identification was made to repeat it in court. It was held that there was no possibility of concoction because common sense dictates that Lucas would not have sat in his car concocting a lie about the identity of his assailant, but would be sitting there getting over the shock of the attack. Lawton LJ said that Lord Wilberforce's test for evidence being part of the res gestae excluded statements where there was a serious possibility of the witness having made a mistake, as well as if he deliberately concocted or distorted matters.

O'Connor LJ took the explanation of *Ratten* v *R* a little further in *Turnbull* (1984) 80 Cr App R 104. A man who was mortally wounded named his attacker as 'Ronnie Tommo'. People to whom he had said this were allowed to give evidence of that fact. O'Connor LJ said, after having referred to the passage from *Ratten* v *R* cited above:

> 'What Lord Wilberforce was saying is that the danger is that the person making the statement may have had time to make a false statement to exculpate himself or to incriminate somebody else, or alternatively, if he has not been quite as wicked as that, he may have adapted the matter in a way favourable to himself and antagonistic to another. Those are the risks one is looking for.'

The House of Lords has been asked to approve the principle stated in *Ratten* v *R* on two occasions. The first was *Blastland* [1986] AC 41 in which Lord Bridge said that he would follow it if it were directly relevant to the case before the House. That was not the case, so *Ratten* v *R* was not expressly adopted as part of English law. Another chance to address the question of this aspect of res gestae arose in *Andrews* [1987] AC 281 in which *Ratten* v *R* was applied and *Bedingfield* disapproved. A man called Morrow was stabbed and about 10 minutes afterwards the police arrived at the scene. Morrow said to one officer 'Don'; Andrews' name was Donald. The House of Lords upheld the judge's decision to allow evidence of what the victim had said. Lord Ackner expressly approved *Ratten* v *R* and stated five principles by which the admissibility of evidence under this part of the res gestae can be judged:

'1) The primary question which the judge must ask himself is: can the possibility of concoction or distortion be disregarded?

2) To answer that question the judge must first consider the circumstances in which the particular statement was made, in order to satisfy himself that the event was so unusual or startling or dramatic as to dominate the thoughts of the victim, so that his utterance was an instinctive reaction to that event, thus giving no real opportunity for reasoned reflection ...

3) In order for the statement to be sufficiently 'spontaneous' it must be so closely associated with the event which has excited the statement that it can be fairly stated that the mind of the declarant was still dominated by the event. Thus the judge must be satisfied that the event which provided the trigger mechanism for the statement was still operative. The fact that the statement was made in answer to a question is but one factor to consider under this heading.

4) Quite apart from the time factor there must be special features in the case, which relate to the possibility of concoction or distortion ...

5) As to the possibility of error in the facts narrated in the statement, if only the ordinary fallability of human recollection is relied on, this goes to the weight to be attached to and not to the admissibility of the statement and is therefore a matter for the jury. However, here again there may be special features that may give rise to the possibility of error. In the instant case there was evidence that the deceased had drunk to excess ... Another example would be where the identification was made in circumstances of particular difficulty or where the declarant suffered from defective eyesight. In such circumstances the trial judge must consider whether he can exclude the possibility of error.'

Andrews clarifies the way in which trial judges should approach arguments that evidence is admissible as part of the res gestae. Lord Ackner said that the person whose statement is in issue should be called if possible and only if that is not possible should hearsay evidence of it be allowed. *Andrews* was applied in *Edwards and Osakwe* v *Director of Public Prosecutions* [1992] Crim LR 576. In that case, at the scene of the offence the victim of a 'mugging' identified the defendants to a police officer. The victim failed to attend the trial, but it was decided that his statement to the police had been admissible as part of the res gestae.

5

The Statutory Admissibility of Hearsay

5.1 The Crown Court

5.2 The High Court and county courts

5.3 The magistrates' courts

5.4 Child proceedings

5.1 The Crown Court

History

Some hearsay evidence contained in documents has been admissible for many years, such as certificates of birth, marriage and death (Evidence Act 1845 s1) and certificates that someone has been convicted of a criminal offence (Evidence Act 1851 s14 and Criminal Procedure Act 1865 s6). But these are not wide-ranging exceptions to the hearsay rule.

The evidence which was rejected in *Myers* v *DPP* was so reliable that Parliament acted swiftly to allow the reception of hearsay which was contained in certain business records. The Criminal Evidence Act 1965 was restricted in its application to records compiled in the course of a trade or business. A number of decisions of the Court of Appeal showed the limitations of the 1965 Act. For example, Home Office records of immigrants were not rendered admissible (*Patel* [1981] 3 All ER 94) nor were those of a National Health Service hospital (*Crayden* [1978] 1 WLR 604), because the organisations concerned were not businesses.

The 1965 Act was repealed by the Police and Criminal Evidence Act 1984, ss68 and 69 of which allowed documents compiled under a duty, whether or not they were compiled in the course of a trade or business. Section 68 laid down conditions of admissibility which were applicable to all documents and s69 added further conditions for documents emanating from computers. Section 68 of the 1984 Act was in turn repealed by the Criminal Justice Act 1988, although s69 remains in force.

Criminal Justice Act 1988, s23

A comprehensive code for the reception of documentary hearsay evidence in criminal proceedings in the Crown Court and magistrates' courts is contained in ss23 to 30 of the Criminal Justice Act 1988. It should be noted and not forgotten that the 1988 Act does not allow for the reception of oral hearsay evidence. The most important sections are 23 and 24.

The effect of s23(1) is to allow hearsay to be given provided it is contained in a document and the maker of the document could give direct oral evidence of the fact which the document is put in evidence to prove. The section talks of statements in documents, emphasising that it is the assertions contained within documents and not the documents themselves which are the relevant evidence. The requirement that the maker of the statement should be able to give direct oral evidence of the matters contained in the statement rules out the admission of a statement where someone has written, for example, 'X told me ...' if the truth of what X said is in issue. The reason it would not be admissible is that if he were to give oral evidence and said 'X told me ...' he would be giving hearsay oral evidence and not direct oral evidence: *Re Koscot Interplanetary (UK) Ltd* [1972] 3 All ER 829. Another way of expressing this point is to say that only first-hand hearsay is admissible under s23, not secondhand or as it is sometimes called, multiple, hearsay.

The difference between first-hand and second-hand hearsay is important in civil as well as criminal cases and it can be illustrated as follows. If the colour of a particular car is in issue and a witness (W) says 'I saw the car, it was blue', he is giving direct evidence. If X gives evidence and says 'W told me the car was blue', he gives hearsay evidence which will be first-hand because the person he got the information from had direct knowledge of the matter. If Y gave evidence and said 'X told me the car was blue', he would give second-hand hearsay because X received the information from W. So, to see what sort of evidence someone gives one must see how many stages there are between the person with direct knowledge and the court. If the person with direct knowledge is the witness, his evidence is not hearsay. If he received the information from a person with direct knowledge it is first-hand hearsay. But if he received it from someone without direct knowledge it is second-hand hearsay.

The same pattern is seen with documents. A document may itself be relevant, for example if in a case it is relevant to know what were the terms of a written contract, the contract itself is direct evidence because it is the very thing in issue. But most documents are not themselves the thing in issue, but are recordings by human beings of information which is in issue. So if W writes on a piece of paper 'The car was blue', the paper is first-hand hearsay because it passes information to the court from its original source through only one intermediary, the piece of paper. If, however, X writes down, 'W told me the car was blue', the document is second-hand hearsay because the person who supplied the information to the document did not have direct knowledge. One can assume that the piece of paper is itself a witness and ask whether it is directly probative of the facts in issue or only probative because someone has told it about those facts. If someone told it of the facts one then asks whether that person had direct knowledge about those facts. If he did, the paper is first-hand hearsay; if not, it is second-hand (or, of course, third, or fourth, etc).

Hearsay is not admissible under s23(1) unless one of the requirements of subs(2) is satisfied or both of the requirements of subs(3). The construction of s23(2) gives rise to several problems, although it is clear that the burden of satisfying the requirements of s23(2)(b) rests on the prosecution and that it is the criminal standard of proof: *R* v *Case* [1991] Crim LR 192.

Paragraph (a) of subs(2) provides that a written statement is admissible from someone who is unfit to give evidence because of his mental state. We saw in Chapter 1 that those whose mental state does not allow them to understand the nature and sanction of the oath are incompetent to testify: *Hill* (1851) 2 Den CC 254. But, of course, a dead person could not be called, yet his statement is admissible. While a person may be 'unfit to attend as a witness' even after he has gone into the witness box, if due to his mental illness he is unable there to recall relevant events his previous statements may be read unless medical evidence casts doubt on the quality of those statements: see *R* v *Setz-Dempsey* (1993) The Times 20 July.

In *R* v *MacGillivray* (1993) 97 Cr App R 232 the Court of Appeal held that where a person had been injured and died before the trial but after having made a statement to a police officer recorded contemporaneously by that officer, that was a statement made by that person in a document and was admissible under s23 of the 1988 Act if it was signed by the deceased. It was also admissible if – as here – the deceased had clearly indicated by speech or otherwise that the record was accurate, he being unable to sign the record owing to some physical disability, in this case, severe burns. The court also decided that the judge's exercise of his discretion under s26 of the 1988 Act to admit the document in question had been correct.

One question which is not clearly answered by subs(2) is whether an anonymous document can be admissible. Paragraph (c) is ambiguous in this regard because it says that documentary evidence is admissible if it is not possible to find the person who made the statement. This may mean that it is admissible if it is known who made the statement but it is not possible to discover his whereabouts; or it may mean both. It is likely that the maker of the statement must be identifiable otherwise the court cannot possibly know how much weight to give to what he has said. Nor could it be said, for example, whether the document contains privileged information which the maker would not have been allowed to repeat on oath (as to privilege see Chapter 8, below).

The requirements of subs(3) are that the statement was made to a police officer or someone charged with the duty of investigating offences or charging offenders, and the maker does not give oral evidence through fear or because he is kept out of the way. This is designed to counteract witness 'nobbling'. It will be for the prosecution to prove beyond reasonable doubt the reason why its witness does not attend court before it will be able to rely on subs(3).

A witness's statement may be admitted in evidence in committal proceedings under s23 of the 1988 Act on the ground that she did not give evidence through fear, even though she has already entered the witness box and started to answer questions. A justice can satisfy herself that a witness is not giving evidence through fear by her own observation of the witness's demeanour: *R* v *Ashford and Tenterden Justices, ex parte Hilden* [1993] 2 All ER 154. The criminal standard of proof must be satisfied and the court must also exercise its discretion under s26 of the 1988 Act: *R* v *Acton Justices, ex parte McMullen* (1991) 92 Cr App R 98.

Nothing in s23 allows the prosecution to use a confession made by a defendant unless that confession would be admissible under s76 of the Police and Criminal Evidence Act 1984 (as to which see paragraph 6.2, below).

Criminal Justice Act 1988, s24

Section 24 is not restricted to documents which contain first-hand hearsay, and is therefore somewhat wider in scope than s23. There are four conditions which must be satisfied before s24 allows hearsay evidence:

1. The document must contain a statement of a fact or facts which, were a witness available, could be proved by direct oral evidence.
2. The document must have been created or received in the course of a trade, business or occupation.
3. The supplier of the information must have had, or could reasonably be supposed to have had, personal knowledge of the truth of the fact or facts.
4. If the information was not supplied direct to the creator by a person with personal knowledge of the truth of the fact or facts stated, it must have been supplied through intermediaries each of whom received it in the course of a trade, business or occupation.

Each of these must be examined.

The first requirement is phrased differently from the equivalent requirement under s23. In s23 the requirement is that direct oral evidence from the maker of the document would be admissible. By contrast s24 simply requires the statement in the document to be of a fact of which direct oral evidence would be admissible. Such evidence need not come from the maker of the statement. In this way it is clear at the outset that second-hand hearsay is admissible under s24 because the direct oral evidence could come from anyone with direct knowledge, whether or not he is the maker of the document.

The purpose of the requirement that direct oral evidence could be given of the fact, is probably to ensure that all rules of exclusion except for the hearsay rule are left unaltered by the section. One must look at the fact which the document states and ask whether it is a fact which is capable of proof by direct oral evidence. If it falls foul of a rule of exclusion such as the rule that the prosecution is generally not entitled to inform the jury of any previous convictions of the defendant, or the rule against non-expert opinion evidence, it cannot be proved by *admissible* direct oral evidence. Thus hearsay evidence about it is not allowed.

The second condition involves a significant change from the position under the Police and Criminal Evidence Act 1984. Both that Act and the Criminal Evidence Act 1965 allowed hearsay which was contained within business documents, provided that those documents were 'records'. In *Tirado* (1974) 59 Cr App R 80 it was doubted whether a file of correspondence which built up over a period of time constituted a record for the purposes of the 1965 Act, and there is authority under the Civil Evidence Act 1968 which limits the meaning of record to documents which an historian would regard as an original source of information: *H v Schering Chemicals Ltd* [1983] 1 All ER 849, *Savings & Investment Bank Ltd* v *Gasco Investments (Netherlands) BV* [1984] 1 All ER 296. No such limitation appears in s24, so any document compiled in the course of a business comes within the section.

But also any document received in the course of a business is admissible. This make an enormous number of documents admissible because there is no need for the maker to make it in the course of a business provided the recipient receives it in the course of a business. There is no definition in the Act of the manner in which a document must be 'received' to come within s24. The term must therefore be given a literal interpretation resulting in every document received by a business being admissible. Professor Smith has suggested that letters to The Times newspaper would come within the section and on the wording of the Act it is hard to refute his view: Di Birch 'The Evidence Provisions' [1989] Crim LR 25 n48.

Transcripts of information given to liquidators, on a confidential basis, are admissible evidence under s24 of the 1988 Act as they had been received by the liquidators in the course of their profession and as holders of the office of liquidator: *R v Clowes* [1992] 3 All ER 440.

The third condition requires the supplier to be someone who had or could reasonably be supposed to have had personal knowledge of the fact or facts stated in the document. In order for any statement to assert a fact there must be someone from whom the assertion originated, even if he was simply the source of a totally unfounded rumour. The person who was the origin of the statement may have been the maker of the statement or may have been someone who passed the information on to the maker either directly or through one or more intermediaries. The requirement is not that there must be someone who knows that the matters dealt with in the statement are true, simply that there must be someone with personal knowledge of the matters dealt with. He could, for example, have personal knowledge that they are wholly untrue. Because there will always be someone with personal knowledge of the matters dealt with in the statement, it is hard to see what this condition attempts to achieve. Perhaps its aim is to ensure that a document can only be admitted under s24 where it is possible to identify the source of the information.

The suggested purpose of the third condition links with the fourth condition, that all intermediaries acted in the course of a trade, business or occupation. If the origin of the statement cannot be identified it cannot be said who had personal knowledge and it cannot be proved that all of the intermediaries received the information in the course of a trade, business or occupation. The fourth condition raises a potential problem in that it may introduce questions of agency and vicarious liability into the law of evidence. For example, does someone receive information in the course of his employment if he receives information about something wholly outside his work but within that done by other employees of the same company? The answer may revolve around whether he acted in the scope of his authority as an agent of his employer, or it may turn on the question whether he acted in the course of his employment or was 'on a frolic of his own'. It is hoped that these niceties of the law of obligations will be avoided by the courts when construing the 1984 Act, but it is difficult to see that they can be wholly ignored.

The admissibility of evidence under s24 is not generally subject to any of the conditions contained in s23(2) and (3) being satisfied. In principle, therefore, a first-hand hearsay document which is not admissible under s23 may be admissible under s24 provided it was made or received in the course of a trade or business and the person who supplied the information may reasonably be supposed to have had direct knowledge of it.

Like s23, nothing in s24 allows the prosecution to rely on a confession made by the defendant which is not admissible under s76 of the Police and Criminal Evidence Act 1984: s24(3) of the 1988 Act. However, in *R* v *Iqbal* [1990] 1 WLR 756 the Court of Appeal decided that, by virtue of s68 of the Police and Criminal Evidence Act 1984, which was replaced by s24 of the 1988 Act, an affidavit and signed statement of a police inspector in Lahore, Pakistan, and accompanying confession statements by persons other than the accused, should have been admitted in evidence. Woolf LJ stressed, though, that the court would be vigilant, especially in cases of this kind, to ensure that any relaxation of the rules of hearsay evidence did not lead to any abuse of the due process of law.

On its face s24 allows the prosecution to read its witnesses' statements in court because in practice they will have been made to a police officer who received the information or compiled the statement in the course of an occupation. To prevent this, subs(4) provides that a statement made for the purposes of pending or contemplated criminal proceedings or of a criminal investigation shall not be admissible under s24(1) unless one or more of the requirements of s23(2) or the requirements of s23(3) are satisfied, or the person who made the statement cannot be expected to have any recollection of the matters dealt with in the statement by reason of the time which has elapsed since he made it and all the circumstances.

The vast majority of statements made in the course of a criminal investigation are first-hand hearsay because the statement of the witness is signed by him and is his document, even though it may have been dictated to a police officer who wrote it down. If it is to be admitted in evidence it would normally be admitted under s23. But the final part of s24(4) allows witness statements to be read if the maker cannot be expected to have any recollection of the matters recorded in it. This is not one of the requirements of admissibility under s23(2) or (3), so s24(4) widens the admissibility of documents in quite a significant manner: *Martin* [1988] 3 All ER

440. It seems to allow, for example, a police officer's notebook or statement to be used as evidence of the facts stated in them if he is unable to remember the events recorded.

Furthermore, it would seem to allow the same officer to repeat his note of what another witness told him. He might for example say, 'A lady who called herself Mrs Andrea Fox-Hiley told me that she saw the accident and that the blue car was on the wrong side of the road when it occurred.' This note would be the officer's document, not that of Mrs Fox-Hiley, because she neither wrote it down nor adopted it by her signature. The admissibility of the note under s24(4) would depend not upon whether Mrs Fox-Hiley remembered the events, but upon whether the policeman remembered them. Thus if Mrs Fox-Hiley attends court as a witness but is unable to remember events, any document of hers would be inadmissible, but the policeman would be allowed to repeat what she told him because it was in his statement. This construction of s24(4) is not necessarily correct, however. What the subsection allows is the maker of a statement to repeat it if he cannot remember the event recorded. It is arguable that the event recorded by the officer is not the collision but the making of a statement to him by Mrs Fox-Hiley. If he is unable to remember whether she said anything or is unable to remember what she said, he may repeat her statement from his note. But this only makes the fact that she spoke the words admissible and does not make the words themselves evidence of their truth.

Computer printouts

Where hearsay evidence emanates from a computer it is not enough for it to satisfy the requirements of either ss23 or 24, it must also satisfy s69 of the Police and Criminal Evidence Act 1984. Supplementary provisions are to be found in Pts II and III of Schedule 3 to the 1984 Act.

These provisions were considered by the House of Lords in *R* v *Shepherd* [1993] 1 All ER 225. The Court of Appeal had certified a point of law of general public importance as follows: 'Whether a party seeking to rely on computer evidence could discharge the burden under section 69(1)(b) of the 1984 Act without calling a computer expert, and if so how?'

In answering this specific question, Lord Griffiths concluded that s69(1) could be satisfied by the oral evidence of a person familiar with the operation of the computer who could give evidence of its reliability and such a person need not be a computer expert. In the case which had given rise to the appeal a store detective had given evidence regarding till rolls from tills connected to a central computer. Although she was thoroughly familiar with the operation of the tills and of the computer, she did not claim to have any technical understanding of the computer's operation. Nevertheless, her evidence had been properly admitted as part of the prosecution case, even though she had not been qualified to sign a certificate under Schedule 3, Pt II, para 8.

Lord Griffiths acknowledged that computers varied immensely in their complexity and in the operations they performed. The nature of the evidence to discharge the burden of showing that there had been no improper use of the computer and that it had been operating properly would inevitably vary from case to case. The evidence had to be tailored to suit the needs of the case, but his Lordship suspected that it would rarely be necessary to call an expert. In the vast majority of cases it would be possible to discharge the burden by calling a witness who was familiar with the operation of the computer in the sense of knowing what the computer was required to do and who would say that it was doing it properly.

His Lordship also made, or clarified, other important points in relation to this whole matter and they may be summarised as follows:

1. The duty to show that the computer was operating properly could not be discharged without evidence by the application of the presumption that the computer was working correctly expressed in the maxim onmia praesumuntur rite esse acta, as appeared to be suggested in some of the cases.
2. It did not make any difference whether the computer document had been produced with or without the input of information provided by the human mind and thus might or might not be hearsay. If the document produced by the computer was hearsay it would be necessary to comply with the provisions of s24 of the Criminal Justice Act 1988 before the document could be admitted as evidence and it would also be necessary to comply with the provisions of s69 of the 1984 Act.
3. There was no warrant for an interpretation of the Act which limited the operation of s69 to cases that fell within s24 of the 1988 Act. If the prosecution wished to rely upon the document produced by a computer they had to comply with s69 in all cases.
4. Proof that the computer was reliable could be provided in one of two ways, either by calling oral evidence or by tendering a written certificate in accordance with Schedule 3, Pt II, para 8.

Although the point did not then call for a decision, in *R v Blackburn* (1992) The Times 1 December the Court of Appeal said that they would have been extremely reluctant to accept that a document produced on a word processor, rather than on a typewriter or by a quill pen, thereby became a document to which s69 of the 1984 Act applied, that is to say a document produced by a computer rather than a document produced by the writer. If such documents were covered by s69, the welcome reforms found in s24 of the 1988 Act would be greatly diminished and marginalised. Now, with the almost universal use of word processors, if that were to be the case, almost every business document would become subject to s69 which, in their Lordships' view could not have been Parliament's intention when it passed that statute.

The discretion to exclude

In Chapter 9 below, we shall see that there is a substantial body of law about the discretion of a judge to exclude admissible evidence. In addition to that, ss25 and 26 of the 1988 Act specifically empower the court to exclude certain evidence which is admissible under ss23 or 24. Nothing in the 1988 Act detracts from the power of the court to reject within the discretions it has at common law and under s78 of the Police and Criminal Evidence Act 1984.

Section 25 applies to all evidence which is admissible under ss23 or 24. Section 25(1) gives the court the discretion 'in the interests of justice' to refuse to allow a document to be used even though it is admissible under ss23 or 24. There is no definition of the interests of justice, although subs25(2), which is expressly stated to be without prejudice to the generality of subs(1) requires the court to have regard to specified matters.

Where evidence has been obtained from outside the United Kingdom in response to a letter of request issued under s3(1) of the Criminal Justice (International Cooperation) Act 1990, in exercising its discretion under s25 of the 1988 Act the court must have regard to whether it was possible to challenge by questioning the person who made it; and if proceedings have been instituted, to whether the local law allowed the parties to the proceedings to be legally represented when the evidence was being taken: s3(8) of the 1990 Act.

Section 26 of the 1988 Act applies only to statements contained in documents prepared for the purposes of pending or contemplated criminal proceedings or a criminal investigation. This provides that such a statement may only be admitted in evidence with leave of the court and that leave shall not be given unless the court is of the opinion that it is in the interests of justice to do so. Before making its decision, the court must be apprised of the statement's contents; it does not need to have seen and read it: *R* v *Ashford and Tenterden Justices, ex parte Hilden* [1993] 2 All ER 154.

The contrast between ss25 and 26 is important. The former gives the court a discretion to exclude but does not require it to consider the question whether to exclude. In effect it will therefore be for the defence to raise objections if it has any. The latter section, by contrast, requires the prosecution to obtain leave if it is to adduce evidence prepared for the purposes of pending or contemplated criminal proceedings or a criminal investigation. The evidence is not admissible unless leave is given and it is not for the defence to object to it but for the Crown to ask that it be admitted.

In *R* v *Cole* [1990] 1 WLR 865 it appeared that the judge had allowed to be read a formal witness statement of a security guard who had since died. The Court of Appeal decided that the judge had been entitled to make this decision and to take the view that it was in the interests of justice for the jury to be given the fuller picture provided by the statement, subject to the necessary warning. The nature of the discretion to be exercised by the court under ss25 and 26 of the 1988 Act, and the matters to which, in exercising that discretion, the court was required to have regard, had been laid down by Parliament and, in the view of the court, were clearly expressed.

Attendance of witnesses

Nothing in ss23 or 24 specifically states that their provisions only apply where the maker of the statement does not give evidence, although certain parts of s23 obviously only apply in such circumstances. It is possible for hearsay evidence to be given even where the maker of the statement is a witness. Paragraph (d) of s25(2) allows for this possibility and para 2 of Schedule 2, which must be considered because of s28(2), provides that hearsay evidence of a statement admitted under the 1988 Act cannot corroborate the evidence of the person who made the statement. These paragraphs would be entirely otiose unless hearsay evidence originating from a person who gives evidence is admissible.

Whether or not the maker of the document gives evidence, his character may be attacked under the provisions of the Criminal Procedure Act 1865 in the same way as if he were a witness giving entirely non-hearsay evidence. Therefore evidence can be called about his character where this is allowed, including evidence about any inconsistent statement made by him: Criminal Justice Act 1988, Schedule 2 para 1.

In principle the provisions of the 1988 Act apply equally to the defence as they do to the prosecution. In practice, however, it is likely to be the prosecution which will rely on them more as was the case under the 1965 and 1984 Acts. Section 24(4), which limits the admissibility of statements made for the purposes of pending or contemplated criminal proceedings, is not expressly limited to statements made to the police or the Crown Prosecution Service. There is no reason to suppose that witnesses' statements which are taken by defence solicitors are not in exactly the same position – the statements may only be used by the defence in the circumstances outlined above.

Experts' reports

Section 30 of the Criminal Justice Act 1988 allows experts' reports to be used in evidence whether or not the expert who compiled it gives oral evidence: s30(1). The report is admissible as evidence of the truth of the facts or opinions it asserts: s30(4). An expert's report is a written report by a person dealing wholly or mainly with matters on which he is qualified to give expert evidence or would be qualified if he were alive: s30(5).

If the party who proposes to use the expert's report does not intend to call him to give oral evidence, his report is admissible only with leave: s30(2). Section 30(3) contains the matters the court should consider when deciding whether or not to give leave. As always, all relevant circumstances must be taken into consideration, but the specific matters to which the court must direct its attention are the contents of the report, the reason why the expert is not to give evidence and the risk of unfairness to the accused. Perhaps the most important of these matters is the last because absence of the opportunity to cross-examine could make it unfair to allow the Crown to rely on a report the accuracy of which is challenged.

Section 30 was enacted because of the regular and considerable waste of experts' time in criminal cases when they attend court simply to read out a report which they have compiled and the accuracy of which no one challenges.

Experts' reports are hearsay evidence because they are statements made by the experts in which they assert facts or opinions. There is no reason why an expert's report should not be admitted under ss23 or 24 where the requirements of one or both of those sections are met. Insofar as experts' reports contain statements of opinion they are not within ss23 or 24, because those provisions apply to statements admissible to prove 'facts' and an opinion is not a fact unless it is directly in issue whether the witness holds the opinion rather than whether that opinion is true.

Confessions

His written or oral confession is admissible against a defendant: s76 Police and Criminal Evidence Act 1984. There are considerable technicalities defining the admissibility of confession statements, and they form the subject matter of paragraph 6.2 below.

Apart from written or oral confession statements in which the accused admits his guilt, specific admissions may be made on certain issues so as to prevent those issues having to be proved. Section 10 of the Criminal Justice Act 1967 provides that a formal admission may be made for the purposes of the proceedings. It may be made in court or out of court, but if made out of court it must be in writing and signed by the accused's solicitor or counsel: s10(2).

Formal admissions are frequently made orally in court in order to save time. Once made, whether orally or in writing, the admission may be withdrawn with the court's leave: s10(4).

Criminal Justice Act 1967

A development was made in 1967, although it did not amend the 1965 Act in any way. Section 9(1) of the Criminal Justice Act 1967 allows written statements of evidence to be read in court rather than the witness who made the statement having to go to court. The purpose of the section is to allow evidence which is unchallenged to be read so as to save time in court and save the time of the witness who would otherwise be inconvenienced unnecessarily. There are certain conditions to the admission of what are commonly known as 's9 statements'.

First, such a statement should be signed: s9(2)(a). The witness's signature will usually be at the foot of each page and his initials alongside any amendment or correction in the body of the statement, but the only requirement of the statute is that the statement should be signed. Secondly, the statement should contain a declaration by the maker that it is true to the best of his knowledge and belief and that he made it knowing that if it is used in evidence he might be liable to prosecution if he wilfully stated in it anything which he knew to be false or did not believe to be true: s9(2)(b). There is no need for the declaration to be signed, although it usually will be: *Chapman* v *Iyleton* [1973] Crim LR 296. The declaration takes the place of an oath, although strictly speaking it is not an oath.

Thirdly, the party wishing to rely on it must then serve it on all other parties, even if it is only to be used against one of them, before the hearing: s9(2)(c). Fourthly, if, within seven days of service, no objection is taken to it being used, it may be used as of right: s9(2)(d). Failure to serve it in time or at all before trial is not necessarily fatal because statements can be read if all parties agree, or the judge may adjourn the hearing to allow time for it to be served properly. Normally objection is not taken to late service of a statement unless personal attendance by the witness is required. It should be noted that the court has no power to allow either party to read a statement pursuant to s9 if the conditions in s9(2) have not been complied with, unless it is done by agreement of the other parties.

If a statement which one party proposes to read contains inadmissible material, it is common practice to edit it and read the remainder. The editing should be done by a Crown prosecutor, who is a legally qualified employee of the Crown Prosecution Service: *Practice Direction* [1986] 2 All ER 511. Judges are frequently asked for guidance on the admissibility of certain parts of s9 statements, in the same way as they are asked to rule on the admissibility of proposed oral evidence, and editing will comply with the judge's ruling.

The jury does not see the written statements, it merely has them read either by counsel for the Crown or by the clerk of the court, depending on the practice adopted at the particular court. A s9 statement is unchallenged evidence which should be treated as though it had been given on oath from the witness box. The practical effect of allowing one's opponent to read a statement pursuant to s9 is that one admits the truth of the contents of the statement: *Lister* v *Quaife* (1982) 75 Cr App R 313.

Prior to a Crown Court trial the prosecution's evidence will have been served on the defence in the form of the witness statements used at committal. Sometimes, however, evidence additional to that used at committal will be relied on. Notice of all such evidence must be served on the defence in the form of 'notices of additional evidence'. These are not specifically dealt with by statute and there is no prescribed form. They usually take the form of statements which could be read if no objection is raised, that is, statements which comply with s9(2) of the 1967 Act. There is no time limit in which they should be served, and it is not uncommon to be served with notices of additional evidence at court during the course of the trial. If the defence requires the witness to attend, the prosecution will not be allowed to read his statement. There is no special rule allowing evidence served by way of notices of additional evidence to be read. If the statement is not in the form required by s9 or if it is in the right form but is not agreed, it may not be read. Again the judge may adjourn the case to allow time for it to be served, or for the defence to decide whether to agree to it, or to allow the prosecution to call its witness.

The Criminal Justice Act 1988 affects s9 quite significantly. Every time it is considered whether to edit out hearsay evidence it must also be asked whether that hearsay is now admissible. If it is admissible it may be decided not to edit it but to seek to rely on it as hearsay. It is likely that leave will be required pursuant to s26 of the 1988 Act because the statement will almost certainly have been prepared for the purpose of the trial in which it is proposed to use it. In the event that the judge refuses his leave, the offending hearsay passages will be edited and the remainder read to the jury.

Criminal Justice Act 1925

A number of statutes allow a criminal court to receive evidence which was given on oath in previous proceedings but is not repeated on oath before the later court. The most important in practice is s13(3) of the Criminal Justice Act 1925 which overlaps considerably with s9 of the Criminal Justice Act 1967.

Section 13(3) allows a committal statement or deposition (written record of evidence given by a witness at committal) to be read at trial in the Crown Court provided that the witness is dead, insane, too ill to travel, or kept out of the way by the defendant (see *R* v *O'Loughlin* [1988] 3 All ER 431), or at the committal hearing neither prosecution nor defence asked the court to make an order for him to attend at the trial and he has not subsequently been served with a notice requiring his presence at trial. In *R* v *Bateman* [1989] Crim LR 590 the Court of Appeal decided that statements from witnesses in Ireland and New Zealand which had been put in evidence at commital had, in effect, become depositions in the case and, by virtue of s13(3) of the 1925 Act, were admissible in evidence at the trial without further proof.

In passing, it should be noted that the Criminal Justice (International Co-operation) Act 1990 makes it possible to issue a 'letter of request' asking for assistance in obtaining outside the United Kingdom specified evidence for use in proceedings or investigations within the United Kingdom. Indeed, the court has inherent jurisdiction to issue such a letter in relation to particular documents which, had they been in England, could properly have been made the subject of a subpoena: *Panayiotou* v *Sony Music Entertainment (UK) Ltd* [1994] 1 All ER 755. As to the English court's power to comply with letters of request from a foreign court, see the Evidence (Proceedings in Other Jurisdictions) Act 1975 and, eg, *Re Pan American World Airways Inc* [1992] 3 All ER 197.

It is often thought that witnesses' statements may be read at trial where their presence has not been required, only if their evidence has been served pursuant to s9 of the 1967 Act. In fact s13 of the 1925 Act is the basis for the prosecution reading witness statements in a great number of criminal trials. To save confusion it is common practice for the Crown Prosecution Service to serve the defence with copies of the statements of witnesses whom no body intends to call to give live evidence. These copies are served in addition to the copies served at committal and the covering letter specifically says that it is intended to rely upon the statement pursuant to s9 of the Criminal Justice Act 1967, and invites the defence to tell the prosecution if attendance of the witness is required. Once this is done the statement could be read pursuant to either s9 of the 1967 Act or s13 of the Act of 1925.

Section 13 cannot be relied upon unless the statement was used by the prosecution at committal. Therefore any statements served as notices of additional evidence do not come within its provisions. Nor does the section allow hearsay evidence within the statement itself. Naturally any statement which is read in order to prove the truth of assertions contained in it is itself hearsay evidence, but that hearsay must be first-hand otherwise it is outside the 1925 Act. In theory a statement could come within both s24 of the 1988 Act and s13 of the 1925 Act. In that situation second-hand hearsay could be allowed, but it is unrealistic to say that s13 makes any difference to its admissibility.

Furthermore, if the defence asks at a very late stage, such as at trial itself, for the witness to attend in order that he can be cross-examined, the judge should not allow the Crown to read his witness statement under s13 because the result of doing so is that the jury would have to try to weigh a written statement against oral evidence, a virtually impossible task in many cases. The proper course is to require the witness to attend, adjourning the hearing if necessary in order to allow him to get to court: *Collins* (1938) 26 Cr App R 177.

5.2 The High Court and county courts

Civil Evidence Act 1968 – introduction

The admissibility of hearsay evidence in the High Court and the county courts is governed by the provisions of the Civil Evidence Act 1968. Prior to its enactment the Evidence Act 1938 allowed certain documentary hearsay to be used in civil proceedings. That Act still applies in the magistrates' courts and its limitations will be considered in 5.3.

The effect of the Civil Evidence Act 1968 is that first-hand and second-hand hearsay are both admissible subject to notice being given to all parties in the case. There are certain limits to the admissibility of second-hand hearsay because of the need to ensure so far as possible that it is reliable. Documents produced by computers are admissible provided that a huge array of technicalities is satisfied. Certain common law exceptions to the hearsay rule are preserved by s9, but those which are not preserved have been abolished because s1 of the Act says that hearsay evidence is admissible under the Act or by agreement of the parties but not otherwise.

The scope of the Act was extended by the Civil Evidence Act 1972 such that hearsay evidence of opinions is admissible as well as hearsay evidence of statements of fact: 1972 Act, s1.

The admission of hearsay evidence in civil proceedings is particularly useful where expert evidence is required because it allows their reports to be used as evidence rather than having them read out each word so as to make it evidence in the case. There are special provisions for the admission of experts' reports, which are discussed in Chapter 10 below, when the law on opinion evidence is examined.

There is a growing trend to require parties to exchange their witnesses' proofs of evidence before trial. This practice started in the Commercial Court and the Official Referees' Court and has resulted in considerable saving of time because examination in chief is virtually redundant. The practice does not mean that everything in the proofs is necessarily admissible. The 1968 Act still applies, so that anything in a proof which is inadmissible hearsay must be ignored by the judge.

First-hand hearsay

First-hand hearsay evidence is admissible by reason of s2(1) of the Act; s23(1) of the Criminal Justice Act 1988 uses similar wording, although it is not as lengthy as s2(1). The wording of s2(1) allows for hearsay evidence to be given whether the original statement was made orally, in a document or in any other way, such as by gesture. The wording of s2(1) is in essence repeated in s10(1) where 'statement' is defined as including any representation of fact whether made in words or otherwise, and by s1 of the Civil Evidence Act 1972 it also includes statements of opinion.

The admissibility of hearsay is subject to the remainder of s2 and to rules of court, both of which are examined below, and to the fact being one of which direct oral evidence could be given by the maker of the statement which is repeated. The person whose original statement is being repeated must be able to give admissible direct oral evidence if he were to give evidence at trial. In *Re Koskot Interplanetary (UK) Ltd* [1972] 3 All ER 829 Megarry J held that a letter from a lawyer in a government department to another employee of that department about the affairs of a company which the department was investigating did not come within s2(1) because the writer of the letter would not be able to give direct oral evidence about the contents of the letter; his evidence would have been hearsay. Therefore, s2(1) is restricted to first-hand hearsay documents, that is, documents which contain statements made by people with actual knowledge of the truth of the statements.

Where the statement which is repeated is in a document it is normally quite simple to discover whose statement it is; all one has to do is ask who wrote the document. But it is not always simple because the definition of 'document' in s10(1) includes items the maker of which may not always be readily identifiable, such as a map, plan, graph or drawing, photograph, disc, tape soundtrack, film negative or video tape.

If the statement was made orally it is arguable that s2(1) does not clearly state that only first-hand hearsay is admissible. This can be illustrated as follows. If A says 'I saw X hit Y' and B hears this being said, B could repeat it because he would be repeating the statement of someone (A) who could give direct oral evidence about the subject matter of the statement. If B tells C, 'A told me he saw X hit Y', evidence by C could be seen as putting A's statement before the court, because he would be repeating A's statement, albeit he heard of it from B and not directly from A. In such a case if C is seen as repeating A's statement, C's evidence falls within s2(1) because he is repeating someone else's (A's) statement, and that person could give direct oral evidence of the subject matter of the statement.

The reality, of course, in such a case is that C would give second-hand hearsay evidence and this carries the risk that B did not hear A correctly or did not remember A's statement properly when he told C about it. It is only if B gives evidence in court that the accuracy of what he told C could be tested. Section 2(3) ensures that its accuracy can be tested. The effect of this is that evidence about what A told B could only be given by A ('the person who made the statement') or by B ('any person who heard or otherwise perceived it being made').

An alternative analysis of the example above is that C repeats B's statement about what A said, and does not repeat A's statement at all. If this view is correct s2(3) is otiose because s2(1) is quite sufficient to ensure that only first-hand hearsay is admissible. Section 2(1) would disallow C's evidence because his repetition of B's statement is only permissible if B could give direct oral evidence of the facts stated: see the final ten words of s2(1). B, of course, could not give direct oral evidence about whether X hit Y, all he could give is hearsay evidence, thus the final ten words of s2(1) render C's evidence inadmissible. This was the analysis adopted by Robert Goff J in *The Ymnos* [1981] 1 Lloyds Rep 550 where a written report repeated oral statements made by someone to the author of the report. It was held that the only statements made in the report were made by its author and therefore one must ask whether the author of the report could give direct oral evidence of the facts stated to him by the other person. He was unable to give that evidence; all he could give was hearsay evidence, therefore the last ten words of s2(1) applied and the hearsay evidence in the report was inadmissible.

On the authority of *The Ymnos*, therefore, s2(3) is meaningless and s2(1) is all that is required to ensure that only first-hand hearsay is admissible under s2.

Provided that either proper notice has been given or leave is obtained (as to both of which, see below) a party may use first-hand hearsay evidence whether or not the maker of the statement of which hearsay evidence is given, himself gives evidence. But if he does give evidence his previous statement may not be used without leave: s2(2)(a). The reason for this is that his direct evidence will normally be preferable to hearsay. If leave is given the hearsay evidence should not be put before the court until the conclusion of the examination in chief of the witness, although the court does have a discretion to allow it to be given by a previous witness and it may allow the witness himself to repeat his previous statement if this is required in order to make his evidence intelligible: s2(2)(b).

In *Ventouris* v *Mountain (No 2), The Italia Express* [1992] 3 All ER 414 the Court of Appeal concluded that statements tape-recorded with the speaker's knowledge and intention are made 'in a document' as well as 'orally' and are therefore admissible under s2 of the 1968 Act, subject to production and proof of the tapes or authenticated copies, ie, copies authenticated as true copies. However, statements so recorded without the speaker's knowledge or intention are not made 'in a document' and are therefore not so admissible in civil proceedings unless proved in accordance with s2(3) by direct oral evidence by the person who made the statements or by someone who had heard or otherwise perceived them being made. Where an out-of-court statement is contained in a document, it may be proved by any lawful means, including second-hand hearsay evidence (eg, another out-of-court statement introduced under s2 in which the maker of the first statement stated facts concerning the making of the first statement) made admissible by the Act itself.

Second-hand hearsay

As we have seen, s2 allows first-hand hearsay only. Second-hand is allowed by s4, but its admissibility is subject to more complex conditions being met than need be met by first-hand hearsay. The requirements which must be satisfied before evidence is admissible under this section are five in number:

1. Direct oral evidence of the facts stated in the document must be admissible.
2. The document must be or form part of a record.
3. It must have been compiled by someone acting under a duty.
4. The information contained in the record must have been supplied by a person who had personal knowledge of the information or who may reasonably be supposed to have had such knowledge.
5. If the supplier did not supply the information direct to the compiler of the record, it must have been supplied through intermediaries each of whom acts under a duty.

The first condition ensures that the fact stated in the document is one evidence of which would not be excluded by any rule other than the hearsay rule. There is no requirement that the supplier of the information should be able to give direct oral evidence, merely that the fact stated by the document is one which in principle can be proved by direct oral evidence.

The second condition requires the document to be or form part of a record. There is no definition of record in the 1968 Act. Two first instance decisions hold that a record for the purposes of the 1968 Act is a document which a reputable historian would regard as a primary source of information. In *H* v *Schering Chemicals Ltd* [1983] 1 WLR 143 Bingham J said that in order for documents to be records they should be:

'... documents which either give effect to a transaction itself or which contain a contemporaneous register of information supplied by those with direct knowledge of the facts.'

Articles in medical journals which summarised the results of drug tests were held not to be records because they were not an original source of the information obtained by the drug tests.

Peter Gibson J in *Savings and Investment Bank Ltd* v *Gasco Investments (Netherlands) BV* [1984] 1 All ER 296 accepted as correct what Bingham J said. The evidence in issue in the *Gasco* case was a company inspector's report. He had been appointed to investigate the affairs of a company and his report contained summaries of some of the submissions made to him as well as his opinions on the affairs of the company. The report was held not to be a record because it did not simply record the information given to the inspector. In *Taylor* v *Taylor* [1970] 1 WLR 1148 it was said, obiter, by Davies LJ that a transcript of a judge's summing up to a jury would be a record of the evidence which was given at trial. This must be in some doubt following the two cases just cited because a summing up does not have to record all of the evidence and, indeed, it should be a summary only.

The third condition requires the compiler to have acted under a duty when compiling the record, the fifth condition also requires any intermediaries between the supplier and the compiler to have acted under a duty. Acting under a duty is partially defined in s4(3) which states that it includes acting in the course of a trade, business, profession or other occupation in which the person is engaged or employed or acting for the purposes of any paid or unpaid office held by him. This is not an exhaustive definition because acting under a duty is said to 'include' these matters, which implies that it also includes other duties. Arguably, any duty under which someone acted counts for the purposes of s4, including a moral duty. The definition of 'record' is so restrictive that there is unlikely to be any harm done by having a wide definition of 'duty'.

The supplier of the information must have had personal knowledge of the matters dealt with in it or must reasonably be supposed to have had such knowledge. As was said above in connection with s24 of the Criminal Justice Act 1988, there must always be someone who was the original supplier of the information. He may know the information to be true, he may know it to be false, he may have guessed that it was true without knowing whether or not it was; but if the chain of communication is traced back, the origin of the information will be a person and that person will have personal knowledge of the information he supplied. This was impliedly accepted as being correct by Goulding J in *Knight* v *David* [1971] 1 WLR 1671. The question arose whether an old document compiled by a borough official was compiled from information supplied by a person who could reasonably be supposed to have had personal knowledge. The judge held that the nature of the document was such that it was proper to infer that the information was supplied to the official by someone with knowledge of whether it was true.

The decision in *Knight* v *David* recognises that where it is impossible to tell whether information was supplied directly to the compiler of the record by someone with personal knowledge, reasonable inferences can be drawn. The drawing of reasonable inferences is expressly allowed by s6(2). It is implicit in this that reasonable inferences can be drawn about whether any intermediaries through whom the information was passed acted in the course of a duty.

If the supplier gives evidence the record may still be used, although not until the end of his examination in chief and not without leave of the court: s4(2). The court may allow a second-hand hearsay record to be put in evidence before the person whose statement it contains has completed his evidence in chief. Unlike cases coming within s2, there are no limits to the times when this may be done.

Although it does not fit very comfortably with the wording of s4, the section does allow a record to be used where the compiler is also the supplier, in other words, where the record is first-hand hearsay. In such cases s2 would allow its admission in any event.

Section 4 of the 1968 Act only provides for the admissibility of the record itself and not for the admissibility of information tendered to the recorder who, in the performance of his duty, does not include it in his record: *Ventouris* v *Mountain (No 2), The Italia Express*, [1992] 3 All ER 414.

Computer print-outs

Statements contained in documents produced by computers may be admissible as original or hearsay evidence, depending upon the function performed by the computer. In either case, a computer print-out's admissibility is subject to s5 of the Civil Evidence Act 1968. Section 5 contains numerous conditions and is recognised as being unnecessarily complicated. It is notable that s69 of the Police and Criminal Evidence Act 1984 manages to lay down strict requirements about the way in which the computer was operated without having to go into the sort of detail which appears in s5.

The main requirements of s5 are that the computer was in regular use and was not operating in a way which would affect the accuracy of its print-out: s5(2). Proof that these requirements were met need not come from a witness in court, because a certificate signed by a person responsible for the computer will suffice: s5(4).

Previous statements of witnesses

Sections 2(2) and 4(2) envisage that a witness who gives evidence on oath in court can have his evidence supported by hearsay evidence of what he said on a previous occasion provided the hearsay evidence falls within s2 or s4.

Section 3 of the Act eliminates some of the more opaque common law rules about previous statements of witnesses. The rule that a witness's memory-refreshing note may be an exhibit but is not evidence of its truth does not apply to memory-refreshing notes which are exhibits in civil cases to which the 1968 Act applies. Such notes become evidence of the truth of what they say: s3(2). But it is important to note that the Act does not alter the circumstances in which such a note becomes an exhibit, it simply says that once it is an exhibit it is evidence of its truth.

The witness is liable to be treated like any other, so he can be cross-examined about any previous inconsistent statements he has made or about any criminal convictions he has. A previous inconsistent statement of a witness is not just evidence that he has been inconsistent, it is evidence of the truth of its contents: s3(1)(a). The same applies to a previous consistent statement which it put in evidence to contradict an allegation that the witness invented his evidence at a particular time: see further 6.5 below.

If the maker of the hearsay statement is not called as a witness, evidence may be called to discredit him by showing that he has been inconsistent, or by showing his bad character in just the same way as if he were called as a witness: s7(1). Any inconsistent statement is admissible as evidence of the truth of the facts stated: s7(2).

Common law exceptions

Certain common law exceptions to the hearsay rule are preserved by s9. They are the exceptions applicable to admissions, public documents, works of reference and public records: s9(2). In addition the obscure and little used hearsay exceptions applicable to evidence of reputation, evidence of pedigree and evidence of family tradition where relevant are preserved (s9(3)), although these latter matters are of minimal importance.

The only significant common law exception to the hearsay rule which is not preserved by s9 is that evidence which is hearsay but forms part of the res gestae. The vast majority, if not all, of the evidence within that category is first-hand hearsay and is therefore admissible under s2, so no great hardship results from it not being preserved as a specific common law exception.

Evidence admitted by virtue of s9 does not have to comply with the rules which are discussed below about giving notice. Therefore one's right to use hearsay evidence is not subject to any preconditions. This has the effect that evidence which is admissible both under s2 or s4 and under s9 is admissible as of right. This would cover, for example, an admission by one party which is proved by calling the person to whom he made the admission. Notice may, however, be given as a tactical device to put pressure on one's opponent to settle the case, but no such notice is required by the Act or rules of court.

Notice

Section 8(1) requires rules of court to be made regulating the admission of evidence under ss2, 4 and 5. Subsections (2), (3) and (4) state in general terms what the rules may state. Those subsections need not be considered in any detail because the rules themselves are what determine what should be done. The relevant rules RSC Ord 38 rr21-34 for the High Court and, for the county courts, CCR Ord 20 rr14-24.

RSC Ord 38 r21 provides that notice must be served within 21 days of the case being set down for hearing, or 14 days in the county court: CCR Ord 20 r15. In the county court no notice need be served if the defendant has not filed a defence. The prescribed contents of the notice differ according to whether the statement is admissible under ss2, 4 or 5. The High Court rules on contents of notices are applied to the county court by CCR Ord 20 r16.

Notice of a statement admissible under s2 must set out the time, place and circumstances at or in which the statement was made, who made it, to whom it was made and the substance of the statement or the words used if they are material: Ord 38 r22(1). A copy of any document in which the statement is contained must be annexed to the notice: (r22(2)).

The notice required before a second-hand hearsay record is admissible – a document within s4 – must have annexed to it a copy of the document, or the relevant parts, if not all of it is relevant. It must contain particulars of the person by whom the record was compiled and the duty under which he acted, the person who originally supplied the information and all intermediaries, along with the duty under which they acted. It must also describe the nature of the record if this is not apparent from the document, and must give details of the time, place and circumstances in which the record or the relevant part of it was compiled. All of these requirements are in r23(1).

As with documents admissible under s4, a copy of the document admissible under s5 must be annexed to the notice, stating the intention to rely on it. The notice must contain particulars of a person who was responsible for management of the computer, a person who was responsible for supplying information to the computer, and a person who was responsible for the operation of the computer: r24(1). The notice must state whether the computer was operating properly throughout the material time, that is the time when the relevant information was supplied, stored and reproduced; or if it was not operating properly, the notice must state whether this affected the production of the print-out or its accuracy: r24(2).

The service of notice is designed to give all parties the opportunity of agreeing to the admission of the hearsay evidence if they wish. This has the advantage at trial of saving time, and consequently, costs. If any party who is served with a notice does not agree to the use of hearsay, he may serve a counternotice requiring the maker of the statement to give evidence: RSC Ord 38 r26(1), CCR Ord 20 r17(1). In order to avoid this being done in cases where there is a good reason for not calling the maker, RSC Ord 38 rr22(3), 23(2) and 24(3) require the notice which is served to state whether any of the list of reasons contained in RSC Ord 38 r25 applies (RSC Ord 38 r25 applies in the county court, CCR Ord 20 r16). If the notice states that one or more of those reasons does apply, no counternotice may be served unless it contends that the person in question can attend as a witness: RSC Ord 38 r26(2), CCR Ord 20 r17(2).

The reasons set out in r25 are that the person in question is dead or beyond the seas or unfit to give evidence by reason of his bodily or mental condition, or that despite the exercise of reasonable diligence it has not been possible to identify or find him, or that he cannot reasonably be expected to remember the matters contained in his statement. It should be noted that the ability to identify the person and the ability to find him are separate matters under this provision, whereas the Criminal Justice Act 1988 refers only to inability to find the maker of the statement.

The meaning of most of the reasons is clear. It is not necessary to prove that the maker of the statement is both beyond the seas and unable to attend as a witness; simply being beyond the seas is sufficient: *Rasool* v *West Midlands Passenger Transport Executive* [1974] 3 All ER 638. 'Beyond the seas' means outside those parts of the United Kingdom in which a writ of sub poena can be effected: the result is that the Isle of Wight is not beyond the seas but the Channel Islands and the Isle of Man are: *Rover International Ltd* v *Cannon Film Sales (No 2)* [1987] 1 WLR 1597.

Where there is a dispute whether a r25 reason applies the court may determine that question as a preliminary issue: RSC Ord 38 r27(1), CCR Ord 20 r18(1). If it is held that the r25 reason does not apply, a counternotice requiring the attendance of the witness will be effective and, subject to the court's discretion to allow hearsay evidence, he must attend or his evidence will not go before the court. On the other hand, where a r25 reason is proved to apply the person serving notice may as of right utilise the hearsay evidence.

There are special provisions for cases where the hearsay statement which a party intends to use was made in the course of giving evidence in previous proceedings. The court has a virtually free hand to make what directions it wishes about the use of that hearsay evidence: RSC Ord 38 r28, CCR Ord 20 r19. The reason for this is that the court may feel it right to accept the hearsay evidence without requiring the original maker of the statement to give evidence, on the ground that when he testified before he would have done so on oath and the opportunity for cross-examination would, normally, have been present. There may be exceptional cases where the witness should attend anyway, such as where he was not cross-examined on the previous occasion or where new evidence has come to light which casts doubt on the truth of what he said before, or where the parties to the previous hearing were different. Where the statement was made on oath in previous proceedings no counternotice may be served, whether or not a r25 reason is given in the notice. The proper procedure is for the party who wants the maker of the statement to give evidence to apply to the court for such a direction: RSC Ord 38 r26(3), CCR Ord 20 r17(3).

Service of a counternotice should not be made just to be awkward because the court may, and in practice will, order any party who unreasonably requires a witness to attend after service of a notice to pay the costs wasted by calling him: RSC Ord 38, r32, CCR Ord 20 r23.

As we have seen, one effect of s7 of the Act is that previous inconsistent statements of a witness are evidence of their truth once they have been used to contradict him. They are, in effect, hearsay documents adduced by the cross-examining party. There is no need to give notice of one's intention to use such a document in cross-examination unless the witness is not to be called. Therefore if a party, P, calls a witness, W, he may be taken by surprise by having W's previous inconsistent statement put to him in cross-examination. But, if W is not to be called and a notice is served stating an intention to give his evidence in a hearsay form, the recipient of the notice may not introduce W's previous inconsistent statement unless he himself serves a notice to that effect within 21 days of receipt of the notice from P (RSC Ord 38 r31(1)), or seven days in the county court (CCR Ord 20 r22(1)). If the previous inconsistent statement is itself admissible under s2, the notice which is served about it must contain the information prescribed by RSC Ord 38 r22. In addition, no other evidence may be adduced to discredit W unless either P gave a r25 reason for not calling him, or the other party served a counternotice requiring W to attend: RSC Ord 38 r30, CCR Ord 20 r21.

The court has a discretion to allow hearsay evidence where no notice has been given, or the notice was not in the proper form, or was served too late, or a counternotice was served but the witness has not attended: RSC Ord 38 r29(1), CCR Ord 20 r20(1). This discretion should not be used so as to allow one party to take another by surprise. In *Ford* v *Lewis* [1971] 1 WLR 623 the plaintiff was injured in a road traffic accident in 1960. The case came to trial in 1970 and at trial the defence wished to adduce a statement of the defendant under s2 and certain hospital records under s4. No notice was given because it was thought that the plaintiff or her witnesses would change their evidence if they had notice. The judge was not told that this was the reason for not giving notice, and exercised his discretion to allow the evidence to be given. The Court of Appeal overturned this ruling, holding that the purpose of the notice procedure it to ensure that a party against whom hearsay evidence is to be adduced has the opportunity to consider his position in the light of that evidence. The whole purpose of the notice procedure was flouted by the defendant in this case and the judge should not have allowed the hearsay evidence to be given.

By contrast, in *Morris* v *Stratford-on-Avon RDC* [1973] 1 WLR 1059 the plaintiff called an eyewitness who was wholly unable to remember events. The plaintiff was allowed to adduce the witness's proof of evidence under s2 despite having served no notice. The Court of Appeal upheld the trial judge's ruling because on the facts of the case no prejudice was caused to the defendant. Megaw LJ said that it would be wrong to expect a party to serve notice every time there was a remote possibility of having to rely on hearsay evidence because something might happen at trial which required it.

Where the effect of refusing to allow hearsay evidence to be given would be that one party would have to call one of the opposing parties or a servant or agent of an opposing party, the trial judge should normally exercise his discretion in favour of allowing the hearsay. RSC Ord 38 r29(2) and CCR Ord 20 r20(2) specifically give the judge a discretion on this matter, but in practice the discretion should normally be exercised so as to allow the hearsay in such a situation. In *Tremelbye (Selangor) Ltd* v *Stekel* [1971] 1 WLR 226 the judge allowed a transcript of evidence from a criminal trial to be used by the plaintiff as hearsay because the witnesses at that trial were defendants in the civil proceedings. But in *Greenaway* v *Homelea Fittings Ltd* [1985] 1 WLR 234 the judge refused to allow the plaintiff to use hearsay evidence of a former employee of the defendant because the purpose of the discretion was to prevent embarrassment, yet if the witness was no longer the defendant's employee it could not embarrass him to give evidence for the plaintiff.

Section 6

Section 6 of the 1968 Act contains general guidance about how judges should approach hearsay evidence. Most of its provisions are superfluous because all it does is lay down general principles which judges would follow in any event. The superfluous subsections are subs(2), which says that judges may draw reasonable inferences from the circumstances in which a statement was made in order to determine its admissibility, subs(3) which says that when assessing the weight to be given to hearsay evidence the court must look at all of the circumstances including whether the statement was contemporaneous with the matters of which it speaks, and subs(4) which says that a hearsay statement cannot corroborate the evidence of the maker of that statement or the supplier of the information contained in a hearsay record.

Section 6(1) provides that a document admissible under ss2, 4 or 5 may be proved by production of the original or a copy authenticated in such a way as the court may approve. In practice originals are adduced in the great majority of cases.

5.3 The magistrates' courts

Criminal cases

When hearing criminal trials magistrates' courts are subject to the provisions of the Criminal Justice Act 1988 and s9 of the Criminal Justice Act 1967. They cannot rely on s13 of the Criminal Justice Act 1925 because they may not hear a case after it has been committed for trial to the Crown Court.

There are no statutory provisions applicable to the admissibility of hearsay evidence in the magistrates' courts which do not apply also in the Crown Court.

Civil cases

The provisions of the Civil Evidence Act 1968 relating to hearsay evidence do not apply in the magistrates' courts. But the Evidence Act 1938 does apply. This allows certain first-hand and second-hand hearsay contained in documents, but it does not allow any oral hearsay evidence.

In order for a document to be admissible under the 1938 Act the maker of the statement must be called to give evidence. Either he must have have personal knowledge of the matters dealt with by the statement, or the statement must be or form part of a continuous record which was compiled by him under a duty from information which was supplied by a person who had, or might reasonably be supposed to have had, knowledge of the matters dealt with: s1(1). The requirement that the maker of the statement gives evidence makes this Act of very narrow scope as an exception to the hearsay rule. It does not apply where the maker is 'dead, unfit to attend as a witness by reason of his bodily or mental condition, beyond the seas, or if it is not reasonably practicable to secure his attendance, or if all reasonable efforts have been made to find him but he has not been found.

In cases where the witness is available, the court may dispense with the need to have him called if it would cause undue delay or expense: s1(2). The original of the document should be used in evidence (s1(1)), although a copy which is certified to be a true copy is admissible at the discretion of the court where it would cause undue delay or expense to use the original: s1(2).

5.4 Child proceedings

High Court and county courts

In *H v H and C (Kent County Council intervening) (child abuse: evidence)* [1989] 2 FLR 333 the Court of Appeal decided that:

1. The county court when exercising the matrimonial jurisdiction in custody and access applications could not waive the evidential requirements of the hearsay rule as those proceedings were not within the exception in s18 of the Civil Evidence Act 1968.
2. The wardship jurisdiction as exercised in the High Court did come within the exception and in the wardship jurisdiction the hearsay rule could be waived by the agreement of the parties.
3. In the High Court and in the county court in child proceedings a welfare officer directed by court order to investigate and report had a duty to give to the court all the information which was considered relevant and was not constrained by the hearsay rule from including relevant but otherwise inadmissible information.

1993 Order

Section 96(3)-(7) of the Children Act 1989, empowered the Lord Chancellor to make provision for the admissibility of evidence in certain civil proceedings concerning children, where such evidence would otherwise be inadmissible under any rule of law relating to hearsay. Accordingly, the Children (Admissibility of Hearsay Evidence) Order 1991 provides that in civil proceedings in the High Court or a county court or in family proceedings in a magistrates' court the hearsay rule does not apply to any evidence given in connection with the upbringing, maintenance or welfare of a child. To this extent the effect of *H v H and C*, above, has been reversed. See also *R v B County Council* [1991] 1 WLR 221. The 1990 order (which was revoked and replaced by the 1991 order, the 1990 order having given only qualified exemption in the case of magistrates' courts) also applied where a Crown Court heard an appeal against the making of a child care order under s1 of the Children and Young Persons Act 1969 by a juvenile court: *B* v *X County Council* (1991) The Times 16 December.

Applications under s25 of the Children Act 1989 for secure accommodation orders are 'family proceedings' for the purposes of the 1991 order and hearsay evidence is therefore admissible in such cases: *R(J)* v *Oxfordshire County Council* [1992] 3 All ER 660.

An applicant seeking to rely on the hearsay evidence of a child in civil proceedings pursuant to the 1991 order has to demonstrate that the evidence has a substantial connection with the upbringing, maintenance or welfare of the child. It is a matter of fact in each case whether the connection is sufficiently substantial: *Re C and others (minors) (hearsay evidence: contempt proceedings)* [1993] 4 All ER 690. In that case the county court judge had held that the hearsay evidence of a mother's children contained in a report of a court welfare officer and an affidavit by the minister of the mother's church were inadmissible under the 1991 order, in proceedings to commit the mother's former husband for contempt for, inter alia, breach of a non-molestation injunction. While the Court of Appeal accepted that contempt proceedings as such could be within the scope of the order, here the judge's decision would be upheld on the ground that the injunction had not been granted for the protection of the children and they had not been seriously affected by their father's alleged actions.

The 1991 order was revoked and superseded by the Children (Admissibility of Hearsay Evidence) Order 1993 but the only difference between them in effect is that the 1993 order extends to civil proceedings in magistrates' courts under the Child Support Act 1991. The 1993 order reproduces the provisions of the 1991 order in relation to the High Court and county courts and those provisions are sufficiently general to embrace Child Support Act proceedings in those courts.

6

Common Law Admissibility of Hearsay

6.1 Confessions and admissions: the common law

6.2 Confessions and admissions: the statutory rules

6.3 Res gestae

6.4 Declarations by persons now dead

6.5 Self-serving statements

6.6 Public documents

6.7 Reference works

6.1 Confessions and admissions: the common law

Definitions

An admission is the acceptance by a person of the truth of an allegation. He need not be involved in litigation or be subject to any charge at the time he makes the admission. Anyone who heard or otherwise perceived it being made will be entitled to give evidence of it, and any document in which it is contained is admissible. Admissions can be made formally, as we have seen, by virtue of the Criminal Justice Act 1967 in criminal cases, or on the pleadings in the county court or High Court. But formal admissions also encompass concessions made in court. For example in a landlord and tenant case the landlord may assert on the pleadings that the occupant of his house is a licensee not a tenant, but in court it may be conceded by his legal representative that the occupation is pursuant to a tenancy. Such a concession is binding on the party whose solicitor or counsel makes it.

It is mainly with informal admissions that this part of this chapter is concerned. The term 'informal admission' to describe an admission made otherwise than on the pleadings or as a concession in court is useful but not entirely accurate. The difference in practical terms between formal and informal admissions is that a formal admission may not be contradicted by evidence whereas an informal one may be. However, a formal admission may be withdrawn with leave of the judge and pleadings may be amended with leave so as to retract an admission. It is only those

147

formal admissions or concessions which are made and not withdrawn which may not be contradicted by evidence. But a concession made during a court hearing does not involve any formality, and 'informal admissions' are often made in a very formal context such as during an interview with the police. It would be better if formal admissions were known as conclusive, and informal as rebuttable admissions.

Informal admissions are sometimes described as 'out-of-court admissions'. This is not always accurate, although in the vast majority of cases they are made out of court to someone who later gives hearsay evidence by repeating what he was told. But a party to any case may admit something during the course of his evidence. Such an admission may be contradicted by that party correcting himself – although this often results in disaster as he tries to climb out of the hole he has dug himself into – or by evidence from other sources which shows that the admission was not correctly made. It is not where or to whom it is made which determines whether an admission may be contradicted, but the way in which it is made. In this respect 'formal admission' is accurate to describe a conclusive admission because it is the form in which it is made which makes it conclusive.

A statement made by an accused person during interview with the police in which he admits his guilt is normally known as a confession. This is not a term of art (subject to what is said below about the Police and Criminal Evidence Act 1984), but it is in common usage to describe a complete admission as opposed to an admission of part but not the whole of the prosecution's case.

Admissions can arise in various ways. In a criminal case the accused may fully admit guilt to the police during interview (a confession), or he may admit that he was present at the scene of the crime, while denying that he was the offender (an example of a partial admission), or he may make an admission to someone other than a policeman. In each of these instances any person who heard the admission being made may give evidence about it, subject to certain limitations which will be explained below: *Commissioner of Customs & Excise* v *Harz and Power* [1967] AC 760. These examples are all of cases where evidence will be called to prove that the accused has made either a partial or an entire admission of guilt. But admissions can also be made in court. We have seen in chapter 5 that formal admissions may be made in criminal trials under the provisions of s10 of the Criminal Justice Act 1967 and that allowing a statement to be read to the court pursuant to s9 of the 1967 Act is in reality an admission that what is said in the statement is true. Admissions can also be made by conduct.

Admissions can be made in civil cases and two sorts of formal admission are possible. First, there may be an admission in the pleadings. In this circumstance no evidence will be called to prove that the admission was made. Secondly one party may serve on another a notice admitting certain facts. A notice of admission may be given voluntarily (RSC Ord 27 r1, CCR Ord 20 r1), or in response to a Notice to Admit, which is a formal request by one party that another admits the truth of certain facts or the authenticity of certain documents: RSC Ord 27 r2, CCR Ord 20 rr2 & 3.

Informal admissions in civil cases may be made by a party admitting the truth of allegations to another person, in which case that person can give evidence about it; or one party may have made admissions in documents; or he may have acted in such a way that it can be inferred from his conduct that his opponent's case is correct.

Admissions by conduct

Admissions by conduct may be made in a variety of ways. In *Moriarty* v *London, Chatham & Dover Railway* (1870) LR 5 QB 314 the plaintiff tried to suborn false witnesses, that is, get people to give false evidence in his favour. Evidence of this activity was held admissible against him because it was possible to infer from his conduct that he had no case. It is a matter of fact in each case whether conduct by a party is properly seen to amount to an admission that he is in the wrong. In *Bessela* v *Stern* (1877) 2 CPD 265 a woman accused a man to his face of having promised to marry her daughter. He did not answer the allegation directly, but offered the woman money to go away. His silence was an admission that the allegation was true because, it was held, in the circumstances the natural reaction of someone who has a false allegation made to his face is to deny what is said. The offer of money for the woman to go away was a further admission by conduct.

In other circumstances the court is unable to draw the inference that the reason for silence in the face of an allegation is the truth of the allegation: see, eg, *Wiedemann* v *Walpole* [1891] 2 QB 534.

The criminal courts adhere quite strictly to the right of a defendant to remain silent. No inference of guilt can be drawn from his failure to give evidence, nor from his failure to answer questions: see paragraph 1.5. In *Christie* [1914] AC 545 the defendant was accused of indecent assault on a boy. Evidence was given that the boy approached Christie and said, 'That is the man.' Christie said, 'I am innocent.' The House of Lords held that this evidence was properly admitted because the defendant answered the allegation and it was for the jury to decide whether his answer amounted to acceptance of its truth. Lord Atkinson said:

> 'The rule of law undoubtedly is that a statement made in the presence of an accused person, even upon an occasion which would be expected reasonably to call for some explanation or denial from him, is not evidence against him of the facts stated save so far as he accepts the statement, so as to make it, in effect, his own. If he accepts the statement in part only, then to that extent alone does it become his statement. He may accept the statement by word or conduct, action or demeanour, and it is the function of the jury which tries the case to determine whether his words, action, conduct or demeanour at the time when a statement was made amounts to an acceptance of it in whole or in part.'

Two principles about admissions in criminal cases emerge from *Christie*. First, evidence may not be given of an allegation which is met by silence. Secondly, if there is any answer to the allegation it is for the jury to decide whether the answer amounts to an acceptance of the truth of the allegation. If it does amount to acceptance of its truth, it is an admission, but if it does not, the defendant admits nothing. The case is not authority that silence is never an admission, because silence may be accompanied by actions which show that the accused accepts the truth of the allegation.

In *Hall* v *R* [1971] 1 All ER 322 someone told the police that drugs found in a house had been brought there by Hall. This allegation was put to him and he said nothing in answer to it. The passage from *Christie* cited above was held by the Privy Council to be a correct statement of the law, and so Hall's silence was not an admission of the truth of the allegation. But it was said that in 'very exceptional circumstances' an inference may be drawn from failure to give an explanation or a disclaimer. It was not said what might amount to very exceptional circumstances. Five years later in *Parker* v *R* [1976] 2 All ER 380 the Privy Council held that Parker's failure to answer an allegation that he had stabbed the accuser's daughter was an admission because it was accompanied by conduct, namely lunging at the accuser with a knife, from which it could be inferred that the accusation was true. There were very exceptional circumstances accompanying the accused's silence. In reality it was not Parker's silence from which an admission was inferred, but his conduct.

The dictum of Lord Diplock in *Hall* in which 'very exceptional circumstances' were mentioned reads as follows:

> 'It is a clear and widely known principle of the common law ... that a person is entitled to refrain from answering a question put to him for the purpose of discovering whether he has committed a criminal offence ... It may be that in very exceptional circumstances an inference may be drawn from a failure to give an explanation or a disclaimer, but in their Lordships' view silence alone on being informed by a police officer that someone else has made an accusation against him cannot give rise to an inference that the person to whom this information is communicated accepts the truth of the accusation.'

In *Chandler* [1976] 3 All ER 105 the Court of Appeal said that this dicum was in conflict with what Lord Atkinson said in *Christie*. The supposed conflict is that Lord Diplock suggested that silence in answer to a police officer's question can never be construed as acceptance of the truth of what the officer said. In *Chandler* the accused was accompanied by his solicitor when questioned by the police. Both before and after he was cautioned he answered a number of questions but refused to answer others. The Court of Appeal held that the jury was entitled to hear about the whole of the interview and should approach those answers where there was silence by asking whether the defendant was accepting the truth of what the officer put to him and then asking whether an inference of guilt could be drawn if he was accepting the truth of the accusations.

There is in fact no conflict between *Christie* and *Hall* v *R* because Lord Diplock said that no admission is made by 'silence alone' in answer to a questions. If silence is the answer to some questions but not to others there is not 'silence alone' – there is silence in the context of a series of questions some of which are answered.

Lawton LJ, who delivered the judgment of the court in *Chandler*, approved *Bessela* v *Stern* as setting out the correct test for whether silence in the face of an accusation is an acceptance of the truth of the accusation. He approved the following dictum of Cave J in *Mitchell* (1892) 17 Cox CC 503:

> 'Undoubtedly, when persons are speaking on even terms, and a charge is made, and the person charged says nothing, and expresses no indignation, and does nothing to repel the charge, that is some evidence to show that he admits the charge to be true.'

This approach was also adopted in *Parker* v *R*. It was held to be significant that the accuser was not a police officer but the mother of the victim of the stabbing. The phrase used by Lord Diplock was that accuser and accused 'were speaking on even terms'.

The result of these authorities is that the law is not entirely clear. Certainly in civil cases one must ask whether the circumstances in which the accusation is made are such that one can infer from failure to reply that the accused is accepting the truth of the accusation. In criminal cases absolute silence to all allegations is not something from which it can be inferred that they are accepted as true and, therefore, evidence may not be given about what allegations were put to him. But where he answers some questions but not others, or accompanies his silence with conduct from which acceptance of the allegations may be inferred, it is a matter for the jury whether they draw that inference. They should always be directed to approach the evidence they hear in two stages. First, they should consider whether the defendant accepted the truth of the allegations and secondly they should ask themselves whether that acceptance is something from which they can infer guilt.

Admissions and the hearsay rule

An admission by one party is something of which hearsay evidence is admissible at common law because, as Parke B said in *Slatterie* v *Pooley* (1840) 6 M & W 664, 'What a party himself admits to be true may reasonably be presumed to be so.' In other words this exception to the hearsay rule arises from the reliability of the hearsay evidence. At common law there were various limitations on the admissibility of admissions made by an accused person to a person in authority, that is, a person who had responsibility for prosecution. The general principle being that hearsay evidence of an admission can be given because it is likely to be reliable, it follows that if there was something in the circumstances in which the admissions was made which rendered it unreliable, no hearsay evidence should be allowed. The hearsay evidence about an admission was an exception to the general rule against hearsay. Accordingly, the rationale of the exception had to be satisfied, and the circumstances in which the admission was made had to be such that it was reliable.

The formula adopted in the criminal court was laid down by Lord Sumner in *Ibrahim* v *R* [1914] AC 599. He said:

> 'It has long been established as a positive rule of English criminal law, that no statement by an accused is admissible in evidence against him unless it is shown by the prosecution to have been a voluntary statement, in the sense that it has not been obtained from him

either by fear of prejudice or hope of advantage exercised or held out by a person in authority.'

The requirement that a statement by the accused must be voluntary has been refined over the years by definition of its elements, and restated with minor amendments in *DPP* v *Ping Lin* [1976] AC 574. However, it was far from perfect because it contained too many technicalities. Today s76 of the Police and Criminal Evidence Act 1984 governs the admissibility of confessions and admissions in criminal trials in both the Crown Court and the magistrates' courts.

In civil cases no conditions of admissibility have to be satisfied before hearsay evidence could be given about an admission by a party. The principle cited above from *Slatterie* v *Pooley* was first authoritatively stated in *Maltby* v *Christie* (1795) 1 Esp 340 in which an auctioneer who advertised the goods he sold as belonging to a bankrupt had this advertisement proved against him when he sued the bankrupt for damages but claimed the man was not bankrupt.

Section 9 of the Civil Evidence Act 1968 preserves the common law as it relates to hearsay evidence of admissions in civil proceedings in the High Court and county court. First-hand hearsay may be given of a statement made by a party in which he admits the truth of facts alleged by another party, or in which he admits the falsity of the facts alleged in his own pleadings. Only first-hand hearsay is admissible at common law. This appears most clearly in *Attorney-General's Reference (No 4 of 1979)* [1981] 1 All ER 1193. The question arose whether money received by the accused was part of the proceeds of a theft. When asked whether it represented her share of the proceeds she answered, 'I suppose it was.' The trial judge ruled that this was no evidence that the money was part of the proceeds because the accused did not know where the money came from, she merely stated her belief. The Court of Appeal upheld this ruling.

Evidence of an admission is subject to other rules about the admissibility of evidence, therefore it may not be given if it would breach rules on privilege (see chapter 7), or if it would be unfairly prejudicial. For example, in *Turner* v *Underwood* [1948] 2 KB 248 the defendant admitted guilt by saying, 'I've done time for this before.' This would, necessarily, have informed the court that the accused had a criminal record and might have led to the justices being prejudiced against him by assuming that because he had committed similar offences before so he was guilty of the present offence. As we will see in chapter 8, this line of reasoning is not generally acceptable. The Divisional Court held that evidence of the admission was not admissible.

Admissions by non-parties

Not only may hearsay evidence be given about admissions made by a party, but also admissions made by a non-party are admissible in certain limited circumstances. The most obvious case is where the person making the admission is the agent of a party and acts within his authority in making the admission. We have already seen that admissions made by a party's legal representative in pleadings or during court proceedings are binding on him. This is a special instance of an admission by a non-party because it is so closely connected with litigation and the admissions are formal rather than informal.

Whether evidence may be given about an informal admission made by an agent of a party depends upon whether that agent was acting within the scope of his authority. This raises questions of agency law which are outside the scope of this book, but a few of the more obvious examples are useful. A stationmaster was held to have authority to make admissions about the loss of a parcel at his station in *Kirkstall Brewery Co* v *Furness Railway* (1874) LR 9 QB 468, but in *GW Railway* v *Willis* (1865) 18 CBNS 748 an inspector of cattle at a railway station was not authorised to make admissions about the loss of cattle. More recently, in *Edwards* v *Brookes (Milk) Ltd* [1963] 1 WLR 795 admissions made by a depot manager about the contents of cartons of milk were held to be admissible against his employer.

Certain relationships between the person making an admission and the party to litigation do not normally give any authority to make admissions. For example the admissions of a man are not normally admissible against his wife, nor vice versa: *Clifford* v *Barton* (1823) 1 Bing 199.

The admissions of one defendant to criminal proceedings are not normally admissible evidence against a co-defendant. This rule overlaps with the law on competence. Because one defendant is not normally competent to give evidence for the prosecution against another, so his admissions may not be relied upon against that other defendant. But where the charge is conspiracy, anything done by one defendant in the course of the conspiracy may be treated by the jury as evidence against a co-conspirator. In *Blake and Tye* (1844) 6 QB 126 the defendants were charged with conspiracy to defraud the Customs & Excise by importing goods without declaring them, thereby reducing the liability to pay duty. One defendant was a customs officer who made false entries in a book. These entries were admissible against both defendants, although entries in the first defendant's chequebook which showed what he did with his share of the proceeds of the conspiracy were admissible against him only because they were not made as part of the execution of the conspiracy.

6.2 Confessions and admissions: the statutory rules

Conditions of admissibility

The admissibility at common law of hearsay evidence of admissions is subject to the conditions of admissibility set out in s76 of the Police and Criminal Evidence Act 1984. Section 76(1) introduced a statutory rule identical to the primary common law rule, namely, that hearsay evidence of any confession or admission made by an accused person is admissible in evidence against him. In fact s76(1) is careful not to limit itself to hearsay evidence of confessions, because there may be cases where the jury is given direct evidence of a confession, such as where tape recordings of an interview containing admissions are played in court. The section only refers to confessions, not to admissions. But s82(1) defines 'confession' as including 'any statement wholly or partly adverse to the person who made it'. It is therefore clear that s76(1) makes hearsay evidence of both admissions and confessions admissible in the Crown Court and the magistrates' courts. The provisions of the Act do not apply in civil proceedings. Section 76(1) is expressly stated to be subject to the conditions of admissibility in the remainder of the section.

A juvenile's confession may be 'unreliable' in this sense if the adult accompanying him at the interview, in accordance with the relevant Code of Practice, was incapable of giving him advice (*R v Morse* [1991] Crim LR 192), although a father may still be an 'appropriate adult' for these purposes if he encourages his son to tell the truth: *R v Jefferson* [1994] 1 All ER 270.

Where the court found that a person being interviewed by the police had been 'bullied from first to last', evidence of the interview (which gave rise to a confession) was excluded on the grounds of unreliability as the judge felt that the interview had 'stepped into the realms of oppression': *R v Beales* [1991] Crim LR 118.

Section 76(2) sets out both procedural and substantive conditions of admissibility. The procedural conditions are that it is for the prosecution to prove the admissibility of the confession, and that proof of admissibility is needed whenever it is represented to the court that the confession may not be admissible. Where it is proposed to challenge the admissibility of a confession, or indeed any evidence, it is common practice for defence counsel to tell prosecuting counsel in advance that objection is being taken, so that when the time comes for the confession to be used the prosecution can inform the judge that a point of law arises. The jury will then be sent out of court and argument will take place on the question of admissibility. Thus it will be represented to the court that the confession may not be admissible without evidence being given about the confession and, indeed, without the jury ever hearing that a confession was made.

Section 76(3) allows the court to raise the issue of admissibility. This is a useful provision for cases where the defendant is unrepresented. If he is represented, his counsel may feel for tactical reasons that it would be best for the jury or justices to hear that there was a confession in order to attempt to gain sympathy for the defendant by showing that it was obtained improperly. In practice the majority of judges and justices leave it to the judgment of defence counsel to decide whether to challenge the admissibility of a confession. Section 76(3) therefore is used primarily in cases where the defendant is not represented.

Where it is represented that a confession is inadmissible, what the prosecution must prove beyond reasonable doubt is that the confession was not obtained in either of the ways set out in paras (a) and (b) of s76(2).

In *Lam Chi-ming* v *R* [1991] 3 All ER 172 Lord Lowry said it was the Privy

Council's view that:

> '... the more recent English cases established that the rejection of an improperly obtained confession is not dependent only upon possible unreliability but also upon the principle that a man cannot be compelled to incriminate himself and upon the importance that attaches in a civilised society to proper behaviour by the police towards those in their custody'.

His Lordship added that all three of these factors have combined to produce the rule of law applicable in England that a confession is not admissible in evidence unless the prosecution establish that it was voluntary and that this, perhaps the most fundamental rule of the English criminal law, now finds expression in s76 of the Police and Criminal Evidence Act 1984.

Sections 23 (first-hand hearsay) and 24 (business etc documents) of the Criminal Justice Act 1988 do not render admissible confessions made by accused persons that would not be admissible under s76 of the Police and Criminal Evidence Act 1984: ss23(4), 24(3) and 28 and para 6, Schedule 2 to the 1988 Act.

Oppression

Paragraph (a) requires it to be proved beyond reasonable doubt that the confession was not obtained by oppression. This is defined in s76(8) as including 'torture, inhuman or degrading treatment, and the use or threat of violence (whether or not amounting to torture)'. This definition speaks for itself, but it is only a partial definition because it says that oppression 'includes' these things. It follows from this that it also includes other things. The common law requirement that a confession had to be voluntary before it was admissible, included a requirement that it was not obtained by oppression. The definition of oppression was directed to cover cases where the accused was kept under conditions which sapped his will, that is, which led him to confess simply in order to be released from custody, such as long periods of questioning without adequate breaks or refreshment. Inhuman or degrading treatment would cover most of these matters.

In *Fulling* [1987] 2 All ER 65 the accused said that she was questioned by the police and after two interviews in which she said nothing she was questioned for a third time. During that interview there was a short break during which, she said, she was told that her lover had had an affair with the woman in the cell next to her cell at the police station. She said that she could no longer stand being in the cells and confessed because of what she was told. The trial judge did not make any finding whether the accused's version of events was true, but he assumed it to be so for the purposes of the argument on admissibility. He and the Court of Appeal held that the confession was not obtained by oppression because the circumstances described by the accused did not amount to oppression.

The Court of Appeal adopted the definition of oppression found in the Oxford English Dictionary, which reads:

'Exercise of authority or power in a burdensome, harsh or wrongful manner; unjust or cruel treatment of subjects, inferiors etc; the imposition of unreasonable or unjust burdens.'

It was said by Lord Lane CJ that the court found it hard to envisage any circumstances in which oppression would not involve some impropriety on the part of the person carrying out the interrogation. On the assumption that the defendant's version of what happened at the police station was true, the court held that what the police did fell far short of the high standard of misbehaviour which amounts to oppression.

A further important point made in *Fulling* is that common law definitions of oppression are not relevant to the construction of s76(2)(a) because the Police and Criminal Evidence Act 1984 is a consolidating statute and has to be construed according to its wording and not to the law as it stood before its enactment, an approach endorsed by the Court of Appeal in *R* v *Smurthwaite* [1994] 1 All ER 898.

Fulling was followed by the Court of Appeal in *R* v *Emmerson* (1991) 92 Cr App R 284 where police questioning, with raised voice and some bad language, which was 'rude and discourteous' and gave the impression of 'impatience and irritation', was not considered to amount to oppression. The Court of Appeal arrived at the opposite conclusion, though, when it appeared that the police had shouted at a suspect what they wanted him to say after he had denied involvement over 300 times: see *R* v *Miller* (1992) The Times 24 December.

That paragraph (a) renders inadmissible any confession unless the prosecution proves that it was not obtained 'by' oppression, makes clear that there must be a causal link between the oppression and the obtaining of the confession. If it is proved beyond reasonable doubt that the confession would have been made regardless of the oppressive treatment of the accused, it will be admissible.

Things said or done

Paragraph (b) is of greater practical importance. It is not very carefully phrased but seems to mean that the court must look at all the circumstances in which the confession was made and ask whether anything was said or done which was likely to make any confession given by the accused person unreliable. In other words, one should not ask whether the confession which was made is unreliable, nor whether it is true; instead one should approach the matter in the abstract and ask whether any confession made by the accused is likely to be unreliable. This requires an investigation into the circumstances existing at the time the confession was made and also an investigation into the character of the defendant. If he is a very hardy individual the judge may find that he was not likely to give an unreliable confession as a result of what was said or done. But a person of weak character may feel pressurised far more easily.

Where a promise has been made to the defendant that, for example, he will be given bail if he confesses, it will clearly be open to the court to hold that the confession is inadmissible. In such circumstances the court is unlikely to bother asking whether anything in the defendant's character would make him resilient to such an offer because the very nature of the offer is that it is made in order to induce a confession whether or not the accused is guilty.

There is a considerable overlap between s76(2)(b) and s78 of the 1984 Act. We will see in chapter 12 that s78 prevents the prosecution from relying on evidence where to allow the evidence would have an adverse effect on the fairness of the proceedings. One relevant factor in the effect of evidence upon the fairness of the proceedings is the way in which it was obtained because it is unfair to rely on evidence which has been obtained by trick or by threat. Many of the cases in which evidence of confessions has been excluded consider s78 in preference to s76 because the test for unfairness is wider than that in s76(2)(b), in that it may be unfair to rely on a confession even though it was not unreliable: *Mason* [1987] 3 All ER 481.

Both provisions were considered by the Court of Appeal in *R v Crampton* [1991] Crim LR 277. The appellant had been convicted of drugs offences. He had made admissions at interview in the police station 19 hours after his arrest when he might have been undergoing withdrawal. The defence contended that the confession was thereby rendered unreliable and should have been excluded by the trial judge either under s76(2)(b) of the Police and Criminal Evidence Act 1984 or through the exercise of his discretion under s78 of that Act. The appeal was dismissed as their Lordships could see no reason on the evidence to conclude that the trial judge had come to a wrong conclusion on the facts in refusing to exclude the confession either under s76 or 78 of the 1984 Act. It was in fact doubtful whether the mere holding of an interview at a time when the appellant was withdrawing was within s76(2)(b) as the words of the subsection seemed to postulate some words spoken by the police or some acts done by them which were likely to induce an unreliable confession.

In *R v Barry* (1991) The Times 11 December the Court of Appeal underlined some important points as to the reliability of confessions.

1. Everything said or done by the police which was likely in the circumstances to render the confession unreliable should be taken into account: s76(2) of the 1984 Act requires a broad approach.
2. The test is hypothetical; it relates not to the particular confession but to any confession.
3. The judge should ask whether the prosecution had proved beyond reasonable doubt that the confession had not been made as a consequence of things said or done.
4. While breaches of a Code of Practice do not necessarily mean that the evidence should be excluded, it does not follow that such breaches are irrelevant.

On the same day the Court of Appeal delivered judgment in the cases *R v Silcott, R v Braithwaite, R v Raghip* (1991) The Times 9 December: successful appeals against convictions of the murder of PC Blakelock and riot on the Broadwater Farm estate. Their Lordships said, inter alia, that the circumstances to be considered by the trial judge upon a submission under s76(2)(b) of the 1984 Act include the mental condition of the defendant at the time of the interview and the decision is to be taken upon the medical evidence rather than the trial judge's own assessment of the defendant's performance in interview. The judicial approach should not be governed by whether the defendant's IQ is above an arbitrary figure. In *Raghip's* renewed application for leave to appeal in December 1988 the Court of Appeal had been wrong to conclude that psychological evidence as to his intelligence and susceptibility would not have assisted the jury in determining the reliability of his confession pursuant to s76(2)(b).

In *R v Cox* [1991] Crim LR 276 the Court of Appeal stressed that, in accordance with s76 of the 1984 Act, the judge should ask himself not whether a confession in a police interview was true but whether it was made in consequence of anything (eg, a breach of a Code of Practice) likely to render it unreliable.

Applying the guidance in *R v Galbraith* [1981] 1 WLR 1039, in *R v McKenzie* [1993] 1 WLR 453 the Court of Appeal considered that where (i) the prosecution case depended wholly upon confessions, (ii) the defendant suffered from a significant degree of mental handicap and (iii) the confessions were unconvincing to a point where a jury properly directed could not properly convict upon them, then the judge, assuming that he had not excluded the confessions earlier, should withdraw the case from the jury.

Procedure

The admissibility of a confession may be challenged at any time before evidence of that confession is given. No court is bound to consider the admissibility of a confession simply because a suggestion has been made that it was obtained improperly. In *R v Liverpool Juvenile Court, ex parte R* [1987] 2 All ER 668 the Queen's Bench Division said, obiter, that a magistrates' court need only enquire into the admissibility of a confession if it is represented that such an inquiry should take place. In other words, suggestions may be made to prosecution witnesses in cross-examination that the confession was obtained improperly without thereby representing that the confession is inadmissible. In effect this means that it is for the defence to challenge admissibility if it thinks fit. As is stated above, there are many cases where for tactical reasons no challenge is made to the admissibility of a confession. *Ex parte R* repeats the long-standing rule in *Anderson* (1929) 21 Cr App R 178 that such tactics are permissible.

Once the defence has represented that the confession is inadmissible the court must hold a trial within a trial, or as it is usually known, a trial on the voir dire or, for short, a voir dire. This is a hearing simply on the question of admissibility. The defendant may give evidence without being asked about his guilt because the only question for the court is whether the confession is admissible and s76(2) expressly provides that the truth of the confession is irrelevant to its admissibility. In *Wong*

Kam Ming v *R* [1980] AC 247 the defendant, who was charged with murder, gave evidence on the voir dire about how a confession made by him was obtained. During cross-examination he was asked about the truth of the confession and gave certain answers which implicated him in the murder. The judge ruled that the confession was inadmissible but at the trial allowed the prosecution to call evidence about what was said by the accused on the voir dire. This resulted in a conviction. The Privy Council held that evidence was inadmissible about what happened at the trial-within-a-trial, and the conviction was quashed: see also *R* v *Cox* [1991] Crim LR 276.

In *Brophy* [1982] AC 476 the House of Lords upheld *Wong Kam Ming* v *R*, but said, obiter, that a defendant who says something at the voir dire which is irrelevant to the question of admissibility of the confession may in exceptional circumstances be questioned about it at the main trial. The sort of exceptional circumstances envisaged by the House were cases where the accused deliberately abuses the right to give evidence on the voir dire by boasting about having committed the offences with which he is charged, or uses the witness box as a platform for a political speech. If in front of the jury he is inconsistent with such boasting or such a speech, he may be asked about the evidence he gave at the trial-within-a-trial. In effect the statement made on the voir dire is separate from the confession which was being considered during the trial-within-a-trial, and in the same way that evidence may be given of an admission made by a defendant in an earlier trial (*McGregor* [1968] 1 QB 372), so evidence may be given about his admission in the trial-within-a-trial.

The court has no option about holding a trial-within-a-trial if the defence asks it to do so: *R* v *Liverpool Juvenile Court, ex parte R*. And if a confession is ruled to be admissible after such a trial, the defence is still entitled to question witnesses in the presence of the jury so as to try to undermine the confession by reference to the way in which it was obtained.

In many cases the defence is unable to challenge the way in which the confession was obtained, but wishes to assert that it is not true. Necessarily this involves the defence putting forward some reason for a false confession having been given. Often this is difficult, but everything depends upon the circumstances of the case and it is sometimes possible to raise a doubt and thereby gain an acquittal.

Where it is said by the defence that an alleged confession was never made at all and has been invented by the prosecution witnesses, it is a question for the jury whether the confession was made. There will be no trial-within-a-trial on such an issue. This is the result of the Privy Council's decision in *Ajodha* v *The State* [1982] AC 204. However, one must examine exactly what is put forward by the prosecution and the defence in order to know whether the issue of admissibility arises. In *Ajodha* v *The State* there were four appellants. Each said that he had been forced to sign a confession statement which he did not write, either by threats of violence or misrepresentations about the nature of the document put before him being made by police officers. The Privy Council held that in these cases the judge first had to rule whether the defence objections on the ground of threats or misrepresentation made the confessions inadmissible. Once he ruled that the confessions were not inadmissible in law, it was for the jury to assess whether the defendants were the authors of the statements. Because the appellants admitted signing the confession statements – thereby, on the face of things, making them their own statements – the question arose whether the signatures were obtained in such circumstances that the confessions were inadmissible. In the state of the law today this requires an examination of whether the prosecution can prove that the confessions were not obtained in such circumstances that s76 renders them inadmissible. Once the trial judge had ruled that the way in which the confessions were made did not make them inadmissible, it was a question for the jury whether the confessions were true.

The Privy Council identified four commonly occurring situations in which questions arise about the relative functions of judge and jury where the prosecution wishes to rely on a confession. In the following quotation from Lord Bridge's opinion, the position was stated as it was at common law, with references to voluntariness as the test for admissibility. (It should be borne in mind that where Lord Bridge referred to the common law test of admissibility the statutory requirements of s76 now apply.)

'1) The accused admits making the statement (orally or in writing) but raises the issue that it was not voluntary. This is a simple case where the judge must rule on admissibility, and, if he admits the evidence of the statement, leave to the jury all questions as to its value or weight.

2) The accused ... denies authorship of the written statement but claims that he signed it involuntarily. Again, ... the judge must rule on admissibility, and, if he admits the statement, leave all issues of fact as to the circumstances of the making and signing of the statement for the jury to consider and evaluate.

3) The evidence tendered or proposed to be tendered by the prosecution itself indicates that the circumstances in which the statement was taken could arguably lead to the conclusion that the statement was obtained by fear of prejudice or hope of advantage excited or held out by a person in authority. In this case, irrespective of any challenge to the prosecution evidence by the defence, it will be for the judge to rule, assuming the prosecution evidence to be true, whether it proves the statement to have been made voluntarily.

4) On the face of the evidence tendered or proposed to be tendered by the prosecution, there is no material capable of suggesting that the statement was other than voluntary. The defence is an absolute denial of the prosecution evidence ... In this situation no issue as to voluntariness can arise and hence no question of admissibility falls for the judge's decision. The issue of fact whether or not the statement was made by the accused is purely for the jury.'

At the end of the evidence the judge has an opportunity to review his decision to allow the prosecution to rely on a confession. If evidence is given during the course of the trial which changes his view on admissibility he should direct the jury to disregard the confession: *Watson* (1980) 70 Cr App R 273. The admissibility of a confession is always for the judge and not the jury to decide. Therefore, what he must not do is to direct the jury to consider the question of admissibility and disregard the confession if they feel the prosecution has not proved its admissibility.

A judge who reviews his decision on admissibility and concludes at the end of the trial that the confession is inadmissible, may feel that the confession is so prejudicial to the accused that he should discharge the jury and a fresh trial should take place. In such circumstances there is no estoppel requiring the judge at the retrial to exclude the confession.

Confessions by the mentally handicapped

Section 77(1) of the 1984 Act requires the judge at a trial in the Crown Court to direct the jury of the special need for caution where the defendant is mentally handicapped and the case against him depends wholly or substantially on a confession by him. Magistrates should also treat such a case as requiring special need for caution: s77(2). These requirements for caution do not apply if the confession was made in the presence of an independent person.

A person is mentally handicapped for these purposes if he is in a state of arrested or incomplete development of mind which includes significant impairment of intelligence and social functioning: s77(3). In establishing whether a defendant was mentally handicapped within the meaning of s77(3) of the 1984 Act it is not appropriate to attempt to take figures produced by intelligence tests in one case and to apply them slavishly to another in order to define some sort of rigid and unswerving line, the crossing of which leads automatically to the exclusion of confession evidence. Each case has to be looked at on its own facts: *R* v *Kenny* (1993) The Times 27 July.

An independent person is someone who is not a police officer or a person employed for or engaged on police purposes: also s77(3). Special constables, police cadets undergoing training and civilians employed by the police are all engaged in police purposes: Police Act 1964 s64. In summary, an independent person is someone who is not a police officer either on a permanent or a temporary basis and is not employed by the police force.

The use of inadmissible confessions

The police sometimes find valuable evidence as a result of following-up information given to them by an accused person. If he gives that information in the course of a confession which is ruled inadmissible, s76(4)(a) allows the prosecution to use any evidence discovered as a result of the confession. For example, if the accused charged with murder is tortured and tells the police that the knife he used in the killing is in his garden shed, evidence may be called about the finding of the knife even though the confession itself may not be used. The prosecution may not, however, refer to the confession: s76(5); cf *Lam Chi-ming* v *R* [1991] 3 All ER 172. In the example just given, this prevents them from saying why they were looking in the shed. If only part of the confession is inadmissible, and it is that part which caused the knife to be found, no reference may be made to that part: s76(6)(b).

To extend the example further, there may be cases where the accused gives evidence, or calls a witness who gives evidence, about the finding of the knife as a result of the inadmissible confession. This does not lead to the trial having to be abandoned and the jury discharged, because s76(5) specifically states that evidence that a fact was discovered as a result of an inadmissible confession is admissible if it is given by the defendant or is given on his behalf.

An inadmissible confession may be useful in another way. Section 76(4)(b) provides that where it is relevant that the accused speaks, writes or expresses himself in a particular way, an inadmissible confession may be used if necessary to show how he speaks, writes or expresses himself. This is a limited provision because it only allows so much of the confession to be used as it is necessary to use and it only allows the confession to be used if it is necessary to use it. If other evidence is available, that other evidence should be used.

Section 76(4)(b) would apply where, for example, it is in issue whether a document was written by the accused and the only available evidence of his handwriting is his signature at the bottom of a confession statement or his writing in the body of the statement. The statement should be edited so as to exclude any material which would suggest to the jury that it is a confession – it should be presented simply as an example of his handwriting. Where it is not possible to edit the statement so as to exclude material which is adverse to the accused, the judge may exercise his discretion under s78 to prevent the prosecution from using the confession at all.

Normally, a defendant may not be questioned about his confession once it has been ruled inadmissible: *Treacy* [1944] 2 All ER 229. Thus, ss4 and 5 of the Criminal Procedure Act 1865, which allow cross-examination about previous inconsistent statements, do not apply where the previous inconsistent statement is an inadmissible confession. But this is subject to an exception in that one defendant is allowed to cross-examine another about a previous inconsistent statement no matter how it was made. In *Rowson* [1986] QB 174 one defendant gave evidence which was inconsistent with what he had said in a confession which the judge had ruled to be inadmissible. A co-defendant was allowed to cross-examine him about the confession in order to show his inconsistency. The Court of Appeal upheld this ruling, holding that once one defendant has said something inconsistent with a previous statement made by him he may be freely cross-examined about his inconsistency. In fact the Court of Appeal went further than the trial judge because he imposed restrictions on the cross-examination. The Court of Appeal followed a dictum from Lord Donovan in *Murdoch v Taylor* [1965] AC 574 and held that the only permissible restriction was that cross-examination should not deal with matters which are irrelevant to any issue in the case. The decision in *Rowson* was approved by the Privy Council in *Lui Mei Lin v R* [1989] 2 WLR 175.

Where one defendant's confession has been used by a co-defendant, as in *Rowson*, the jury must be directed not to treat the confession itself as evidence against its maker save in so far as it shows him to have been inconsistent.

6.3 Res gestae

In chapter 4 the question whether evidence admitted as part of the res gestae was hearsay evidence was considered in relation to each example of such evidence given in that chapter. Reference should be made to chapter 4 for this discussion.

6.4 Declarations by persons now dead

Dying declarations

Where a defendant is tried for murder or manslaughter, evidence may be given of a statement made by the deceased about the cause of his death provided certain conditions are fulfilled. Almost always the statement will be an identification of the defendant as the killer, but this is not necessarily so. For example, in *Scaife* (1836) 1 Mood & R 551 a declaration that the deceased had provoked the defendant was admissible for the accused.

This exception to the hearsay rule derived from days when the courts could safely presume that someone who thought he was about to die would not say anything other than the truth for fear of going to hell. Today such a presumption would not necessarily be drawn, nevertheless the rule remains. The basis for it is clear from the following words of Eyre CJ in *Woodcock* (1789) 1 Leach 500 which were approved by the Court of Criminal Appeal in *Perry* [1909] 2 KB 697:

> 'The general principle on which this species of evidence is admitted is, that they are declarations made in extremis, when the party is at the point of death, and when every hope in this world is gone: when every motive to falsehood is silenced, and the mind is induced by the most powerful considerations to speak the truth; a situation so solemn, and so awful, is considered by the law as creating an obligation equal to that which is imposed by a positive oath administered in a court of justice.'

The conditions which must be fulfilled are four in total. First, the declarant must have expected to die and must have had no hope of recovery at the time he made his statement. This is the requirement of a 'settled hopeless expectation' of death. In *Jenkins* (1869) LR 1 CCR 187 the declarant identified her assailant and said that she had no hope of recovery 'at present'. This disallowed hearsay evidence of her identification because her expectation of death was not hopeless. That the expectation of death holds out no hope for recovery does not mean that the deceased must believe that he is going to die immediately provided he believes that his death is not far away. Evidence of other things said by the declarant are admissible on the question whether his expectation of death was hopeless: see *Spilsbury* (1835) 7 C & P 187.

The second condition is that the declarant would be a competent witness had he or she lived. In *Pike* (1829) 3 C & P 598 the declaration was inadmissible because the declarant was aged only four. If live evidence of the declarant would have required a corroboration warning, such a warning should be given about his declaration: *Austin* (1929) 8 Cr App R 27. The Privy Council held in *Nembhard* v *R* [1982] 1 All ER 183 that there is no requirement for a corroboration warning simply because the only evidence against the accused is a dying declaration. But, because dying declarations usually involve identification it may be necessary for the judge to direct the jury in accordance with the well-established principles about identification evidence which are discussed in detail in Chapter 11.

Thirdly, the declaration must not have been obtained by the asking of leading questions: *Mitchell* (1892) 17 Cox CC 503. The fourth and final condition is that the statement must have been complete. In *Waugh* v *R* [1950] AC 203 the declarant fell into a coma while describing how he was attacked; the Privy Council held evidence of the declaration to be inadmissible.

The extension of the res gestae doctrine in *Blastland* and *Andrews* effectively prevents it being necessary to satisfy the strict requirements of the dying declaration cases in many cases. But, unless the statement was made almost immediately after the attack it will not count as part of the res gestae and the conditions set out above will have to be satisfied.

Declarations of public or general rights

Evidence of a statement that it was reputed that a public or general right existed may be given where it is in issue whether such a right did exist. A public right is one which may be enjoyed by any person, for example a public right to use a footpath. A general right is a right which may be enjoyed by any member of a class, such a right of the inhabitants of a village to graze sheep on particular land.

The declaration must have been made by someone who could be expected to have had knowledge of the existence of the right and who would themselves have been entitled to exercise it if it existed: *Duke of Newcastle* v *Hundred of Broxtowe* (1832) 4 B & Ald 273. The declaration must have been made before any dispute about the right existed: *Moseley* v *Davies* (1822) 11 Price 162.

Only general statements about the right may be repeated under this hearsay exception, not statements about particular facts. Statements which show that a public or general right was reputed to exist are admissible but statements that show that certain individuals acted as though the right existed are not. In *Bliss* (1837) 7 A & E 550 the statement by someone that he had planted a tree to mark the boundary of a road was not admissible to prove that the road was a public road. It was evidence of a particular act by a person which was consistent with the road being a public road, but it was equally consistent with the person being mistaken or the road being open to only certain people. Similarly, in *Earl Dunraven* v *Llewellyn* (1850) 19 LJ QB 388 the question arose whether a number of tenants of the lord of the manor had a right of common over certain ground. Statements by certain tenants that they exercised such a right were not admissible because they were statements consistent with there being a number of individual rights and not necessarily a general right. In *Mercer* v *Denne* [1905] 2 Ch 538 documents which asserted usage of a seashore for the drying of nets by fishermen were not admissible to establish a general right because they did not establish a reputation that there was a public or general right to do so.

Section 9(4)(c) of the Civil Evidence Act 1968 retains this little used common law exception to the hearsay rule in cases covered by that Act.

Declarations in the course of duty

Oral or written statements or records made by someone in the course of a duty are admissible provided he was under a duty to state or record exactly the facts which he did state or record. In *Price* v *Earl of Torrington* (1703) 1 Salk 285 a written record of deliveries compiled by a drayman was admissible to prove the truth of what he had written because he was under a duty in the course of his employment to record deliveries he had made, and he was dead. Only first-hand hearsay is admissible under this rule: *Brain* v *Preece* (1843) 11 M & W 773.

In *Smith* v *Blakey* (1867) LR 2 QB 326 it was held that the duty of the deceased must have been to do a particular act and then to report about it to another or to make a written record of it. That other person's oral evidence or that written record were admissible to prove that the act was done. If one person reported that he had done an act which he was legally obliged to do and report, and the person to whom he reported wrote it down, the written record would not be admissible unless countersigned by the person whose act it describes: *Price* v *Earl of Torrington*. It is only those parts of a statement by the deceased which he was under a duty to make that are admissible under this rule. In *Chambers* v *Bernasconi* (1834) 3 LJ Exch 373 a police officer's record of when and where he arrested someone was admissible only so far as it said when the arrest took place, because he was under no duty to record where he made it.

There is an additional requirement for the admission of evidence of such declarations in criminal cases. It is that the statement, whether it be an oral report or a written record, must be contemporaneous or nearly contemporaneous with the act which was done. In *The Henry Coxon* (1878) 3 PD 156 records compiled two days after the events to which they referred were not admissible. In civil cases in the High Court and County Courts the common law has been superseded by s2(1) of the Civil Evidence Act 1968.

Declarations against interest

Hearsay evidence may be given of a statement which was against the financial or proprietary interest of the maker at the time it was made provided he is dead at the time it is repeated in court. This exception to the hearsay rule has much in common with the law on admissions, but is subject to several technical restrictions on admissibility which do not apply where the declarant is himself a party to the case.

In *Higham* v *Ridgway* (1808) 10 East 109 an entry in a book kept by a midwife in which he recorded that he had been paid for his services was admissible to prove that he had been paid. It was also evidence of the date of birth of the child because that was all part of the same entry and it qualified and explained the statement that the midwife had been paid.

Declarations against proprietary interest are only evidence against persons who derive their title from the declarant. In *Papendick* v *Bridgwater* (1855) 24 LJ QB 289 a tenant's declaration that he did not have a right of pasture was not admissible against his landlord, whereas it was said, obiter, that if the litigation had involved a sub-tenant or assignee of the tenant the declaration would have been admissible against that party.

6.5 Self-serving statements

Introduction

The general inadmissibility of hearsay evidence prevents a party from giving hearsay evidence about what a non-witness in the case has asserted. But the rule also prevents a party from giving or calling evidence about what a witness has asserted unless the assertion is contradicted by the witness in court. Witnesses who have made previous inconsistent statements may be cross-examined about them under the provisions of the Criminal Procedure Act 1865 ss4 and 5: see, for example, *R* v *Funderburk* [1990] 1 WLR 587. There are no equivalent statutory rules allowing the giving in evidence of previous consistent statements.

Evidence of statements which are admissible as part of the res gestae are admissible on behalf of a party whom they favour just as much as such statements which go against one party may be called by the other. We have seen the present limits of the res gestae rules and it is not proposed to repeat the discussion here.

The rule excluding repetition of previous consistent statements, otherwise known as self-serving statements, is conventionally referred to as the rule against narrative. The reason for the embargo on self-serving statements is that it adds little to the weight of the evidence and may involve a considerable waste of court time. The rule is the same in civil and criminal cases and applies alike to the parties when giving evidence and to their witnesses. In *Corke* v *Corke and Cooke* [1958] P 93 a wife accused of adultery in divorce proceedings gave evidence that when her husband found her in the bedroom with their lodger she telephoned the doctor to get him to examine her to ascertain whether she and the lodger had had sexual intercourse. The Court of Appeal held that evidence of the telephone call was inadmissible because it was evidence of an assertion made by the wife that she did not commit adultery and was given by her in order to prove its truth. A good example from the criminal courts is *Roberts* [1942] 1 All ER 187 in which the accused's defence to a charge of murder of a girl was that he shot her by accident in that his gun fired while he was cleaning it. He was not allowed to call his father to give evidence that he had said it was an accident shortly after the shooting happened.

Not only can the rule against self-serving statements be said to be based on the general prohibition against hearsay evidence, but it can also be said to be derived from the rule against self-corroboration. In *Fox* v *General Medical Council* [1960] 1 WLR 1017 the Privy Council recognised that to allow a witness's evidence to be supported by evidence that he had said the same thing on occasions outside court as he said on oath in court adds little to his veracity, because that is best judged by the way he reacts to cross-examination.

There are some occasions, however, on which it is relevant to show that the witness has been consistent, either because of the nature of the case or because of the way it has been conducted. One such occasion which arises most frequently in criminal cases is where a witness has identified the accused as being the offender. This is dealt with in chapter 11. The other three occasions on which self-serving statements are admissible are where someone has made complaint of a sexual assault, where it is alleged that a witness has invented his evidence at a particular time, and certain limited cases where the accused has been questioned.

Complaints in sexual cases

In every case where a person is accused of a sexual offence, whether against a female or a male, evidence is admissible that the 'victim' complained of it at the first reasonable opportunity. In *Lillyman* [1896] 2 QB 167 the defendant was charged with attempted rape and indecent assault against a 16-year-old girl. She gave evidence of what occurred and the Crown was allowed to call evidence from the girl's employer that the girl had reported the matter to her shortly after the assault was alleged to have happened. The employer was allowed to say not just that a complaint had been made, but also the terms in which it was made. The Court for Crown Cases Reserved upheld the trial judge's ruling, holding that evidence that such a complaint had been made was always relevant because it enabled the jury to assess the credibility of the complainant as a witness.

Where consent is in issue the fact of the complaint having been made can take on special significance, particularly when it is borne in mind that corroboration of the complainant is required as a matter of practice where a sexual offence is alleged. But whether or not consent is in issue, evidence of the complaint may be given: see, eg, *R* v *Osborne* [1905] 1 KB 551.

In both of the cases cited so far the complainant was female. But the same rule applies to trials where someone is accused of a sexual offence committed against a male. For example, in *Camelleri* [1922] 2 KB 122 the allegation was of indecency with a boy of 16. There is no clear authority that the same rule applies to complaints made by grown men, although in *Wannell* (1923) 17 Cr App R 53 the male complainant was 19 and the Court of Criminal Appeal held that evidence of his complaint was admissible.

In order for evidence about it to be admissible, the complaint must have been made at the first reasonable opportunity. Whether this is so in any case involves consideration of not only the time lapse between the alleged offence and the complaint but also of whether the complainant had an opportunity to make a complaint at any earlier time: see, eg, *R* v *Cummings* [1948] 1 All ER 551.

Evidence of a complaint is not itself evidence that the facts complained of occurred, so it is not admitted as an exception to the hearsay rule. Its use is two-fold. First, it is evidence that the complainant has been consistent, and secondly, it may be considered by the jury to be inconsistent with consent where that is in issue. It follows from this that if the complainant does not given evidence, the person to whom she complained may not give evidence with a view to showing the complainant's consistency, because her consistency or inconsistency is not in issue. In both *Brasier* (1779) 1 Leach 199 and *Wallwork* (1958) 42 Cr App R 153 the defendant was charged with indecent assaults of various kinds on young girls. The girls concerned did not give evidence about what happened, although the girl in *Wallwork* was called as a witness. It was held that evidence of their complaints should not have been given because it could only have been relevant to their credibility, yet that was not an issue unless they gave evidence.

There is no authority in which evidence of a complaint has been given where consent is in issue despite the complainant not giving evidence. In principle evidence of the complaint would be admissible because, as was held in *Lillyman*, the fact that a complaint was made shortly after the incident complained of may be considered by the jury to be relevant as showing lack of consent. Almost inevitably, however, a prosecution based on absence of consent to an admitted act will be in difficulties if the 'victim' concerned does not give evidence himself or herself.

Fabrication of evidence

It is sometimes alleged in cross-examination that a witness has invented the whole or part of his evidence and that it is false. Such an allegation does not of itself allow the party calling the witness to try to support the evidence by proof that he has said the same thing at some time in the past. However, if the allegation is more specific and asserts that the evidence was fabricated at a particular time or after a particular time, evidence to rebut such an assertion may be given.

This is often said to be the rule allowing a self-serving statement to rebut an allegation of 'recent fabrication'. The use of 'recent' is misleading. In *Oyesiku* (1971) 56 Cr App R 240 the defendant was charged with assaulting a police officer. His wife made a statement about the assault in which she said that the officer started the fight. This was also the husband's account of events. It was put to her in cross-examination that she invented this story after having seen her husband in custody. The Court of Appeal held the trial judge to have been wrong to refuse the defence leave to adduce her original statement. The statement was made before she saw her husband and this proved that the allegation put to her in cross-examination was not correct. It could not properly be said that the allegation that Mrs Oyesiku invented her story when visiting her husband was in any way a 'recent' fabrication.

Nevertheless, because a specific time at which it was alleged the story was invented was put in issue, her previous statement was admissible.

That a witness has been consistent does not mean that he is truthful. But if it is specifically alleged that he invented his evidence on or after a particular time, that allegation may be rebutted. The previous statement is admissible in its entirety. The jury is not restricted to hearing that a statement was made which is consistent with what is said in court; they may see the written statement or hear it being repeated if it was made orally. The previous statement is not evidence of its truth, merely evidence of the consistency of the witness. It is for the jury to decide what weight they give the oral evidence, and if they believe the whole thing is an invention they will decide the case accordingly, because a witness does not become truthful by repeating a lie on two or more occasions.

In *Oyesiku* the Court of Appeal approved the following dictum from *Nominal Defendant* v *Clements* (1961) 104 CLR 476:

'If the credit of a witness is impugned as to some material fact to which he deposes upon the ground that his account is a late invention or has been lately devised or reconstructed, even though not with conscious dishonesty, that makes admissible a statement to the same effect as the account he gave as a witness, if it was made by the witness contemporaneously with the event or at a time sufficiently early to be inconsistent with the suggestion that his account is a late invention or reconstruction.'

In civil cases a previous consistent statement may be used to rebut an allegation of recent fabrication: *Fox* v *General Medical Council*. Section 3 of the Civil Evidence Act 1968 provides that a statement admitted for this purpose is admissible as evidence of the truth of assertions contained in it.

Statement by the accused

It is common practice for a jury to be given copies of a transcript of the defendant's interview or interviews with the police. The most common occasion when this will not happen is where he refused to answer questions, or answered all questions with an answer which made clear that he was not prepared to give any information, such as 'No comment' or 'My solicitor has told me not to answer questions'. In addition, however, some interviews are inadmissible where they are purely self-serving.

Where the interview contains admissions the jury may hear about it by virtue of the common law and statutory rules examined in the first two parts of this chapter. Many interviews contain some admissions and some self-serving answers. In such cases the whole statement should be put before the jury. If they were to hear of admissions without seeing the context in which they were made a misleading impression could be obtained. Not only must the jury hear of the whole statement, but they may treat it all as evidence of its truth. This is a fairly recent principle and is a new exception to the hearsay rule.

In the past judges had to direct juries that where, for example, evidence was given that a defendant said in interview 'I stabbed him but he provoked me', the words 'I stabbed him' were evidence that he did stab the victim but the words 'but he provoked me' were not evidence of provocation. This was of particular significance where the defendant did not give evidence and no suggestion of provocation was made otherwise than in the interview. In such a case there would be no evidence of provocation and the judge would not have to leave that issue to the jury, the evidential burden not having been satisfied by the calling of some evidence to make it a live issue.

This was an absurd exercise because it was only in rare cases that a jury could be expected to fully understand what the judge meant when he said that some parts of the interview were evidence of their truth whereas others were not. In *Duncan* (1981) 73 Cr App R 359 the Court of Appeal held that a 'mixed' statement, containing some admissions and some self-serving statements, could all be left to the jury to make what they would of it. In appropriate cases the judge will be entitled to direct them that the admissions are likely to be true but that the self-serving parts may have been an invention by the accused to try to save his skin. In *Duncan* the accused admitting hitting his wife with a hammer but claimed to have been provoked. He did not give evidence and the question arose whether the judge should have directed the jury to consider provocation. The only evidence which made any reference to provocation was the hearsay evidence of what was said in interview. The Court of Appeal held that the judge should have directed the jury to consider provocation because all parts of a mixed statement were admissible as evidence of their truth. The House of Lords approved *Duncan* in *Sharp* [1988] 1 WLR 7, without laying down any qualifications or exceptions to what the Court of Appeal said in the earlier case.

In other circumstances a purely self-serving statement by a defendant may be admissible. The first such case is where the statement is given in order to show the reaction of the accused on first being accused. This overlaps to some extent with what was said above about admissions by conduct. If someone is accused of an offence and accepts that he committed it, what his reaction to the charge is may be repeated in court because it is an admission: see, eg, *R v Pearce* (1979) 69 Cr App R 365.

At first sight it is rather difficult to see how this fits in with the common law on admission. In *Christie*, the House of Lords held that if the defendant accepted the truth of an allegation made to him, evidence about it may be given, whereas if he did not accept its truth, the fact that the allegation was made may not be repeated in court. But *Christie* was a case where the allegation in question was not the first allegation. *Pearce* holds that the defendant's reaction when first accused is always relevant and it is a matter entirely for the jury what inferences they draw from it. Thus *Pearce* is not inconsistent with *Christie*. The first allegation may be made by the police or by someone else. In either event, his first reaction is relevant.

The time when the answers given in interview by the accused are not admissible is when those answers are wholly self-serving and the interview is not the first time accusations were made. For example, in *Newsome* (1980) 71 Cr App R 325 the defendant was interviewed three times about an allegation of rape. He then made a written statement to the police in which he gave a full explanation that intercourse took place but was consensual. The prosecution did not give evidence of this statement and on the defendant's application to be allowed to give evidence about it the trial judge ruled that it was inadmissible because it was wholly self-serving. The Court of Appeal held that the trial judge was correct. They applied *Pearce* in which it was said:

> '... there may be a rare occasion when an accused produces a carefully prepared written statement to the police, with a view to it being made part of the prosecution evidence. The trial judge would plainly exclude such a statement as inadmissible.'

Pearce and *Newsome* were applied by the Court of Appeal in *Tooke* (1989) 90 Cr App R 417. It was held that a full self-serving statement which was not relevant to show the accused's reaction when first accused of the offence was inadmissible. His first reaction was proved by other evidence, so the answers given in interview did not take matters any further.

Self-serving statements made to people other than the police are not admissible unless they are in answer to the first allegation of the offence. In *Steel* (1981) 73 Cr App R 173 the defendant confessed to the police and then saw his solicitor in private and told him the confession was false. And in *Kurshid* [1984] Crim LR 288 the defendant told his solicitor that he was going to make a false confession in order to obtain bail, then confessed guilt to the police. In neither case was the solicitor allowed to repeat what he had been told. Both statements were purely self-serving. Had the defendants made those statements during the course of their interviews they would have been admissible because they would have placed the answers given in interview in context. The strictness of these decisions could be unfair in extreme cases, but the defendant can always give evidence about why he confessed and the jury should be able to assess his truthfulness without having to hear that he had previously given an explanation to his solicitor.

6.6 Public documents

Definition

Statements made in public documents are admissible as evidence of their truth without the compiler of the document having to give evidence. Public documents take several forms but there is no list of documents which are public, rather any document which fits the following definition is a public document. The document must be a record of information about matters affecting the public and which has been compiled by someone acting under a public duty to record that information. This definition comes from *Sturla* v *Freccia* (1880) 5 App Cas 623 in which the House of Lords held that a report compiled by a committee of the Genoese government in which the age of a person was stated, was not admissible to prove that person's age. The report was not available for public inspection, was not compiled under any duty to record the person's age and was not intended to be retained. It was therefore inadmissible on the issue of his age.

Many examples of public documents can be given, such as registers of births, marriages and deaths, registers of electors, reports of official enquiries, Ordnance Survey maps, Public General Acts of Parliament, Statutory Instruments, Royal Proclamations and declarations of war. In fact, any document which satisfies the *Sturla* v *Freccia* definition is a public document.

Evidential value

Public documents are admissible evidence of the truth of facts stated in them: Civil Evidence Act 1968 s9(2)(c), *Irish Society* v *Bishop of Derry* (1846) 12 Cl & F 641. But they are not conclusive evidence of the truth of assertions they contain. An entry in the register of marriages is not conclusive proof that the people named in it are validly married.

It is not necessary to use the original of a public document; any copy which is certified to be a true copy may be used. Many statutes make special provision for the admission in evidence of copies of certain public documents. For example, s2 of the Documentary Evidence Act 1868 provides that a Statutory Instrument may be proved by a copy printed by HMSO, s9(2) of the Public Records Act 1958 allows a public record to be proved by a certified copy of the entry in the record, entries in the registers of birth and death may be proved by a certified copy of the register (Births and Deaths Registration Act 1953 s34(6)), and marriage can be proved by a certified copy of an entry on the register of marriages: Marriage Act 1949 s65(3).

Where no statute specifically provides for the proof of the contents of a public document by production of a certified copy of it, s14 of the Evidence Act 1851 allows proof by these means.

6.7 Reference works

Definition

Works which are written or compiled for public reference will only be public documents if they satisfy the criteria set out in *Sturla* v *Freccia*. Many reference works, however, are not compiled under any public duty and therefore are not public documents. Obvious examples include dictionaries and maps.

A book which claims to be an authoritative reference work may contain comment and analysis rather than a simple recitation of fact. In order to ensure that the work is an authoritative statement of fact rather than of opinion, evidence may be received about the qualifications and experience of the author.

Admissibility

The courts are able to make reference to authoritative works and to take judicial notice of their contents. Modern examples include the meaning of the word 'or' as defined in Fowler's Modern English Usage (*R* v *Agricultural Land Tribunal (South Western Province) ex p Benney* [1955] 2 QB 140) and the meaning of 'oppression' in the Oxford English Dictionary: *Fulling*.

Section 9(2)(b) of the Civil Evidence Act 1968 retains the right of the court to consult works of reference in civil proceedings.

7

Character

7.1 Similar fact evidence in criminal cases

The meaning and significance of character

When the jury or magistrates have to decide between the case presented by the prosecution and that presented by the defence they may approach the comparison in various ways depending upon what the issues are in the case and how the evidence has been presented. Sometimes their task is simple because the version of events given by one side's witnesses is obviously ridiculous and falls of its own volition. Generally, however, the court must compare the performance of witnesses, asking itself whether witnesses called by the same side contradicted each other, and whether they seemed from their demeanour in the witness box to be truthful.

We have already seen that witnesses may be asked about their criminal record pursuant to s3 of the Criminal Procedure Act 1865. Cross-examination about the character of a witness is designed to undermine his truthfulness by inviting the court to say that it cannot rely on him to tell the truth. Whether such a conclusion should be drawn depends on the nature of the convictions. If they are for offences of dishonesty it may be a proper conclusion to draw that the witness's evidence should be treated with circumspection. But offences of assault may not indicate much about his truthfulness unless he gave evidence in the previous proceedings and his evidence was rejected. There are, in fact, no rules of law about what conclusions should be drawn from the fact that a witness has convictions, nor about whether

174

different convictions should be treated in different ways. But it is inevitable that the more dishonest he appears from his record the more likely it is that his evidence will be undermined by that record.

Someone's character involves more than his criminal record, it also includes his conduct and reputation. Cross-examination about these matters is not subject to statutory rules, except where cross-examination of the accused is concerned. A police officer giving evidence in a criminal trial could be asked about another case in which he gave evidence against the same defendant but in which the accused was acquitted. Similarly, a witness could be asked about his reputation for being a liar. Whether this sort of cross-examination is possible depends upon the circumstances of each case. But the character of a witness is always relevant if it affects his credibility.

Section 3 does not apply to the defendant because of the risk that a court which hears that he has criminal convictions may infer that he is more likely to be guilty of the offence with which he is charged than he would be if he had no record. Indeed, the same point applies to any questions about the accused's bad character. We will see later in this chapter that in some circumstances the defendant may be asked about his convictions and other aspects of his character due to the provisions of the Criminal Evidence Act 1898. That Act governs the position where the defendant gives evidence. If he does not give evidence his record is generally of no significance at all because his truthfulness as a witness is not in issue.

The basic rule

In some limited circumstances the defendant's character assists the court in deciding his guilt or innocence. But in general it does not. Not only does this mean that he may not be asked about his convictions or other bad character, it also means that evidence may not be given about his character as part of the prosecution case.

The basis of this rule is the following dictum from Lord Herschell LC in *Makin v A-G for New South Wales* [1894] AC 57:

> 'It is undoubtedly not competent for the prosecution to adduce evidence tending to show that the accused has been guilty of criminal acts other than those covered by the indictment, for the purpose of leading to the conclusion that the accused is a person likely from his criminal conduct or character to have committed the offence for which he is being tried.'

This dictum was cited in many cases after 1894 and was last authoritatively approved by the House of Lords in *DPP v Boardman* [1975] AC 421, which is examined and discussed below.

The exception

The basic rule stated by Lord Herschell is subject to an exception which he described in general terms. Immediately following the above dictum, he said,

'On the other hand, the mere fact that the evidence adduced tends to show the commission of other crimes does not render it inadmissible if it be relevant to an issue before the jury, and it may be so relevant if it bears upon the question whether the acts alleged to constitute the crime charged in the indictment were designed or accidental, or to rebut a defence which would otherwise be open to the accused.'

In other words the general rule against evidence of the accused's bad character being put before the court does not apply where his character is relevant to his guilt. Lord Herschell did not refer to 'bad character' as that phrase is used today, instead he referred to evidence which tends to show the commission of other crimes. This is wide enough to cover not just evidence of the defendant's previous convictions, but also evidence of other offences which he is alleged to have committed but for which he has not been tried.

Lord Herschell recognised two instances in which evidence of other offences may be relevant to guilt: first, where the defendant claims that the act of which complaint is made did take place but that it was an accident and, secondly, where the defendant puts forward some defence but his character shows that that defence is not open to him. In *Makin* v *A-G for New South Wales* Mr and Mrs Makin were accused of the murder of a child. The child had been left with the Makins by its mother who paid a fee for them to adopt it. The mother later returned and wanted her child back, but the Makins said that it had died. Its body was found buried in their garden. During the search of the garden by the police the bodies of several other young children were found. The prosecution discovered that those children had also been left for adoption and a fee paid to Mr and Mrs Makin. They were charged with the murder of one child only, the defence being that it had died of natural causes after an illness. The prosecution wished to prove the finding of the other bodies and the fact that the Makins had been paid to adopt them, in order to prove that the death was not of natural causes but was murder. The Privy Council held that this evidence was admissible because it was relevant to the issues which arose.

It was not said clearly what the relevance of the evidence was. But the second dictum of Lord Herschell cited above suggests that the relevance was that it rebutted the defence raised, that death occurred by natural causes. One could speculate about circumstances in which the evidence would probably not have been relevant. For example, if the defence had been that the child was run over by a train it would probably not be proper to prove the deaths of other adopted children. All that would be necessary would be expert medical evidence about the state of the body. Similarly, if the child's body had been dismembered in any way the defence of natural causes would almost certainly fail in any event. And if the causes of death of the other children were proved to have been by natural causes, it would not have assisted one way or the other on the question whether the relevant child died of natural or unnatural causes.

The facts of the *Makin* case illustrate two important points about this area of the law. First, there was no direct evidence that any of the children were murdered, that was simply an inference which could have been, and was, drawn by the jury. The evidence was not direct evidence that the defendants had committed other offences, but was circumstantial evidence from which it could be concluded that they had engaged in a course of criminal conduct with a view to profit – to adopt children, receive fees and then kill them, thereby not having to incur expenses. Lord Herschell's dictum applies not just to direct evidence of other offences, but also to indirect or circumstantial evidence of other offences having been committed. Secondly, the admissibility of evidence of other offences depends entirely upon the issues in the case in that the relevance of the evidence can only be judged by reference to the issues which arise for decision.

The evidence in *Makin* was not normally known as similar fact evidence. This is not always an appropriate term to use in cases governed by the dictum from *Makin*, but it is in almost universal usage. It is used whenever the prosecution wishes to prove that on one or more occasions other than that forming the subject-matter of the charge or charges, the accused has acted in a way similar to that alleged in the charge or charges.

Two questions remained unanswered by *Makin* v *A-G for New South Wales:* how does the rule apply to evidence of the defendant's character which does not disclose the commission of offences, and what degree of relevance is required before the evidence is admissible? The first of these questions will be answered immediately, and the second after the subsequent House of Lords cases have been examined.

Evidence other than commission of offences

In *Thompson* [1918] AC 221 the appellant was charged with offences of indecency towards small boys. Evidence was allowed that he was homosexual and that he possessed, amongst other things, indecent photographs and powder puffs. This evidence did not prove either directly or indirectly that he had committed any offences, it merely proved his sexual disposition.

The issue in the case was whether the appellant was the man who had committed acts of gross indecency in a public lavatory three days prior to Thompson's arrest. The man who committed the offences arranged to meet the boys at the same place three days later and at the appointed time and place the appellant turned up. The issue was one of identity because the appellant's defence was that it was pure coincidence that he turned up at the agreed time. In that context evidence of the defendant's sexual predeliction for young boys was held to be relevant to rebut the suggestion that it was just coincidence that he arrived at the time arranged by the offender.

The subsequent cases

The House of Lords has had four opportunities to consider the rules on similar fact evidence since the decision in *Makin* v *A-G for New South Wales*. The first was *Ball*

[1911] AC 47 in which a brother and sister were charged with incest. The House of Lords applied the law as stated by Lord Herschell in *Makin* and held that evidence was admissible that they had a child two years before the date on which they were alleged to have committed incest. The evidence was held to be relevant because it proved 'the existence of a sexual passion between them' (per Lord Loreburn LC). This case did not refine the law in any way, it simply accepted that Lord Herschell's dictum was correct and represented English law.

In *Thompson*, to which reference has already been made, the speeches in the House were concerned specifically with the evidence in the case, and not with stating general principles applicable in other cases. Lord Parker said that the decision in that appeal should not be treated as laying down any principle capable of general application. But in the only fully reasoned speech in the case, by Lord Sumner, it was recognised that a jury may be prejudiced against an accused by hearing that he has committed other offences or that he has a disposition towards a particular type of crime. The prejudice referred to takes the form of the jury jumping to the conclusion that the accused is guilty because of his criminal record or his disposition. Lord Summer said that because of this risk of prejudice the prosecution is not normally allowed to call such evidence, but that it may do so where it is relevant to an issue in the case. But whether it is relevant to an issue depends, of course, on what the issues are. Lord Sumner said that a plea of not guilty does not raise all potential defences, so that the prosecution is not entitled to rely on potentially prejudicial evidence unless it is relevant to the defence raised by the accused.

The major importance of *Harris* v *DPP* [1952] AC 694 is that it develops the analysis of the part prejudice plays in similar fact evidence. The appellant was charged with eight theft offences committed over a period of time in a market. He was a policeman who was on duty at the market on the occasion of the eighth theft, but not when the previous seven were committed. He was convicted only on the eighth count. The judge directed the jury that they could consider the evidence on the first seven counts when deciding whether the eighth was proved. The House of Lords held this to be a misdirection. The issues were first, whether there was a theft on the relevant date and secondly, if so, was Harris the thief? On the first issue evidence on the first seven counts did not help one way or the other. On the second issue the fact that he was acquitted on the first seven counts made clear that he did not commit any offence on those occasions, therefore the jury should have been told that the evidence on the first seven counts could only possibly have been relevant if he was convicted of those counts. The appeal was allowed because the trial judge did not direct the jury to discount the evidence on the first seven counts unless they were satisfied of his guilt on those charges. The House did not hold that the evidence on the first seven counts would have been admissible had the jury been satisfied of his guilt on those occasions, because it was not necessary to do so in order to determine the appeal.

Viscount Simon cited Lord Sumner's dictum about prejudice saying:

'Evidence of similar facts involving the accused ought not to be dragged in to his prejudice without reasonable cause.'

He then described when there would be reasonable cause to adduce similar facts evidence.

'A criminal trial in this country is conducted for the purpose of deciding whether the prosecution has proved that the accused is guilty of the particular crime charged, and evidence of "similar facts" should be excluded unless such evidence has a really material bearing on the issues to be decided.'

Viscount Simon also referred to the rule of practice requiring a judge to disallow reliance on admissible evidence if its probable effect would be out of proportion to its true evidential value. This rule of practice is examined in more detail in chapter 12. Its relevance to the present chapter is that the judge must disallow prejudicial evidence unless it is so probative of his guilt that the prejudice is outweighed. *Harris v DPP* marks a significant advance in the law because for the first time the House of Lords brought together the need for similar fact evidence to be probative on one or more of the issues in the case, and the need for the judge to consider the overall effect of the evidence on the jury.

These principles were drawn together and fully explained in *DPP v Boardman* [1975] AC 421. The appellant, the headmaster of a school, was convicted of buggery of one boy and of inciting another boy to bugger him. The trial judge ruled that the evidence in relation to each boy was relevant to the charge relating to the other. The House of Lords upheld this ruling. The facts of the case are examined in a little more detail below. Lord Wilberforce summed up the principles as follows,

'Whether in the field of sexual conduct or otherwise, there is no general or automatic answer to be given to the question whether evidence of facts similar to those the subject of a particular charge ought to be admitted. In each case it is necessary to estimate (i) whether, and if so how strongly, the evidence as to other facts tends to support, ie to make more credible, the evidence given as to the fact in question, (ii) whether such evidence, if given, is likely to be prejudicial to the accused. Both these elements involve questions of degree. It falls to the judge ... to estimate the respective and relative weight of these two factors and only to allow the evidence to be put before the jury if he is satisfied that the answer to the first question is clearly positive, and, on the assumption, which is likely, that the second question must be similarly answered, that on a combination of the two the interests of justice clearly require that the evidence be admitted.'

A shorthand re-statement of this principle is that the judge must weigh the probative force of similar fact evidence against its prejudicial effect and only allow it if it would not be unfair to the defendant to allow it to be given.

The types of similar fact evidence

Similar fact evidence only takes one form, although there are many variations of the form. The form it takes is of evidence that the defendant has acted in a particular way on an occasion other than the occasion which forms the subject-matter of the charge. In some cases the prosecution proves that the defendant has been convicted of an offence which bears similarity to the charge he faces. On other occasions it is proved that he has been accused of similar offences, and on others still it is proved that he is disposed to a particular type of activity whether or not he commits a crime by possessing that disposition.

The degree of prejudice to the defendant by proving his disposition is sometimes enormous, but this is justified where his disposition is of particular relevance. For example in *Straffen* [1952] 2 QB 911 the defendant was charged with the murder of a young girl. She had been strangled and her body was left in the open, there was no sexual interference and no sign of a struggle. Straffen was in the area where she was killed, having escaped from a nearby secure hospital. The question which arose for decision in the case was whether Straffen was the killer. He had previously killed two young girls in exactly the same way. The prosecution was allowed to prove that he had committed two identical offences in order to prove that it was Straffen who was the murderer on this occasion. Apart from a short discussion with a police officer on arrest in which the accused said something which could have been construed as an admission, the only evidence against Straffen was that he was in the vicinity. But that, of course, did not single him out as the killer any more than it pointed to any inhabitant of the local village being the offender. His disposition towards committing offences of the type charged was so unusual that it was contrary to common sense to suggest that there could have been another person in the area who would commit a murder in the same way. Therefore his disposition pointed to him being the killer. The conclusion which the jury was asked to draw was that Straffen committed an offence on this occasion because he had committed similar offences on previous occasions. Such a conclusion is not normally permissible, but there was such a remarkable similarity between the ways the two previous murders had been carried out and the way the offence for which he was tried was carried out that his disposition identified him as the killer.

Thompson was relied upon in *Straffen*, it being held by the Court of Criminal Appeal that Straffen's disposition towards a certain type of conduct identified him as the offender in the same way that Thompson's sexual taste for young boys identified him as the man who had approached the accusers previously.

In other cases there is no direct evidence of the disposition of the defendant, but the facts of the present case and of other incidents in his life make clear that he has committed the crime with which he is charged. The classic example of this is *Smith* (1915) 11 Cr App R 229, often known as the 'brides in the bath' case. A woman (M) went through a ceremony of marriage with Smith and made a will in his favour. She was taken to the doctor by Smith who told the doctor that she had been suffering from epileptic fits. She took a bath in a room which could not be locked and drowned in the bath. Medical experts were unable to give an explanation as to the way in which she met her death and Smith's explanation that she had probably met it by having a fit in the bath was initially persuasive. Evidence was given that subsequent to the death of M, two other women, B and L, met their deaths in identical mysterious circumstances shortly after they had gone through a ceremony of marriage with Smith. The Court of Criminal Appeal held that evidence of the subsequent deaths and all the circumstances surrounding them was admissible as evidence that Smith had killed M. He was not charged with or convicted of the murder of B or L, but the evidence about their deaths was admitted because it disproved the defence of accident which had been put forward in relation to M. In other words, to have lost one wife by drowning may have been misfortune, but to lose three in the same unusual way indicates a deliberate course of conduct.

Both *Straffen* and *Smith* have extraordinary facts. The issues in the cases were different, and the 'similar fact' evidence which was admitted was of a different type in each – in *Straffen* it was of other offences which the accused had been proved to have committed previously, in *Smith* it was of subsequent incidents affecting the defendant. But despite these differences there can be little doubt that the decisions were correct on the facts of the cases, and the fundamental reason why they are correct is that the evidence of other events in the defendants' lives was relevant to the issues which arose for decision. In *Smith* it was implicit that the defendant was being accused of the murder of B and L as well as that of M. It will be remembered that in *Boardman* there were two charges and the allegation made by each alleged victim was held relevant and admissible on the charge relating to the other. Like *Smith* the similar fact evidence took the form of allegation of other similar wrongdoing, but in *Boardman* that other wrongdoing formed the subject-matter of a charge, whereas in *Smith* it did not. This difference between the cases is not of any significance; they are both cases where similar fact evidence took the form of unproved allegations of wrongdoing.

There are some authorities in which the importance of looking at the issues which arise for decision by the jury when determining whether evidence of other incidents affecting the defendant is admissible, was overlooked. The practice grew of allowing similar fact evidence to be given as a matter of course where certain defences were raised or certain offences alleged. It is not necessary to investigate these in any detail because it was made clear in *Boardman* that it does not automatically follow that similar fact evidence may be used wherever certain defences are raised. But a few examples will illustrate how the law used to operate.

The old categories

Many similar fact cases involve allegations of homosexual activities or disposition. In *Thompson* Lord Sumner likened homosexuality to a physical attribute which differentiates one person from another such that if it is in question whether the defendant was the person who perpetrated a homosexual offence, the fact that he is of a homosexual disposition will always be relevant, and proof of that disposition will be admissible against him. The high point of this was *Sims* [1946] KB 531 in which the Court of Criminal Appeal held that in every case where the allegation is made of a homosexual offence the fact that the accused has homosexual propensities is admissible evidence against him. This approach gradually lost credence and was finally disposed of in *Boardman*. Now evidence of the accused's homosexual tendencies is only admissible where it is of sufficient relevance.

The second category is where it is alleged by the defence that something happened by accident, for example the death of M in the brides in the bath case, *Smith*. Indeed, *Makin v A-G for New South Wales* is also an 'accident' case. In *Makin* Lord Herschell said that evidence of the accused's disposition towards the type of offence charged may be admissible where the defence is accident.

In *Sims* evidence of the accused's homosexual propensity was admissible to rebut his defence of innocent association. He was alleged to have committed homosexual offences with four men on different occasions. He said that on each occasion he met the men but nothing improper occurred. There was no suggestion that the men had conspired together to concoct false evidence, so the Court of Criminal Appeal held that the evidence of each of the four men was admissible on every charge, not just on the charge relating to the man giving evidence, because of the inherent improbability that four men would make identical allegations if they were not all speaking the truth. In *Sims* the defence of innocent association took the form of a denial that the acts alleged had occurred. By contrast, in *Hall* [1952] 1 KB 302 the defence took the form of a denial of the mens rea of the crime alleged. Hall was charged with eight counts of gross indecency. His defence in relation to certain of the counts was that the acts complained of did occur but were part of a course of medical treatment which he was giving the men concerned. The Court of Criminal Appeal held that once the defence of innocent association was raised the Crown was entitled to call similar fact evidence. This rather bold statement illustrates the major difficulty with the law prior to *Boardman*. It says that the defence of innocent association is in some way special such that similar fact evidence is admissible whether or not that evidence really goes to disprove the defence.

The defence of mistake was held to allow similar fact evidence for the prosecution in *Francis* (1874) LR 2 CCR 128. The defendant was alleged to have said that a ring contained real diamonds in order to induce a pawnbroker to make a substantial advance using the ring as security for the loan. It was in fact worthless. The defence was that Francis did not know that the stones in the ring were not diamonds and was honestly mistaken when he asserted them to be diamonds. Evidence that he had previously made similar false statements in order to attempt to induce other pawnbrokers to make advances was held to be admissible to disprove the assertion of honest mistake. The reasoning behind the decision was that although someone might be mistaken once, it is unlikely that he would make the same mistake on several occasions. The Court for Crown Cases Reserved held the evidence of the other false statements to be admissible to show that the accused was operating a system of dishonest conduct.

The rejection of categorisation

In *Boardman* the House of Lords held that there are no special rules applicable to certain defences. It was held that in every case the court must examine the issues and ask whether the similar fact evidence which the Crown wishes to adduce goes to prove the crime alleged. The defence which is raised may make similar fact evidence admissible which would not be admissible if another defence were raised. But, it was held, it is not possible to categorise defences such that some automatically allow similar fact evidence. It was recognised that the categories which appellate courts had previously applied are illustrative of the most commonly occurring situations in which similar fact evidence is admitted, but it was stressed that each case must be looked at individually and the relevance of the similar fact evidence stressed.

Because similar fact evidence discloses material to a jury which they may consider to be more probative than it really is, the court should only admit it if its relevance is clearly such that unfair prejudice can be avoided. *Straffen* is a case where the prejudice which arose from the similar fact evidence was absolute but was also justified and therefore not unfair. The jury drew the conclusion that the defendant was guilty because of the way he had acted in the past, but because his behaviour was so unusual it identified him as the murderer and the conclusion of the jury was therefore justified. As we shall see below, the proper approach is to ask first whether the similar fact evidence is of any real probative value and then to consider whether it would be fair to allow it to be adduced.

Because the general rule is that the jury should not be told of the defendant's bad character, the admission of similar fact evidence is rare and must be justified by a high degree of relevance. Lord Wilberforce stated the principle in this way in *Boardman*:

> 'The basic principle must be that the admission of similar fact evidence (of the kind now in question) is exceptional and requires a strong degree of probative force. This probative force is derived, if at all, from the circumstance that the facts testified to by the several witnesses bear to each other such a striking similarity that they must, when judged by experience and common sense, either all be true, or have arisen from a cause common to all the witnesses or from pure coincidence.'

Boardman was a case where allegations were made by two boys about sexual misconduct on the part of a teacher. It was in that context that Lord Wilberforce's statement of principle was made. That is why he spoke of similar fact evidence 'of the kind now in question'. In such a case, whether each allegation helps to prove the truth of others depends upon whether it should properly be concluded that if one is true the other must also be true. The more peculiar the incident described by the witnesses the less chance there is of each having fabricated stories which by pure coincidence are identical. But the fabrication of identical and strange allegations by witnesses does not necessarily lead to the conclusion that they are both true because the witnesses concerned may have put their heads together and conspired to concoct false stories. As Lord Simon explained in *DPP* v *Kilbourne* [1973] AC 729, it is for the trial judge to ask himself whether he can discount the possibility of the witnesses having conspired. If he can, he must then ask himself whether the allegations being made bear such similarity to each other that a jury could properly conclude that if one is true they are both true.

It is when deciding whether there is sufficient similarity between the allegations being made by the witnesses that the judge has his most difficult task. As we have seen, Lord Wilberforce said the judge must look for 'striking similarity'. In the same case Lord Hailsham explained the test of admissibility in the following way:

> '... it is for the judge to ensure as a matter of law in the first place ... that a properly instructed jury, applying their minds to the facts, can come to the conclusion that they are satisfied so that they are sure that to treat the matter as pure coincidence by reason of the "nexus", "pattern" "system", "striking resemblance" or whatever phrase is used in an "affront to common sense" '.

This statement of principle is perhaps the clearest that there has ever been on the subject. Lord Hailsham made clear that it is a matter of law for the judge whether evidence of one allegation can be used by a jury when determining the truth of another. The way the judge must test admissibility is by asking whether the jury could decide that as a matter of common sense there is no possibility of the accusers having by pure coincidence made the same false allegation. The more strange the allegation which is made, the less chance there is of it having been invented by two or more witnesses independently of each other. Lord Hailsham went on to say, correctly, that the same principle must be applied where the similar fact evidence in question does not take the form of two or more witnesses making similar allegations. If it is alleged, for example, that the disposition of the accused to a particular form of conduct is relevant, the judge must ask whether a jury could say that it is pure coincidence that the defendant has that disposition and that he faces the charge in question.

Admissability of SFE *

Thus, the judge when ruling on the admissibility of similar fact evidence must ask two questions:

1. Can I rule out any possibility of similar fact evidence having been concocted – this is to be judged by investigating the circumstances in which the evidence came to light?
2. Can I rule out the possibility of it being a pure coincidence that the accused faces the charge in question and that the similar fact evidence in the case exists?

Once the judge has satisfied himself that he can answer both of these questions in the affirmative, the similar fact evidence is admissible. But he must then ask a third question, whether he should disallow the use of the similar fact evidence because it may be unduly prejudicial. It was clear in all speeches in *Boardman* that this discretion arises only once the judge is satisfied that the similar fact evidence is sufficiently probative to assist the jury in their deliberations. We have seen already that the 'prejudice' which must be avoided is the risk of the jury giving more weight to similar fact evidence than it actually deserves. Lord Herschell expressed this matter in *Makin's* case by saying that the jury should not hear evidence which might lead them to the conclusion that because the accused has been guilty of offences other than those charged, so he is guilty of the present offence, unless that is a proper conclusion to draw. In *Boardman* Lord Hailsham said that what the similar fact rules are designed to prevent is 'the inadmissible chain of reasoning' that because someone has misbehaved in the past so he must have done on the occasion in question. However, where the similar fact evidence is extremely probative, as it was in *Straffen* for example, that chain of reasoning is justified. In other cases the similar fact evidence may be less probative, and where that is the case the judge must be careful to prevent it from being adduced if the jury may give it undue weight.

It is arguable that this 'discretion' is not a discretion at all because any judge who allows the jury to hear evidence which is unfair to the defendant will undoubtedly be overturned on appeal. In some cases judges are able to avoid much of the possible prejudice to the accused by a careful direction to the jury, stressing that they should examine in detail whether the evidence of similar allegations or of the accused's disposition really does prove guilt. It is in this way that the judge has a discretion on the matter. If he gives a clear direction so that undue prejudice is avoided, he can safely allow the evidence, but if he does not give such a direction he will have exercised his discretion incorrectly and will be open to review by the Court of Appeal.

'*Striking similarity*'

It has proved little easier to assess the admissibility of similar fact evidence since the decision in *Boardman* than it was before. In *Rance & Herron* (1975) 62 Cr App R 118 the Court of Appeal said that to ask whether similar fact evidence bore a 'striking similarity' to the offence charged was often misleading because it leads the judge to asking whether there is something unusual about the crime alleged and allowing similar fact evidence only where there is something unusual about it. In that case the question arose whether Rance had signed a document knowing what it was. Evidence was given that he had signed similar documents twice in the past in circumstances where he must have known what they were. The Court of Appeal refused his application for leave to appeal. The court held that what must be asked is whether the similar fact evidence is 'positively probative in regard to the crime now alleged'.

This added yet another catch-phrase to those used in *Boardman* and in this way perhaps did more harm than good. It was repeated by the Court of Appeal in *Scarrott* [1978] QB 1016 in which Scarman LJ said:

'Positive probative value is what the law requires, if similar fact evidence is to be admissible. Such probative value is not provided by the mere repetition of similar facts; there has to be some feature or features in the evidence sought to be adduced which provides a link – an underlying link as it has been called in some of the cases. The existence of such a link is not to be inferred from mere similarity of facts which are themselves so commonplace that they can provide no sure ground for saying that they point to the commission by the accused of the offence under consideration.'

In *Boardman* Lord Hailsham gave a useful example of the sort of evidence which might show an underlying link between the similar fact evidence and the commission of the charge faced by the accused.

> '... whilst it would certainly not be enough to identify the culprit in a series of burglaries that he climbed in through a ground floor window, the fact that he left the same humorous limerick on the walls of the sitting room, or an esoteric symbol written in lipstick on the mirror, might well be enough. In a sex case ... whilst a repeated homosexual act by itself might be quite insufficient to admit the evidence as confirmatory of identity or design, the fact that it was alleged to have been performed wearing the ceremonial head-dress of a Red Indian chief or other eccentric garb might well be in appropriate circumstances suffice.'

A case which does not sit easily with Lord Hailsham's examples is *Johanssen* (1977) 65 Cr App R 101. The defendant was alleged to have committed offences against five teenage boys whom he picked up at an amusement arcade. In each instance he was alleged to have picked up the boys by offering them food or money and then to have committed various sexual acts with them. There was similarity not just in the way the accused was meant to have importuned boys in amusement arcades but also in the nature of the sexual acts performed with them, but none of the allegations was so unusual as to warrant the epithet 'strikingly similar'. The decision was probably justified, however, by the sheer number of allegations made by boys who did not know each other.

In *Lewis* (1982) 76 Cr App R 33 the accused was charged with sexual offences involving the two children of his girlfriend. Each child gave evidence of the accused masturbating in his or her presence and of indecent assaults committed in various ways. The defence was a complete denial that the events occurred. The Court of Appeal upheld the decision of the trial judge to allow evidence that the defendant had links with an organisation which promoted sexual conduct with children. It was conceded by counsel for the appellant that if the defence had been one of accident or innocent association the evidence would have been rightly admitted. This concession was held to have been correctly made and seems to have influenced the court in its decision that the evidence was admissible where the defence was a complete denial. *Lewis* has been criticised and should not be relied on in so far as it attempts to re-introduce the old categories of defence in which similar fact evidence is always admissible.

A more recent case than *Lewis* makes it clear that whether similar fact evidence will be admitted depends upon whether it is relevant to the issue or issues in the case, and that it is impossible to say in general terms that if the defendant puts forward a particular defence similar fact evidence either will or will not be admissible to rebut that defence: see *R v Lunt* (1987) 85 Cr App R 241.

When a headmaster was charged with sexual offences against girl pupils, it was held that evidence as to his conduct towards the girls at PE classes was relevant and admissible for the purpose of the jury's deliberations about his conduct on buses and at the swimming pool: *R* v *Shore* (1989) 89 Cr App R 32.

The whole question was reviewed by the House of Lords in *Director of Public Prosecutions* v *P* [1991] 2 AC 447. A man was charged with rape of and incest with his two daughters. He applied for the counts relating to each daughter to be tried separately. The judge refused his application and he was convicted. The Court of Appeal allowed his appeal on the ground that there had not been such striking similarities between the girls' accounts to permit the evidence of one girl properly to be admitted on the trial of the counts relating to the other. See also 2.1 *The legal definition*, above.

Applying *DPP* v *Boardman*, the House of Lords allowed the Crown's appeal and restored the conviction. In the Law Lords' view, there was strong probative force to the evidence of each of the girls in relation to the incidents involving the other which was sufficient to make it just to admit that evidence and it had therefore been unnecessary for the charges to be tried separately. As Lord Mackay of Clashfern LC explained, 'there was sufficient connection between the circumstances spoken of by the two girls ... for their evidence mutually to support each other'. See also *R* v *Laidman* [1992] Crim LR 428.

Incidental points

We saw above that participants in similar fact offences are considered to be accomplices for the purpose of the rules on corroboration: *Davies* v *DPP* [1954] AC 378. This principle is upheld by *DPP* v *Kilbourne* [1973] AC 729, which makes clear that the similar fact rules are no less stringent against the prosecution where corroboration of a prosecution witness is required than they are in other cases. *DPP* v *Kilbourne* also shows that whatever the reason why corroboration of one witness is required, it can be provided by similar fact evidence linking the accused to the offence charged.

After some doubt, raised by the case of *Novac* (1976) 65 Cr App R 107, it was held in *Barrington* [1981] 1 WLR 419 that the striking similarities which identify the accused as the offender may lie not in the acts complained of but in the surrounding circumstances.

It is sometimes denied that the similar facts about which evidence is given are true. For example, in *Rance & Herron*, where it was alleged that Rance paid a bribe to Herron, the evidence that Rance had made payments to two other people in allegedly corrupt circumstances, was said by Rance not to disclose that he had done anything wrong. The Court of Appeal held that where there is a challenge to the truth of similar fact allegations it is for the jury to assess whether those allegations are true and only to treat them as probative if they are satisfied that they are true. This point is further illustrated by cases such as *Boardman*, where the defendant is accused of two or more similar offences. Unless the jury is satisfied so that it is sure that one allegation is correct, it cannot use it as evidence on another charge.

It is never sufficient to show similarity between two similar charges faced by the accused unless there is also sufficient evidence that it was the defendant who committed them. In *Tricoglus* (1976) 65 Cr App R 16 there was clearly striking similarity between the two offences alleged against the defendant such that it was clear that each rape was committed by the same man. But there was insufficient evidence to prove that Tricoglus was that man.

In *R* v *Ryder* (1993) The Times 16 March the Court of Appeal referred to four possible situations relating to similar fact evidence and collusion, using that word to encompass not only deliberate but also unconscious influence of one witness by another. First, where a real possibility of collusion was apparent to the judge on the face of the documents, he should not allow the similar fact evidence to be led. Second, if a submission was made raising the suggestion of collusion the judge might find it necessary to hold a voir dire. Third, if the evidence was admitted but at the end of the case the judge took the view that there was a real possibility of collusion he should tell the jury in summing-up not to use the evidence as corroboration. Finally, even if the judge himself was of the view that there was no real possibility of collusion, but the matter had been argued, he should leave the issue to the jury.

7.2 Criminal Evidence Act 1898 s1

The effect of the Act

Prior to the enactment of the Criminal Evidence Act 1898 a defendant in criminal proceedings was not entitled to give evidence. By s1, the defendant was made generally competent, but limitations were imposed on his compellability and upon the way in which he could be cross-examined. Section 1 does not follow the normal drafting pattern of having numbered sub-sections. Instead it contains a general statement of principle and then the limitations on it appear as lettered sub-sections.

The general statement of principle reads:

> 'Every person charged with an offence ... shall be a competent witness for the defence at every stage of the proceedings, whether the person so charged is charged solely or jointly with any other person.'

Although it is said that the defendant is competent at every stage of the proceedings, s2 of the Act says that where he is the only defence witness of fact the accused must be called immediately after the close of the prosecution case. This does not mean that he must be called in every case, simply that where he chooses to give evidence, his evidence must come first if he is the only witness to fact. Character witnesses, if they are to be called, must come after the defendant. Section 2 was extended in effect by s79 of the Police and Criminal Evidence Act 1984 which provides that where the defence proposes to call more than one witness of fact and the defendant is one of the witnesses, his evidence must be given before that of the others. The court has a discretion to allow him to give his evidence after other witnesses have given theirs, but this is rarely exercised.

Character witnesses at common law

At common law the accused was entitled to call character witnesses, but they were only allowed to speak of his reputation. Evidence was not allowed of specific incidents involving the accused or of the witness's opinion as to the likelihood of him having committed the offence charged. In *Rowton* (1865) 34 LJ MC 57 the accused called a character witness who spoke of his good reputation. The prosecution called in rebuttal a witness who admitted that he knew nothing of the defendant's character but did know that when they were at school together the accused was capable of committing the sort of indecency offence charged. On appeal it was held that this rebuttal evidence should not have been allowed, Cockburn CJ saying:

> 'It is laid down in the books that a prisoner is entitled to give evidence as to his general character. What does that mean? Does it mean evidence as to his reputation amongst those to whom his conduct and position are known, or does it mean evidence of his disposition? I think it means evidence of reputation only.'

Once the defence has called evidence of good reputation the prosecution is entitled to call any evidence it may have of bad reputation. But, as *Rowton* demonstrates, only evidence of reputation is relevant unless the case comes within the similar fact rules. Indeed, if the prosecution's evidence of the accused's character is admissible as similar fact evidence it should be led during the prosecution case and not left to be brought out in rebuttal.

The principle behind *Rowton* is that the limited right of the defence to call character evidence must be subject to a right in the prosecution to call evidence directly in rebuttal, otherwise a false impression may be given by the defence witnesses and left unanswered. It is only where the defendant puts his character in issue that the prosecution may call evidence on that issue: *R v Butterwasser* [1948] 1 KB 4.

The character evidence which is called by the defence must be relevant to the charge in order to be admissible. For example, evidence that someone is reputed to be honest and trustworthy with money does not throw any light at all on his likelihood to commit an offence of indecency. This is implicit in the passage from *Rowton* cited above. But there is authority that once the accused has put his character in issue by calling evidence of relevant good reputation, the prosecution is entitled to call evidence not just about the accused's bad reputation but about any aspect of his bad character. In *Winfield* [1939] 4 All ER 164 the accused was charged with indecent assault on a woman. He called a witness who gave evidence as to his good reputation with women. That witness was asked in cross-examination about the accused's criminal record, including offences of dishonesty. The Court of Criminal

Appeal held this to be perfectly proper, holding that once the defendant put his character in issue the whole of his character was in issue.

It is very rare these days for the defence to call evidence of the accused's good reputation or to ask prosecution witnesses about it without the defendant himself giving evidence. It sometimes happens that a witness will volunteer evidence of the accused's character without being invited to do so. In *Redd* [1923] 1 KB 104 a defence witness who was called simply for the purpose of producing some documents to the court said that the defendant held a good position in the Army and was all right as far as he knew. This was held not to justify the witness being asked about the accused's previous convictions. The defendant had not chosen to put his character in issue, therefore evidence of his bad character was not relevant at the trial.

Section 1 of the 1898 Act

Where the accused does not give evidence the prosecution is not allowed to pass comment on this fact: Criminal Evidence Act 1898, s1(b); see also 1.5 'The defendant in criminal proceedings' above. The judge, however, may pass comment although he should be careful not to suggest that the defendant was under any sort of duty to give evidence (*Bathurst* [1968] 2 QB 99). Indeed, while acknowledging that there were presently proposals for altering the law relating to comment on a defendant's failure to testify and on his failure to answer questions put by the police (subsequently included in the Criminal Justice and Public Order Bill, published 17 December), in *R v Martinez-Tobon* [1993] 2 All ER 90 the Court of Appeal enunciated the principles to be applied where a defendant failed to testify. In particular, the judge should give the jury a direction on lines as follows:

> 'The defendant does not have to give evidence. He is entitled to sit in the dock and require the prosecution to prove its case. You must not assume that he is guilty because he has not given evidence. The fact that he has not given evidence proves nothing, one way or the other. It does nothing to establish his guilt. On the other hand, it means that there is no evidence from the defendant to undermine, contradict, or explain the evidence put before you by the prosecution.'

Sections 1(e) and 1(f)

The effect of s1(e) is that the defendant cannot claim privilege against self-incrimination so far as the charges he faces at trial are concerned. But he may still claim such a privilege as regards other offences.

The sub-paragraphs of s1(f) are examined in detail in the following sections of this book. What is important at this stage is to establish exactly what the purpose of s1(f) is, and how it relates to s1(e). The general part of s1(f) does not merely provide for a privilege against self-incrimination, it provides that no questions at all may be put about the accused's bad character unless one of the numbered sub-paragraphs comes into play. The way this is normally expressed is to say that the accused has a shield which protects him from cross-examination about his character.

Section 1(f) prevents four types of question being asked of the defendant in cross-examination. First, he may not be asked any question which tends to show that he has committed any offence other than the offence or offences with which he is charged. Secondly, he may not be asked any question which tends to show that he has been convicted of any offences. Thirdly, he may not be asked about any other charges he has faced. And, fourthly, he may not be asked about his bad character. The drafting of the sub-section raises three preliminary points. First, it does not affect the admissibility of evidence proposed to be called by the prosecution, it merely prevents the four types of question being asked during cross-examination of the accused. It follows from this that section 1(f) only applies if the accused gives evidence. If he calls witnesses but does not testify himself, s1(f) does not prevent them from being asked any of the four types of question described above, but it is necessary for the defendant's character to be put in issue in the manner set out in *Rowton* before any such questions might be allowed. Secondly, the sub-section refers to questions 'tending to show' that the defendant has convictions, without defining 'tending to show'. And thirdly, the sub-section does not say what is to happen if a question incriminates the defendant on the charge for which he is being tried and also tends to show convictions, offences, charges or bad character. In that situation s1(e) allows the question but s1(f) does not and nothing in either sub-section says which is to take precedence.

The term 'tending to show' originates in Lord Herschell's opinion in *Makin v A-G for New South Wales*. It will be remembered that he said that the prosecution may not usually adduce evidence tending to show that the accused has been guilty of other offences in order to prove his guilt on the present charge. But he used the phrase in a different context to that in s1(f) because he was speaking about the calling of evidence by the Crown, not about the asking of questions in cross-examination. In *Jones v DPP* [1962] AC 635 the defendant was charged with murder of a girl guide. His defence was an alibi, namely, that he had spent the night in question with a prostitute. This was the same defence that he had raised, successfully, on a previous occasion when he had been acquitted of rape of a girl guide. He said during his evidence in chief that he had been 'in trouble' with the police before. The prosecution was allowed to cross-examine him about the rape charge in order to show that he raised the same defence and to suggest to the jury that his present defence was untrue. The House of Lords held that the questioning of the defendant did not 'tend to show' that he was of bad character or that he previously faced a criminal charge because 'tending to show' in s1(f) means 'tending to show to the jury for the first time'. The accused raised his character by saying that he had been in trouble before, therefore when the prosecution asked him about the previous charge they were not raising a new issue but were following up the issue raised by the defendant.

'To show' means 'to reveal' and paragraph (f) prohibits questions which tend to reveal to a jury that a defendant has committed other offences: *R* v *Anderson* [1988] 2 WLR 1017.

The decision on this point in *Jones* v *DPP* was by a majority of 3 to 2. The minority took at face value the words of s1(f), that the prosecution must not ask any question which suggests that the accused has committed, been convicted of or been charged with any offence or is of bad character unless one or other of the numbered sub-paragraphs applies. The minority view is usually applied in practice. The majority decision would allow the prosecution to cross-examine the accused freely about his criminal record if, for example, his defence was that he could not have committed the offence charged because at the time he was committing another offence. Indeed, were he to say 'I was nowhere near the scene of the crime in London and I can prove it because I got a speeding ticket in Manchester at the time', he could be cross-examined as to his character because he had admitted the commission of some crime other than that presently charged. This seems an absurd result.

Jones v *DPP* also answers the third general point on s1(f), namely, the relationship between s1(e) and s1(f). Prior to that decision there were two views in the authorities about the relationship. The first was that s1(e) allows questions which tend to incriminate the accused directly or indirectly and s1(f) is concerned with questions which go to credit only. On this view of matters questions about Jones's previous rape trial would be permitted by s1(e) because they indirectly implicated him in the alleged murder by undermining his defence. The second view was that s1(e) only allows questions directly implicating the accused in the offence charged. On this view, if, like Jones, he raises a defence which could be undermined by reference to his criminal record or bad character, s1(e) will not allow questioning because his record or character does not directly show his guilt, it merely shows it indirectly because of the defence he has chosen to put forward. Therefore, reliance will have to be placed on s1(f). The majority of the House held that the second of these views is correct. It was previously said to be correct by Viscount Sankey LC in *Maxwell* v *DPP* [1935] AC 309, whose dictum was approved by the majority in *Jones* v *DPP*. Viscount Sankey said:

> 'In section 1, proviso (e), it has been enacted that a witness may be cross-examined in respect of the offence charged, and cannot refuse to answer questions directly relevant to the offence on the ground that they tend to incriminate him: thus if he denies the offence he may be cross-examined to refute the denial. These are matters directly relevant to the charge on which he is being tried. Proviso (f), however, is dealing with matters outside, and not directly relevant to, the particular offence charged.'

It is not always easy to know whether evidence of the accused's character is directly relevant or only indirectly relevant to guilt. The best test of this is to ask whether the prosecution would be able to call evidence about it regardless of the defendant giving evidence. If they could, then his character is directly relevant; but if they could not his character is only relevant indirectly. The decision of the House in *Jones* v *DPP* restricts section 1(e) so that only questions which directly implicate the accused are allowed. It should be noted that a question cannot implicate the accused, only the answer. But the normal terminology in this area is to ask whether the question implicates the accused, because it is assumed that any assertion in a question asked of the accused is true and that the answer will implicate him. The effect of the narrow construction of s1(e) favoured in *Jones* v *DPP* is that the prosecution may ask the defendant about matters upon which evidence called by the prosecution would be admissible. It is not always the case, however, that the prosecution is in a position to call such evidence, so asking questions of the defendant can be a way of proving matters which could not otherwise be proved.

The four impermissible questions

In practice it is the accused's criminal record which is considered to be the most important part of his character. But once his shield is thrown away any aspect of his character may be adduced, subject to the judge's discretion to disallow cross-examination (which is discussed in paragraph 7.4, below). It is clear that s1(f) only comes into play if the accused gives evidence. The effect of this is that answers given to any of the four types of impermissible question are normally relevant only to his credibility as a witness and not to his guilt. The first two of the four types of question which may not be asked speak for themselves – it is obvious what is meant by questions about offences he has committed or has been convicted of. It is equally obvious how questioning about such matters might undermine the defendant's credibility. If he is shown to have a criminal record or to have committed offences for which he has not been convicted, the jury may feel him to be someone who cannot be trusted to tell the truth. Whether they do feel that his criminal activities undermine his truthfulness is a matter for them, but they may feel that it does.

But it is not obvious why it should ever be thought relevant to ask him about previous charges which did not lead to conviction. In *Stirland* v *DPP* [1944] AC 315 the defendant was charged with an offence of forgery. He gave evidence of his good character and said specifically that he had never been 'charged' before. The trial judge allowed the prosecution to ask the accused about an incident where his former employer had suspected him of forgery. That incident did not lead to a formal charge for any offence, but did involve a direct allegation by the employer that Stirland had committed one. The House of Lords held that when s1(f) says that someone may not be asked whether he has been charged with any offence, it means that he should not be asked whether he has been brought before a court. Viscount Simon LC said:

> 'It is no disproof of good character that a man has been suspected or accused of a previous crime. Such questions as "Were you suspected?" or "Were you accused" are inadmissible because they are irrelevant to the issue of character and can only be asked if the accused has sworn expressly to the contrary.'

As we will see below, where an accused asserts his good character when giving evidence, s1(f)(ii) allows the Crown to cross-examine him in order to dispel any false impression he may have made. In *Stirland* v *DPP* Viscount Simon said that the only time when it will be possible to cross-examine him about charges which did not lead to conviction is where he expressly asserts that he has never been before a court. The jury are entitled to know that he has been charged if his assertion to the contrary is false. Apart from that situation, previous charges will normally be irrelevant. There are, however, one or two examples in the authorities where a previous charge was relevant otherwise than in the way envisaged by Viscount Simon. In *Waldman* (1934) 24 Cr App R 204 the defendant was asked about two previous similar charges, one of which resulted in acquittal and the other in conviction. The Court of Criminal Appeal upheld his conviction, holding that the questions about the charge of which he was acquitted were relevant because they showed that the accused was or ought to have been aware of the dangers of receiving goods in suspicious circumstances.

The fourth type of question which is impermissible is questions about the accused's 'bad character'. At common law someone's character is his reputation: *Rowton*. The Act does not define bad character, but there is ample authority that in the Act it means not just bad reputation but also specific acts done by the accused. In fact the word 'character' appears four times in s1(f); once in the general prohibition against asking the accused about his bad character and three times in sub-paragraph (ii). In all four places where the word is used it means the same thing and in *Selvey* v *DPP* [1970] AC 304 the House of Lords held that someone's character is not just his reputation, but also his disposition towards certain types of conduct. In that case the accused gave evidence that a prosecution witness had offered to commit buggery with him. This was held to be an imputation on the character of the witness. Evidence by the accused of a specific act by the witness was held to be evidence about the witness's character.

7.3 Criminal Evidence Act 1898 s1(f)(i)

Similar fact evidence and proviso (i)

The first proviso to s1(f) allows the accused to be cross-examined as to other offences committed by him or of which he has been convicted where proof that he has committed or been convicted of that offence is admissible to prove the present offence.

On the face of things, this proviso applies to similar fact cases where proof of one offence is admissible to prove that with which the defendant is charged. In such cases the prosecution would normally prove the commission of the earlier offence as part of its case, so that cross-examination about that offence does not tend to show to the jury for the first time that it was committed. Where the prosecution is allowed to prove a similar fact offence as part of its case, the effect of *Jones* v *DPP* is that s1(f) does not come into play and the prosecution may ask the accused any of the four types of question which are normally permitted, without having to rely on proviso (i). Indeed, the same point can be made about cases where statute allows the proof of one conviction at the trial for another offence, such as s27(3) of the Theft Act 1968. Because it is already before the jury that the accused has a criminal record, any questions about previous offences do not raise that issue for the first time.

If the Crown chooses not to prove the conviction as part of its case it will have to rely on section 1(f)(i) if it wishes to ask the accused about it. The normal standard of admissibility for similar fact evidence will then be applicable, and if the previous conviction is not sufficiently probative of guilt to out-weigh the prejudice which may be caused by evidence being given about it, the question may not be asked in cross-examination.

Proviso (i) only allows questions about the commission of or conviction for other offences. It does not allow questions to be asked about the accused's disposition nor about previous charges which did not result in conviction: *Coker* [1960] 2 QB 207. However, if evidence of disposition has been given by witnesses for the Crown, the accused may be asked about it in the same way that he may be asked about any other part of the evidence called by the Crown.

Non-similar fact evidence

Questions may sometimes be asked of the defendant about non-similar fact convictions. Although this would bring out that he has a criminal record, in some cases this is inevitable. The most obvious examples are cases where the offence charged can only be committed by someone with a previous conviction. For example, someone charged with driving while disqualified may be asked about his disqualification. Not all disqualifications arise from convictions for offences, because any person under the age of 17 is disqualified. But where, as is usually the case, the charge of driving while disqualified arises from disqualification for an offence, the accused may be asked about the disqualification. If the prosecution failed to call evidence of disqualification as part of its case the accused would be entitled to have the charge dismissed on a submission of no case to answer, so it is vital that the previous disqualification is proved and this inevitably will bring to light the fact that he has a record.

The effect of *Jones* v *DPP* is that s1(f) does not come into play in such cases. Once the prosecution has proved the fact of disqualification, the court will have heard that the accused has a criminal record, so that any questions about his record would not tend to show for the first time that he has convictions. This point is not limited to cases of driving while disqualified; it applies to any non-similar fact offence which is relevant and proved at trial by the prosecution.

The overall effect of what is said above about s1(f)(i) is that it is effectively redundant save for those rare cases where the prosecution asks the defendant about relevant convictions without proving those convictions first as part of its case. Where s1(f)(i) does come into play, the answers given by the accused are relevant not just to his credibility as a witness but also to his guilt because if they were not relevant to guilt the questions which elicited them would not be permitted by s1(f)(i).

7.4 Criminal Evidence Act 1898 s1(f)(ii)

An over-view

Section 1(f)(ii) allows the accused to be asked any of the four types of questions which are generally not permitted provided he has made his character a relevant issue in the case. This can be done in two ways, either by attacking the character of prosecution witnesses, or by putting forward the assertion that the defendant is of good character. It will be remembered that in *Butterwasser* it was held that a defendant does not put his character in issue by attacking the character of prosecution witnesses. But the context in which the question of character arose in *Butterwasser* was that the accused did not give evidence. The Court of Criminal Appeal held that in those circumstances his character was not in issue so the mere fact that he attacked the character of prosecution witnesses did not entitle the prosecution to put in evidence his criminal record.

That position still prevails where the accused does not give evidence, but under the Act the defendant is liable to be asked about his character if he attacks the character of prosecution witnesses, or asserts his own good character. In other words, if he chooses to throw away the shield given by the first part of s1(f) he is liable to be cross-examined like any other witness. The defendant in *Butterwasser* would have been liable to cross-examination about his criminal record had he given evidence, but, as that case shows, the defendant's shield can only be thrown away if he goes into the witness box.

Proviso (ii) is the most important sub-paragraph of s1(f) in practice, because there are relatively few cases where sub-paragraphs (i) or (iii) come into play. Furthermore, the major importance of section 1(f)(ii) is in relation to the defendant's criminal record rather than in relation to any other matter about which questions are not normally permitted. To a great extent, it is a matter for the defence whether the shield is lost and many barristers conducting criminal trials are of the view that it is usually best to have the jury know of their client's criminal record in order to prevent speculation about it. But where the shield is not deliberately cast aside by the accused being asked about his record during examination in chief, the Crown will only be allowed to cross-examine him about his record if the accused has asserted his own good character, or imputations have been cast on the character of the prosecutor or of one or more prosecution witnesses.

Asserting good character

Section 1(f)(ii) stipulates the circumstances in which the shield will be lost. There are two ways in which the defendant's good character can be asserted. Either it can be elicited from prosecution witnesses, or it can be asserted directly by the accused. It is not clear on the face of the Act whether the calling of a character witness amounts to the defendant giving evidence of his good character, but it would make no difference to the defendant's position whether that loses his shield, because the character witness could be asked about the defendant's convictions at common law: *Winfield*. In *Redd* [1923] 1 KB 104 a witness called by the defence volunteered that the accused was of good character. He was not asked to give such evidence but took it upon himself to do so. The Court of Criminal Appeal held that the defendant's shield was not lost because the defendant did not ask the witness to give evidence of his good character. It is, however, implicit in this decision that questions asked of a defence witness may lead to the shield being lost.

Not every question asked of a prosecution witness which elicits an answer about the accused's good character will lead to the loss of the shield. For example, the principle in *Redd* may apply to prosecution witnesses as it does to defence witnesses. In addition, the accused may freely ask questions with a view to setting-up his defence. This will always involve an assertion that he is not guilty of the offence charged, but merely denying the charge and putting forward one's version of events does not also involve an assertion that one is of good character.

Evidence given by the accused himself may involve a direct assertion that he is of good character, for example by asserting that he is not the sort of person who would commit the type of offence charged. It would be absurd if the prosecution were not entitled to show that such an assertion is false. Therefore, if the prosecution has evidence that he is the sort of man who might commit the type of offence charged, s1(f)(ii) allows him to be cross-examined in order to show that his assertion was not true. In such cases the evidence about his disposition is relevant not just to his credibility but also to his guilt, because the issue whether he is the sort of man who would commit the type of offence in question has been made an issue by the accused himself.

Indirect assertions of good character by the accused when giving evidence do not lead to the loss of the shield if all he does is to put forward his version of events. In *Ellis* [1910] 2 KB 746 the defendant was charged with obtaining cheques by false pretences. He gave evidence about the transactions whereby he obtained the cheques and also gave evidence of other transactions with a view to showing the way his business worked. The Court of Criminal Appeal held that he did not give evidence of his own good character by simply explaining what had happened, even though this necessarily involved him saying, in effect, 'The way I have acted in the past shows that I was not dishonest on this occasion' – impliedly asserting his good character. The same point was made by the Privy Council in *Malindi* v *R* [1967] AC 439. The defendant was charged with various offences including conspiracy to commit arson. The conspiracy was alleged to have occurred at two political meetings. The defendant gave evidence that he attended the first of the meetings but that it dispersed after he spoke against the use of violence. The Privy Council held that he had not given evidence of his good character. Lord Morris said:

> 'All the appellant did was to give a narrative of what he says took place at the meetings in question. He records what he asserted was said at those meetings. He gave his version of events and of conversations. He did no more. He did not, independently of giving his account of what actually happened and of what had actually been said, assert that he was a man of good character.'

Malindi v *R* is the clearest possible authority that the accused does not lose his shield simply by putting forward his version of events. But the case was concerned only with that part of s1(f)(ii) which says that the shield is lost if the accused gives evidence of good character. It does not apply to that part of s1(f)(ii) which refers to the casting of imputations on prosecution witnesses. The distinction between the giving of evidence of good character and the giving of a version of events is usually quite easy to draw. What must be asked is whether the accused is giving evidence directly about the incident which the prosecution alleges constitutes an offence. If he is, he is simply giving his version of events.

The accused does not assert his own good character by asserting that others are of bad character. This was clearly illustrated in *Butterwasser*, but the same point was made in *Lee* [1976] 1 WLR 71 where the defendant asserted that others, who were not witnesses in the case, had committed the offences with which he was charged. The Court of Appeal held that he had not asserted his own good character.

Casting imputations

Imputations might be cast directly or indirectly on the prosecutor or witnesses for the prosecution. Direct imputations take the form of allegations that they are of bad character. Indirect imputations arise where it is implied that evidence has been deliberately fabricated by prosecution witnesses.

The accused is allowed a certain amount of freedom to assert his innocence without throwing away his shield. For example, in *Rouse* [1904] 1 KB 184 the defendant's assertion that a prosecution witness was a liar was held not to involve an imputation on the character of that witness. Rather it was an emphatic denial of guilt, albeit in rather clumsy terms. By contrast, the assertion in *Rappolt* (1911) 6 Cr App R 156 that a prosecution witness was such a horrible liar that his brother would not talk to him, was held to involve an imputation on his character.

But the latitude he is allowed is limited to emphatic denials of guilt; where he puts forward his defence and this expressly or impliedly accuses prosecution witnesses of deliberately giving false evidence, the shield will be lost. In *Hudson* [1912] 2 KB 464 it was held that whether the defendant has cast imputations on the character of the prosecutor or prosecution witnesses is to be judged by applying the words of s1(f)(ii) literally. The section does not say that the casting of imputations does not lead to the loss of the shield if it is necessary to cast them in order to advance the defence, nor does it say that the shield is only lost if it is unreasonable to cast imputation. Therefore one must examine the evidence put forward by the defence and ask whether it alleges that the prosecutor or prosecution witnesses have deliberately given false evidence.

In *Preston* [1909] 1 KB 568, Channell J said:

> 'If the defence is so conducted, or the nature of the defence is such as to involve the proposition that the jury ought not to believe the prosecutor or one of the witnesses for the prosecution upon the ground that his conduct – not his evidence in the case, but his conduct outside the evidence given by him – makes him an unreliable witness, then the jury ought also to know the character of the prisoner who either gives that evidence or makes that charge, and it then becomes admissible to cross-examine the prisoner about his antecedents and character with the view of showing that he has such a bad character that the jury ought not to rely upon his evidence.'

That statement of principle remains true today. It was cited with approval by Lord Hewart CJ in *Jones* (1923) 17 Cr App R 117 and by Lord Goddard CJ in *Clark* [1955] 2 QB 469. The same principle was restated in *Selvey v DPP* by Viscount Dilhorne.

The defendant in *Selvey v DPP* [1970] AC 304 was charged with buggery. He said that the main prosecution witness had offered to commit buggery with him but that the offer had been refused. He said, further, that the same witness had admitted having committed buggery with someone else earlier in the day. This evidence was held to amount to the casting of imputations against the witness so that cross-examination of the accused about his own homosexual tendencies was justified. A more relaxed view was taken by the Court of Appeal in *Nelson* (1978) 68 Cr App R 12 where the accused denied that he had made admissions which prosecution witnesses had recounted. It was held that the trial judge was wrong to rule that the accused had cast imputations upon the character of the prosecution witnesses because all he had done was to assert his defence, which was that he had not committed the offences and had not admitted committing them. *Nelson* reflects what had become quite a common practice, which was not to accuse prosecution witnesses of lying, but to suggest that they were mistaken. That line of defence was held in *Tanner* (1977) 66 Cr App R 56 to give rise to imputations where it was not possible to explain the discrepancy between the prosecution and defence versions of events otherwise than by finding that either the prosecution witnesses had deliberately conspired to fabricate evidence or the defendant had done so. However, *Nelson* held that it is the form in which evidence is given and suggestions made to witnesses rather than the substance of the evidence or questions which determines whether the shield is lost: if one says that a witness is mistaken the shield is not lost even if there is obviously no scope for genuine mistake.

The apparent conflict between *Tanner* and *Nelson* was clarified in *Britzman* [1983] 1 All ER 369 in which *Nelson* was disapproved. The defendant, who was charged with burglary, denied that he had made certain admissions in the course of an interview. The only possible explanations for the police officers giving evidence of these admissions were that either that evidence was true, or it was deliberately fabricated. It could not possibly have been given by mistake because the admissions were not just single words which might have been misquoted by the policemen, but were whole sentences and, in one instance, a series of three questions and answers. The Court of Appeal held that where the defence suggests that a prosecution witness is mistaken, the shield is not necessarily safe. It will be lost if the true import of what is said is that the witness is deliberately lying. The distinction recognised in *Malindi* v *R* between simply asserting one's defence and making assertions of good character is not carried over into the part of s1(f)(ii) which deals with the casting of imputations. The assertion of his defence may lead to his shield being lost if the defendant's version of events is so radically different from that of prosecution witnesses that the only conclusion to be drawn is that he or the witnesses are lying.

In rape cases an assertion by the accused that the complainant consented to intercourse does not involve any imputation being made against her character (*Turner* [1944] KB 463). This is not in line with the strict rule in *Britzman*, but it is a rule of long standing and was approved by the House of Lords in *Stirland* v *DPP*. The best explanation for this is that the issue of consent is a special matter which deserves rules of its own.

The wording of the part of s1(f)(ii) being considered here provides that the shield is lost where the 'nature or conduct of the defence is such as to involve imputations on the character of the prosecutor or witnesses for the prosecution'. This has been construed as requiring the defendant to make it part of his case that the prosecutor or a prosecution witness is of bad character. If he makes that sort of allegation during cross-examination in direct answer to a question like 'Are you saying the prosecution witness is deliberately lying?' he will not lose his shield: *Jones* (1910) 3 Cr App R 67. The prosecutor is the complainant who instigated the charge for the purpose of s1(f)(ii) and not counsel for the Crown or anyone who works for the Crown Prosecution Service. The prosecutor will almost always be a prosecution witness, so in practice the casting of imputations against the prosecutor takes the form of allegations being made against a prosecution witness.

Permissible questions

When the accused's shield is lost he may be asked not just whether he has convictions, but also what those convictions are and what the facts behind them were: *Duncalf* (1979) 69 Cr App R 206. Some doubt must exist whether this is a proper approach to adopt, because the result of it is that the jury may be told about various details of the previous convictions which would not be admissible as similar fact evidence yet which might be considered by the jury to be probative of guilt. In *Duncalf* the earlier decision of the Court of Appeal in *France* [1978] Crim LR 48, in which cross-examination about the details of previous convictions was held to be improper, was disapproved. In *Watts* (1983) 77 Cr App R 126, *France* was against disapproved, so *Duncalf* must be taken to be correct, subject to the judge's discretion to limit or prevent cross-examination.

Because the main purpose of cross-examination about previous convictions is to undermine the credibility of the accused as a witness, it is common practice to investigate whether the accused gave evidence at his previous trials. It is often very effective to ask the defendant in cross-examination: whether he pleaded guilty or not guilty at his previous trial, whether he gave evidence and whether that evidence was believed.

The discretion

In *Selvey* v *DPP* the question arose directly whether the trial judge has a discretion under s1(f)(ii) to prevent the prosecution from cross-examining about certain previous convictions once the shield is lost. It was held that such a discretion does exist and that it should be exercised where it would be unfairly prejudicial to allow all previous convictions to be put to the accused. This discretion is effectively the same as the rule preventing evidence of previous misconduct of the defendant to be put before the jury where it would be considered to be more probative than it really is. It was expressed in the following way by Viscount Sankey LC in *Maxwell* v *DPP*:

> '... the question whether a man has been convicted, charged or acquitted ought not to be admitted, even if it goes to credibility, if there is any risk of the jury being misled into thinking that it goes not to credibility but to the probability of his having committed the offence of which he is charged.'

Whether there is 'any risk' of previous convictions being taken by the jury as evidence of guilt depends to an extent upon the direction which the judge gives. In *Powell* [1985] 1 WLR 1364 the Court of Appeal held that in general the loss of the shield leads to the prosecution being entitled to cross-examine about all previous convictions, whether they are similar or dissimilar to the offence charged.

In *R* v *McLeod* (1994) The Times 14 April Stuart-Smith LJ said that, although the authorities were not always easy to reconcile, for the general principles upon which the discretion whether to permit cross-examination of a defendant on his previous convictions, the Court of Appeal could not improve upon the analysis contained in the judgment of Ackner LJ in *R* v *Burke* (1986) 82 Cr App R 156, as supplemented by the observations of Neill LJ in *R* v *Owen* (1986) 83 Cr App R 100. As to the nature of the questions that might properly be put, the following propositions should borne in mind:

1. The primary purpose of the cross-examination on previous convictions and bad character of the accused was to show that he was not worthy of belief. It was not, and should not be, to show that he had a disposition to commit the type of offence with which he was charged. However, the mere fact that the offences

were of a similar type to that charged or because of their number and type had the incidental effect of suggesting a tendency or disposition to commit the offence charged would not make them improper.

2. It was undesirable that there should be prolonged or extensive cross-examination in relation to previous offences: this would divert the jury from the principal issue in the case, which was the guilt of the accused on the instant offence and not the details of earlier ones. Unless the earlier ones were admissible as similar fact evidence, prosecuting counsel should not seek to probe or emphasise similarities between the underlying facts of previous offences and the instant one.

3. Similarities of defences which had been rejected by juries on previous occasions, eg false alibis or the defence that an incriminating substance had been planted, and whether or not the accused pleaded guilty or was disbelieved having given evidence on oath, could be a legitimate matter for questions. These matters did not show a disposition to commit the offence in question but they were clearly relevant to credibility.

4. Underlying facts that showed particularly bad character over and above the bare facts of the case were not necessarily to be excluded. However the judge should be careful to balance the gravity of the attack on the prosecution with the degree of prejudice to the defendant which would result from the disclosure of the facts in question.

   Details of sexual offences against children were likely to be regarded by a jury as particularly prejudicial to an accused.

5. If objection was to be taken to a particular line of cross-examination about the underlying facts of a previous offence, it should be taken as soon as it was apparent to defence counsel that it was in danger of going too far. There was little point in taking it subsequently since it would not normally be a ground for discharging the jury.

6. While it was the duty of the judge to keep cross-examination within proper bounds, if no objection were taken at the time, it would be difficult thereafter to contend that the judge had wrongly exercised his discretion. In any event, the Court of Appeal would not interfere with the exercise of the judge's discretion save on well-established principles.

7. In every case where the accused had been cross-examined as to his character and previous offences, the judge had in the summing up to tell the jury that the purpose of the questioning went only to credit and that they should not consider that it showed a propensity to commit the offence they were considering.

'Spent' convictions

The Rehabilitation of Offenders Act 1974 provides that after a certain period of time has passed convictions become 'spent' and the convicted person should be treated as not having been convicted and, when giving evidence in civil proceedings, he should not be asked any question which cannot be answered without acknowledging or referring to a spent conviction: s4(1). Offences for which a custodial sentence of life or more than 30 months was imposed are never spent. Where the sentence was more than six but not more than 30 months, the conviction becomes spent after 10 years, the rehabilitation period for custodial sentences of six months or less is seven years, it is five years for fines or community service orders, one year where a probation order or conditional discharge was imposed and six months where the accused was discharged absolutely: s5. The effect of s4(1), (2) and 3(b) of the Rehabilitation of Offenders Act 1974 is restricted where the offence involved fraud or dishonesty or was under legislation relating to companies, building societies, banking or other financial services: s95 of the Banking Act 1987.

By a *Practice Direction* [1975] 1 WLR 1065 the Court of Appeal had provided that reference to spent convictions should be avoided wherever possible in criminal courts, even though the Act does not specifically extend to criminal proceedings. It is therefore for the judge to decide in the exercise of his discretion whether to allow cross-examination about previous convictions which are spent.

7.5 Criminal Evidence Act 1898 s1(f)(iii)

Giving evidence against

Section 1(f)(iii) allows cross-examination of the defendant as to character where he has given evidence against any person charged in the same proceedings. Originally the section only applied where the accused gave evidence against someone charged with the same offence, but it was amended by the Criminal Evidence Act 1979 so that the giving of evidence against someone charged in the same proceedings loses the accused his shield, regardless of whether the charge faced by the co-accused is the same as that faced by the defendant himself.

Whether he has given evidence against a co-defendant is to be judged by asking whether the evidence he had given has strengthened the prosecution case or weakened the case of the co-accused on a material issue: *Murdoch* v *Taylor* [1965] AC 574.

Cross-examination under s1(f)(iii) is usually undertaken by the co-defendant who runs the risk of being adversely affected by the evidence given. It was held in *Murdoch* v *Taylor* that the trial judge has no discretion to prevent the co-defendant from cross-examining the accused who gives evidence against him. The role of the judge is to assess whether the evidence goes against the co-defendant. Once he is satisfied that it does, he must allow the co-defendant to cross-examine, subject only the rule which affects every field of evidence, that irrelevant matters may not be raised. The prosecution may cross-examine under s1(f)(iii) where the co-defendant chooses not to: *Seigley* (1911) 6 Cr App R 106. But in such a situation the trial judge has a discretion if he feels such cross-examination may be unfairly prejudicial: *Murdoch* v *Taylor*.

One problem which frequently arises in the context of s1(f)(iii) comes about where it is clear that one or other of two defendants committed the offence charged and they each deny that they committed it. It is implicit in such a denial that the other must be the guilty man. One such case was *Davis* [1975] 1 WLR 345. The appellant was asked in cross-examination whether he was saying that the co-defendant was guilty of a theft with which they were both charged. He answered that he was not saying that the co-defendant was guilty, but he did not steal the item in question so the co-accused must have stolen it. In *Stannard* [1965] 2 QB 1 Winn J said:

'Mere conflict between a version of fact given by one is quite insufficient to amount to evidence given by one against the other.'

This was held in *Davis* not to apply where the conflict between the versions of events given by the two accused was so fundamental that if the version of one was accepted the other must stand little chance of acquittal.

In *Bruce* [1975] 1 WLR 1252, on the other hand, the evidence given by one defendant (Bruce) asserted one defence and that given by another (McGuinness) asserted a different line of defence. These defences were inconsistent in that if Bruce were believed the version of events given by McGuinness would be false. But, if Bruce were believed, the defence he put forward would also be available to McGuiness. The conflict between the two accused did not make the conviction of each other more likely, it made it less likely. Therefore the evidence of Bruce was not evidence against McGuiness. It was accepted by the Court of Appeal that there might be cases where the putting forward of inconsistent defences might lead to a jury being sceptical about both. But this was not such a case, therefore the trial judge was wrong to rule that s1(f)(iii) applied.

The law was restated by the Court of Appeal in *Varley* [1982] 2 All ER 519. It was necessary for there to be a restatement because the application of s1(f)(iii) to cases where defendants put forward inconsistent defences was proving difficult despite the assistance given by *Davis* and *Bruce*. In *Varley*, the co-defendant (Dibble) said that he took part in a robbery because Varley forced him to. Varley denied any involvement and asserted that Dibble's version of events was entirely untrue. The Court of Appeal held that the trial judge was correct in holding that Varley had given evidence against Dibble. The following restatement of the law was made:

'(1) If it is established that a person jointly charged has given evidence against the co-defendant that defendant has a right to cross-examine the other as to previous convictions and the trial judge has no discretion to refuse an application. (2) Such evidence may be given either in chief or during cross-examination. (3) It has to be objectively decided whether the evidence either supports the prosecution case in a material respect or undermines the defence of the co-accused. A hostile intent is irrelevant. (4) If consideration has to be given to the undermining of the other's defence care must be taken to see that the evidence clearly undermines the defence. Inconvenience or inconsistency with the other's defence is not of itself insufficient. (5) Mere denial of participation in a joint venture is not of itself sufficient to rank as evidence against the co-defendant. For the proviso to apply, such denial must lead to the conclusion that if the witness did not participate then it must have been the other who did. (6) Where the one defendant asserts or in due course would assert one view of the joint venture which is directly contradicted by the other such contradiction may be evidence against the co-defendant.' (Kilner Brown J).

The relationship to s1(f)(ii)

We have seen that where s1(f)(iii) applies the judge has no discretion to prevent or restrict the co-defendant's cross-examination. This is a clear distinction between provisos (ii) and (iii) to s1(f). In general, loss of the shield will occur either where the prosecution applies pursuant to proviso (i) or (ii), or where the co-defendant applies pursuant to proviso (iii). It is clear from *Seigley* that the prosecution may ask for leave to rely on s1(f)(iii). But it is probably also the case that a co-defendant may be able to apply for leave to cross-examine under proviso (ii).

In the normal sort of case which arises under s1(f)(ii) the prosecution will ask the judge for leave to cross-examine because one of its witnesses has been attacked. But where both defendants give evidence and one of them makes allegations about the other, the case may not come within s1(f)(iii) but may be within proviso (ii). An example will illustrate a potential situation where this would happen.

D1 is charged with burglary and D2 with dishonestly handling goods which were stolen during the same burglary. Property which was stolen during a burglary was found in D2's possession. D1 says that he bought the property legitimately but cheaply from X and sold it equally legitimately but at a small profit to D2. D2 admits during cross-examination that when he bought the goods he suspected them to have been stolen because they were offered at a very low price and D1 would not give him a receipt.

In this example neither D1 nor D2 gives evidence which directly supports the prosecution case against the other, nor does either give evidence clearly undermining the defence of the other. But D2 does make an imputation about D1's honesty because he suggests that D1 may have come by the property dishonestly. This does not of itself indicate that he was the burglar because he may have been a mere handler himself. In as much as D1 says that he sold the property to D2 he is a prosecution witness against D2, because he gives evidence linking D2 to the goods. When D2 suggests that D1 may have been dishonest, he casts an imputation on the character of a prosecution witness. That D1 counts as a prosecution witness when being called in his own defence is clear from *Lovett* [1973] 1 WLR 241. D1 would need leave to rely on s1(f)(ii) and whether that leave will be granted depends upon the same considerations as apply to the prosecution in such a situation.

7.6 Judge's direction as to character

The judge should give the jury a proper direction as to a defendant's good character and, although it is not vital, should point out, in an appropriate case, that good character demonstrates that the defendant was less, rather than more, likely to commit a crime: *R* v *Cohen* (1990) 91 Cr App R 125. A defendant's good character should be put to the jury with clarity and impartiality and without exaggeration or sarcasm (*R* v *Berrada* (1989) 91 Cr App R 131n) and in no case of any seriousness can a neglect of that duty be excused: *R* v *Kabariti* [1991] Crim LR 450.

In *Berry* v *R* [1992] 3 All ER 881, it appeared that the accused's defence to a charge of murder had been that the shooting of the deceased woman was an accident. The trial judge in Jamaica had failed to direct the jury that the accused's previous good character was primarily relevant to the question of credibility and, applying, inter alia, *R* v *Cohen* and *R* v *Berrada*, the Privy Council held that this had been a material misdirection.

Where there are two defendants, one of good character and one with previous convictions, it is usually advisable for the judge to say little, if anything, about the good character of the one. However, if that one insists on a full direction as to his or her good character, it can hardly be refused, even though it might lead to the necessity for separate trials, even at that late stage: *R* v *Shaw* (1992) 97 Cr App R 218. In *R* v *Vye* [1993] 3 All ER 241 the Court of Appeal said, inter alia, that a defendant of good character is entitled to have the judge direct the jury as to its relevance in his case even if he is jointly tried with a defendant of bad character. What the judge then says, if anything, about the character of the defendant of bad character is for him (the judge) to decide in all the circumstances of the case.

When a defendant otherwise of good character pleaded guilty to the second count (assault occasioning actual bodily harm) but not guilty to the first (causing grievous bodily harm with intent) and much depended upon the credibility of her account of the incident, applying *Vye* the Court of Appeal said that the trial judge should have directed the jury as to the materiality of her otherwise good character: *R* v *Teasdale* [1993] 4 All ER 290.

In a case where a defendant's character is in issue, unless the trial judge reaches a clear conclusion that the defendant is not a person of good character, the standard direction as to the relevance of good or bad character should be given: *R* v *Micallef* (1993) The Times 26 November. Specimen directions issued by the Judicial Studies Board should be used by judges with the greatest care and adapted as may be appropriate in the particular case: *R* v *Taylor* (1993) The Times 15 June.

The trial judge has a discretion to allow a defendant who has spent convictions to be put forward or treated as a person of good character, but there must be no question of the jury being misled and they must certainly not be told that he has no previous convictions: *R* v *O'Shea* (1993) The Times 8 June. Where a judge regards the spent convictions of a defendant, disclosed by him in evidence, as lacking in significance to the extent that he should be regarded as a person of good character, the judge should give to the jury the directions to be found in *R* v *Vye* above as to the relevance of good character to the defendant's credibility and to his propensity to have committed the offence charged: *R* v *Heath* (1994) The Times 10 February.

7.7 Similar fact evidence in civil cases

Evidence of good character

Parties to civil disputes may not normally call character witnesses in support of their case. No reason has ever clearly been given for this in the authorities. The leading case is *A-G* v *Bowman* (1791) 2 Bos & P 532n in which a character witness was not allowed to be called by the defendant to support his defence. Also, in *Holcombe* v *Hewson* (1810) 2 Camp 391 the question arose whether the plaintiff brewer had supplied bad beer to the defendant. Evidence tendered by the plaintiff that he had supplied good beer to other publicans was held to be inadmissible.

When civil disputes were decided by juries there was no reason why the rules of evidence should be any different in this regard to those in criminal courts. However, the distinction between *A-G* v *Bowman* and *Rowton* is clear. Now that the vast majority of civil disputes are heard by judges sitting alone, the ban on character evidence makes more sense. It is unlikely that many judges would feel that it helps them to assess the truthfulness of a witness to know what reputation he has. Nevertheless, it frequently occurs that parties volunteer information about their character with a view to influencing the judge. Only rarely does it do so.

Evidence of bad character

Parties and witnesses in civil disputes may be cross-examined about their criminal records pursuant to s6 of the Criminal Procedure Act 1865. This is a comparatively rare event in civil disputes because one party is not often in a position to prove his opponent's convictions, unlike the parties in criminal cases who can ask the police officers in the case to check the other side's witnesses on the criminal records office computer. Sections 1(e) and (f) of the Criminal Evidence Act 1898 do not apply in civil courts, so parties and witnesses are in the same position. Cross-examination about bad character will normally only be relevant to credibility.

Similar fact evidence is admissible in the civil courts as it is in the criminal courts. There is less risk of undue prejudice because judges are usually able to ignore the prejudice which might arise in the minds of juries when hearing of other misdeeds of a party. In *Hales* v *Kerr* [1908] 2 KB 601 a customer of a barber sued him claiming that as a result of the use of an unsterilised razor the customer contracted ringworm. Evidence was allowed that a later customer also contracted ringworm because it was held to be relevant to the issue whether the first customer was infected through negligence of accident. A commonly occurring use of similar fact of evidence used to be in order to prove adultery where there was little direct evidence of it. For example, if the divorce petition claimed that the respondent committed adultery with X on 1 January, evidence would frequently be admitted that throughout the following year the respondent and X committed adultery because this may throw light on the likely conduct of the respondent and X on 1 January.

There are many authorities that similar fact evidence is usually inadmissible in civil courts as in criminal: see, eg, *Hollingham* v *Head* (1858) 4 CB (NS) 388.

Two true similar fact cases were decided in civil courts. In *Mood Music Publishing Co Ltd* v *De Wolfe Ltd* [1976] Ch 119 the question arose whether the defendant had copied tunes to which the plaintiff owned the copyright. The defendant company's case was that it was mere coincidence that a tune which it published called 'Girl in the Dark' was similar to a tune called 'Sogno Nostalgico' which had been published by the plaintiff many years before. The plaintiff called evidence that on three other occasions the defendant had sold tunes in breach of someone else's copyright. The Court of Appeal held the evidence to be sufficiently probative to be admissible, but said that as a matter of practice similar fact evidence ought not to be allowed in civil courts unless notice was given of an intention to adduce it in order that the other side might have a chance to investigate the matter. The *Mood Music* case was decided shortly after *Boardman* but the Court of Appeal said that similar fact evidence is admissible more easily in civil cases. No reason was given for this, but the probable reason was that the risk of a judge who is accustomed to sifting the relevant from the irrelevant being prejudiced by similar fact evidence is less than the risk of a jury being prejudiced.

In *Berger* v *Raymond Sun Ltd* [1984] 1 WLR 625 it was held by Warner J in the Chancery Division that similar fact evidence which aimed to prove that certain documents had been forged by one of the defendants was inadmissible. The evidence in question took the form of expert handwriting evidence which compared the defendant's handwriting to that on other documents which it was alleged he had forged in the same way that he was alleged to have forged documents in the instant case. Warner J applied the test in *Mood Music Publishing Co Ltd* v *De Wolfe Ltd*, saying that although the evidence was probative it should not be admitted because it had only been served on the defendant the day before the trial started.

Because the prejudice which the courts are careful to avoid in the adduction of similar fact evidence in civil disputes is the prejudice of having the evidence served very late in the day, thereby making it difficult or impossible to test it, the way the law in this area works depends to an extent upon the rules of court which cover disclosure of evidence. It is not within the scope of this book to examine in any detail the Rules of the Supreme Court and the County Court Rules. But in outline the position is that any documents which are to be relied on must be disclosed in advance and expert evidence is only admissible if the court directs in advance of trial that it may be called. A direction allowing expert evidence will always require experts' reports to be exchanged to allow both sides to prepare properly. The law on similar fact evidence aims to uphold the principle behind the disclosure of evidence – civil litigation should be conducted openly with all parties being in a position to assess documentary evidence intended to be relied upon by the other parties.

8

Privilege

8.1 Definition and effect

8.2 Legal professional privilege

8.3 'Without prejudice' correspondence

8.4 Privilege against self-incrimination

8.5 Statutory modifications

8.6 Public interest privilege

8.1 Definition and effect

The general principle

A party does not have to disclose documents or answer questions if he is able to rely on privilege. Privilege takes several forms, the four most important of which are: legal professional privilege, privilege of confidential communications, the privilege against self-incrimination and public interest privilege. It will be seen below how these privileges have developed their own rules to such an extent that the only thing they now have in common is that they are justifications for the non-disclosure of information.

Paragraph 1.5 dealt with competence and compellability. Those topics bear a degree of similarity to privilege, in that a witness who is not competent is not allowed to give evidence and one who is not compellable may not be forced to give evidence. Privilege deals with the position where a witness is giving evidence. Of course, a witness must be competent before he may give evidence, but once he is in the witness box he must usually answer all questions put to him. The only occasion on which he can refuse to answer a question which is relevant and not subject to a rule of exclusion, such as the hearsay rule or the rule against opinion evidence, is when he can rely on privilege.

Disclosure of documents

In civil litigation each party to the proceedings must usually disclose all relevant documents to all other parties. This procedure is known as giving discovery. There

209

are lengthy provisions in the Rules of the Supreme Court (Ord 24) and the County Court Rules (Ord 14) for the disclosure of documents. Discovery has two stages. First, lists of documents are exchanged. Every document which is or has been in the possession, custody or control of a party, and which is or might be relevant to the proceedings, must be listed. The details of the documents are not given in the list, simply a general description, such as 'Letter dated 1 April 1989 from plaintiff to defendant'. The second stage to discovery is inspection of documents listed. The usual method of inspection where there are not enormous numbers of documents is for each party's solicitor to write to the other parties' solicitors asking for photocopies of the documents he wishes to see. These are then sent by post. Where there are enormous numbers of documents or where it is important to see the original rather than a photocopy, inspection may take place at the office of the solicitor of the party whose documents are being inspected.

Lists of documents must be divided into two schedules, the first of which is in two parts. Part 1 of schedule 1 lists those documents which are in the possession, custody or control of a party, and which he is content for all other parties to see. Part 2 of schedule 1 lists those documents which are in his possession, custody or control, and which he is not prepared to allow his opponents to see. Schedule 2 lists those documents which were once, but are no longer, in his possession, custody or control, such as the originals of letters which have been sent to other parties.

There are two possible penalties for not disclosing a relevant document. The first is that the trial judge may refuse to allow it to be used at trial. This sanction is rare because it may lead to a miscarriage of justice. The second, and more important penalty, is that any costs which are wasted by reason of the non-disclosure may be ordered to be paid by the party who was at fault in failing to give full disclosure. It is not always the case that costs are wasted, but sometimes it may be necessary to adjourn the hearing in order to allow the document which ought to have been disclosed earlier to be inspected, and for full instructions to be taken about it. This involves extra work and extra costs.

For the purposes of this chapter it is Part 2 of schedule 1 which is important. The only grounds upon which one can properly place a relevant document in Part 2 of schedule 1 is where one can rely on privilege. If privilege is claimed by one party, but another disputes that the document in question is covered by privilege, the issue should be resolved by an application for an order that the document be disclosed. At the hearing of that application the arguments for and against privilege being applicable will be aired. It is possible to leave arguments about whether a document is privileged until the hearing of the trial, but this is only appropriate where it is the central issue in the case. If one party would win if the document were disclosed and then used in evidence, but the other would win if it were not, the outcome of the case depends upon the single issue of whether the document should be disclosed. In such cases there is no need for an application to be made prior to trial, although it would lead to a speedier and possibly cheaper resolution of the case if application were made.

A plaintiff will not be granted an order for discovery against a person who is not a party to the action unless he is able to demonstrate a real prospect that the information might lead to the location or preservation of assets which he is claiming and that the potential advantage to him outweighs any detriment to the person against whom the order is sought: *Arab Monetary Fund* v *Hashim (No 5)* [1992] 2 All ER 911.

It was explained in paragraph 1.2 how in criminal cases the prosecution is normally under a duty to disclose its case to the defence: see also 10.4 'Material relied upon by the expert'. It was also shown that in limited circumstances the defence must disclose its case to the prosecution. There is no discovery by exchange of lists and inspection of documents in criminal proceedings, although judges do have power to give directions about the conduct of a case and these may include directions about the disclosure of documents. The judge does not have power to order that the defendant discloses his case in advance of trial otherwise than in the two instances prescribed by statute, namely, where the defence is alibi and where it wishes to adduce expert evidence. There is no scope for the Crown to rely on privilege as a ground for refusing to disclose a document or statement to the defence if it intends to rely on it at trial. The trial judge may refuse to allow either prosecution or defence to rely on evidence if it is covered by public interest privilege.

8.2 Legal professional privilege

Communications between lawyer and client

A party to litigation does not have to answer a question when giving evidence if to do so would be to disclose anything said by him to his solicitor or by his solicitor to him. But this privilege only extends to communications which involve the giving of legal advice or which are made with a view to the obtaining or giving of advice. The foundation of the modern law is *Wheeler* v *Le Marchant* (1881) 17 Ch D 675 in which the issue was whether communications between the defendants' solicitor and their surveyor were privileged. The Court of Appeal held that they were not privileged, and in the process Sir George Jessel MR laid down the following general rule:

> '... it must not be supposed that there is any principle which says that every confidential communication which, in order to carry on the ordinary business of life, must necessarily be made, is protected. The protection is of a very limited character. It is a protection in this country restricted to obtaining the assistance of lawyers, as regards the conduct of litigation or the rights of property. It has never gone beyond the obtaining of legal advice and assistance; and all things reasonably necessary in the shape of communication to the legal advisers are protected from production or discovery...'

It will be seen from this dictum that the privilege applies to communications to solicitors as well as communications from solicitors. It will also be seen that there need not be any litigation in process for the privilege to arise. But there is a significant difference between the position when litigation has already started or is contemplated compared to cases where advice is sought about one's rights without any thought of there being litigation about those rights. Where litigation has not started and is not contemplated, as in *Wheeler* v *Le Marchant* itself, communications between the solicitor and third parties will not be privileged. But where it has been started or is contemplated, such communications can, in some circumstances, be privileged. Communications between solicitors and third parties will be considered below.

Many solicitors employ clerks and legal executives. They have varying degrees of legal qualification and many have none. However, the more experienced they are the more freedom they sometimes have to give advice to clients. Indeed there are some solicitors' firms who have a retired solicitor as the nominal head of the firm but are actually run day-to-day by non-professionally qualified clerks. It would be absurd for the existence of privilege to depend upon whether the person giving advice is a solicitor or an employee of a solicitor. Legal professional privilege was said by Sir George Jessel MR in *Wheeler* v *Le Marchant* to extend to communications between solicitors' agents and clients. He also said that it extends to communications between solicitors or their agents and the agents of the party who is seeking advice. This, again, is a sensible and necessary provision because many clients, such as limited companies, are not able to give instructions nor receive advice personally and therefore must do so via servants or agents.

Barristers are not employed by their lay clients (see, however, s61 of the Courts and Legal Services Act 1990), but the absence of a contractual relationship between the barrister and either the solicitor or the lay client does not prevent legal professional privilege from attaching to communications with barristers as it does to communications with solicitors.

The communications which are covered by privilege are those made with a view to the obtaining of advice: see, eg, *Minter* v *Priest* [1930] AC 558 where, on the facts, it was found that, at the material time, the relationship of solicitor and client had not existed. Communications between a person and his legal advisers for the purpose of gaining advice are construed widely. Not only communications which directly result in the giving of written or oral advice are covered but also communications prior to a trial in which the solicitor or barrister receives instructions to enable him to present the case properly.

It is often a difficult matter to decide whether a solicitor speaks in his capacity as a solicitor. Some situations are obviously privileged because there is no relationship between the solicitor and the person to whom he speaks other than that of solicitor and client. Equally other situations are obviously not privileged because the solicitor is not acting as such, for example if he is simply chatting to a friend at a party. In each case it is a matter of fact whether the relationship existed at the relevant time, but it is an issue for the judge, not the jury, because it is a matter of law whether a conversation is privileged. In *Minter* v *Priest* the judge left it to the jury to decide whether the relationship of solicitor and client existed when the defendant spoke the words of which the plaintiff made complaint. The House of Lords held this to have been wrong.

Privilege does not arise unless the communications are made in confidence. If anyone other than the solicitor, his agents and the client and his agents are present, no privilege attaches. Similarly, if a client says something to his solicitor and expressly instructs him that he may repeat it to anyone he wishes, the necessary confidentiality is missing.

In *Parry* v *News Group Newspapers Ltd* (1990) The Times 22 November the Court of Appeal decided that a note made by the plaintiffs' solicitor of a telephone conversation with the defendants' solicitor, containing nothing in the nature of a communication to the plaintiffs, was not a privileged document, even if the subject matter of the conversation had been 'without prejudice'.

For recent examples of cases where pleas of legal professional privilege have been rejected, see *Re Konigsberg (a bankrupt)* [1989] 1 WLR 1257 and *Dubai Bank Ltd* v *Galadari* [1990] 3 WLR 1044. See also *R* v *Governor of Pentonville Prison, ex parte Osman* [1990] 1 WLR 277.

Communications between lawyer and third parties

In order to be able to advise their clients properly it is sometimes necessary for solicitors to seek the assistance of other professionals. For example, if Mr A is injured in a road traffic accident and he wishes to take action against a driver, it may be necessary for doctors to report on his condition in order for it to be possible for Mr A's lawyers to advise him on the amount of damages he might expect to recover. Such reports may be prepared before the proceedings are started or only after issue of the writ or summons. Indeed it is not uncommon for one or more reports to be prepared before issue of proceedings and then further reports afterwards in order to bring the position up to date. The same is seen in other sorts of litigation, such as reports from surveyors where questions arise about the state of a building or of works carried out by a builder.

In order for an expert to prepare a thorough report it will often be necessary to give him details about the case of the party who instructs him. Communications between solicitors and third parties will be privileged if the dominant purpose of the communication is to prepare for litigation. This obviously means that statements made to solicitors by witnesses are privileged, but the contentious issue is whether communications between solicitors and other experts will always be privileged.

In *Waugh* v *British Railways Board* [1980] AC 52 the House of Lords held that an accident report would have been privileged if the dominant purpose for it being made was the preparation of a case in the event that there was litigation. But that was not the dominant purpose for its production and therefore it had to be disclosed.

No litigation had been commenced at the time the report was prepared. The House of Lords held that this did not of itself prevent privilege attaching provided litigation was anticipated. No clear test was laid down for the degree of anticipation which is required. Is it enough if it is contemplated that litigation is possible? Or is it necessary that it is contemplated as probable? In any event, how are these matters to be tested? Such questions were not addressed at any length in *Waugh* v *British Railways Board*, although Lord Simon said that it would suffice if future litigation was contemplated as a possibility. On this basis, a report prepared without a thought to the possibility of it later being used in a court case would not be privileged, but provided the dominant purpose of preparing the report was to use it in court if the need arose, no matter how remote the possibility of it arising, it would be privileged. Necessarily, the less likely it is that litigation will be started the less likely it is that a report will be prepared with a view to litigation.

Cases since *Waugh* v *British Railways Board* have shown the courts adhering strictly to the 'dominant purpose' test. For example, in *Neilson* v *Laugharne* [1981] 1 QB 736 an investigation was carried out after Nielson complained about the conduct of police officers. In the course of the investigation statements were taken from witnesses. Legal professional privilege was held not to apply to these statements because the dominant purpose for taking them was the carrying out of the investigation and not the preparation for anticipated litigation. See also *Peach* v *Metropolitan Police Commissioner* [1986] 2 WLR 1080 and *Halford* v *Sharples* [1992] 3 All ER 624.

The report in *Waugh* v *British Railways Board* was prepared by an internal inquiry, and therefore was a somewhat different type of communication from that in *Wheeler* v *Le Marchant* because it did not involve an independent third party. However, for the purpose of the law of privilege it was treated by the House of Lords as though it was a communication between British Rail's legal advisers and a wholly independent inquiry.

Organisations like British Rail have many different branches and internal offices. The same, of course, applies to many companies. It seems, following the *Waugh* case, that communications between in-house legal advisers and other offices of a company or between independent solicitors and such other offices will be privileged if the sole or dominant purpose of the communication is to prepare for litigation. A difficult situation which can arise is to decide who is to be treated as the client. One problem is that communications between legal advisers and their client will be privileged whether or not litigation is contemplated, provided the purpose of the communication is to receive legal advice; whereas communications between the same legal advisers and any person other than the client will only be privileged if the dominant purpose for which it is made is the preparation for litigation. There is no authority on what part, if any, of a company is the client for the purposes of legal professional privilege. Although certain positions within a company carry with them certain well-recognised powers, and the holders of certain offices within a company have certain rights and duties as agents of the company either at common law or by statute, there is no general recognition by English company law of any office or person as being 'the company'.

In *Alfred Crompton Amusement Machines Ltd* v *Customs and Excise Commissioners (No 2)* [1974] AC 405 the House of Lords held legal professional privilege to attach to some communications between the Customs and Excise Commissioners (the heads of the Customs and Excise government department) and the department's solicitor, because the only purpose of the communications was to obtain advice. Legal professional privilege was held not to attach to other communications, even though litigation about the subject matter of the communications was contemplated, because the dominant purpose for the communications was to assess what purchase tax was payable by a taxpayer and not to prepare for any litigation which might in the future have been started.

The recognition of the heads of the department as 'the client' so far as the giving of advice is concerned should not be seen as limiting the offices or persons whose communications for the purpose of gaining advice will be privileged. Although there is no clear authority on this matter, it is submitted that the proper approach is to consider the nature of the communication between one office or employee and the company or organisation's legal advisers.

If it is made solely for the purpose of obtaining advice it is privileged whereas if it is for any other purpose one should ask whether the dominant purpose is the preparation for litigation which has either started or is contemplated as a possibility at some time in the future.

To what does privilege attach?

The purpose of legal professional privilege is to protect confidential communications between lawyers and clients. But to state the effect of privilege in such wide terms would allow any person to make all sorts of documents privileged simply by sending them to his solicitor and asking for advice on them. The true effect of privilege is to protect original confidential communications and documents which come into effect for the purpose of gaining advice, or as we have seen, for the dominant purpose of preparing for litigation. A letter written to a solicitor asking for advice will be privileged but the same letter written to an accountant and then, only as an afterthought, sent to a solicitor will not be privileged.

The same point carries over into the field of communications between solicitors and third parties. Letters written to a potential expert witness asking for his advice and disclosing the case of the client will be privileged. But documents which were not privileged when created will not become privileged by being sent to an expert for his opinion with a view to preparing a report for trial.

There are both civil and criminal authorities on this – the rule is the same no matter the type of proceedings. In *Harmony Shipping Co SA* v *Saudi Europe Line Ltd* [1979] 1 WLR 1380 a document was sent to a handwriting expert for his opinion to be given about its genuineness. He advised that it was not genuine. Some time later the defendant sent the same document to the same expert and he repeated his opinion. By an oversight the expert had forgotten that he had acted for the plaintiff, but when he realised that he had acted for both sides he told the defendant that he was not prepared to give evidence for him. The defendant issued a sub poena requiring the expert to attend court and the plaintiff applied for the sub poena to be set aside on the ground that legal professional privilege applied to what the expert would say in evidence. The Court of Appeal refused to set aside the sub poena holding that legal professional privilege cannot prevent a witness from being sub poenaed, it can only allow him to refuse to answer questions which would divulge confidential communications where those communications were privileged. Thus, the handwriting expert could be called and could be shown the document, which was not privileged, and could be asked to give his opinion on it. What he could not be asked about was communications between himself and the plaintiff's solicitors.

In *Frank Truman Export Ltd* v *Metropolitan Police Commissioner* [1977] QB 952 Swanwick J expressed the view, obiter, that documents left with solicitors by the defendant in a criminal case would be privileged and, therefore, that the prosecution would not be able to use them at trial. The Divisional Court in *R* v *Peterborough Justices, ex p Hicks* [1977] 1 WLR 1371 had to decide whether documents left with a solicitor by a defendant to a criminal charge could be seized under a search warrant. It was argued that the documents were covered by privilege. Although it was not necessary for the court to say whether the documents were privileged, the view was expressed that they were not. The *Frank Truman* case was cited to the court but no reference was made to Swanwick J's dictum in the judgment. The Court of Appeal has held that the view expressed obiter in *ex p Hicks* is to be preferred to that expressed obiter in *Frank Truman Export Ltd* v *Metropolitan Police Commissioner*. In *King* [1983] 1 WLR 411 the Court of Appeal held that documents sent to a handwriting expert by the defendant's solicitors were not privileged. It was clear that they would not have been privileged if they had been in the defendant's possession and did not become privileged by being handed to his solicitor. Although the handwriting expert could not be asked about what was said to him by the defendant's solicitors, he could be asked in court to give his opinion about the document.

Harmony Shipping Co v *Saudi Europe Line Ltd* and *King* illustrate a further principle. It is clear that any written report made by an expert who is consulted by solicitors with a view to preparing a report for possible use in court could not be compelled to disclose that report. But it was also made clear in that case that once the expert is in the witness box any document which is not privileged can be shown to him and he can properly be asked to give his opinion on it. This may, of course, mean that he gives in evidence the same view which he expressed in his privileged report. But it is the report itself and not the opinion of the expert which is privileged. It must be remembered that he could not be asked "What documents were you shown by the solicitors?" because such a question asks about privileged communications. However, if the documents are available to be shown to him in the witness box there is no reason why he should not give his expert opinion there and then.

Legal professional privilege attaches not just to communications between solicitor and client but also to communications between a third party and the solicitor where the solicitor is told something in order to pass it on to his client. In *Re Sarah C Getty Trust* [1985] 2 All ER 809 a solicitor was given information by members of the board of directors of an oil company. He was given the information because he was the solicitor of someone with an interest in the oil company and received the information in his capacity as that person's solicitor. It was held by Mervyn Davis J that the communications between the members of the board and the solicitor were privileged just as much as were the conversations between the solicitor and his client in which he passed on that information. Therefore the solicitor could not be compelled to answer questions about what he was told by the members of the board.

It is arguable that the result in *Re Sarah C Getty Trust* would not have been the same had the members of the board been called as witnesses and asked about their conversations with the solicitor. To ask the solicitor about what he was told amounted to asking him what he told his client. But the members of the board would not be able to rely on privilege because they were not in a lawyer–client relationship with either the solicitor or his client. Had they been approached by the solicitor and asked to give statements those statements would, obviously, be privileged. But they approached the solicitor and not vice versa.

In *Ventouris* v *Mountain, The Italia Express* [1991] 3 All ER 472 the Court of Appeal decided that legal professional privilege could not be claimed for original documents which were not previously in the possession, custody or power of a party to actual or contemplated litigation and which had not come into existence for the purposes of that litigation but which had been obtained by the solicitors of that party for that purpose. Bingham LJ could see no reason in principle why a pre-existing document obtained by a solicitor for purposes of litigation should be privileged from production and inspection, save perhaps in the *Lyell* v *Kennedy* (1884) 27 Ch D 1 situation which, in an age of indiscriminate photocopying, could not often occur. However, his Lordship stressed that the process of discovery is not an uncontrollable juggernaut: see RSC, Ord 24, r13(1). In *Science Research Council* v *Nasse* [1980] AC 1028 the House of Lords and in *Dolling-Baker* v *Merrett* [1990] 1 WLR 1205 the Court of Appeal made plain that production and inspection were not automatic once relevance and the absence of entitlement to privilege were established. Indeed, in the latter case the court explained that inspections of documents under Ord 24, r11(2) cannot be ordered unless it is necessary for the fair disposal of the action. See also *Dubai Bank Ltd* v *Galadari (No 7)* [1992] 1 All ER 658, *Lubrizol Corporation* v *Esso Petroleum Ltd* [1992] 1 WLR 957 and *Macmillan Inc* v *Bishopsgate Investment Trust Ltd* [1993] 4 All ER 998.

Once a document or discussion is privileged it normally remains privileged unless and until the client waives privilege. In *The Aegis Blaze* [1986] 1 Lloyd's Rep 203 a report was prepared for possible use in court, although in the end it was not used in the case. Subsequently there was other litigation in which the party who had earlier had the report prepared was a party, although his opponent was a different party. The Court of Appeal held that the report remained privileged. It was originally prepared for the dominant purpose of being used in court. It was held that the privilege which arose when it was prepared was not limited to the particular case.

The illegality exception

There is a limited exception to the privilege which normally attaches to communications between solicitor and client. If the client's purpose in consulting his solicitor is to use him in the perpetration of a fraud no privilege will attach to their conversations and documents prepared by the solicitor as a result of having been consulted. The classic case on this is *Cox & Railton* (1884) 14 QBD 153 in which a solicitor's client asked him to draw up a legal document which, unknown to the solicitor, was a false document and was to be used by the client in the course of a fraud. The solicitor was called to give evidence and was asked about what he was told when consulted by his client. It was held that he could not refuse to answer the question on the ground of privilege because the client had not consulted him in good faith for legal advice, but had tried to use him to assist in the commission of an offence. See also *Derby & Co Ltd* v *Weldon* (No 7) [1990] 3 All ER 161.

There is a logical difficulty with this principle of law. Legal professional privilege will require the solicitor to refuse to answer unless the client used him in order to commit a fraud or other crime. But where it is in issue whether a fraud or other crime was committed, how is one to know whether the solicitor should answer the question? The answer was given in *Cox & Railton* by Stephen J, who said:

'In each particular case the court must determine upon the facts actually given in evidence, or proposed to be given in evidence, whether it seems probable that the accused person may have consulted his legal adviser, not after the commission of the crime for the legitimate purpose of being defended, but before the commission of the crime, for the purpose of being guided or helped in committing it.'

This dictum should not be read as allowing the judge to compel the solicitor to disclose what was said to him in the hope that it might show the commission of a crime. Instead he should decide whether there is other prima facie evidence from which it could be inferred that a crime may have been committed and that the solicitor inadvertently assisted in its commission. For example a solicitor who is asked to draw up a document for his client may be called to give evidence about that document and what his client told him, once there is evidence that the document was fraudulent or was used for the commission of a crime. What is not allowed, however, is to call the solicitor as part of a 'fishing expedition' hoping that his evidence will bring to light an offence where there is no other evidence of an offence having been committed and no evidence that the solicitor in any way assisted in the commission of an offence.

The rule in *Cox & Railton* does not extend so far as to allow a party in civil litigation to compel a wholly innocent person to disclose what passed between him and his solicitor. In *Banque Keyser Ullmann SA* v *Skandia (UK) Insurance Co Ltd* [1986] 1 Lloyd's Rep 536 an insurance company refused to pay on certain policies claiming that a fraud had been practised on them. It was alleged that gems had been insured for far more than their true value and that a claim for payment on the policies once the gems were lost was a fraud. Banks who held the gems for safe keeping had had certain discussions with their solicitors about the gems and their value. The Court of Appeal refused to allow the banks to be compelled to disclose what they had said to their solicitors. The banks themselves were not in any way part of the fraud, either innocently or dishonestly. The court stressed that the rule in *Cox & Railton* only allows for overreaching of legal professional privilege where the communication which would normally be privileged is part of the fraud. Therefore a purely innocent party like the banks in this case could not lose their privilege by reference to *Cox & Railton*.

It is important to note that where a person consults his solicitor and uses the solicitor to perpetrate a fraud or other crime, no privilege arises. It is not the case that there is privilege but the court requires that privilege to be breached. Rather, there is no privilege at all because communications with a solicitor with a view to using him in the perpetration of a crime or fraud are not communications with him in the normal course of his business as a solicitor.

However, it is in the normal course of business of lawyers to advise their clients on how to carry out an intended transaction lawfully. Therefore if someone consults his solicitor and asks him, for example, how he can best avoid having to pay tax on a transaction which he intends to carry out, the solicitor will be acting perfectly properly by advising him to carry out the transaction in one way rather than in a way which gives rise to a tax liability. Indeed, the solicitor may have to say to his client that there is no way of lawfully avoiding paying tax on the transaction. Such advice does not involve the solicitor, directly or indirectly, in assisting the commission of an offence and therefore the communications will be privileged.

Multiple clients

Where more than one person consults the same solicitor in relation to the same matter each of them is entitled to rely on privilege for his own communications. This, obviously, follows from the nature of the privilege which we are discussing. But a problem which sometimes arises is to what extent one person's privilege can be relied upon by another or to what extent one client is entitled to waive privilege, where to do so involves disclosing what another of the solicitor's clients has told him.

In *Minter* v *Priest*, to which reference has been made already, two people, Thomas and Simpson, consulted a solicitor together. Lord Buckmaster doubted whether one could waive privilege without the other also waiving it. This view incorporates two arguments. First, where two or more people consult a solicitor at the same time each can claim privilege provided advice was being sought. Secondly, because the disclosure by one of those people of the contents of the meeting with the solicitor would inevitably mean that the privileged communications of the others would be disclosed, so none is entitled to waive privilege unless they all waive it.

Where two or more people who have an identical interest in litigation and share the same solicitor, communicate with each other with a view to preparing for that litigation, each can claim legal professional privilege for their communications. This was the position in *Buttes Gas and Oil Co* v *Hammer (No3)* [1981] QB 223 where the dispute was about which of two countries owned an oilfield. The litigation was complex, but basically involved competing claims by Buttes and Occidental about which country owned the oilfield. If one country owned the field, it belonged to Buttes because of an agreement between that country and Buttes. Similarly, if the other country owned the field, an agreement between that country and Occidental meant that Occidental would reap the benefits of the oil. The oil companies were the parties to the litigation, but it was really the rights of the countries which were in dispute. The Court of Appeal held that there was an interest in the proceedings shared by Buttes and the country with which it had made its agreement, and that communications between them which were made with the dominant purpose of preparing for litigation, were privileged. This, of course, is the same test as that applied by the House of Lords in *Waugh* v *British Railways Board* for communications between third parties and solicitors. The *Buttes* case went to the House of Lords, but only on grounds concerned with the questions of public international law which arose and not on the questions of legal professional privilege.

Privilege and witnesses

We have seen that communications between solicitor or clients and witnesses, which were made with the dominant purpose of preparing for pending or anticipated litigation, are privileged. In practical terms this means that a party to litigation does not have to give discovery of any document which went to or came from the witness, and the witness when giving evidence does not have to answer any question which asks him to disclose what he was told in confidence by the solicitor or the party. We have also seen that once the witness is called he may be asked questions which overlap with the privileged communications: see, for example, *King*.

There is no property in a witness. Each party is entitled to interview and take statements from the same witnesses. Similarly, one party (A) may call as a witness someone (C) whom another party (B) has interviewed. That witness may not, of course, be asked about confidential discussions he has had with B's solicitors, but he may be asked about the facts of the case and in answering such questions may indirectly make known what he said to B's solicitors.

In some rare situations it is possible for a party to apply for an order that someone who is not a party to existing litigation gives discovery of documents. There are two common examples of this. The first arises where a right such as a patent has been infringed and an order is sought requiring someone who is suspected of having breached the patent to disclose documents from which the question whether he has has breached it can be determined. This is known as an 'Anton Piller order' after the case of *Anton Piller KG* v *Manufacturing Processes Ltd* [1976] Ch 55. The primary purpose of Anton Piller orders is to preserve evidence which might be destroyed unless an order is made. The second common order requiring someone who is not a party to litigation to disclose documents may be made in personal injury cases pursuant to s33 of the Supreme Court Act 1981. This allows pre-action discovery against those who may become parties to personal injury litigation: see *Harris* v *Newcastle-upon-Tyne Health Authority* [1989] 1 WLR 96. Such orders are designed specifically to allow patients who come out of hospital in a worse state of health than when they went in to discover exactly what treatment they received.

Someone against whom an Anton Piller order or an order under s33 of the 1981 Act is made may refuse to disclose documents which are privileged. But he may only normally do so to the extent that the privilege is his. He may not normally, for example, say that he refuses to hand over a document because it came into existence for the dominant purpose of someone else's litigation. Similarly, someone who is sued cannot rely on privilege which arose in entirely separate proceedings to which he was not a party. Where A sues B and consults C as an expert witness who prepares a report in which he defames B, in a subsequent libel action by B against C, C cannot claim that the report is privileged by virtue of having been prepared with the dominant purpose of assisting A to prepare his case. This was the position in *Schneider* v *Leigh* [1955] 2 QB 195. In that case the person whom we have called A was not a party to the libel action between B and C and therefore was not able to object to the report being disclosed. The Court of Appeal held that in the absence of objection by A to the report being disclosed, C was not entitled to assert privilege – he had none to assert.

In *Schneider* v *Leigh*, C was a party and therefore could be ordered to make discovery. With the exception of the two cases cited above (Anton Piller orders and s33 orders) the court is not normally able to order that C gives discovery unless he is a party. There is some authority that unless C is being sued he can rely on the privilege of whichever party approached him. In *Lee* v *South West Thames Regional Health Authority* [1985] 1 WLR 895 a child suffered brain damage during medical treatment. The damage occurred either when he was in an ambulance operated by Hillingdon Regional Health Authority, or while he was in a hospital administered by South West Thames Regional Health Authority. Proceedings were started against Hillingdon, and Hillingdon asked South West Thames to provide them with a memorandum about what happened in hospital. The plaintiff applied for an order that South West Thames provide a copy of that memorandum. The application was made under s33 of the Supreme Court Act 1981. Because the memorandum came into being at the request of a party to proceedings (Hillingdon) it was privileged.

On the face of things the application for an order against South West Thames was similar to the position in *Schneider* v *Leigh* in that the child plaintiff (A) wanted an order against a non party (C), and the question arose whether C had to give discovery. The Court of Appeal held that the document prepared by South West Thames was privileged. It distinguished *Schneider* v *Leigh* on the ground that the application against C arose in the course of proceedings between A and B, whereas in *Schneider* v *Leigh* the application for discovery against C was made in wholly separate proceedings to which C himself was a party.

Schneider v *Leigh* was distinguished in *The Aegis Blaze* where there was an action between A and B in which A sued over damage caused to a cargo of steel during a voyage. At some later time D sued B over damage to a cargo while being carried on the same ship, albeit at a different time and on a different voyage. A report prepared by C for B for use in the first action was privileged in that action and the Court of Appeal held that it was privileged in the second action also. Unlike *Schneider* v *Leigh*, the question of privilege arose in the course of proceedings to which the person who originally had privilege (B) was a party. It was held that once a document is privileged it remains privileged and that privilege can be asserted in subsequent proceedings just as much as if C had been consulted specifically for the purpose of the second proceedings.

Where a witness has his own privilege it seems that he can assert it even though he is not a party to the litigation in which he gives evidence or is asked to give discovery. For example, if A sues B and calls D as a witness, D may refuse to answer questions if to do so would be to disclose privileged communications between him and his own solicitor. There is little authority directly on this point, although it is implicit in such cases as *Barton* [1973] 1 WLR 115: see below.

Waiver

Legal professional privilege may be waived, although the right to do so is that of the client not the lawyer: *Wilson* v *Rastall* (1792) 4 Term Rep 753. It is important to distinguish between waiver of privilege and cases in which there is no privilege. If the necessary ingredients for the privilege to arise do not exist then there is no privilege and no question of waiver arises. For example, if the communication between solicitor and client was not confidential there is no privilege.

The right of the client to waive privilege is not absolute. We have seen that in *Minter* v *Priest* there are dicta from Lord Buckmaster that one party may not waive privilege if the result of him doing so is the disclosure of information to which another party can claim privilege. An unusual position arose in *Barton* [1973] 1 WLR 115. The defendant in a criminal trial served a solicitor with a sub poena requiring him to produce documents which were privileged. The privilege was not that of the defendant, and the client of the solicitor was not a party to the case at all. Caulfield J held that legal professional privilege could not be relied upon where to do so may be to deprive someone charged with a criminal offence of evidence which may prove of value in his defence. It is doubtful whether the position would have been the same if the solicitor's client had been a defendant as well and had objected to the disclosure of the documents, although such a situation could be averted by having separate trials and requiring the solicitor to disclose the documents in the case in which he did not act, but upholding privilege in the trial of his client.

Waiver can be express or can be implied from the conduct of a party or his legal advisers. It is obvious that a party can expressly waive privilege for one or more documents, and if authority is needed for that proposition it can be found in *Lyell* v *Kennedy (No 3)* (1884) 27 Ch D 1 where Cotton LJ said:

> '... the defendant ... said "Whether I am entitled to protect them or not I will produce certain of the documents for which I had previously claimed privilege – I will waive that, and I will produce them", but that did not prevent him relying on such protection with regard to others which he did not like to produce. It is not like the case of a man who gives part of a conversation and then claims protection for the remainder ...'

There are many examples of implied waiver. In *Re Briamore Manufacturing Ltd* [1986] 3 All ER 132 a privileged document was, by mistake, included in Part I of schedule 1 of a party's list of documents, and was inspected by the solicitor for the other party. Some time later he wished to take a copy of it and it was then discovered that a mistake had been made and he was refused the opportunity to make a copy. An application was made for an order that he be allowed to take a copy and it was held that by including it in the list of documents for which no privilege was claimed and allowing inspection, privilege was waived. Hoffman J said, obiter, that had the solicitor not inspected the document, the list could have been amended so as to correct the mistake. But once he had inspected it it was too late to amend and so the privilege was lost. For recent examples of the losing of privilege by mistake, see *Webster* v *James Chapman & Co* [1989] 3 All ER 939 (consulting engineer's original report), and *Kenning* v *Eve Construction Ltd* [1989] 1 WLR 1189 (expert engineer's covering letter).

Again, in *Pizzey* v *Ford Motor Co Ltd* (1993) The Times 8 March the Court of Appeal decided that unfavourable medical reports obtained confidentially by a plaintiff for the purposes of personal injury litigation which were inadvertently disclosed on discovery to the defendants could be used by them at the trial. On the facts, the defendants' solicitor reasonably believed that the plaintiff's solicitor had waived the privilege that attached to the reports so the plaintiff could not rely on his solicitor's mistake to prevent their use. Mann LJ stressed that it was of the utmost importance in the context of litigation that a party should be able to rely on the discovery of his adversary. Exceptions to that ability must not extend beyond fraud and mistake. Cases of mistake were stringently confined to those which were obvious, ie those which were evident to the recipient of the document.

Where a solicitor has been permitted to see a document only by reason of an obvious mistake, the court has power to intervene for the protection of the mistaken party by the grant of an injunction in exercise of its equitable jurisdiction: *Derby & Co Ltd* v *Weldon (No 8)* [1990] 3 All ER 762. In that case it appeared that, in inspecting documents and, at their request, being supplied with copies of them, the defendants' solicitors had 'knowingly taken advantage of an obvious mistake' by the plaintiffs' solicitors. Accordingly, the Court of Appeal decided that the plaintiffs were entitled to the return of the copies and an injunction restraining reliance upon them.

The defendant in *Tomkins* (1977) 67 Cr App R 181 wrote a note when in the dock to be passed to his counsel. The note was dropped onto the floor of the courtroom and during an adjournment was picked up by the prosecutor. When the defendant gave evidence he was shown the note, which was inconsistent with what he said on oath, and asked if he wished to change his evidence. The trial judge ruled that the prosecution could use the note in this way although no express reference should be made to its contents. The Court of Appeal upheld this ruling – privilege was lost when the note came into the hands of the Crown without the Crown acting in any way improperly.

Privilege will also be waived by use of a document in court, even if only part of the document is used. In *Great Atlantic Insurance Co v Home Insurance Co* [1981] 1 WLR 529 a privileged memorandum was read out in court by counsel for the party who owned the privilege. By an oversight it was not at first noticed that there was more to the memorandum than just the part read in court. When this was noticed, privilege was claimed for the remainder of the document. The Court of Appeal held that by reading out part of the document privilege in all of it was waived. It was also held that the decision by counsel to read out the memorandum amounted to a waiver of privilege by his client in that he had ostensible authority to bind his client in matters related to the conduct of the case in court. A question which was touched on by the Court of Appeal was whether a document can be severed so that privilege is waived for part only. It was said that this is possible but the document must deal with different matters in different parts if it is to be severed. This is a necessary rule, otherwise a misleading impression could be given about the meaning of the document by part of it being taken out of context, as was recognised by Cotton LJ in the passage quoted above from *Lyell* v *Kennedy (No 3)*. See also *Derby & Co Ltd v Weldon* (No 10) [1991] 2 All ER 908.

Once privilege has been waived with regard to a document, no privilege can be claimed for other documents which it is necessary to consult in order to understand the document about which privilege has been waived. Hobhouse J held in *General Accident Fire and Life Assurance Corp Ltd* v *Tanter* [1984] 1 WLR 100 that once privilege is waived in relation to a document, no privilege can be claimed for otherwise privileged documents or conversations about the transaction dealt with in the first document. He did not explain in any detail what he meant by the 'transaction', but it is submitted that the essential point is that waiver of privilege should not be so selective as to lead to a document being considered out of context. This was recognised by Mustill J in *Nea Karteria Maritime Co Ltd* v *Atlantic and Great Lakes Steamship Corp* [1981] Comm LR 138. In a passage approved by the Court of Appeal in *Great Atlantic Insurance Co* v *Home Insurance Co* Mustill J said:

'... where a party is deploying in court material which would otherwise be privileged, the opposite party and the court must have an opportunity of satisfying themselves that what the party has chosen to release from privilege represents the whole of the material relevant to the issue in question. To allow an item to be plucked out of context would be to risk injustice through its real weight or meaning being misunderstood.'

The uses of a document which lead to privilege being waived include calling a witness who produces the document as original evidence or refreshes his memory from it, and using the document as hearsay evidence under the provisions of the Civil Evidence Act 1968 or the Criminal Justice Act 1988.

In *Lillicrap* v *Nalder & Son* [1993] 1 All ER 724 the Court of Appeal said that the institution of civil proceedings against a solicitor by his client constitutes an implied waiver of professional privilege in relation to all relevant documents concerned with the suit to the extent necessary to enable the court to adjudicate the dispute fully and fairly. However, such waiver extends only to matters relevant to an issue in the proceedings and cannot be used as a roving search into anything else in which the solicitors may have happened to have acted for the client.

Secondary evidence

It sometimes happens that privilege is not waived by the party entitled to rely on it, but a copy of a privileged document finds its way into the hands of another party. Where that happens, *Calcraft* v *Guest* [1898] 1 QB 759 holds that the copy can be used. In that case it was held that the original only is privileged and a dictum was approved from Parke B in *Lloyd* v *Mostyn* (1842) 10 M & W 478 in which he said that a party can use a copy of a privileged document even if he obtained that copy by theft. The principle behind *Calcraft* v *Guest* is that privilege entitles a party to withhold a privileged document, but does not make that document inadmissible in evidence. A copy of it, or evidence about its contents, are both admissible. In *Calcraft* v *Guest* itself the defendant came across privileged documents innocently and took copies. At trial he proposed to use the copies and the question of whether they were privileged arose.

Shortly after the decision in *Calcraft* v *Guest* it was held that a party who finds that one of his opponents has obtained originals or copies of privileged documents may apply for and be granted an injunction preventing use at trial of the originals or copies. In *Ashburton* v *Pape* [1913] 2 Ch 469, Pape was bankrupt and Ashburton opposed his application to be discharged from bankruptcy. Ashburton found out that Pape had obtained privileged documents and started proceedings separate from the bankruptcy proceedings in which he claimed an injunction preventing the use of copies of the privileged documents in the bankruptcy proceedings. The Court of Appeal allowed an injunction requiring all originals and copies to be handed back, and preventing use of any copies at trial. *Calcraft* v *Guest* was distinguished because in that case the question whether copies of privileged documents could be used only arose as a side issue, whereas in *Ashburton* v *Pape* the only question in the proceedings was whether an injunction should be granted. It was held that Ashburton had an interest which deserved to be protected, so the injunction was issued.

Injunctions are discretionary remedies and the court must consider all the circumstances before deciding whether to grant one. In *Butler* v *Board of Trade* [1971] Ch 680 Goff J expressed the opinion, obiter, that it would be an improper use of the discretion to prevent a prosecuting authority from using a copy of a privileged document which provides evidence that an offence may have been committed. He expressly reserved his opinion on whether an injunction could properly be granted preventing a private prosecutor from using a privileged document.

The decision in *Ashburton* v *Pape* involves a palpably ridiculous distinction to be drawn between applications for injunctions made by instituting separate proceedings and applications made at trial for an order in the nature of an injunction that one party may not use certain evidence in his possession. *Calcraft* v *Guest* holds that once the trial of an action has started the judge has no power to prevent one party from using a copy of another party's privileged document. But *Ashburton* v *Pape* holds that if separate proceedings are started in which an injunction is sought to prevent use of the copy, the court may grant such an injunction. There is absolutely no reason why such a distinction should exist.

A small exception to the rule in *Calcraft* v *Guest* was recognised in *ITC Film Distributors Ltd* v *Video Exchange Ltd* [1982] Ch 431 in which one of several defendants tricked the plaintiff's courier into handing over privileged documents which were being carried from court back to the plaintiff's solicitors' office. Warner held that because the documents had been brought into court it would be wrong to allow the defendant to use copies where he obtained the original by trick. He said that a party to litigation ought to be able to bring documents into court without fear that they will be taken by his opponent and used in evidence. *Tompkins* was distinguished because in that case the document came into the hands of the prosecution without any wrongdoing.

The Court of Appeal in *Goddard* v *Nationwide Building Society* [1987] QB 670 considered both *Calcraft* v *Guest* and *Ashburton* v *Pape* and held that the true explanation of the two cases is that a party who has not yet used a copy of a privileged document in evidence may be prevented from doing so by an injunction. However, once he has used the document in evidence the court has no power to disregard it simply because of the way it was obtained. Both May and Nourse LJJ suggested that it may not be necessary to start separate proceedings as had been done in *Ashburton* v *Pape*. One might apply for an injunction at any time until the privileged document or copy of a privileged document had actually been used in evidence. *Goddard* v *Nationwide Building Society* seems to relax the law a little from the procedural strait-jacket it was in after *Ashburton* v *Pape*. The position now is as follows: where privilege has not been waived, an injunction may be granted at any time until the privileged document or a copy of it has been used as evidence preventing such use. Once the document is proffered for use the party who owns the privilege may not object to its use simply because its use involves disclosing a privileged document.

Nourse LJ in the *Goddard* case said, obiter, that there was much to be said for *Ashburton* v *Pape* having the upper hand over *Calcraft* v *Guest*. He seemed to be suggesting that the trial judge ought to be able to refuse to allow one party to rely on a copy of a privileged document if the party owning the privilege objected to its use. At the moment *Calcraft* v *Guest* holds that the trial judge has no such power.

Application to other relationships

At common law there is no privilege for confidential communications between professionals and their clients unless the professionals concerned are lawyers. In *Chantrey Martin* v *Martin* [1953] 2 QB 286 no privilege was held to exist between an accountant and his client. The same applied between banker and client (*Tournier* v *National Provincial and Union Bank of England* [1924] 1 KB 461), between doctor and patient (*Duchess of Kingston's Case* (1776) 20 How St Tr R 355) and between employers and a firm of non-legally qualified personnel consultants (*New Victoria Hospital* v *Ryan* (1993) ICR 201). Communications with a journalist were held not to be privileged in *Attorney-General* v *Mulholland* [1963] 2 QB 477 and also in *British Steel Corporation* v *Granada Television* [1981] AC 1096. In *Wheeler* v *Le Marchant* it was said that the only relationship privilege attaches to is that of lawyer and client and all of the cases just cited uphold that principle. In *Goddard* v *Nationwide Building Society* Nourse LJ doubted that the rule in *Ashburton* v *Pape* could be relied upon in order to obtain an injunction preventing the use in evidence of confidential communications between priest and penitent or doctor and patient. He said that in order to protect confidential communications by injunction there must be some legal basis for upholding the confidence. That something was said in confidence is not sufficient although a contract between parties requiring information to be kept secret might be.

When s63 of the Courts and Legal Services Act 1990 is fully in force, the privilege enjoyed by communications between solicitors and their clients will be extended to authorised advocates and litigators and conveyancing and probate practitioners.

Judges frequently protect confidential communications or information which it is desirable should remain secret without directly holding them to be privileged. For example, in a trial of an alleged bank robber the judge may disallow questions about the bank's security system unless they are directly relevant to issues in the case. For obvious reasons it is sensible not to disclose such information and under the basic rule that only relevant questions need be answered the judge can protect the desired secrecy of the bank. There is no privilege for the bank to rely on and it is not even a party to the case, but common sense says that its secrecy should be protected unless it is absolutely necessary to do otherwise. Similarly, the courts normally only require a doctor or priest to divulge confidential communications if it is absolutely necessary to do so. Indeed, the existence of a discretion in the judge to protect confidences was recognised in *Attorney-General* v *Mulholland* by Lord Denning MR (see also *Arab Monetary Fund* v *Hashim (No 5)* [1992] 2 All ER 911), and in *British Steel Corporation* v *Granada Television Ltd* Lord Wilberforce said that such a discretion arises in both civil and criminal cases whenever a witness is asked to disclose something which was told to him in confidence.

The power of a judge to rely on irrelevance as a reason for disallowing questions which require a witness to breach a confidence or disclose information which he would prefer not to disclose, is a discretionary power. The judge does not have to respect the confidence, but he may if he chooses to exercise his discretion in that way, and he normally will respect the confidence. There are, however, some professional privileges created by statute which are true privileges and do not rely for their existence on exercise of any judicial discretion. For example, s15 of the Civil Evidence Act 1968 created a privilege for the communications between a patent agent and his client for the purpose of preparing for patent proceedings. This privilege was later contained in s104 of the Patents Act 1977, but it is now found in, and it has been extended by, s280 of the Copyright, Designs and Patents Act 1988.

A more commonly applicable privilege is contained in s10 of the Contempt of Court Act 1981 which provides that no witness has to answer a question in court if to do so would involve him in disclosing the source of information contained in a publication for which he is responsible. But the court may require him to answer the question if it is established to the satisfaction of the court that disclosure is necessary in the interests of justice or national security, or for the prevention of disorder or crime. In *Secretary of State for Defence* v *Guardian Newspapers* [1985] AC 339 the House of Lords held that s10 must be interpreted widely so as to uphold the right of publishers to publish without naming their sources save where it is proved that it is necessary to identify the source in order to protect justice, national security, the prevention of disorder or the prevention of crime.

In their own circumstances, it has been held that a journalist's notes (*X Ltd* v *Morgan-Grampian (Publishers) Ltd* [1990] 2 All ER 1), a welfare report (*Brown* v *Matthews* [1990] 2 All ER 155), social work records (*Re M (A Minor) (Disclosure of Material)* [1990] 2 FLR 36) and a psychiatrist's report (*W* v *Egdell* [1990] 2 WLR 471) were not protected against disclosure. In *Re Manda* [1993] 1 All ER 733 the Court of Appeal upheld an order for the disclosure of wardship documents as, in the circumstances, the public interest outweighed any detriment to child proceedings generally. Balcombe LJ reviewed the principles to be applied in such cases and added:

> 'Certainly if social workers and others in a like position believed that the evidence they gave in child proceedings would in all circumstances remain confidential, then the sooner they were disabused of that belief the better.'

Their Lordships explained that, in exercising its discretion, in the case of a minor the court would also take into account the prospects of success in the litigation for which disclosure was sought, but (as in the case which was then before them) in the case of a ward who had attained his majority he was to be taken as being able to make up his own mind as to what was in his best interests and the court merely had to satisfy itself that his proposed action was not bound to fail.

On the other hand, in *Re X and Others (Minors) (Wardship: Disclosure of Documents)* [1992] 2 All ER 595 Waite J refused a newspaper's application for access to the wardship court's files for the purposes of a libel suit as the evidence filed in support of the application fell a long way short of showing that the public interest in the administration of justice in the libel action outweighed the damage which disclosure of the wardship court's files would cause to the family jurisdiction.

In *Re R (a minor) (disclosure of privileged material)* [1993] 4 All ER 702, Thorpe J said that in cases under the Children Act 1989 a judge of the Family Division has power, arising out of the court's responsibilities where the welfare of a child is in issue, to order a party to disclose a report to which legal professional privilege attaches which contains material relevant to the determination of the case, even if the material is adverse to the party's case. Indeed, legal representatives in possession of material adverse to their client's case are under a positive duty to disclose it to the other parties and to the court and not to resist disclosure by relying on legal professional privilege. This decision was approved by the Court of Appeal in *Oxfordshire County Council* v *M* [1994] 2 All ER 269. In that case their Lordships decided that, by the Children Act 1989 and under the wardship jurisdiction, the interests of the child were paramount; therefore legal professional privilege which attached to medical reports had to yield to that overriding principle. However, Steyn LJ added that it did not follow that legal professional privilege had no role to play. Communications between lawyer and client should not be disclosed. Such advice was not material which arguably could affect the judgment of the court.

Excluded material and special procedure material

By s9 of the Police and Criminal Evidence Act 1984 a police officer investigating an alleged offence may apply to a circuit judge for an order authorising him to obtain access to 'excluded material' (see s11) and 'special procedure material' (s14).

It is outside the scope of this book to investigate the full range of circumstances which must be present before such an order may be made, but they include reasonable grounds for belief that a serious offence has been committed, that the documents will be of substantial value in the investigation, that the documents are likely to be relevant evidence, that other methods of obtaining the documents have been tried and have failed, and that it is in the public interest to authorise them to be seized: see Police and Criminal Evidence Act 1984, Schedule 1 paragraphs 2 and 3.

The power of a judge under s9 is limited in that the conditions which must be fulfilled before he may make an order for the seizure of privileged material are numerous and apply in only a few cases. However, if the judge makes the order, neither a solicitor nor his client may rely on legal professional privilege to frustrate it.

A bank is not in breach of duty to its customer if it fails to resist the making of an access order under s9 of the 1984 Act: *Barclays Bank plc* v *Taylor* [1989] 1 WLR 1066.

Hospital records of patients' admission to and discharge from hospital are 'excluded material' under ss11 and 12 of the Police and Criminal Evidence Act 1984 as they relate to the physical or mental health of persons who could be identified from them: *R* v *Cardiff Crown Court, ex parte Kellam* (1993) The Times 3 May.

By virtue of the Prevention of Terrorism (Temporary Provisions) Act 1989, Schedule 7, para 3, a constable may, for the purposes of a terrorist investigation, apply to a circuit judge for an order for the production of 'excluded material' or 'special procedure material'. For example, in *R* v *Crown Court at Middlesex Guildhall, ex parte Salinger* [1993] 2 All ER 310 the Divisional Court upheld a circuit judge's order requiring the production by an American journalist, resident in England, of video recordings of interviews of two Libyan citizens suspected of the Lockerbie aircraft bombing.

8.3 'Without prejudice' correspondence

General rule

Correspondence between parties to litigation or their legal advisers will not normally be privileged because they are not confidential. If one party admits the correctness of all or part of his opponent's case in correspondence, the letter may be used in court as an admission.

There has grown up a practice of heading letters 'without prejudice' if it is desired to ensure that they will not be used in evidence. Without prejudice correspondence is of particular importance where efforts are being made to settle a dispute. For example, in a landlord and tenant dispute where the landlord sues for possession and the tenant claims that he has been harassed, the tenant may wish to avoid costly proceedings by saying that he is willing to leave the premises provided the landlord pays him suitable compensation. Any letter making such a proposal could be considered to be an admission by the tenant of the landlord's right to possession, and a similar letter written by the landlord may be considered to amount to an admission that he has harassed the tenant. The courts do not wish to have their time taken up by cases which the parties are able to settle to their mutual satisfaction. Therefore bona fide proposals of settlement which are headed 'without prejudice' are privileged unless both writer and recipient waive the privilege.

The principles stated above were held to represent English law by the Court of Appeal in *Walker* v *Wilsher* (1889) 23 QBD 335 in which a case was settled on agreed terms and the defendant wished to refer to correspondence headed 'without prejudice' in which at an early stage of negotiations he had suggested a settlement on the terms which were finally agreed. His argument was that the plaintiff should have accepted the offer when first made and should therefore have to pay all the costs incurred between the time the offer was first made and the time settlement was eventually reached. The Court of Appeal held that the defendant was not entitled to refer to the letter because it was a bona fide offer of settlement; it was headed 'without prejudice' and the plaintiff did not consent to the court seeing it.

In *Rush & Tompkins Ltd* v *Greater London Council* [1988] 3 WLR 939 the House of Lords decided that 'without prejudice' correspondence entered into with the object of effecting the compromise of an action remains privileged after the compromise has been reached. Accordingly, the correspondence is inadmissible in any subsequent litigation connected with the same subject matter whether between the same or different parties and is also protected from subsequent discovery by other parties to the same litigation.

Where there is a series of correspondence it is not necessary for every letter to be headed 'without prejudice' in order for every letter to be privileged. In *Paddock* v *Forrester* (1842) 3 Man & G 903 an offer of settlement was headed 'without prejudice', but the reply was not, although it was a continuation of the negotiations of settlement which were started by the 'without prejudice' letter. It was held that once negotiations have started on a 'without prejudice' basis the whole of the correspondence is privileged provided that it involved negotiations for settlement.

It is competent for one party to reply to a 'without prejudice' letter by writing a letter which he expressly states is not 'without prejudice'. This may allow him to refer to it at trial provided that to do so does not lead to disclosure of the 'without prejudice' letter. However, unless the communication of a change in the basis of negotiations is made in such circumstances as would bring home the change to the mind of a reasonable person in the position of the recipient, the change must be made absolutely clear to the other side: see, eg, *Cheddar Valley Engineering Ltd* v *Chaddlewood Homes Ltd* [1992] 4 All ER 942.

On the ground of public policy, 'without prejudice' correspondence is admissible on an interlocutory application for dismissal of an action for want of prosecution: *Family Housing Association (Manchester) Ltd* v *Michael Hyde and Partners Ltd* [1993] 1 WLR 354.

In appropriate circumstances the court will hold written or oral negotiations to be privileged even if the words 'without prejudice' are not used. But in order to do so it will require clear evidence that the parties understood their negotiations to be on a 'without prejudice' basis. For example, in *McTaggart* v *McTaggart* [1949] P 94 negotiations took place between husband and wife and a probation officer with a view to effecting a reconciliation between them. At trial of the divorce both husband and wife gave evidence about what was said to the probation officer and the Court of Appeal held that in those circumstances any privilege which existed was waived. Denning LJ expressly said, however, that the negotiations with the probation officer were 'without prejudice' negotiations because that is how they were understood by all persons taking part.

While, as a general rule, admissions made in the course of negotiations for a settlement will not be admitted in evidence, such evidence may be admitted if it contains an unambiguous admission of impropriety: *Alizadeh* v *Nikbin* (1993) The Times 19 March.

Once agreement has been reached in 'without prejudice' negotiations, that agreement is binding in the same way that it would be if the negotiations were not on a 'without prejudice' basis. In *Tomlin* v *Standard Telephones and Cables Ltd* [1969] 1 WLR 1378 correspondence headed 'without prejudice' continued between the parties for some time, and in the course of it the parties agreed that the case should be settled on the defendant paying one half of the loss suffered by the plaintiff as the result of an injury at work. The Court of Appeal held that because agreement was reached in the 'without prejudice' correspondence, neither party was entitled to claim that no agreement had been reached. The court could therefore see the correspondence, despite its heading, because the heading 'without prejudice' only created a privilege for so long as the parties were negotiating. Once they reached agreement to settle the case on particular terms the purpose of the privilege disappeared and so did the privilege itself. In that case there were subsequent letters headed 'without prejudice' in which the quantum of damages was discussed. No agreement was reached about quantum, so those subsequent letters remained privileged. But the issue of liability had been agreed and no privilege remained for the letters which comprised that agreement.

In *McDowall* v *Hirschfield Lipson & Rumney* (1992) The Times 13 February Judge Eric Stockdale held that 'without prejudice' correspondence between solicitors was admissible in evidence where severance of a joint tenancy as a result of that correspondence was sought to be established as an independent fact. His Lordship observed that it was difficult to see what admission anyone was seeking to rely on here. All that was being said was that during negotiations a legal event had taken place: a severance.

Calderbank letters

It is common practice for defendants to civil actions to pay money into court as an offer to settle the case. If the payment-in is accepted, the case is over. But if it is not accepted and the case goes to trial, the fact that there has been a payment-in and the size of that payment-in must not come to the attention of the trial judge until after he has given judgment and has assessed damages. In effect a payment-in is a 'without prejudice' offer to settle. If the plaintiff recovers less than the amount of the payment-in or exactly the same amount, the defendant will be awarded his costs from the date of payment-in because the plaintiff has wasted the court's time by continuing with the action. He should have accepted the offer. However, if the plaintiff recovers more than the payment-in he will be awarded his costs, because he was acting perfectly reasonably by rejecting the defendant's offer to settle.

Some cases are not suitable for payments into court, perhaps because the claim is not concerned with money, or because it is the plaintiff who wishes to propose terms for settlement, or because the defendant does not have access to money to pay into court. In such situations it is common practice to make an offer of settlement in a 'without prejudice' letter and to say in that letter that the right to refer to the letter on the question of costs is reserved. This practice is followed in all types of litigation, but is perhaps most frequently encountered in divorce proceedings where the issue of the division of the parties' property arises. Proceedings about divisions of property on divorce are known as ancillary relief proceedings, because they are ancillary to the divorce itself.

The sort of situation in which ancillary relief proceedings involve a 'without prejudice' offer to settle would be where the former husband (H) and the former wife (W) own a house which, after the mortgage is paid, is worth, say, £50,000. H's solicitors may write to W's solicitors proposing that the house be sold and the proceeds divided in shares of 60 per cent to W and 40 per cent to H. It is unrealistic to expect H to have £20,000 which he could pay into court. Therefore the offer of settlement would be made in a letter which is headed 'without prejudice' and which expressly states that the right to refer to it on the question of costs is being reserved. If, at the end of the day, W is awarded 60 per cent or less of the net proceeds of sale, she had done worse than what was offered and therefore will be ordered to pay H's costs. If, however, she is awarded more than 60 per cent she will only be entitled to her costs if she had made a counter-proposal, because unless she has made a counter-proposal H has had no option but to take the matter to court. The court would usually require H and W to pay their own costs in such a situation.

Without prejudice correspondence in which an offer is made to settle the case and the right is reserved to refer to the correspondence on the question of costs are known as 'Calderbank letters' because the Court of Appeal approved of the power of the court to refer to such letters despite their being headed 'without prejudice' in *Calderbank* v *Calderbank* [1976] Fam 93. It will be remembered that in *Walker* v *Wilsher* the defendant was not entitled to refer to a letter headed 'without prejudice' in order to argue that the plaintiff should have to pay costs by virtue of having refused the offer. This case was not referred to in *Calderbank* v *Calderbank*, but that does not undermine the authority of the *Calderbank* decision because the defendant in *Walker* v *Wilsher* did not expressly or impliedly reserve the right to refer to his letter, he simply headed it 'without prejudice'.

It remains to be decided whether a letter headed 'without prejudice' in proceedings in which a payment into court is not appropriate, may be treated as though it stated that the right to refer to it is reserved. It seems to follow from Denning LJ's dictum in *McTaggart* v *McTaggart* that where it is clear that everybody understood the letter to be a 'Calderbank letter' it should be treated as such.

8.4 Privilege against self-incrimination

Definition

In favour of every witness there exists a privilege against self-incrimination. This derives from the fundamental tenet of English law that a suspect has a right to silence when questioned about an offence; 'nemo tenetur prodere seipsum' – no-one is obliged to give himself away.

The rule was stated by Goddard LJ in *Blunt v Park Lane Hotels Ltd* [1942] 2 KB 253, in the following terms:

> '… no one is bound to answer any question if the answer thereto would, in the opinion of the judge, have a tendency to expose the deponent to any criminal charge, penalty or (in a criminal case) forfeiture which the judge regards as reasonably likely to be preferred or sued for.'

This principle exists in relation to both civil and criminal case and it applies to the production of documentary and real evidence as well as to answers to questions (*Spokes v Grosvenor Hotel Co* [1898] 2 QB 124 CA), although the provisions of the Civil Evidence Act 1968 have modified its application to civil cases. These provisions will be discussed in more detail below.

It is important to note that the privilege exists in relation to offences which are likely, in the future, to be preferred or sued for; it cannot be relied upon in instant proceedings. Section 1(e) Criminal Evidence Act 1898 specifically provides that the accused 'may be asked any question in cross-examination notwithstanding that it would tend to incriminate him as to the offence charged'. Thus it can be said that when the accused gives evidence in an offence with which he is charged he cannot rely upon the privilege against self-incrimination: certainly Lord Mustill took this view in *Smith v Director of Serious Fraud Office* [1992] 3 All ER 456.

When does privilege arise?

Whether in any proceedings a witness can rely on the privilege against self-incrimination, is not to be decided upon by the individual witness. It is a matter of law to be decided upon by the judge, and can be considered in camera, so that if the information is in fact privileged it will not become generally known. The judge should have regard to the following two matters: Would the answer tend to expose the witness to criminal charge etc, as a matter of law? Is there a real and substantial danger to the witness, of the same?

The exposure must be to criminal charge, penalty or forfeiture. This excludes the risk of affiliation proceedings (*S v E* [1967] 1 QB 367) and the risk of proceedings in bankruptcy (*ex parte Hayes* [1902] 1 KB 98 CA), neither of which are penalities or forfeitures, nor does it apply to exposure to liability for a civil remedy: see below. In *Re Thomas (Disclosure Order)* [1992] 4 All ER 814 Leggatt LJ said that the disclosure of assets, following the making of a restraint order under the Drug

Trafficking Offences Act 1986, was not self-incriminating. Although the disclosure of assets could lead to a confiscation order of a greater amount than would otherwise be the case, by making reparation of proceeds of drug trafficking a person would not incur punishment.

The first question involves nothing more than an evaluation by the judge of the elements of the offence charged, and therefore whether the fear can be reasonable in apprehending potential legal liability. The second issue involves a determination upon whether there is more than a simple danger of a legal charge. The danger must be 'real and substantial, something more than a remote possibility'. In *R* v *Boyes* (1861) 1 B & S 311 QB, a witness had been granted a pardon in respect of a particular offence. Nevertheless, he sought to rely on the privilege against self-incrimination, saying that the pardon did not confer protection against being further impeached for the offence. Lord Cockburn CJ said:

> 'We are of the opinion that the danger to be apprehended must be real and appreciable with reference to the ordinary operation of the law in the ordinary course of things – not as danger of an imaginary or insubstantial character, having reference to some extraordinary and barely possible contingency, so improbable that no reasonable man would suffer it to influence his conduct. We think that a merely remote and naked possibility, out of the ordinary course of the law and such as no reasonable man would be affected by, should not be suffered to obstruct the administration of justice ... it would be to convert a salutary protection into a means of abuse if it were to be held that a mere imaginary possibility of danger, however remote and improbable, was sufficient to justify the withholding of evidence essential to the ends of justice.'

Whether or not the danger must simply exist or be substantial, has been a matter of some controversy. The House of Lords in *Rio Tinto Zinc Corporation and Others* v *Westinghouse Electric Corporation* [1978] AC 547 finally dispensed with the idea that the risk in question could be anything less than 'real or substantial'. In the Court of Appeal Lord Denning MR said that 'great latitude should be allowed (to the witness) in judging for himself the effect of any particular question'. He added:

> 'It may be improbable that proceedings will be taken but nevertheless if there is some risk of their being taken – a real and appreciable risk, as distinct from a remote or insubstantial risk – then he should not be made to answer or disclose the documents.'

The House of Lords agreed with this assessment of the degree of apprehended risk. Viscount Dilhorne commented:

> 'Lord Denning contrasted a real and appreciable risk with a remote or insubstantial one, and once it appears that the risk is not fanciful then it follows that it is real. If it is real then there must be a reasonable ground to apprehend danger, and, if there is, great latitude is to be allowed to the witness and a person required to produce documents.'

In *Rank Film Distributors* v *Video Information Centre* [1981] 2 WLR 668, the defendants were permitted to rely on privilege to justify non-disclosure of documents and answering questions regarding breach of copyright in films owned by the plaintiffs since if they had complied there was a real and appreciable risk of criminal proceedings for conspiracy to defraud being brought against them. However, Parliament immediately legislated to deal with the position by providing that defendants in intellectual property actions could not resist production of documents on the grounds of self-incrimination, but that the documents so produced could not be used in any subsequent prosecution: see s72 of the Supreme Court Act 1981. A similar position obtains where the danger apprehended relates to a prosecution for a substantive crime under the Theft Act 1968: see s31 of the 1968 Act, below.

In *Sociedade Nacional de Combustireis de Angola UEE* v *Lundqvist* [1990] 3 All ER 283 the Court of Appeal decided that the privilege against self-incrimination could be invoked to resist the making of an order for discovery ancillary to a Mareva injunction where, on the facts alleged by the plaintiff, there was a reasonable apprehension on the part of the defendant that a prosecution for conspiracy to defraud might be brought in the United Kingdom and that, if the documents or information were produced, there was a real risk that they might incriminate the defendant. This decision applies equally to all aspects of discovery in a fraud action, including the making of an ex parte Anton Piller order, and the right to resist discovery on the grounds of self-incrimination only now applies where there is a serious risk of prosecution for conspiracy: *Tate Access Floors Inc* v *Boswell* [1990] 3 All ER 303.

However, the courts may substitute a different protection for the privilege against self-incrimination when requiring a person to comply with a disclosure order, provided the alternative is adequate to protect that person against the information divulged being used in a criminal prosecution: *AT & T Istel Ltd* v *Tully* [1992] 3 WLR 344. In that case the plaintiffs in an action involving alleged fraud applied for and were granted a wide-ranging order for Mareva injunctions and discovery. The order was made, provided no disclosure made in compliance with it was used as evidence in a criminal prosecution of the person making the disclosure. By letter, the Crown Prosecution Service said it did not wish to intervene in relation to the material covered by the order and in this particular case. In all the circumstances, the order was allowed to stand as the condition and the letter afforded the defendants adequate protection. The order would not have been saved by s72 of the Supreme Court Act 1981 or s31 of the Theft Act 1968 as the proceedings did not concern 'commercial property' or theft.

In *United Norwest Co-operatives Ltd* v *Johnstone* (1994) The Times 24 February the Court of Appeal affirmed that where people are charged in civil proceedings with having committed a criminal offence (here, fraudulent trading), they are not to be deprived, in the absence of statutory provision, of their traditional privilege against self-incrimination.

While there is no privilege in the case of offences under the criminal law of a foreign state, there is no reason why the possibility of self-incrimination or the incrimination of others should not be taken into account in deciding whether and, if so, in what terms, a disclosure order should be made: *Arab Monetary Fund* v *Hashim* [1989] 1 WLR 565.

Effects

Before the privilege is asserted, the question may be put to the witness and he may refuse to answer it on the grounds that it is privileged: *Boyle* v *Wiseman* (1855) 10 Exch 647. If he successfully claims privilege then no adverse inference can be drawn against him by reason of his asserting that right.

In *Wentworth* v *Lloyd* (1864) 10 HL Cas 589 the court stated:

'... the keeping back of evidence must be taken most strongly against the person who does so. When I say this I wish to distinguish between the case of the suppression of evidence by a witness and the case where he declines to answer the question on the ground that he is not bound to incriminate himself; in which case no presumption of guilt can fairly be drawn from his refusal to answer or the privilege would be at once destroyed ...'

If the witness claims privilege and his claim is wrongly rejected then any information given by him in consequence of that wrongful rejection cannot be used against him: *R* v *Garbett* (1847) 1 Den CC 236.

Exposure to charge, penalty or forfeiture

The privilege against self-incrimination requires exposure to 'criminal charge, penalty or forfeiture'. For the most part privilege in relation to a penalty is obsolete but continues to exist in relation to some penalties in civil proceedings. Forfeiture was abolished in civil cases by s16(1)(a) of the Civil Evidence Act 1968.

There is no privilege from answering questions which would expose the witness to civil liability to any person or at the suit of the Crown: see s1 of the Witnesses Act 1806.

There is some authority to suggest that at common law a privilege exists in relation to communications or answers which would expose their maker to liability under foreign law – see *United States of America* v *McRae* (1868) LR 3 Ch App 79 – although there is converse authority: see *The King of the Two Sicilies* v *Willcox* (1851) 1 Sim NS 301, and *Re Atherton* [1912] 2 KB 251. It is surely in the best interests of maintaining consistency between civil and criminal cases, that the common law rule applied to criminal cases be the same as that applied in civil proceedings by s14(1)a of the Civil Evidence Act 1968, requiring exposure to penalties and/or criminal charge under the law of the UK, and the law of the EC.

In *Redfern* v *Redfern* [1891] P 139 Bowen LJ said:

'It is one of the inveterate principles of English law that a party cannot be compelled to discover that which if answered would tend to subject him to any punishment, penalty, forfeiture or ecclesiastical censure.'

While acknowledging that the notion of ecclesiastical censure may be anachronistic in a society of increasing secularity he added that:

'Adultery is a charge of such gravity as to render it not unnatural that we should find the doctrine still applicable to it that no is bound to incriminate himself.'

The notion that ecclesiastical censure for adultery is included within a 'penalty' was formally dispensed with in *Blunt* v *Park Lane Hotels Ltd* and the privilege clearly no longer exists in relation to such questions.

A fine imposed by the court for a civil contempt is a penalty for the purposes of s14(1)(a) of the 1968 Act and a party to proceedings can therefore refuse to answer questions or produce information where to do so would expose him to the risk of proceedings for contempt: *Bhimji* v *Chatwani (No 3)* [1992] 4 All ER 912.

However, since failure to pay the poll tax was not a criminal offence, the privilege which allows a person to refuse to answer questions which might be self-incrimatory did not attach to questions put by justices to establish the payer's means, as part of the procedure for enforcing the payment of poll tax: *R* v *Highbury Corner Magistrates, ex parte Watkins* (1992) The Times 22 October. As Henry J explained, s14 of the 1968 Act was declaratory of the common law and the privilege applies only to criminal proceedings.

Exposure of spouse

Section 14(1)(b) of the Civil Evidence Act 1968 provides privilege against questions tending to expose the husband or wife of the person questioned to any penalty. 'Husband' or 'wife' does not include references to a person who is no longer married to that person: s18(2).

The provisions of s14 serve to resolve in civil cases matters which are confused in relation to criminal cases. Not only has s14 restricted the ambit of privilege but it has clearly indicated that where such privilege does exist it should encompass exposure to liability of the spouse of the person being questioned. It is thought that in the interests of consistency the common law would apply the same rule to criminal cases.

8.5 Statutory modifications

Limitation Act 1980

The general principle of legal professional privilege has become modified in so far as it is apparently undermined by statute. The Limitation Act 1980 s34 is an apparent exception to such privilege.

In *Jones* v *Searle & Co* [1979] 1 WLR 101 CA, Eveleigh J said:

'I think that the court would be slow to take away a well established privilege ... and certainly would require some positive indication that the legislation so included ... However, the wording of the section refers specifically to the nature of any such advice he may have received. Thus the position is that the court is under a duty to consider the nature of advice received by the plaintiff and (therefore) ... must be in a position to demand evidence as to what the nature of the advice was.'

Civil Evidence Act 1972

The Civil Evidence Act 1972 s2(3) states that provision may be made by rules of court for enabling the court in civil proceedings to direct with respect to medical matters the disclosure of expert evidence which would otherwise be privileged. See also '*10.3 Rules of court*', below

Statutory abolition

In addition to the above provisions which either remove or severely limit the privilege against self-incrimination in certain circumstances, there are several statutory provisions by which certain bodies are empowered to hear and receive evidence. The right of an individual to rely on privilege is severely curtailed in those statutes, but the statutes have correspondingly provided that any information given cannot be used against the person giving it, in certain subsequent proceedings. While removing the protection against being compelled to make incriminatory statements the statutes have also partly eliminated the danger for which that protection originally developed. See, eg, s31 of the Theft Act 1968.

Self-incriminating statements made by a bankrupt during his public examination may be used against him in proceedings under the 1968 Act and are not protected by s31 of that Act as the privilege has been specifically abrogated by relevant provisions of the Insolvency Rules 1986 and the Insolvency Act 1986: *R* v *Kansal* [1992] 3 All ER 844.

The Criminal Damage Act 1971, s9 contains a provision with wording identical to that in s31(1) Theft Act 1968 and intended to have the same effect on a charge of criminal damage rather than a charge of theft, with a prohibition against using evidence obtained against those persons or their spouses in proceedings for a subsequent offence under the Criminal Damage Act.

By necessary implication, s42(1) of the Banking Act 1987 provides that a person coming within the section has a duty to provide information or disclose documents as stipulated and is not excused from doing so because the result would tend to show that he had contravened the 1987 Act or any other provision of the criminal law: *Bank of England* v *Riley* [1992] 1 All ER 769.

Section 98(1) of the Children Act 1989 provides that in any proceedings in which a court is hearing an application for an order under Parts IV (care and supervision) or V (protection of children) of that Act, no person shall be excused from giving evidence on any matter, or answering any question put to him in the course of his giving evidence, on the ground that doing so might incriminate him or his spouse of an offence. However, a statement or admission made in such proceedings is not admissible in evidence against the person making it or his spouse in proceedings for an offence other than perjury: ibid, s98(2).

Statutory prohibition

Certain statutes make it compulsory to answer all questions and do not provide the witness with a corresponding protection by prohibiting or limiting further use of those answers in other proceedings. Thus it can be used in subsequent proceedings and the witness cannot object to it being used on the ground that he was compelled to give the answers, and unable to rely upon his privilege against self-incrimination.

In *R* v *Scott* (1856) Dears & B 47, the witness had been made to answer questions 'touching all matters relating to his trade dealings or estate' under the provisions of s117 in the Bankruptcy Law Consolidation Act 1849. The answers were subsequently admitted against him in criminal proceedings. Lord Campbell said:

> 'When the legislature compels parties to give evidence accusing themselves and means to protect them from the consequences of giving such evidence, the course of legislation has been to do so by express enactment.'

R v *Scott* is clear authority for the fact that in any inquiry where answers are made compulsory by statute, and the statute places no restriction on the further uses to which those answers may be put, then there is no objection to those answers being used in subsequent proceedings. Provisions for compulsory answers without corresponding statutory prohibitions on use are found in s1 Official Secrets Act 1911 and statutes dealing with road traffic offences and taxation matters.

When inspectors have been appointed under ss431 or 432 of the Companies Act 1985, no person considered by them to possess relevant information is entitled to invoke the common law privilege against self-incrimination when required to answer relevant questions: *Re London United Investments plc* [1992] BCC 202.

Admissions made to inspectors conducting an investigation pursuant to s432 of the 1985 Act are admissible as evidence in criminal proceedings against the person making the admissions even though they might be self-incriminating: *R* v *Seelig* [1991] 4 All ER 429.

A director of a company is not entitled to rely on the privilege against self-incrimination to refuse to answer questions put to him by provisional liquidators under ss235 and 236 of the Insolvency Act 1986, but such privilege is available to a fiduciary from whom the principal is seeking information about dealings with trust money under the general law: *Bishopsgate Investment Management Ltd* v *Maxwell* [1992] 2 WLR 991.

The restrictions imposed by s2(8) of the Criminal Justice Act 1987 on the use of statements obtained under that section (investigation powers of the Director of the Serious Fraud Office) do not apply to documents obtained in an examination under s236 of the 1986 Act: *Re Arrows Ltd (No 4)* [1993] 3 All ER 861. On the other hand, where documents relating to an examination under s236 are relevant to a prosecution, the defence has no right to the production of those documents: *Re Headington Investments Ltd* [1993] 3 All ER 861. The right of the Serious Fraud Office to require the production of documents under s2 of the 1987 Act is exercisable against a person who has been charged with a criminal offence: *Re Bishopsgate Investment Management Ltd* [1993] 3 All ER 861.

In *Smith* v *Director of Serious Fraud Office* [1992] 3 WLR 66 the House of Lords decided that the Director's powers of investigation under s2 of the 1987 Act were not subject to any implied qualification that a person charged with an offence (in this case, carrying on the business of a company with intent to defraud its creditors) could invoke the right to silence once he had been so charged.

In *Morris* v *Director of Serious Fraud Office* [1993] 1 All ER 788 Sir Donald Nicholls V-C said that, in the ordinary way when an application is made or is proposed to be made against the Serious Fraud Office for an order under s236 requiring disclosure of documents acquired by the office under its compulsory powers, a third party who might be affected by the disclosure ought to be notified of the application and the Serious Fraud Office's attitude to disclosure, and asked whether he objects to an order being made. If his assent is not forthcoming, he should be joined as a respondent to the application. However in exceptional cases, if it is just to do so, the court may make an order under s236 in the exercise of its discretion even though the third party has not been notified.

Advice to others

It is not unlawful to advise a person to remain silent when he is being questioned by the police: *Green* v *Director of Public Prosecutions* [1991] Crim LR 782.

8.6 Public interest privilege

Definition

Evidence which is both relevant and admissible may be excluded on the grounds of public policy following objection at trial, on the basis that it is in the public interest to do so. A party who contends for the disclosure of information must not be engaged in a mere 'fishing' exercise. He must show that the information in question would actually help his own case or damage that of his opponent: *Air Canada* v *Secretary of State for Trade (No 2)* [1983] 1 All ER 910 HL.

The exclusion of evidence in the public interest is often referred to as a branch of the law of privilege. This is a confusing classification, because where evidence is inadmissible on the grounds of public policy it cannot be admitted for any purpose and, unlike privilege, no act or election by the party protected can render it admissible. In the words of Lord Simon in *Duncan* v *Cammell Laird* [1942] AC 624):

> 'The withholding of documents on the grounds that their production would be contrary to the public interest is not properly to be regarded as a branch of the law of privilege connected with discovery ... privilege in relation to discovery is for the protection of the litigant, and could be waived by him, but the rule that the interest of the state must not

be put in jeopardy by producing documents which would injure it is a principle to be observed in administering justice, quite unconnected with the interests or claims of the particular parties in litigation, and indeed it is a rule on which the judge should, if necessary, insist, even though no objection is taken at all.'

Moreover, whereas secondary evidence of privileged communications is admissible in evidence, secondary evidence of evidence excluded on the grounds of public policy is not. '... If it is contrary to public interest to produce the original documents, it must be equally contrary to public interest to produce copies which the maker of the documents has kept for his own information': Lynskey J: *Moss* v *Chesham UDC* (1945) January 17 (unreported).

The exclusion of evidence on the grounds of public policy, in the public interest, may be conveniently divided into two main categories:

1. Matters of public interest, affecting the state;
2. Ancillary matters such as evidence of informants, judges, advocates, jurors, arbitrators, only the first of which will be dealt with in this text.

In addition it must be considered to what extent confidentiality should be respected when privilege is claimed as being in the public interest.

It is important to remember that in excluding evidence on the grounds of public interest courts are only too aware of the omnipresent requirement that it is often in the best interest of justice that the whole truth should be disclosed: see Lord Hailsham in *D* v *National Society for the Prevention of Cruelty to Children* [1978] AC 171. This always acts as a counterbalance to the arguments in favour of exclusion.

Although there are limits on the use to which documents seized by the police under the Police and Criminal Evidence Act 1984 can properly be put, there is no reason why the police should not produce such documents to the court for use in civil proceedings in obedience to an order of subpoena duces tecum if the owner of the documents could have been required to produce them under such an order had they still been in his possession: *Marcel* v *Commissioner of Police of the Metropolis* [1992] 1 All ER 72. This does not apply to documents which are the subject of legal professional privilege: ibid.

Similarly, in *Re Barlow Clowes Gilt Managers Ltd* [1991] 4 All ER 385 Millett J said that it would be against public policy for the liquidators of a company to assist its directors in defending criminal charges by disclosing information given to them (the liquidators) voluntarily and in confidence in the course of the winding up although, after weighing the competing interests, the Crown Court could order such disclosure which, in fact, it did: see *R* v *Clowes* [1992] 3 All ER 440. In *Macmillan Inc* v *Bishopsgate Investment Trust Ltd* [1993] 4 All ER 998 the Court of Appeal said that a court should not order the production of documents unless it is of the opinion that it is necessary either for disposing fairly of the cause or matter or for saving costs. In that case the plaintiff's only purpose in seeking to obtain transcripts of a witness's private examination under s236 of the Insolvency Act 1986 by the liquidators of a company closely associated with one of the defendants was to see if the witness had made statements to the liquidators which were inconsistent with his evidence under cross-examination. Distinguishing *R* v *Clowes*, an order for production was refused as it had not been shown that the production of the documents was necessary for the fair disposal of the action.

Where the court orders disclosure of information to a plaintiff for a particular purpose it is only in exceptional circumstances that it will authorise the plaintiff voluntarily to make use of it for any other purpose: *Bank of Crete SA* v *Koskotas (No 2)* [1993] 1 All ER 748. In reaching this conclusion, Millett J gained assistance from the Court of Appeal's decision in *Marcel*.

The balancing process

In *Duncan* v *Cammell Laird* [1942] AC 624 HL, the defendants were prevented from disclosing documents which showed the plans and specifications of the submarine Thetis. Such documents could have given vital information to a foreign agent and it would therefore be clearly injurious to the public interest that they be disclosed. The House of Lords excluded them on the basis that a document could be withheld on the grounds of public interest either as a result of its particular contents or because it belonged to a particular class of documents which justified it being withheld. But they said that to come within these heads it was not enough to exclude documents that they were marked 'state documents', 'confidential' or 'official', nor that their production would provoke criticism of a government department.

Matters of public policy are not limited to war-time secrets. It is clear that the test for exclusion which had been developed in the war-time cases was far too wide, as the contents of virtually any document could be excluded on the say-so of the minister concerned, and much dissatisfaction was expressed with the finality of the decision of the individual minister. In *Ellis* v *Home Office* [1953] 2 QB 135, reports prepared by doctors and police officers on the mental condition of a prisoner awaiting trial were excluded on the grounds of public policy in that it would not be in the public interest to order their disclosure. Nevertheless Devlin J confessed to an uneasy feeling that justice had not been done, because of the incompleteness of the material before him.

The rule was finally re-evaluated and reformulated in *Conway* v *Rimmer* [1968] AC 910 HL, which dispensed with the notion that the views of the individual minister must be invariably accepted. It is for the court to decide whether or not to uphold an objection to the production of a particular document. The defendants to an action for malicious prosecution said that reports compiled by them on the defendant's behaviour during his probation as a police constable, and a report on his previous prosecution for theft, should be excluded as injurious to the public interest. Lord Reid said:

> 'I do not doubt that there are certain *classes* of documents which ought not to be disclosed whatever their contents may be. Virtually everyone agrees that Cabinet minutes and the

like ought not to be disclosed until such time as they are only of historical interest ... The business of government is difficult enough as it is, and no government could contemplate with equanimity the inner workings of the government machine being exposed to the gaze of those ready to criticise, without adequate knowledge of the background and perhaps with some axe to grind.

This applies equally to 'all documents concerned with policy making within departments including ... minutes and the like by quite junior officials with outside bodies'.

I do not think that it is possible to limit such documents by any definition. But there seems to me to be a wide difference between such documents and routine reports ... the proper test to be applied is to ask ... whether the withholding of a document because it belongs to a particular class is really necessary for the proper functioning of the public service.'

As regards documents which do not fall within this clearly defined category, the following considerations must apply:

'... the courts have and are entitled to exercise a power and duty to hold a balance between the public interest, as expressed by a minister, to withhold certain documents or other evidence, and public interest in ensuring the proper administration of justice. That does not mean that a court would reject a minister's view: full weight must be given to it in every case, and if the minister's reasons are of a character which judicial experience is not competent to weigh then the minister's view must prevail ... But experience has shown that reasons given for withholding whole classes of documents are not often of that character.'

The criteria to be applied in deciding whether or not the evidence is to be excluded were set out by Lord Pearce:

'... It is a judge's constant task to weigh human behaviour and the points that tell for or against candour. He knows full well that in general a report will be less inhibited if it will never see the light of public scrutiny, and that in some cases and on some subjects this may be wholly desirable. He also knows that on some subjects this fact has little if any important effect. Against this he can consider whether the documents in question are of much or little weight in the litigation, whether their absence will result in a complete or partial denial of justice to one or other of the parties or to both, and what is the importance of the particular litigation to the parties and the public. All these are matters which should be considered if the court is to decide where the public interest lies.'

The balancing process is essentially a matter concerned largely with the exercise of judicial discretion. In *Continental Reinsurance* v *Pine Top* [1986] 1 Lloyd's Rep 8 CA the insurers, under a contract of reinsurance, claimed to avoid liability for misrepresentation of the risk to be covered. In support of this claim they sought discovery of letters and notes of conversations which had passed between the assured and the Department of Trade. The department filed a minister's certificate claiming that the documents should not be disclosed as disclosure was against the public interest.

In *R* v *Governor of Brixton Prison, ex parte Osman (No 1)* [1992] 1 All ER 108 the Divisional Court accepted that the doctrine of public interest immunity applies not only to civil proceedings but also to criminal proceedings. Mann LJ added:

'I acknowledge that the application of the public immunity doctrine in criminal proceedings will involve a different balancing exercise to that in civil proceedings. ... Suffice it to say for the moment that a judge is balancing on the one hand the desirability of preserving the public interest in the absence of disclosure against, on the other hand, the interests of justice. Where the interests of justice arise in a criminal case touching and concerning liberty or conceivably on occasion life, the weight to be attached to the interests of justice is plainly very great indeed.'

On the facts, the court nevertheless concluded that the public interest privilege should not there be set aside in the interests of justice.

Neilson v *Laugharne* [1981] 1 QB 736 was applied in *Makanjuola* v *Commissioner of Police of the Metropolis* [1992] 3 All ER 617 and both decisions were applied in *Halford* v *Sharples* [1992] 3 All ER 624. In *Makanjuola* the plaintiff alleged that she had been assaulted by a police officer. Her allegation was treated as a complaint under s49 of the Police Act 1964. As such, it was duly investigated and subsequently referred to a police disciplinary tribunal. The plaintiff also brought an action for assault and intimidation and in that action sought, inter alia, discovery and production of the evidence at the investigation and tribunal hearings. This application failed on grounds of public policy, but Lord Donaldson of Lymington MR said that the obvious answer to the plaintiff's dilemma was to seek leave to interrogate both defendants (the police officer and his commissioner). Bingham LJ added 'Where a litigant asserts that documents are immune from production or disclosure on public interest grounds he is not (if the claim is well founded) claiming a right but observing a duty. Public interest immunity is not a trump card vouchsafed to certain privileged players to play when and as they wish.'

In *Halford* the assistant chief constable of Merseyside Police Force made a complaint to an industrial tribunal of unlawful sex discrimination. In interlocutory proceedings she sought discovery of, inter alia, the force's complaints and disciplinary files. Her application failed on grounds of public policy. Sir Stephen Brown P said:

'I consider that there is an overriding public interest in maintaining the integrity of the police complaints and disciplinary files. In my judgment this court is bound by the decisions in the *Neilson* and *Makanjuola* cases. The particular position of the applicant ... as a member of the Merseyside Police Force does not alter the essential character of the complaints and disciplinary files. The reasoning of Oliver LJ in the *Neilson* case, to which I have referred, applies in full measure to these files. They should not be opened and used in the course of the proceedings before the industrial tribunal. The effect of the decision will be binding upon all parties.'

However, public interest immunity does not attach to statements made in the course of police grievance procedures which are non-statutory and purely internal: *Commissioner of Police of the Metropolis* v *Locker* [1993] 3 All ER 584.

Documents in the possession of the Police Complaints Authority are not protected by public interest immunity in all circumstances. *In Ex parte Coventry Newspapers Ltd* [1993] 1 All ER 86 it appeared that one Bromell, who had been convicted of unlawful wounding, had alleged that a police officer had fabricated admissions. After the trial, this and another officer had inspected the court file and it was subsequently found that the original interview notes were missing. The matter was investigated by the Police Complaints Authority, but the officers were cleared of suspicion. An article in the applicants' newspaper referred to the suggestion that the notes had been removed from the file by two officers: the two officers who had inspected the file sued for libel. Meanwhile, Bromell's case had been referred to the Court of Appeal and the court ordered the Police Complaints Authority to disclose all relevant documents to the appellant. His appeal was successful and the applicants (proprietors of the newspaper) sought disclosure of those same documents for use in the libel action.

Distinguishing *Makanjuola*, the Court of Appeal granted this application and ordered disclosure. After explaining that the documents would be used 'not as a sword but as a shield', Lord Taylor of Gosforth CJ added:

> 'This court is in no way prejudging any defence of justification which may hereafter be raised in those libel proceedings. All that we are concerned to ensure is that the present applicants have a proper opportunity of obtaining the evidence they seek so that the grave allegations which they make – the very same allegations that troubled this court sufficiently to allow Bromell's appeal – can be properly tested in the courts. Justice in our judgment demands no less. This, we conclude, is the imperative public interest in the case.'

In *R* v *Chief Constable of the West Midlands Police, ex parte Wiley* [1994] 1 All ER 702 the Court of Appeal said that documents which were created and came into existence for the purpose of a police complaints investigation were not to be used for any purpose in civil proceedings except to enable a legal adviser to the police to advise on discovery. In reaching this conclusion their Lordships applied *Neilson* v *Laugharne, Makanjuola* and *Halford* v *Sharples*, above.

Applying *Osman* (*R* v *Secretary of State for the Home Department, ex parte Osman* (1992) The Independent 10 September), in *R* v *Clowes* [1992] 3 All ER 440 Phillips J conducted a balancing exercise and concluded that the interests of the defendants, having regard to the gravity of the offences with which they were charged (theft and fraud), outweighed the interests of the liquidators of the companies concerned in preserving the confidentiality of transcripts of information given to them in confidence for the purposes of the liquidation.

While the Public Order Manual of a police force, containing details of police tactics and techniques, is a privileged document protected from disclosure on grounds of public interest immunity, it is open to the party seeking disclosure to contend that, without production of the manual, he cannot properly present his case: *Goodwin* v *Chief Constable of Lancashire* (1992) The Times 3 November.

Where in a criminal case the prosecution wish to claim public interest immunity for documents helpful to the defence, the prosecution is in law obliged to give notice to the defence of the asserted right to withhold the documents so that, if necessary, the court can be asked to rule on the legitimacy of the prosecution's asserted claim: *R* v *Ward* [1993] 2 All ER 577; see also *R* v *Preston* [1993] 4 All ER 638. Following

Ward, in *R* v *Fergus* (1993) The Times 30 June the Court of Appeal said that a photograph of the appellant taken by the police after his arrest and a crime report containing the first details given to the police by the victim ought to have been forwarded by the police to the Crown Prosecution Service and that it was clear that public interest immunity did not attach to these documents.

In *Re D (minors) (conciliation: disclosure of information)* [1993] 2 All ER 693 the Court of Appeal said that evidence may not be given in proceedings under the Children Act 1989 of statements made by one or other of the parties in the course of meetings held or communications made for the purpose of conciliation, save in the very unusual case where a statement was made clearly indicating that the maker had in the past caused or was likely in the future to cause serious harm to the well-being of a child. The court emphasised that even in the rare case falling within that narrow exception, the trial judge would still have to exercise a discretion whether or not to admit the evidence. He would do so only if, in his judgment, the public interest in protecting the interests of the child outweighed that in preserving the confidentiality of attempted conciliation. While the court stated the law in terms appropriate to the case which was then before them and no other and felt that it was not desirable to attempt any more general statements, it should be noted that Sir Thomas Bingham MR found that the privilege of conciliation information had developed into a new category based on the public interest in the stability of marriage.

In *Lonrho plc* v *Fayed (No 4)* [1994] 1 All ER 870 the Court of Appeal held that documents which related to a person's tax affairs and came into existence with specific reference to his tax liability did not attract public interest immunity where they were held by the taxpayer and he refused consent to their disclosure. On the other hand, the court would give great weight to preserving the confidentiality of such documents in the hands of the Revenue and would only override that confidentiality if, according to settled principles, the applicant showed strong grounds for concluding that, on the particular facts, the public interest in the administration of justice out-weighed the public interest in preserving confidentiality.

For general guidance on the approach to be adopted where the prosecution wish to rely on public interest immunity, see *R* v *Davis* [1993] 2 All ER 643; see also *R* v *Keane* (1994) The Times 15 March.

Inspection of the documents

In order that the court may undertake this balancing process it must be able to see the documents in question if necessary, and evaluate them for itself. In *Burmah Oil* v *Bank of England* [1980] AC 1090 HL, the House of Lords rejected the argument that inspection by the court was contrary to the rules of natural justice. Indeed, in *R* v *K (DT)* (1992) The Times 8 December the Court of Appeal said that where public interest immunity is claimed for a document, the judge could rule on the competing claims of immunity and fairness to the party claiming disclosure only if he had himself examined the evidence in dispute.

In deciding whether or not the public interest requires exclusion, the court's task is to decide the case between the parties on the evidence available to it; it should not seek out evidence of its own accord in order to ascertain its own independent truth of the situation. In *Air Canada* v *Secretary of State for Trade (No 2)* [1983] 1 All ER 910 HL, the judge should not have ordered the documents in question to be produced for his inspection on the grounds that even if they were of no assistance to, or detrimental to, the plaintiffs' case they would be of assistance to the court in finding the true facts of the case.

State security and state interests

There is no more obvious an example than that which is claimed in the interests of state security. In *Asiatic Petroleum Co Ltd* v *Anglo Persian Oil Ltd* [1916] 1 KB 822, the defendants acting under the direction of the Board of Admiralty declined to produce a letter written to their agent containing information on the government's plans in the Middle Eastern Campaigns of the First World War. Swinfen-Eady LJ upheld the non-disclosure and commented:

> 'The foundation of the rule is that the information cannot be disclosed without injury to the public interests and not that the documents are confidential or official, which alone is no reason for their non-production; the general public interest is paramount to the interests of the suitor.'

The case of *Duncan* v *Cammell Laird* is another example of non-disclosure where production would have jeopardised state security. Matters may be prohibited from disclosure, however, on grounds much wider than the threatening of the national security. The principles of *Conway* v *Rimmer* make it clear that the complete area of government activity is capable of being construed as an area in which the public interest requires prohibition rather than disclosure of documents. In determining whether or not the document should be excluded the court should have regard not to the way in which the documents are classified, but whether their contents justify their exclusion in the public interest.

This is well illustrated in *Burmah Oil Co Ltd* v *Bank of England* [1980] AC 1090. The documents in question showed a 'rescue' attempt of Burmah Oil by the Bank of England and subject to the very close scrutiny and control of the government. The documents revealed the formulation of government economic policy both at ministerial and at lower levels; a quite separate category of documents concerned financial or commercial information communicated to the bank.

The House of Lords said that *Conway* v *Rimmer* established that the court could question the finality of a Minister's certificate. In deciding whether or not to exclude the documents in question the court was involved in 'a weighing on balance of the two public interests, that of the nation or the public service in non-disclosure and that of justice in the production of the documents' (per Scarman LJ). While the internal candour of government members and prevention of public criticism are both justifications for protecting government secrecy, neither should be allowed to preclude a legitimate balancing process from taking place.

The House of Lords in upholding the view of the majority in the Court of Appeal emphasised that it was the nature of the documents and not the area of government to which they related which would be relevant. In the final analysis the objection of the Crown to the production of the documents was upheld.

The importance accorded to the Minister's certificate was illustrated in *Lonrho Ltd* v *Shell Petroleum* [1980] 1 WLR 627. The Secretary of State for Foreign and Commonwealth Affairs set up an inquiry to investigate supply of petroleum to Rhodesia during the period of UDI. Documents consisting of evidence given by officials and employees of the defendants to the inquiry, correspondence with the Foreign Office and individual members of the inquiry were all claimed to be privileged in subsequent proceedings, on the grounds of public interest by virtue of the 'class' to which the documents belonged. This claim was supported by a certificate from the Lord Privy Seal in which he made his arguments for non-disclosure. Lord Diplock agreeing with the Court of Appeal and the trial judge said:

> 'While weight ought to be given to this certificate, it was ... not for the minister to decide whether the public interest against disclosure relied on by the minister outweighed the general public interest; that in the administration of justice, whether by courts of law or by arbitrators that decisions should be based on all the facts that are available, to the fullest extent that available procedures enable them to be ascertained ...'

In *Balfour* v *Foreign and Commonwealth Office* (1993) The Times 10 December the Court of Appeal, guided by the speeches in *Conway* v *Rimmer*, concluded that, although a court must be vigilant to ensure that a claim of public interest immunity is only raised in appropriate circumstances and with sufficient particularity, where an appropriate certificate, signed by a Secretary of State, claiming immunity from disclosure of material on the ground of national security is before the court it should not exercise its right to inspect that material. However, documents in a criminal case which are covered by a ministerial certificate claiming public interest immunity may be disclosed voluntarily by the prosecution without a ruling being sought from the court, provided the Treasury Solicitor gives his consent and maintains a record of his approval having been given: *R* v *Horseferry Road Magistrates' Court, ex parte Bennett (No 2)* [1994] 1 All ER 289.

The notion of matters affecting the state and thereby being prejudicial to the public interest is in no way restricted to matters of government or organs of central government. In *Blackpool Corporation* v *Locker* [1948] 1 KB 349, it apparently did not extend to communications between local authority departments although the decision perhaps falls to be re-evaluated in the light of the following authority.

In *D* v *NSPCC* [1978] AC 171, the plaintiff claimed damages in negligence against the NSPCC on the grounds that they had acted on wrong information regarding the plaintiff's ill-treatment of her daughter. She sought the disclosure of the name of their informant. The House of Lords refused such disclosure drawing an analogy with the immunity which is given to police informers, who provide information vital to the detection of crime. Lord Simon of Glaisdale said:

> 'The "state" cannot on any sensible political theory be restricted to the Crown and the departments of central government ... The state is the whole organisation of the body politic for supreme civil rule and government – the whole political organisation which is the basis of civil government. As such it certainly extends to local and as I think also statutory bodies in so far as they are exercising autonomous rule ... There is a recurrent transfer of functions between central, local and statutory authorities; the Crown as parens patrial had traditionally a general jurisdiction over children; a residue is now exercised in the High Court but the bulk has devolved by statute on local authorities.'

Thus it would appear that any statutory body performing an autonomous function falls to be included in this extensive definition, and any internal communications may be excluded on the grounds of their effect upon the public interest.

In *Norwich Pharmacal Co Ltd* v *Customs and Excise Commissioners* [1974] AC 133, the commissioners published information which contained evidence that a patent owned by the appellants had been infringed. The House of Lords ordered disclosure of the documents on the grounds that the information could not be obtained elsewhere, to prevent disclosure would be to afford protection to the wrongdoers, and the commissioners would not be put to any trouble for which they could not be compensated by an order for costs.

It should be noted, though, that the *Norwich Pharmacal* principle does not give a judge jurisdiction to make an order against a party to use all lawful means to obtain possession of documents so that an order for the discovery of those documents, at present not possible, might then be made: *Dubai Bank Ltd* v *Galadari (No 6)* (1992) The Times 14 October.

In *Alfred Crompton Amusement Machines Ltd* v *Customs and Excise Commissioners (No 2)* [1974] AC 405, Commissioners of the Department of Customs and Excise claimed that documents and communications between the commissioners and their staff and the commissioners and third parties should be excluded in the public interest, being communications made by statutory body to enable the commissioners to determine the basis on which a particular company should pay purchase tax, and therefore made in furtherance of a statutory obligation. On balance, the House of Lords upheld this claim.

Informants

Quite independently of the operation of the doctrine of public interest with reference to the state, there exists a rule that all those who provide information to the police or the Inland Revenue which leads to prosecution or further information are entitled to have their identity protected from exposure. In *Rogers* v *Secretary of State for the Home Department* [1973] AC 388, Lord Simon of Glaisdale said:

> 'Sources of police information are a judicially recognised class of evidence excluded on the grounds of public policy unless their production is required to establish innocence in a criminal trial.'

He isolated the reason for this exception to the general rule of immunity in *D* v *NSPCC*:

> 'The public interest that no innocent man should be convicted of a crime is so powerful that it outweighs the general public interest that sources of police information should not be divulged, so that exceptionally such evidence must be forthcoming when required to establish innocence in a criminal trial.'

The obligation to show the necessity for disclosure of such information lies on the accused: *R* v *Hennessey* (1978) 68 Cr App R 419 CA: see also *R* v *Agar* (1990) 90 Cr App R 318. The general rule was expressed in *Marks* v *Beyfus* (1890) 25 QBD 494:

> '... if upon the trial of the prisoner the judge should be of opinion that the disclosure of the name of the informant is necessary or right in order to show the prisoner's innocence, then one public policy is in conflict with another public policy and that which says an innocent man is not to be condemned when his innocence can be proved is the policy that must prevail.'

This approach was approved by Bingham LJ in *Makanjuola* v *Commissioner of Police of the Metropolis* [1992] 3 All ER 617.

As the Court of Appeal explained in *R* v *Slowcombe* [1991] Crim LR 198, if the judge thinks that an innocent man might be convicted, or that there might be a miscarriage of justice, he will order the revelation of an informant's identity, but not otherwise.

The police will not be compelled to disclose the identity of a member of the public who permitted the police to use his premises as an observation post, or to identify the premises so used, for fear that co-operation from the public might be more difficult to gain for the future: *Rankine* [1986] 2 All ER 566: see also *R* v *Johnson* [1988] 1 WLR 1377 and *R* v *Hewitt* (1992) 95 Cr App R 81. Disclosure may be refused on the ground that the occupier fears harassment: *Austin* v *Director of Public Prosecutions* (1992) The Times 26 November.

It seems a logical and inevitable extension of this principle that any acts done by the police specifically for the purpose of obtaining information would also claim non-disclosure in the public interest, and in *R* v *Guildhall Justices ex p DPP* (1983) The Times 8 December, the Divisional Court quashed a summons compelling the police to produce tapes and transcripts made by them as a result of telephone tapping. This information could have equally claimed to be excluded in the public interest on the ground that it consisted of an act by an organ of 'the state'. The Divisional Court said unless the court was satisfied that the private interests of the defendant should override the public interest, the prosecution should not be required to disclose whether telephones had been tapped nor to produce tapes and documents resulting from that interception.

The informants who are protected are no longer simply police informants or those who supply the Inland Revenue. In *D* v *NSPCC* the House of Lords drew an analogy with police informants to prevent the disclosure of the identity of an informant of the NSPCC. In *Alfred Crompton Amusement Machines* v *Customs and Excise* it extended to those customers of a company who had supplied information to the Commissioners of Customs and Excise, on the grounds that 'to say that the ... Commissioners cannot keep such information secret may be harmful to the efficient working of the Act' (per Lord Cross of Chelsea). In *Conerney* v *Jacklin* [1985] Crim LR 234, the Police Complaints Board rejected a complaint made against an individual police officer. The officer then began a civil action for libel, based on the complaint made. The Court of Appeal held that the complaint had to be disclosed: but see *Police Complaints Authority* v *Greater Manchester Police Authority* (1991) 3 Admin LR 757, where Macpherson J decided that a letter to a complainant from the Police Complaints Authority setting out the results of the authority's investigation of her complaint was subject to a right of confidence on the ground of public interest, and *Halford* v *Sharples* [1992] 3 All ER 624.

In *Buckley* v *The Law Society* [1984] 1 WLR 1101, a solicitor was restrained from practising by the Law Society following complaints about his conduct. The solicitor knew the contents of those complaints because he had seen the substance of them. To compel disclosure of those documents would have revealed to him the name of the person who had lodged the complaints. Megarry V-C refused disclosure, applying *D* v *NSPCC* and protecting the source of the complaint. He said: 'At all events I do not think that the solicitor is likely to suffer any grave disadvantage in prosecuting these proceedings by being kept in ignorance of the names of the informants.'

It is clear, however, that the confidentiality of a source of information does not extend beyond statutory bodies to the media.

In *British Steel Corporation* v *Granada Television* the House of Lords stated that no 'privilege' attaches to the relationship of a journalist and his supplier of information, and Granada Television were compelled to disclose the name of the person by whom the information used in a current affairs programme on the steel strike had been supplied. They cited the general principle in *Norwich Pharmacal* in support of their decision:

> 'If through no fault of his own a person gets mixed up in the tortious acts of others so as to facilitate their wrong-doing, he may incur no personal liability but he comes under a duty to assist the person ... wronged by ... disclosing the identity of the wrongdoers.'

There was, however, a single dissenting judgment from Lord Salmon that the freedom of the press depended directly upon its immunity.

Confidentiality

A document or communication may be made in confidence by one party to another. It seems a natural and irrefutable adjunct to the protection of informants that the information of those who communicate in confidence should be a category of possible exclusion. This much was completely rejected by Lord Cross in *Alfred Crompton Amusement Machines* v *Customs and Excise*. He said:

'"Confidentiality" is not a separate head of privilege, but it may be a very material consideration to bear in mind when the privilege is claimed on the grounds of public interest.'

In *D* v *NSPCC*, Lord Edmund-Davies said:

'Where a confidential relationship exists (other than that of lawyer and client) *and* disclosure would be in breach of some ethical or social value involving the public interest, the court has a discretion to uphold a refusal to disclose relevant evidence provided it considers that, on balance, the public interest would be better served by excluding such evidence.'

It is not altogether clear, however, what Lord Edmund-Davies meant by a 'discretion to exclude'. If it is in the public interest to exclude, the court must do so; it cannot decide to admit the evidence in any event.

The dictum of Lord Cross has been approved in several subsequent cases. In *Science Research Council* v *Nasse*; *Leyland Cars* v *Vyas* [1980] AC 1028 HL, Lord Scarman said:

'The confidential nature of a document does not of itself confer "public interest" immunity from disclosure. The confidential nature of a document or of evidence is no ground for a refusal to disclose the document or give the evidence if the court requires it ... (but) it does not follow that because we are outside the field of public interest immunity, the confidential nature of documents is to be disregarded by the court in the exercise of its discretionary power to order discovery of documents.'

9

Improperly Obtained Evidence

9.1 History of the common law

9.2 Police and Criminal Evidence Act 1984

9.1 History of the common law

In this chapter we are concerned with the power of a trial judge to exclude legally admissible evidence at his discretion. The distinction between judgment and discretion discussed in chapter 1 is important here, although as we shall see the difference between the two is not always recognised in the authorities. The cases expressly attempt to define when the judge has a discretion to exclude evidence, but the leading case of *Sang* [1980] AC 402 does not in reality define a discretion, but a rule requiring evidence which is obtained in certain ways to be excluded and evidence obtained in other ways to be admitted. In so far as the appellate courts investigate the exercise of a discretion they should only overturn the trial court's decision if the court misdirected itself in law or took into account irrelevant material, or failed to take into account relevant material, or reached a decision which no reasonable court could have reached. The power of the appellate court is to review the exercise of discretion, not to replace the trial court's discretion with its own: see *Evans* v *Bartlam* [1937] AC 473. It must be borne in mind that the cases which are mentioned below do not always follow this pattern, in that the appellate judges express their view as to how the trial judge should have dealt with the evidence in question. Because the cases expressly talk of discretion, they will be discussed as though they lay down rules of discretion.

The discretion to exclude evidence has developed in stages. In this section we will examine briefly the pre-1962 position and the development from 1962 to 1979, in which year the leading case of *Sang* was decided. The development of the law since *Sang* is the subject matter of paragraph 9.2.

Little time was spent by the courts in discussing judicial discretion to exclude otherwise admissible evidence before 1962. In 1914 the House of Lords in *Christie* [1914] AC 545 mentioned the need to prevent the jury from hearing evidence to which they might attribute an undeserved probative force. These comments were made in the context of a case where the appellant complained about the admission of evidence that he had denied an allegation when it was put to him by the alleged victim of a sexual assault. No general discretion was laid down as applying to all

254

evidence. The House merely stated that the trial judge should not allow the prosecution to adduce evidence which was more prejudicial than probative.

That general principle was repeated by the Privy Council in *Noor Mohamed* v *R* [1949] AC 182 in a case concerning similar fact evidence. The evidence was not obtained improperly, so it is not surprising that the court did not go on to discuss whether there is a discretion to exclude evidence which is more probative than prejudicial on the ground that it was obtained by wrongful means. Eight years earlier (in *Barker* [1941] 2 KB 381) the Court of Appeal had come close to stating that such a discretion existed. Although the court decided *Barker* on the ground that the 'confession' in question was involuntary and therefore inadmissible, one view of the decision is that the court was saying that the trial judge may treat as a confession evidence obtained as a result of a threat or promise. To that extent, and to that extent only, was there authority for the trial judge having a discretion to refuse to admit evidence which was probative. The full picture was that:

1. If evidence was more prejudicial than probative the judge had to exclude it, and
2. If evidence was tantamount to a confession and failed the voluntariness test, the judge had to exclude it.

Apart from that there was nothing he could do if he did not like how it was obtained.

The final case in the first stage of development of the law was *Kuruma* v *R* [1955] AC 197. The appellant was convicted of possessing ammunition. He had been searched by officers who did not have a power to search him, and argued that their evidence should not be admitted. The Privy Council dismissed his appeal, holding that a court was not concerned with how evidence was obtained, merely whether it was relevant. *Noor Mohamed* v *R* and the similar fact case of *Harris* v *DPP* [1952] AC 694 were cited as authority that the judge always has a discretion to exclude evidence which is unfairly prejudicial. It was said (by Lord Goddard CJ), obiter:

> 'If, for instance, some admission of some piece of evidence, eg, a document, had been obtained from a defendant by a trick, no doubt the judge might properly rule it out.'

This dictum seems to refer to cases such as *Barker*, although *Barker* itself was not cited.

A series of decisions between 1962 and 1979 contained dicta that a trial judge had a wider discretion to exclude evidence obtained improperly than was stated in any of the cases cited so far. But they did not describe with any consistency the degree of impropriety required for this discretion to arise. In *Myers* v *DPP* [1965] AC 1001 Lord Reid said in passing that every judge has a discretion to exclude legally admissible evidence if justice so requires. But he cited no authority, did not define when justice would so require, and the point was not one which fell for decision in that case. His dictum, therefore, did not take matters any further.

The high water mark of exclusionary discretion was reached in *Jeffrey* v *Black* [1978] QB 490 in which the appellant was arrested for stealing a sandwich from a pub and his home was searched for drugs without the police first obtaining a search warrant. It is unlikely that a search warrant would have been granted if applied for because it does not follow from the fact that someone steals a sandwich that anything illegal is likely to be found in his home. Certainly the police could not realistically apply for a warrant to search for other stolen sandwiches. A charge of possessing drugs was dismissed in the magistrates' court because the search was unlawful. The Divisional Court sent the case back to the justices with a direction that the evidence of what was found in the search ought not to have been excluded. Lord Widgery CJ said that there is no discretion to exclude evidence simply because it was obtained by unlawful means. He went on to say that where evidence has been obtained by trickery or by misleading someone or in an oppressive manner or in any other manner which is 'morally reprehensible' then the discretion arises. He stressed that this discretion will only arise in rare cases, but his statement of the extent of the discretion was in wide terms.

R v Sang

Sang and Mangan were charged with offences of conspiracy to utter forged bank notes and possession of forged bank notes. They both pleaded not guilty and a trial within a trial took place to decide whether the prosecution's evidence against them should be admitted. The defence was entrapment, in other words that the police had set up the offence and it would never have been committed had the police not instigated it. The trial judge ruled that he had no discretion to exclude evidence obtained by entrapment and the defendants changed their pleas to guilty – of conspiracy in Sang's case and of possession in Mangan's. The Court of Appeal upheld the trial judge's decision, holding that the only discretion to exclude arose where evidence was more prejudicial than probative. A point of law was certified for the House of Lords:

> 'Does a trial judge have a discretion to refuse to allow evidence – being evidence other than evidence of admission – to be given in any circumstances in which such evidence is relevant and of more than minimal probative value?'

The House gave leave to appeal. All five Law Lords delivered reasoned speeches and it is difficult to extract a ratio decidendi from those speeches, although an attempt will be made after each speech is analysed. Both Court of Appeal and House of Lords decisions are reported at *R v Sang* [1980] AC 402. The question asks whether the trial judge has a discretion to exclude evidence, but it does not ask what criteria must be satisfied before he will be justified in exercising the discretion. The speeches concentrate on when the judge has a discretion, but they also discuss how he should exercise it.

Lord Diplock said that there was no discretion to exclude evidence unless its prejudicial effect out-weighed its probative value or it was tantamount to a confession or admission. He treated it as a similar case to *Barker*, that is, as a case where the accused had been tricked into making admissions. He said that the power of a judge to prevent the prosecution leading evidence was based on the principle that 'no one can be required to be his own betrayer'. The answer he proposed to the certified question was as follows:

1. A trial judge in a criminal case has always a discretion to refuse to admit evidence if in his opinion its prejudicial effect outweighs its probative value.
2. Save with regard to admissions and confessions and generally with regard to evidence obtained from the accused after commission of the offence, he has no discretion to refuse to admit relevant admissible evidence on the ground that it was obtained by improper or unfair means. The court is not concerned with how it was obtained.

The proposition in the first paragraph of Lord Diplock's answer is beyond dispute. It is the second paragraph which causes problems. He said that a trial judge had a discretion to exclude admissions or confessions or other evidence obtained from the accused after the commission of the offence, but did not say what criteria had to be satisfied before the discretion should be exercised. This is perhaps not surprising since the question only asked whether a discretion existed. To say that any evidence obtained from the accused after commission of the offence is liable to be disallowed if obtained by improper means, is to state the rule in rather wider terms than he stated it in the body of his speech, where he made it clear that it was only evidence obtained from the accused and which was tantamount to a confession that may be excluded.

Viscount Dilhorne did not expressly draw a distinction between the exclusion of evidence because it was unduly prejudicial and its exclusion because of the way it was obtained. But, he impliedly approved *Barker* and therefore probably felt, as did Lord Diplock, that evidence obtained by the accused and which was tantamount to a confession was subject to a discretion if it was obtained unfairly.

Lord Salmon adopted a radically different approach, but reached a similar conclusion. He said that every trial judge has a discretion to exclude legally admissible evidence if justice so requires. And he cited two examples of when that requirement is met, first where the prejudicial effect of evidence out-weighs its probative force and, second, where a confession has been obtained by threats or promises. But he also said that there is a discretion to exclude any evidence obtained after the commission of the offence if its reception would have an unfair effect on the accused.

Lord Fraser also approved Lord Diplock's answer to the certified question, but it is clear from his speech that he considered the circumstances in which it should be exercised to be more common than did either Lord Diplock or Viscount Dilhorne. The major difference between Lord Fraser's speech and the three which preceded it was that he set out a wider definition of what is 'unfair' or 'improper'. Neither Lord Diplock nor Viscount Dilhorne defined 'unfair' or 'improper'. But both seemed to think that the sort of conduct which would lead to a confession being inadmissible was the sort of conduct which might give rise to a discretion where the evidence was not of a confession. In other words, one should assume that the piece of evidence obtained from the accused was a confession, and then ask whether that confession would be inadmissible. If it would, then the judge had a discretion to refuse to allow the piece of evidence in question to be used. In approving Lord Diplock's answer to the certified question, Lord Fraser qualified it somewhat by saying that in paragraph (2) of that answer was to be included evidence obtained from the defendant's premises as well as from the accused himself. He was careful not to link the availability of a discretion to the common law rules on confessions because of the technicality of those rules.

The final speech was made by Lord Scarman and involved discussion of principle more than authority. He said that the discretion to exclude otherwise admissible evidence is based on the need to ensure a fair trial. He felt the rule preventing unduly prejudicial evidence to be an example of this, a further example being the rule allowing a judge to prevent the prosecution from cross-examining the defendant on his criminal record once the shield is lost. But he went further and emphasised that because it is for the prosecution to prove guilt, so the defendant should not be his own betrayer and a trial may be unfair if the prosecution relies on admissions obtained from the accused by trickery or force. In Lord Scarman's view there is nothing wrong in relying upon admissions, confessions or other evidence obtained from the accused provided it was voluntarily given. He did not expressly approve Lord Diplock's answer to the certified question, and the general tenor of his speech implied that he felt the discretion was wider than Lord Diplock stated.

In so far as a ratio decidendi can be extracted from *Sang*, it is that evidence which infringes the principle 'no one can be required to be his own betrayer' may be excluded at the discretion of the trial judge. But it is important to note the emphasis imported by the words 'required to be'. If the defendant voluntarily submits to a medical examination and the doctor gives evidence of his unfitness to drive, the discretion will not arise. If he voluntarily hands over ledgers or gives fingerprints, the discretion will not arise. But if such evidence is given after a promise or threat is made to the accused, it would not be right to admit it because it is for the prosecution to find evidence and not for the defendant to be forced to give it. The dicta of Lord Salmon, Lord Fraser and Lord Scarman that the discretion is not limited to evidence obtained from the accused personally but may arise in other circumstances, for example where it is obtained from the accused's home, do not accord with the view of all five members of the appellate committee that the discretion arises from the need to ensure that an accused should not be required to be his own betrayer. An unlawful search of his home is rarely in breach of his right not to incriminate himself, save for cases where his consent to a search has been obtained by trick or threat. In addition some dicta of Lords Salmon and Scarman urge the courts not to create categories of evidence which may be excluded, but to approach the issue from case to case by applying two principles:

1. No-one can be required to be his own betrayer.
2. A defendant does not receive a fair trial unless evidence obtained from any source is obtained without deception or pressure being used.

But it cannot be stressed enough that the speeches do not give one clear ratio. On the one hand Lord Diplock and Viscount Dilhorne required the conduct of the police to have been such as would lead to a confession being excluded at common law. On the other hand Lords Salmon, Fraser and Scarman did not impose such a limitation. But Lords Salmon and Fraser agreed with Lord Diplock and Viscount Dilhorne on the answer to the Court of Appeal's question. Furthermore, within the speeches of Lords Salmon, Fraser and Scarman are set different criteria for the exercise of the discretion, so it is only Lord Diplock and Viscount Dilhorne whose speeches can be said to be mutually consistent on all material issues.

It is difficult to see from the speeches in *Sang* why it is that the judges referred to a 'discretion' to exclude evidence. Throughout it was clear that they felt that if evidence was obtained by trick or threat then not only would the trial judge be entitled to exclude it, but he would be required to do so. What he should ask himself is whether the evidence which was obtained from the defendant by trick or threat could have been obtained by lawful means.

One area of discretionary exclusion of evidence which was hardly touched on in *Sang* is the power of a judge to reject evidence obtained in breach of the Judges' Rules. Before the Codes of Conduct made under s66 of the Police and Criminal Evidence Act 1984 were introduced by statutory instrument on 1 January 1986 (revised Codes came into force on 1 April 1991), the way in which suspects should be treated was laid down by the Judges' Rules. These were statements of principles defined by the judges of the Queen's Bench Division from time to time; first in 1912 and the final version in 1964. They were made because the police wanted to know what they should or should not do in order to avoid criticism in court and the possible exclusion of evidence. The Rules were prefaced by a declaration that breach of their requirements might lead to evidence being excluded by the trial judge even if it was otherwise admissible. The evidence which might be obtained in breach of the Judges' Rules almost invariably consisted of admissions by the defendant. Lords Diplock and Scarman did not treat the evidence obtained in breach of the Rules as different from other evidence obtained from the defendant, and Viscount Dilhorne and Lords Salmon and Fraser did not mention the Judges' Rules at all.

There was some authority that the judge had the right to reject a voluntary confession obtained in breach of the Rules. For example in *Straffen* [1952] 2 QB 911 the defendant was questioned while in Broadmoor but was not cautioned. The trial judge allowed his answers to be given in evidence, holding that the Judges' Rules did not apply unless the suspect was being questioned at a police station. The Court of Criminal Appeal upheld this decision but said that in any event breach of the Rules would only give a discretion to exclude. Similarly in *Lemsatef* [1977] 1 WLR 812 the accused was not allowed access to a solicitor when being questioned by officers from the Customs and Excise. The Court of Appeal expressed the view that the Judges' Rules applied to investigations being carried out by the Customs, as well as investigations carried out by the police, and that breach gives the trial judge a discretion to exclude admissions. No authority was relied on and *Lemsatef* itself was not cited in *Sang*. The discretion was used by judges as a matter of practice whether or not the law really recognised it. But it was not a separate discretion from that defined in *Sang*.

9.2 Police and Criminal Evidence Act 1984

The common law discretion to exclude otherwise admissible evidence has been supplemented, but not abolished, by s78(1) of the Police and Criminal Evidence Act 1984.

The discretion under s78 may be wider than the common law discretion identified in *R v Sang*, the latter relating solely to evidence obtained from the defendant after the offence is complete, the statutory discretion not being so restricted. However, the criteria of unfairness are the same whether the trial judge is exercising his discretion at common law or under the statute. What is unfair cannot sensibly be subject to different standards depending on the source of the discretion to exclude it: see *R v Christou* [1992] 3 WLR 228. The speeches in *R v Sang*, and their import, are matters to be taken into account by a judge when applying the provisions of s78 of the 1984 Act: *R v Gill and Ranuana* [1989] Crim LR 358.

By s78(2) it is provided that nothing in s78 prejudices any rule of law whereby a court is required to exclude evidence; and s82(3) provides that nothing in s78 prejudices any power of a court to exclude evidence at its discretion. It is therefore clear that s78(1) does not replace the common law discretion, but is additional to it.

At first sight it may seem odd that the section emphasises the 'fairness of the proceedings' and considers that the way evidence is obtained can affect this. But Lord Scarman's speech in *Sang* adopts the same analysis. Working from the proposition that no one can be required to be his own betrayer, Lord Scarman said that a defendant does not receive a fair trial if the evidence relied upon by the prosecution has been obtained involuntarily from the defendant himself. In order to make sense of s78(1) it is necessary to adopt Lord Scarman's view.

The section contains four important elements. First, it says that the court (which includes the magistrates' court) 'may' refuse to allow evidence. It is thus clear that the section gives the court a discretion in the matter. Secondly it applies only to evidence on which the prosecution proposes to rely. This obviously includes evidence which is called by the prosecution. Thirdly, the circumstances in which evidence is obtained is only one of the factors which the court must consider. In the vast majority of cases it is the only consideration which will be raised by the defence. Indeed it is hard to imagine cases where other circumstances are relevant. Finally the consideration which the court must always have in mind is whether the admission of certain evidence would have an adverse effect on the fairness of the proceedings. This means that there is scope for the judge to allow evidence to be given even though it was obtained improperly if the same evidence could have been obtained by entirely lawful and fair means.

Section 78 is used by the defence most often in cases where the police breached the Codes of Conduct. The Codes are far more detailed than the Judges' Rules and revised Codes of Practice under the Police and Criminal Evidence Act 1984 were approved by Parliament on 13 December 1990 and came into operation on 1 April 1991. These revised Codes are:

1. For the exercise by police officers of statutory powers of stop and search.
2. For the searching of premises by police officers and the seizure of property found by police officers on persons or premises.
3. For the detention, treatment and questioning of persons by police officers.
4. For the identification of persons by police officers.

Persons other than police officers who are charged with the duty of investigating offences or charging offenders must have regard to the Codes: s67(9) of the 1984 Act. This duty applies, for example, to customs officers (*R* v *Okafor* (1993) The Times 10 November), but it is not restricted to officers of central government or to other persons acting under statutory powers. In appropriate circumstances it applies to store detectives: see *R* v *Bayliss* (1993) The Times 16 March.

While it is not practicable to set out the Codes here in full, the principal provisions relating to cautions may be taken as an example of their contents and they are as follows:

'C. CODE OF PRACTICE FOR THE DETENTION, TREATMENT AND QUESTIONING OF PERSONS BY POLICE OFFICERS ...

10. Cautions
a) *When a caution must be given*
10.1 A person whom there are grounds to suspect of an offence must be cautioned before any questions about it (or further questions if it is his answers to previous questions that provide grounds for suspicion) are put to him for the purpose of obtaining evidence which may be given to a court in a prosecution. He therefore need not be cautioned if questions are put for other purposes, for example, to establish his identity or his ownership of any vehicle or the need to search him in the exercise of powers of stop and search ...
10.3 A person must be cautioned upon arrest for an offence unless:
a) it is impracticable to do so by reason of his condition or behaviour at the time; or
b) he has already been cautioned immediately prior to arrest in accordance with paragraph 10.1 above.
b) *Action: general*
10.4 The caution shall be in the following terms:
"You do not have to say anything unless you wish to do so, but what you say may be given in evidence."
    Minor deviations do not constitute a breach of this requirement provided that the sense of the caution is preserved. [See Notes 10C and 10D].
10.5 When there is a break in questioning under caution the interviewing officer must

ensure that the person being questioned is aware that he remains under caution. If there is any doubt, the caution should be given again in full when the interview resumes. [See Note 10A].

c) *Juveniles, the mentally disordered and the mentally handicapped*

10.6 If a juvenile or a person who is mentally ill, disordered or mentally disordered is cautioned in the absence of the appropriate adult, the caution must be repeated in the adult's presence.

d) *Documentation*

10.7 A record shall be made when a caution is given under this section, either in the officer's pocket book or in the interview record as appropriate.

Notes for guidance

10A In considering whether or not to caution again after a break, the officer should bear in mind that he may have to satisfy a court that the person understood that he was still under caution when the interview resumed.

10B It is not necessary to give or repeat a caution when informing a person who is not under arrest that he may be prosecuted for an offence.

10C If it appears that a person does not understand what the caution means, the officer who has given it should go on to explain it in his own words.

10D In case anyone who is given a caution is unclear about its significance, the officer concerned should explain that the caution is given in pursuance of the general principle of English law that a person need not answer any questions or provide any information which might tend to incriminate him, and that no adverse inferences from this silence may be drawn at any trial that takes place. The person should not, however, be left with a false impression that non-co-operation will have no effect on his immediate treatment as, for example, his refusal to provide his name and address when charged with an offence may render him liable to detention ...

16 Charging of detained persons

a) *Action* ...

16.2 When a detained person is charged with or informed that he may be prosecuted for an offence he shall be cautioned in the terms of paragraph 10.4 above ...

IDENTIFICATION PARADES   ANNEX A ...

c) Conduct of the parade

5. Immediately before the parade, the identification officer must remind the suspect of the procedures governing its conduct and caution him in the terms of paragraph 10.4 of the code of practice for the detention, treatment and questioning of persons by police officers.'

The caution is a reminder to the suspect that he does not have to incriminate himself. Failure to use these precise words will not mean that the caution is defective, provided it is made clear to the suspect that he does not have to answer questions or allegations which are put to him: Code C, paragraph 10.4. The caution given on charging a suspect should be supplemented by a written notice of charge on which the caution must be printed: Code C paragraph 16.3. The administering of the caution prior to the suspect taking part in an identification parade is necessary because otherwise the accused may feel it necessary to say something if he is identified by a witness.

In *Smith* v *Director of Serious Fraud Office* [1992] 3 WLR 66 the House of Lords decided that where a person has been charged with an offence (in this case, carrying on a company's business with intent to defraud its creditors) and the Director decides to conduct an investigation under s2 of the Criminal Justice Act 1967, the Director need not issue a further caution.

There are two provisions in the Act itself which supplement the giving of a caution. The first, in s56(1), is that a suspect who is detained in a police station has the right to have the fact of his detention notified to one friend or relative or other person who is known to him or is likely to take an interest in his welfare. This right was first put into statutory form in s62 of the Criminal Law Act 1977, in which the suspect was allowed to have the fact of detention notified to one person 'reasonably named by him'. The change in wording from that general statement to the specific categories of person set out in the 1984 Act does not alter the substance of the suspect's right. The second provision is in s58(1) and is the right to consult a solicitor in private. No obligation is imposed by s58 on the police to tell the suspect that he may see a solicitor or to offer names of local solicitors who could see him. However, Code C paragraph 3.1 requires the officer who has charge of his detention, known as the custody officer and invariably a sergeant, to tell him of his rights under ss56 and 58. If the suspect does not choose to see a solicitor at that time but the police later wish to question him, it is common practice to ask him whether he wants to have a solicitor present at the interview. A solicitor fulfiling the exacting duty of assisting a suspect during police interviews should not remain passive but should discharge his function responsibly and courageously: *R* v *Miller* (1992) The Times 24 December.

In order to allow the police some latitude in their investigations the rights under ss56 and 58 may be delayed if a senior officer authorises this, but it can only be authorised where the offence alleged is one of a number of serious offences specified by s116 and there are grounds to believe that exercise of the rights may hinder investigations

In *R* v *Silcott*, *R* v *Braithwaite*, *R* v *Raghip* (1991) The Times 9 December the Court of Appeal decided that where the police refuse an arrested person access to a legal adviser under s58 of the 1984 Act the relevant officer must believe, on reasonable grounds, that a solicitor would, if allowed to consult the person in police detention, thereafter commit a criminal offence. To sustain such a basis for refusal, the grounds put forward would have to be by reference to specific circumstances including evidence as to the person detained and/or the actual solicitor sought to be consulted.

In accordance with Code C, paragraphs 3.1, 3.2 and 3.6, the suspect must be informed clearly by the custody officer of his continuing rights to have someone informed of his arrest, to consult privately with a solicitor and to have independent legal advice free of charge and to consult the Codes of Practice. Possession of such rights must be confirmed in a written notice and an interpreter must be called as soon as practicable if the suspect does not understand English or appears to be deaf. The decision of the Privy Council in *Attorney-General of Trinidad and Tobago* v *Whiteman* [1992] 2 All ER 924 indicates that the suspect should be informed of these rights as soon as possible after his arrest and, in any event, before any interrogation.

Section 36(1) imposes on chief constables a duty to appoint one custody officer for each designated police station and a power to appoint more in their discretion, which must be exercised reasonably. In s36(4), the expression 'readily available' covers a situation where a custody officer is not actually at the station but could without much difficulty be fetched there: *Vince* v *Chief Constable of the Dorset Police* [1993] 2 All ER 321.

Although failure to comply with any part of the Codes of Practice does not automatically lead to evidence obtained being excluded, s67(11) requires the court to take into account the Codes where they may be relevant to an issue in the trial. This gives a presumption that failure to comply with the Codes has an effect on the evidence which may be used against the defendant, but it is s78 which determines what that effect shall be.

In *Mason* [1988] 1 WLR 139 Watkins LJ said that s78 does no more than restate the powers a judge had at common law. That statement was obiter and is incorrect. In the case law the statements that breach of the Judges' Rules gave the judge a discretion to exclude evidence were obiter, but it is clear that ss67(11) and 78(1) allow evidence to be excluded for breach of the Codes. Furthermore, some situations which arise frequently would not have come within the Judges' Rules but do come within the Codes of Conduct. Also the restrictions on the discretion recognised in particular by Lord Diplock and Viscount Dilhorne in *Sang* are not repeated in s78(1). Therefore s78(1) applies to all evidence whether or not it was obtained by trick or threat and whether or not it could be construed to be an admission or confession. It is also important to note that the Act does not aim to codify the common law in this area, and even if it did it has long been settled that a codifying Act must be construed according to its terms and not by reference to the pre-existing common law: *Bank of England* v *Vagliano Brothers* [1891] AC 107, *Fulling* (1987) 85 Cr App R 136. The court should not strain for an interpretation which either reasserts or alters the pre-existing law: *R* v *Smurthwaithe* [1994] 1 All ER 898.

There are two important cases which give considerable guidance on the proper interpretation of the section. The first is *Samuel* [1988] 2 WLR 920 and the second *Alladice* (1988) 87 Cr App R 380. What these cases establish is that breach of the Codes of Conduct gives rise to a discretion to exclude the evidence, but that the discretion will only be properly exercised against the prosecution if the breach was material, that is, if it made any difference to the way the accused would have behaved. Therefore, if the defendant has a long criminal record and is clearly well aware of his right not to answer questions, a failure to caution him may not be a ground for excluding evidence of answers given to questions from police officers. Similarly, a suspect who is refused access to a solicitor may have no ground for complaining about this if the solicitor gives evidence and says that he would have advised him to answer all questions.

Lord Lane CJ said, obiter, in *Alladice* that where the police have acted in bad faith the court may have little hesitation in rejecting evidence obtained. This illustrates that s78 gives two tests for the use of the discretion where the acts of the police are alleged to have been improper. First, the 'but-for' test set out in *Samuel* and *Alladice*: would the police have obtained the evidence but for the breach of ss56 or 58 or the Codes? Secondly: did the police act in bad faith? This second test can only be relevant if the first is not satisfied. In other words, if the trial judge feels that the evidence which has been obtained improperly would have been obtained anyway, he may still exclude it if he finds that the police deliberately deprived the accused of his rights.

Farquharson LJ added that however strongly and however justifiably the police might feel that their investigation was being hindered by the presence of a solicitor, coupled with the right to silence, they were nevertheless confined to the narrow limits imposed by s58(8) on their right to delay access. If there were significant and substantial breaches of s58 or of the provisions of Code C, to admit the evidence against the defendant could not but have an adverse effect on the fairness of the proceedings. The court's task is to decide whether the effect was so adverse that justice required the exclusion of the evidence. If there was bad faith on the part of the police, the court would have little difficulty in ruling any confession inadmissible under s78, if not under s76, of the 1984 Act.

As was the position at common law, the Court of Appeal has spoken of a discretion to exclude evidence under s78(1) but in reality has made it clear how the discretion should be exercised in most cases. But *Samuel* and *Alladice* were both concerned with the obtaining of evidence in breach of the requirements of the requirements of the Police and Criminal Evidence Act 1984. Cases which fall outside that Act are governed by a true discretion. Such cases are rare, but they do arise from time to time. A good illustration is *O'Leary* (1988) 87 Cr App R 387 in which the accused was charged with indecent assault of a small girl. She had identified him by looking at him briefly while he was being spoken to by her father. The identification was not conducted by the police and therefore was not regulated by, and did not comply with, Code of Practice D. The Court of Appeal allowed O'Leary's appeal on other grounds, but held that the trial judge's decision to allow evidence of the identification to be given was beyond challenge. The court held that the trial judge had a discretion whether or not to exclude the evidence and had to take into account all circumstances. He had taken into account all circumstances which were relevant, had not taken into account anything which was irrelevant and had not reached a decision which was so unreasonable that no reasonable judge could have come to it. This approach to the judge's ruling is the way in which appeals against discretionary decisions are decided in civil courts, following the well-known 'Wednesbury' test of reasonableness: *Associated Provincial Picture Houses Ltd* v *Wednesbury Corporation* [1948] 1 KB 223. It is a test which develops and explains *Evans* v *Bartlam*, to which reference was made at the beginning of this chapter.

A second illustration of the true discretion in *O'Connor* (1987) 85 Cr App R 298 in which the Court of Appeal held that the trial judge was wrong to allow the jury to hear that a man with whom the defendant was alleged to have conspired had himself pleaded guilty to the conspiracy. *O'Connor* is a different type of case from *O'Leary*, being a case where the prejudicial effect of the evidence was very high, whereas in *O'Leary* the prejudice may not have been high but the probative value was doubtful. Once a jury hears of highly prejudicial evidence the damage is done and a direction from the judge in his summing up is unlikely to be able to repair it. But if evidence is simply of limited weight without also being prejudicial the judge can tell the jury to ignore it or give it little force. The result in *O'Connor* would be the same at common law under the first paragraph of the answer to the Court of Appeal's question in *Sang*. The 'Wednesbury' test was not applied in *O'Connor*, but the judge's decision would have been ruled wholly unreasonable in any event.

It was noted above that s78 does not abolish the *Sang* discretion, but supplements it. Whether there is any case in which a judge would not exclude evidence under s78 but would do under his common law powers is doubtful. It is clear that when evidence is challenged because it was obtained by trickery or threats, the circumstances in which it was obtained are investigated. And s78(1) expressly states that these circumstances should be considered when the judge decides whether to exercise his statutory discretion. *Fulling* says that *Mason* is wrong in so far as it says that s78 and *Sang* are identical in effect. This is reinforced by the decision in *O'Leary*, which falls outside *Sang* but inside the Act. Perhaps there could be cases in which s78(1) would give the judge a discretion but *Sang* makes clear how that discretion should be exercised. Even if the judge exercises his statutory discretion properly, a failure to comply with the common law will give a ground of appeal. But such cases will be extremely rare.

Recent cases

Recent cases have illustrated the fact that breaches of other provisions of the 1984 Act or of a Code may (*R v Keenan* [1989] 3 WLR 1193 and *R v Canale* [1990] 2 All ER 187) or may not (*R v Dunford* (1990) 91 Cr App R 150; *R v Gillard* (1991) 92 Cr App R 61; *R v Sparks* [1991] Crim LR 128 and *R v Pall* [1992] Crim LR 126 November) lead to the conclusion that evidence was wrongly admitted. As to the Code of Conduct regarding the recording of police interviews, see *R v Brezeanu* [1989] Crim LR 651. For a consideration of the exclusion of identification evidence, see *R v Quinn* [1990] Crim LR 581. Breaches of the Act and Codes, whether or not substantial and whether or not perpetuated in bad faith, have to be judged against the overall fairness of the proceedings: *R v Kerawalla* [1991] Crim LR 451. As to the relevance of s78 of the 1984 Act to extradition proceedings, see *R v Governor of Pentonville Prison, ex parte Osman* [1990] 1 WLR 277.

In *Director of Public Prosecutions v British Telecommunications plc* [1991] Crim LR 532 it appeared that justices had excluded the only prosecution evidence as to a road trailer's braking system because inspection by a police expert had so altered the braking system that it had become impossible for the defence expert to determine its original state. The High Court decided that the justices' decision had been incorrect and an abuse of the power under s78 of the 1984 Act.

In *R v Crampton* [1991] Crim LR 277 the Court of Appeal upheld the trial judge's refusal so to exercise his discretion under s78 of the 1984 Act as to exclude evidence of admissions on the ground that, at the material time, the appellant could have been undergoing withdrawal from drugs. The Court of Appeal arrived at the same conclusion in *R v McDonald* [1991] Crim LR 122 in relation to the admission by the trial judge of evidence of what the appellant had said to a psychiatrist.

In *R v Ali* (1991) The Times 19 February the Court of Appeal held that recordings of conversations between the accused and his family taken in an interview room where the police had planted a microphone without informing the accused or making any record of the 'bugging', were admissible in evidence. The trial judge had correctly exercised his discretion to admit them under s78 of the 1984 Act. This decision was applied in *R v Bailey* [1993] 3 All ER 513 (in this grave case (robbery), incriminating evidence obtained by tape recording conversations between two accused men while sharing a police station cell was admissible in evidence). See also *Undercover police operations*, below.

Again, in *Director of Public Prosecutions* v *Wilson* [1991] RTR 284 the Queen's Bench Divisional Court decided that the fact that a police officer's reason to believe that a person was driving with excess alcohol was based on an anonymous telephone call rather than on the standard of driving did not amount to malpractice and did not therefore entitle magistrates to exercise their discretion under s78 of the 1984 Act to exclude all the evidence following arrest.

It is only in the clearest case and in exceptional circumstances that magistrates, sitting as examining justices and determining whether to commit an accused for trial on indictment, should exercise their discretion under s78 of the 1984 Act to exclude evidence tendered by the prosecution: *R v King's Lynn Magistrates' Court, ex parte Holland* [1993] 2 All ER 377.

In *R v Preston* [1993] 4 All ER 638 the House of Lords explained that phone-tapping material has by statute to be destroyed as soon as its retention is no longer necessary 'for the purpose of preventing or detecting serious crime': it followed that any evidence so obtained could not be used for the prosecution of serious crime. In reaching this conclusion their Lordships said that *R v Effik* [1992] Crim LR 580 should be overruled. It was also contended that if the physical intercept materials were rightly destroyed and their contents irretrievably lost the interests of fairness demanded that the evidence derived from the 'metering' of the telephone calls should have been ruled out under s78(1) of the 1984 Act. ('Metering' denotes the recording by the telecommunications authorities of the making of telephone calls, though not of their contents.) The trial judge, in the exercise of his discretion, had admitted such evidence and their Lordships were satisfied that his decision had been correct.

Prosecution evidence of interceptions within a police station of telephone calls made from the station is admissible since the calls remain within the private system until routed by the internal switchboard into the public telephone system. Tapping lines which are part of a private section of the system does not involve a breach of s1(1) of the Communications Act 1985: *R v Ahmed* (1994) The Independent 18 April.

While s78 of the 1984 Act applies to breath test procedures (see, eg, *Daniels v Director of Public Prosecutions* [1992] RTR 140), any failure to comply with the statutory requirement that a motorist must be warned that failure to provide a specimen may render him liable to prosecution will make any specimens obtained inadmissible in evidence: *Murray v Director of Public Prosecutions* [1993] RTR 209.

Undercover police operations

This whole question received further consideration in *R v Christou* [1992] 4 All ER 559. The police set up 'Stardust Jewellers' and staffed it with two undercover officers who purported to be shady dealers. Transactions in the shop were recorded by camera and sound recording equipment and the two appellants (amongst others) were convicted of handling stolen goods. On appeal, they contended that the judge should not have allowed evidence resulting from the undercover operation to be admitted. This argument was rejected as the police had not tricked the appellants into committing an offence they would not otherwise have committed and questions asked by the police in the course of their dealings at the shop were not questions about an offence which required a caution. As to the latter point, Lord Taylor of Gosforth CJ said:

'The appellants were not being questioned by police officers acting as such. Conversation was on equal terms. There could be no question of pressure or intimidation by [the police] as persons actually in authority or believed to be so. We agree with the learned judge that [Code C] simply was not intended to apply in such a context.

In reaching that conclusion, we should ourselves administer a caution. It would be wrong for police officers to adopt or use an undercover pose or disguise to enable themselves to ask questions about an offence uninhibited by the requirements of the code and with the effect of circumventing it.

Were they to do so, it would be open to the judge to exclude the questions and answers under s78 of the 1984 Act.'

In the course of his judgment Lord Taylor CJ distinguished cases such as *R v Payne* [1963] 1 All ER 848 and *R v Mason* [1987] 3 All ER 481.

Although the Court of Appeal refused leave to appeal to the House of Lords, it certified that the following points of law of general public importance were involved in the decision: (1) whether evidence obtained by a trick, consisting of words spoken by a defendant in conversation with undercover police officers, should be excluded at common law or under s78 of the Police and Criminal Evidence Act 1984 and (2) whether the Code of Practice for the Detention, Treatment and Questioning of

Persons by Police Officers (issued under ss66 and 67 of the 1984 Act) applies to conversations between undercover police officers and a suspect.

The approach adopted by Lord Taylor CJ in *Christou* was applied by the Court of Appeal in *R v Bryce* [1992] 4 All ER 567 where the evidence against the appellant included a telephone conversation alleged to have taken place with an undercover police officer. It was said that the officer had agreed to buy a stolen Saab, worth £23,000, for £2,800. He arranged to view the car at a market the following day and, when he asked how long the car had been stolen, the appellant allegedly replied that it was two or three days old. At the police station, following his arrest, the appellant made no comments during a recorded interview but, after the tape recorder had been switched off at the appellant's request, he allegedly said that he had bought the car for £1,800. The judge admitted evidence of the telephone conversation, the conversation at the market and the unrecorded interview and the appellant was convicted of handling stolen goods.

The appellant's appeal against conviction was allowed as the Court of Appeal believed that the judge's decision as to the admission of this evidence had been incorrect. As Lord Taylor CJ explained:

'The ... questions [on the telephone and at the market] ... were single, isolated questions in separate conversations. There was no extended interrogation. However, they did go directly to the critical issue of guilty knowledge. Moreover, they were hotly disputed and there was no contemporary record. In *R v Christou* there were questions from the undercover officers as to the area where it would be unwise to resell the goods, the answers being obliquely an indication that the goods had been or may have been stolen from that area to the knowledge or belief of the suspect. However, in that case the whole interview was recorded both on tape and on film. The circumstances to be considered by the learned judge in that case in deciding whether the admission of the evidence would have an adverse effect on the fairness of the trial and how adverse were therefore quite different from those in the present case. The film and sound record eliminated any question of concoction. Not so here. The questions asked were direct, not oblique, the conversation was challenged and the appellant had no means of showing by a neutral, reliable record what was or was not said. For those reasons we consider that the learned judge erred here in admitting those answers ...

If [the unrecorded] interview was correctly admitted, the effect would be to set at nought the requirements of the Police and Criminal Evidence Act 1984 and the code in regard to interviews. One of the main purposes of the code is to eliminate the possibility of an interview being concocted or of a true interview being falsely alleged to have been concocted. If it were permissible for an officer simply to assert that, after a properly conducted interview produced a nil return, the suspect confessed off the record and for that confession to be admitted, then the safeguards of the code could readily be bypassed.

In our judgment there would have to be some highly exceptional circumstances, perhaps involving cogent corroboration, before such an interview could be admitted without its having such an adverse effect on the fairness of the trial that it ought to be excluded under s78.'

Police who leave an insecure and unattended van, with an apparently valuable load on display, and keep it under observation in the hope that a passer-by might act dishonestly and be apprehended, are not acting as agents provocateurs and any evidence gathered is not inadmissible on the ground of unfairness, at common law or under s78 of the 1984 Act: *Williams* v *Director of Public Prosecutions* [1993] 3 All ER 365.

In *R* v *Smurthwaite* [1994] 1 All ER 898 (where the evidence of an undercover police officer posing as a contract killer was held to have been correctly admitted) the Court of Appeal said that the substantive rule of law that entrapment or the use of an agent provocateur did not by itself afford a defence in law to a criminal charge had not been altered by s78 of the Police and Criminal Evidence Act 1984. However, entrapment, agent provocateur or the use of a trick were not irrelevant to the application of s78 because the judge, in his discretion, would exclude the evidence if he considered that, in all the circumstances, obtaining it by those means would have such an adverse effect on the fairness of the proceedings that the court ought not to admit it. 'Fairness of proceedings' involved a consideration not only of fairness to the accused but also of fairness to the public. In exercising his discretion whether to admit the evidence of an undercover officer, some, but not an exhaustive list, of the factors that the judge might take into account were as follows:

1. Was the officer acting as an agent provocateur in the sense that he was enticing the defendant to commit an offence he would not otherwise have committed?
2. What was the nature of any entrapment?
3. Did the evidence consist of admissions to a completed offence or did it consist of the actual commission of an offence?
4. How active or passive was the officer's role in obtaining the evidence?
5. Was there an unassailable record of what occurred, or was it strongly corroborated?

In the light of *R* v *Christou* and *R* v *Bryce* a further consideration for the judge in deciding whether to admit an undercover officer's evidence was whether he had abused his role to ask questions which ought properly to have been asked as a police officer and in accordance with the Codes. Beyond these considerations, concluded Lord Taylor of Gosforth CJ, it was not possible to give general guidance as to how a judge should exercise his discretion under s78, since each case had to be determined on its own facts.

In *Ludi* v *Switzerland* (1992) The Times 13 August the European Court of Human Rights held that, in a drugs investigation, the authorised interception of telephone calls and the intervention of an undercover police officer had not breached article 8 of the European Convention on Human Rights.

10

Opinion Evidence

10.1 Definition of opinion

10.2 The common law

10.3 Civil cases

10.4 Experts

10.1 Definition of opinion

Original evidence and inference

A general rule we have encountered already is that a witness should give evidence of things within his knowledge and not things told to him by others. Another aspect of the rule that a witness should testify as to facts within his own knowledge is that he should not express his opinion about what conclusions the court should draw from those facts. He should testify to facts as he perceives them and should leave it to the court to draw what inferences it sees fit from his evidence.

The drawing of inferences is a matter for the trier of fact. The main aim of the calling of evidence is to prove the primary facts from which the court will be able to reach a decision. It may reach its conclusions directly from those primary facts or it may do so indirectly by drawing inferences from them.

For example, in a trial for robbery a witness may say: 'I saw the robbery. After leaving the bank the robber got into a car with the registration number A123 BCD and drove into Hale Street where he was stopped by a police car registration number B234 CDE. I did not see anything else.' A police officer may then give evidence: 'I was in a police car registration number B234 CDE in Hale Street. I stopped a car registration number A123 BCD. The defendant was driving.'

From what these two witnesses say the court would have no difficulty in deciding that the defendant was the robber. All the court needs to do is take the evidence at face value because it directly implicates the defendant.

By contrast the same case could be proved by evidence other than continuous eyewitness evidence. The first witness might say: 'I saw the robber get into a car registration number A123 BCD and drive it into Hale Street but did not see what happened to him. This was at 3.40 pm on 1 January.' The police officer might then say: 'I saw a car registration number A123 BCD when it was half way down Hale Street. The defendant was the driver. This happened at 3.42 pm on 1 January.'

The evidence is not complete because, in theory, the defendant could have got out of the car between the time the first witness lost sight of it and the time it got to half way down the road. But this will not prevent a conviction if the court is satisfied that the driver did not get out before the defendant was spotted. There is no direct evidence that he did not get out, nor is there direct evidence that he did. So the court must draw inferences, it must consider the likelihood of there being a change of drivers and ask itself whether the chance of there having been a change is so small that it feels sure the defendant was the robber.

The more gaps there are in the evidence the less likely it is that a court will feel able to fill them by saying that the evidence which has been called shows what happened at those times when there were no witnesses on hand.

The drawing of inferences from direct evidence of facts is something no court has difficulty doing provided the subject matter of the direct evidence is ordinary everyday events. But where the evidence is about something which a judge or jury does not have proper experience to deal with, they may need help in deciding what the evidence means. In such cases witnesses may give that help by expressing their opinions of what it means. We will see below that at common law any witness who is called to give his opinion of the significance of other evidence must be properly experienced to give such an opinion.

Opinions which are not opinions

In many cases all a witness can do if he is to help the court is state an opinion. For example a witness to a fight might say, 'I think it was the man in the blue shirt who started the fight'. This appears to be a statement of opinion because it starts 'I think ...'. The reality however is that he is stating what he recalls, and by prefacing it with 'I think' he qualifies the degree of certainty he has about his recollection.

Also a witness to a crime will often say, 'I think the defendant is the man I saw'. This is simply a shorthand way of saying, 'I saw a man with blue eyes and dark hair, about five feet nine inches tall etc'. Any witness who is asked to describe someone whom he believes to look like the defendant may be tempted to look at the defendant and describe what he sees in the dock. It would be artificial for him to give his evidence otherwise than by saying that he identifies the accused as the offender. Of course, he can be questioned about the degree of similarity between the man he saw and the defendant. Evidence of identity is thus not really opinion evidence at all but evidence of what the witness saw.

The ultimate issue

Every case involves many issues, some of more importance than others. In a criminal case where identification is in question the ultimate issue is whether it was the accused who committed the offence. If the defence is self-defence, the ultimate issue is whether he acted in reasonable self-defence. In civil cases the ultimate issue may be whether words spoken were defamatory, whether a contract for occupation of land was a licence or a lease, whether goods were of merchantable quality and so on.

There is little harm in witnesses expressing opinions about issues other than the ultimate issue and in practice they frequently do so. Indeed it is sometimes tactically wise to entice one's opponent's witnesses to give opinionated testimony in order to challenge their credibility as objective witnesses. However, particularly in criminal cases, witnesses should not give an opinion on the ultimate issue but should leave it to the judge or jury to decide whether the case is proved.

10.2 The common law

General rules

We saw in chapter 4 that a witness is allowed to repeat what someone else said if he does so in order to prove that the statement was made rather than to prove its truth. So it is with opinion evidence: a witness may give his opinion if it is relevant what opinion he holds. This is seen commonly where someone is accused of obtaining property by deception. Unless the person from whom the property was obtained believed what the defendant said to him he will not have handed over any property by reason of the deception. The witness must give evidence of the opinion he held about what he was told by the accused.

Except where the witness's opinion is itself relevant, the common law's general rule is that no witness may give his opinion in evidence unless there is no better evidence. There are three aspects to this rule. First, a witness may give his opinion where by doing so he indicates his degree of certainty: see example at paragraph 10.1. As we have seen already, this is not really the expression of an opinion at all. Secondly, a witness may say that in his opinion someone was drunk rather than simply saying, for example, 'his eyes were glazed, his speech slurred and he staggered.' In *Davies* [1962] 1 WLR 1111 the Courts-Martial Appeal Court held that a witness who says that he formed the view that the defendant had taken drink had to support that opinion by giving evidence of the facts on which that opinion is based, but it accepted that the witness could tell the court what inference he drew from what he observed about the defendant's demeanour.

The third aspect of the rule is that a witness may give his opinion where by doing so he expresses in a convenient form a number of facts which he cannot express in any better way. This can occur in many different contexts. A witness who gives an estimate of the speed a car was travelling gives his opinion. Also, to say, 'I recognise the defendant as the offender' is a shorthand way of describing the offender because it amounts to setting out in detail the offender's appearance. Evidence of identification is a type of opinion. In *Fryer* v *Gathercole* (1849) 4 Exch

262 a witness gave her opinion that a document she received from someone was the same one she handed to that person on an earlier date. This opinion evidence was admissible because the witness could be asked about how she formed this opinion, and if the court felt that her inference that it was the same document was not justified, the appropriate finding would be made. Evidence of identification of persons rather than documents is considered in detail in chapter 11.

The rule against a non-expert giving opinion evidence was laid down by the House of Lords in *North Cheshire and Manchester Brewery Co Ltd* v *Manchester Brewery Co Ltd* [1899] AC 83. The question arose whether the appellant company's name was intended to deceive people into thinking that it was the same company as the respondent. It was held that it was for the court to decide whether the intention to deceive was proved and that no witness would be entitled to give his opinion on the matter.

In practice, non-expert witnesses frequently state their opinions and little exception is taken to this because they can always be asked about the facts on which the opinion is based. But careful examination of a witness can prevent him from being tempted to do anything other than describe what he saw or heard. The major exception to the rule against opinion evidence is that experts may give their opinions on relevant matters within their field of expertise.

The need for expertise

Courts are able to draw inferences from evidence in the vast majority of cases. If it is in issue whether witness A or witness B is telling the truth, the judge, jury or bench of justices are able to take a decision by relying on their experience of life and people. Unless trials are turned into examinations in detail of the mental state of witnesses involving the weighing of evidence from psychiatrists, psychologists and lie-detectors, their truthfulness must be assessed by applying instincts built up during the life of the trier of fact.

The same principle applies to most issues of fact – the court is able to assess evidence with a reasonable degree of accuracy by relying on its own experience. But on some issues the court is unable to reach a proper conclusion unless it is given assistance, because its own experience does not allow it to assess the evidence accurately. In fact help is often required in two ways, first, in order to allow the court to know what the basic facts of the case are, and secondly, in order to allow it to know what inferences can be drawn from those facts.

This can be illustrated by a simple landlord and tenant dispute. A tenant who sues his landlord claiming that he has breached a covenant in the lease requiring the premises to be kept in good repair will, of course, have to prove that the premises are not in good repair. If he alleges that the premises are damp the issues for the court will be, (a) is there any damp, and (b) if so, is it caused by something for which the landlord or the tenant is responsible? The tenant's own evidence may be sufficient to establish the first issue in his favour, but not the second. Once the court has found that, for example, there are damp patches around the bottom of the walls of a ground floor room it will have to decide whether these were caused by rising damp or condensation. That will involve certain tests being made of the damp-proof course and of moisture and temperature levels inside and outside the room. Anyone could give evidence about whether there are gaps in the damp proof course, and anyone could use a moisture meter and thermometer. But what those tests establish about the cause of dampness involves a conclusion being drawn from the readings on the meters. Unless someone with expert knowledge explains the significance of the readings the court will not be able to interpret them accurately. Both landlord and tenant may call expert evidence and the court will then have to decide which, if either, is correct in his assessment of the problem. But without at least one expert, no proper resolution of the dispute could be made.

What this means in practice is that an expert is needed to establish not just what conclusions can be drawn from the meter readings, but also what the readings are. Therefore experts can be useful in proving the basic facts in the case as well as in establishing the inferences to be drawn from those basic facts.

That an expert may give his opinion in order to assist the court in the drawing of inferences was first held in *Folkes* v *Chadd* (1782) 3 Doug KB 157 in which an expert engineer was allowed to express his opinion on the cause of a blockage in a harbour. The Court of King's Bench held not only that scientific evidence was admissible on the issue but also that no other evidence was admissible because only an expert could assist the court.

Whether an issue is something which the court is able to use its own experience to decide without the need for reliance on experts may change as 'general knowledge' changes. Some issues call for an application by a jury of its own standards and opinions; in such cases expert evidence is not admissible. For example in *Stamford* [1972] 2 QB 391 the question whether an article was 'indecent or obscene' was held by the Court of Appeal to be one for a jury to assess by applying their standards, so that the definition of 'indecent or obscene' may change from time to time as the standards of society change. Similarly in *DPP* v *Jordan* [1977] AC 699 the House of Lords held that whether publication of an obscene article was for the public good was a matter for the jury. It was argued that expert evidence should have been admitted to show that the item of pornography in question would have benefited certain people, but it was held that it was for the jury to assess whether it was for the public good generally. In the end the case revolved around the proper construction of the phrase 'for the public good' in s4(2) of the Obscene Publications Act 1959. But it was held that whether an article is obscene is within the province of the jury as well as the issue whether it was for the public good.

In *Turner* [1975] QB 834 the accused was charged with the murder of his girlfriend. He said in his defence that he was provoked by her informing him that while he was in prison she had slept with two other men. He was not allowed to call a psychiatrist to give evidence about his opinion of the likelihood of the defendant having been provoked by what his girlfriend told him. There was no suggestion that the defendant suffered from any mental illness, so the issue was whether the sane defendant was provoked. The Court of Appeal held that the jury could properly reach their own conclusion about this by applying their own common sense in assessing the evidence the defendant gave. As Lawton LJ said:

> 'Jurors do not need psychiatrists to tell them how ordinary folk who are not suffering from any mental illness are likely to react to the stresses and strains of life.'

It was emphasised in the court's judgment in *Turner* that expert evidence of a particular type may be inadmissible in one case but admissible in an apparently similar case if the issues are different. A good illustration of this is *Lowery* v *R* [1974] AC 85. A murder was committed by Lowery, or by his co-defendant King, or by both of them acting together. A 15-year-old girl was given a lift by Lowery and King; she was beaten and strangled. Each defendant alleged that the other had done it, and in the course of his evidence Lowery said that he was not the sort of person who would commit such a murder. The trial judge allowed King to call a psychiatrist to give evidence about the character of each defendant so as to show that Lowery was more likely to kill than King. Both defendants were convicted and Lowery appealed on the ground that the psychiatrist's evidence should not have been allowed. The Privy Council held that on the facts of the case the evidence was admissible on two grounds. First, it was in issue whether Lowery was the sort of person who would have committed murder. Secondly, because each defendant claimed that the other had committed the killing, if the jury ruled out a joint enterprise they would have to decide which was the killer, and in that circumstance the character of each man became relevant.

Without Lowery's assertions about his character, the first ground would not have arisen. But once he said he was not the sort of man who would commit a murder of the type in question, it was clearly in issue whether he was such a man. The second ground for allowing the evidence was not as sound as the first because if psychiatric evidence was admissible in that case it would be admissible whenever there was a 'cut-throat' defence – each defendant blames another, a line of defence which almost invariably ends with the conviction for both. In *Turner* the Court of Appeal said that *Lowery* v *R* was restricted to its own facts, and the facts were certainly very unusual. Despite this dictum, it is probably still open in an English court to call psychiatric evidence whenever the relative states of mind of two or more defendants is at issue. It was of particular significance in *Lowery* v *R* that the psychiatrist was called by a defendant, because he would have been entitled to be acquitted if the jury had a reasonable doubt about his guilt; therefore any evidence which could raise such a doubt is relevant. Furthermore, it would not have been open to the prosecution to call the psychiatrist as part of its case, because at that stage of the trial no evidence had been given that either defendant would say that he was not the type of man to commit such a murder.

The importance of examining the issues before being able to say whether expert evidence is needed is also illustrated by *Smith* [1979] 1 WLR 1445 in which the Court of Appeal upheld the trial judge's decision to allow expert psychiatric evidence to rebut the defendant's assertion that he killed while sleepwalking. Somnambulism is outside normal experience, so a properly qualified expert could assist the jury in its deliberations.

A much-criticised case in this area is *DPP* v *A & BC Chewing Gum Ltd* [1968] 1 QB 159. The Divisional Court held that expert evidence was admissible on the question whether certain publications could deprave and corrupt the children who were likely to buy them. The criticism which has been made of the case is that any jury or bench of magistrates would be able to assess what effect there would be on children from their own experience of life. Lord Parker CJ said:

'I can quite see that when considering the effect of something on an adult an adult jury may be able to judge just as well as an adult witness called on the point. Indeed, there is nothing more that a jury or justices need to know. But certainly when you are dealing here with children of different age groups and children from five upwards, any jury and any justices need all the help they can get, information which they may not have, as to the effect on different children.'

This ruling seems to fly in the face of the whole concept of the random jury being the best means of deciding matters of fact in criminal cases. Any jury is likely to contain several people who are parents and, of course, all of its members were children themselves. Why are they not able to judge from their own experience whether a publication is likely to deprave or corrupt young children? In *Anderson* [1972] 1 QB 304 the Court of Appeal distinguished *DPP* v *A & BC Chewing Gum Ltd*, saying that it was restricted to its own facts because it dealt with cards which were inserted in bubble gum packets and were likely to be seen by children as young as five years of age. The effect of such cards on children so young may, it was said, have had an effect not appreciated by an adult jury. The most significant criticism of the case was made in *Turner* where the Court of Appeal said:

' ... psychiatry has not yet become a satisfactory substitute for the common sense of juries or magistrates'.

DPP v *A & BC Chewing Gum Ltd* should not be relied upon as laying down any rule of general application. Nevertheless it does make one important point, albeit obiter. Lord Parker CJ recognised that when experts are called to give evidence they are often asked to give their opinion on the very issue the court has to decide. They are allowed to give their opinion on the ultimate issue. This is contrary to the law as stated in certain old authorities, but Lord Parker recognised the absurdity of disallowing an expert from expressing his opinion on the ultimate issue because it might deprive the jury of the very assistance from the expert which they might find most useful. For example, an expert who gives evidence about the result of a genetic fingerprint test and says that there is only a one million to one chance of the defendant not being the offender, gives evidence on the ultimate issue because his evidence is conclusive. Unless he can give an opinion on the ultimate issue he can say nothing of assistance to the court. And in a case involving an allegation of speeding, someone who gives his opinion about the speed at which a car was travelling gives his opinion on the ultimate issue, that the defendant was exceeding the speed limit. But, there are still many cases in which an expert's evidence does not require him to give an opinion on the ultimate issue. For example, an expert who has analysed blood found at the scene of a crime may say that it is the same type of blood as the defendant's and that 40 per cent of the population is of the same blood type. His testimony does not require him to express an opinion on whether the defendant is the offender – he simply tells the court the result of his analysis and leaves the jury or magistrates to draw whatever conclusion they see fit.

In *R* v *Stockwell* (1993) 97 Cr App R 260 the issue was one of identification and the trial judge had ruled that the evidence of a facial mapping expert could be adduced by the Crown to assist the jury in determining whether the appellant appeared in photographs taken by a security camera during the robbery and attempted robbery. Lord Taylor of Gosforth CJ acknowledged that whether an expert could give his opinion on what had been called the ultimate issue had long been a vexed question. If there was such a prohibition, it had long been more honoured in the breach than the observance and he cited *DPP* v *A and BC Chewing Gum Ltd*, above, as an example. The rationale behind the supposed prohibition was that an expert should not usurp the functions of the jury, but since counsel could bring the witness so close to opining on the ultimate issue that the inference as to his views was obvious, the rule could only be a matter of form rather than substance. In their Lordships' view, an expert was called to give his opinion and he should be allowed to do so. It was, however, important that the judge should make it clear to the jury that they were not bound by the expert's opinion and that the issue was for them to decide. In the present case, the trial judge had done just that and he had put the expert's evidence in its proper perspective. Accordingly, the appeal against conviction was dismissed.

In *R* v *Robinson (Raymond)* (1993) The Times 25 November the appellant had been convicted of indecent assault and rape of a mentally retarded girl aged 15. After the girl had given evidence, counsel for the Crown had applied for and been granted leave to call an educational psychologist to give evidence before the jury whether or not the girl was suggestible, would be likely to pick up suggestions made to her and repeat them and whether she was likely to fantasise. On appeal, counsel for the appellant submitted that the effect of this evidence was to enhance the reliability of the girl's evidence by excluding such possibilities as an inability to remember, or a vulnerability to suggestion. The Court of Appeal concluded that the educational psychologist's evidence should not have been admitted and that the appeal should therefore be allowed. In their Lordships' view, the Crown could not call a witness of fact and then, without more, call a psychologist or psychiatrist to give reasons why the jury should regard that witness as reliable. Here, no specific case had been put in cross-examination that the girl was peculiarly suggestible or given to fantasise as a result of her mental impairment and no evidence was to be called for the defence impugning the girl's reliability.

10.3 Civil cases

The Civil Evidence Act 1972

North Cheshire and Manchester Brewery Co Ltd v *Manchester Brewery Co Ltd* was, of course, a civil case. The prohibition which was held to exist against opinion evidence on the ultimate issue was applicable in both civil and criminal courts. There was a challenge to it in *Hollington* v *Hewthorn & Co Ltd* [1943] KB 587, but the Court of Appeal, without reference to the *Manchester Brewery* case, upheld the prohibition. The common law also applied equally in civil and criminal cases on the question when opinion evidence from an expert was admissible.

Major amendments in the law on opinion evidence in civil cases were recommended by the Law Reform Committee in its 17th report. The Civil Evidence Act 1972 put into effect many of the recommendations. Section 1(1) extends ss2 and 4 of the Civil Evidence Act 1968 so that hearsay evidence of a statement of opinion may be given as well as hearsay evidence of a statement of fact. It will be remembered that s2 of the 1968 Act allows first-hand hearsay evidence of statements of which direct oral evidence by the maker of the statement would be admissible. Section 1(1) of the 1972 Act does not alter the need for the maker's direct oral evidence to be admissible, and at first sight it appears that the common law's restrictions on opinion evidence are preserved. But s3(2) says that on any 'relevant matter' a witness may give his opinion if he gives it as a way of conveying relevant facts which he perceived personally. 'Relevant matter' is defined in s3(3) as including an issue in the proceedings. The combined effect of these subsections is that an opinion is admissible from a non-expert provided he is simply describing what he saw or heard. This gives considerable flexibility, allowing each witness to give his evidence in his own words without undue interruption from the judge. Incidentally, s3(2) also allows witnesses, expert or not, to give their opinion on the ultimate issue.

Section 2 allows rules of court to be made for the admission of expert evidence in civil proceedings. The effects of s2 are threefold. First, the notice provisions of the Civil Evidence Act 1968 do not apply to expert reports: s2(2). Secondly an expert's written report may be used in evidence before the conclusion of his examination in chief (s2(1)), and thirdly rules of court have been made for the disclosure of experts' reports if they are to be relied upon at trial: s2(3)-(6). An expert's report for the purposes of s2 of the 1972 Act means a written report by a person dealing with matters upon which he is (or would be if he were still alive) qualified to give expert opinion evidence: s2(7).

Rules of court

The relevant rules of court are contained in RSC Ord 38 rr35-44 and CCR Ord 20 rr27 & 28: RSC Ord 38 rr37-44 apply in both courts. These rules impose two requirements before expert evidence may be adduced. First, the party seeking to rely on expert evidence must have applied to the court to determine whether it should order that expert's report to be disclosed to other parties, and secondly the party wishing to rely on that evidence must have complied with any direction given about disclosure of the expert's report: Ord 38 r36, Ord 20 r27. The summons for directions is the proper time for considering the need for expert evidence: see *Winchester Cigarette Machinery Ltd* v *Payne* (1993) The Times 19 October.

The court must normally order that reports be disclosed unless there are exceptional reasons for not doing so: Ord 38 r27. Many judges do not like to have to choose between two experts' views, so there is power for the court to order that the experts on each side meet before writing their reports, in order to see if they can come up with an agreed report: Ord 38 r38. Some judges, particularly in the county courts, put considerable pressure on the parties to get their experts to come up with a joint report. This is a sensible practical procedure because the experts are almost always in a better position than a lawyer to judge the correct analysis of, for example, the cause of the collapse of a building or the leakage of a damp proof course or the cause of mechanical failure of an engine.

Affidavit evidence

At the hearing of interlocutory applications in the High Court and the county court affidavit evidence may be used. Interlocutory applications are applications which do not necessarily lead to the case being finally decided: *White* v *Brunton* [1984] QB 570. For example, if the defendant seeks to have the plaintiff's case struck out for delay, the case may end at that stage but it may not. It will do so if the defendant's application is successful but will not do so if it is unsuccessful. The application is interlocutory.

An affidavit may contain evidence which is not within the knowledge of its maker, provided that he states where the information came from – who told him, or what he read – and that he believes it to be true: RSC Ord 41 r5(2), CCR Ord 20 r10(5). In this way opinion evidence about the truth of information supplied to the deponent by others is allowed on interlocutory applications.

10.4 Experts

Who is an expert?

Any person who has the experience to give an informed opinion on a matter outside the experience of the court may give expert opinion evidence. He need not hold any formal qualifications. A solicitor who had studied handwriting for ten years was allowed to give expert evidence about handwriting in *Silverlock* [1894] 2 QB 768. Similarly, in *Oakley* (1979) 70 Cr App R 7 a police officer with experience of investigating motor vehicle accidents was allowed to give his opinion on the cause of an accident. In *Chatwood* [1980] 1 WLR 874 the admission by the defendant that a substance found in his possession was heroin was admissible evidence of the nature of the substance because he was qualified by long term usage to know what it was.

It is for the judge to decide whether someone who is put forward as an expert is properly qualified to assist the court: *Bristow* v *Sequeville* (1850) 19 LJ Ex 289. Normally paper qualifications will be taken as sufficient proof of expertise, but if there is a challenge to the competence of someone with paper qualifications to give an opinion on the fact in issue the judge must determine whether those qualifications or the person's practical experience justify him giving expert opinion.

Material relied upon by the expert

Much expert evidence takes the form of an opinion being given on the basis of research done by the witness. This inevitably means that the expert witness repeats other people's findings in order to justify his own. For example, in *English Exporters (London) Ltd* v *Eldonwall* [1973] Ch 415 valuers gave evidence about the value of property on the basis of comparisons of valuations for similar properties. Necessarily this evidence relied on the opinions of other people as to valuations of other properties. Megarry J said, obiter, that such evidence is permissible and recognised that it is inevitable that experts will rely on what they research when forming their opinions.

These dicta were approved and applied in *Abadom* [1983] 1 All ER 364 where an expert gave evidence about the way fragments of glass found in the defendant's shoes refracted light, and gave evidence that glass from the scene of the crime refracted light in the same way. By reference to statistical research carried out by Home Office scientists, which stated that only about 4 per cent of glass refracted glass in this way, he was able to give his opinion that there was a high likelihood that the glass in the defendant's shoes came from the scene of the crime. The Court of Appeal held that this conclusion was properly given because every expert is allowed to rely on research done by others when forming his own opinion. The witness was giving his opinion about the glass he analysed and was not simply repeating the research of the Home Office in order to prove that their conclusions were true. If there was a challenge to the correctness of the research, evidence should have been called by the defence to undermine it.

Sometimes an expert will simply repeat the research of others without adding anything himself. At first sight this infringes the hearsay rule because he does not give his opinion, he merely repeats the opinion of others. In *H* v *Schering Chemicals Ltd* [1983] 1 All ER 849 Bingham J held that there is a distinction between a witness who simply repeats other people's opinions and a witness who says that he has expertise in a field, and that his expertise satisfies him that the correct answer to a problem is stated by a particular research paper written by others. In the latter case what is put before the court is the witness's opinion of the correctness of the conclusions reached by the researchers, rather than findings of those researchers. This adopted and approved a dictum of Cooke J in *Seyfang* v *GD Searle & Co* [1973] QB 148 which itself adopted a submission made by counsel for Seyfang, Thomas Bingham QC.

In the same way that an expert should justify his opinion, if asked to do so, by stating what research he did in forming that opinion, he should also disclose the factual material which was presented to him. If he was not given all relevant material his opinion may be of little or no use.

In *R* v *Robb* (1991) 93 Cr App R 161 the Court of Appeal decided that evidence of voice identification given by an expert witness, who was well qualified by academic training and practical experience to express an opinion, was admissible even where the expert relied solely on a technique which was accepted by the majority of professional opinion to be unreliable unless supplemented and verified by acoustic analysis. Bingham LJ recalled that the trial judge had directed the jury that the function of an expert was:

> '... to provide a court – that is you, the jury – with possible scientific reasons to allow you to form your opinion and judgment in relation to the matters that you find proved to your satisfaction ... Remember, no expert can usurp your function as the final arbiter of fact. He is available to assist you with his experience.'

In his Lordship's view, that was a sound statement of legal principle.

As to the proof of foreign law in an English court, the judge cannot reject the evidence of expert witnesses, if they agree as to the effect of the foreign law, and instead conduct his own researches: *Bumper Development Corp Ltd* v *Commissioner of Police of the Metropolis* [1991] 4 All ER 638.

A prosecution expert witness is under a duty to disclose material of which he is aware and which might have some bearing on the offence charged and the surrounding circumstances of the case. Disclosure is to be made to the prosecuting authority which must in turn, subject to sensitivity, disclose the information to the defence: *R* v *Maguire* [1992] 2 All ER 433; see also *Berry* v *R* [1992] 3 All ER 881 and the Attorney General's guidelines *Practice Note* [1982] 1 All ER 734 to the effect, inter alia, that (subject to discretionary exceptions) 'all unused material should ... be made available to the defence solicitor if it has some bearing on the offence(s) charged and the surrounding circumstances of the case'. In *R* v *Preston* [1993] 4 All ER 638 the House of Lords said that the test for whether unused material of any kind (except material which should, by law, have been destroyed) should be disclosed by the prosecution to the defence in a criminal trial is materiality, not admissibility. Accordingly, the prosecution is under a duty to disclose to the defence material information even if it would be inadmissible if put in evidence by the defence. See also *R* v *Fergus* (1993) The Times 30 June (police photograph of appellant and victim's first crime report should have been forwarded by police to Crown Prosecution Service), *R* v *Taylor* (1993) The Times 15 June (detective sergeant failed to disclose message to prosecution), *R* v *Crown Court at Harrow, ex parte Dave* [1994] 1 All ER 315 (existence of complainant's husband's previous conviction should have been made known to the defence as it was relevant consideration) and *R* v *Crown Court at Chelmsford, ex parte Chief Constable of the Essex Police* [1994] 1 All ER 325 (evidence inadmissible yet should have been disclosed to defence).

The duties and responsibilities of expert witnesses in civil cases were considered by Cresswell J in *National Justice Compania Naviera SA* v *Prudential Assurance Co Ltd (Ikarian Reefer)* (1993) The Times 5 March. His Lordship stressed the duty to give independent and unbiased evidence and that, if an expert did not have experience in a certain area or had insufficient information on which to base a properly researched conclusion, he should say so.

Handwriting

In *Doe d Mudd* v *Suckermore* (1837) 5 A & E 703 someone who was familiar with his employer's handwriting was allowed to give his opinion that a certain document was written by the employer. The witness was not an expert in handwriting generally, but he had sufficient expertise in the handwriting which mattered in the case, that of his employer, to be able to assist the court.

Where no witness is able to give such evidence of handwriting a comparison may be made between a sample of handwriting and any writing which is in dispute in the case. Section 8 of the Criminal Procedure Act 1865 allows a comparison of handwriting by any witness provided only that the sample which he is asked to compare to the disputed writing is proved to be a sample of a particular person's handwriting. The standard of proof of genuineness of the sample depends upon the nature of the proceedings – in a civil case the balance of probabilities is sufficient, as it is if the defence in a criminal matter relies on the sample. But if the prosecution wishes to prove the sample it must do so beyond reasonable doubt: *Ewing* [1983] QB 1039. Section 8 is used most commonly in criminal prosecutions where it is alleged that the defendant wrote something and he denies that it is his handwriting. The Crown must prove that the sample which a witness is asked to compare to the disputed document is a true sample of the defendant's writing.

Nothing in s8 expressly requires a witness who compares handwriting to be an expert. But his evidence may be of little use unless he is. The jury should not be asked to make the comparison themselves, although justices or a judge may do so: *Harden* [1963] 1 QB 8. Nevertheless, a judge should not appear to be acting as a handwriting expert by comparing examples of the defendant's signature and reaching conclusions on the comparisons: *R* v *Simbodyal* (1991) The Times 10 October.

The opinion of a handwriting expert is admissible in evidence under s8 of the 1865 Act if it is formed after examining a photocopy of the writing, although the fact that the original was not examined could affect the opinion's credibility: *Lockhead-Arabia Corp* v *Owen* [1993] 3 All ER 641.

11

Identification Evidence

11.1 The use of identification evidence

11.2 Methods of identification

11.3 *R* v *Turnbull*

11.1 The use of identification evidence

The admissibility of prior identifications

It has long been the practice to allow prosecution witnesses to say that they picked out the defendant at an identification parade or that in some other way they have identified him prior to the trial. It has also long been the practice for the police officer in charge of an identification parade to give evidence of what happened. For obvious reasons the prosecution will try to rely on evidence that a witness to the offence has identified the defendant because it makes their case stronger. But the question which arises is, on what basis is the evidence of the previous identification admissible?

Christie [1914] AC 545 is the leading authority that when a witness gives evidence identifying the defendant as the offender, evidence may also be given that he has previously identified the accused. In that case the defendant was accused of indecent assault on a boy of five; the boy gave evidence and identified Christie as the assailant. He was not asked about, and did not give evidence about, a previous identification when he pointed out Christie and said 'That is the man' and then described the assault, to which Christie replied 'I am innocent'. We have already seen that one issue which arose was whether what the boy said in Christie's presence could be repeated without falling foul of the hearsay rule. On this issue the House of Lords held that evidence could properly be given that the boy had said 'That is the man' because the jury was entitled to hear how Christie reacted, but they were not allowed to hear of the details of the complaint because it was not accepted by the accused.

It was held that evidence is admissible of an out of court identification in order to support the identification which the boy made in court. No clear reason was given for this, but effect was given to the practice which was by that time already well established. In principle the previous identification could fall foul of three

284

exclusionary rules – the hearsay rule, the rule against self-serving statements and the rule against non-expert opinion evidence.

Where someone who saw a witness pick the defendant out at an identification parade gives evidence about what he saw, his evidence is hearsay if it is given to prove the truth of the identification. There is no difference between evidence from a police officer that someone wrote to him saying 'X is the man who robbed the bank' and evidence from the same officer that that same person attended an identification parade and identified the defendant. In this latter case the officer says, in effect, 'Mr Y attended the identification parade and told me that X is the man who robbed the bank by selecting X from the line of men in the parade'. In *Christie* it seems not to have been fully argued that for one person to say 'Y picked out X' might breach the hearsay rule. Viscount Haldane LC expressed reservations about whether it was right for a witness to give evidence of an act of identification carried out by another. He said that it would have been perfectly proper for the boy to give evidence that he had picked out Christie, but that such evidence should not be given by anyone else. It cannot be said conclusively that Viscount Haldane's reservations about the admissibility of the evidence of the identification in *Christie* were based on the hearsay rule, but it is an argument which seems to hold weight.

In *Sparks* v *R* [1964] AC 964 the Privy Council held that there is no exception to the hearsay rule where evidence of identity is concerned. It will be remembered that in that case the mother of the victim of an assault was not allowed to give evidence for the defence to the effect that her daughter told her that the man who assaulted her was coloured, whereas the defendant was white. The facts of the case were rather unusual because they involved evidence of identity in order to show that it was not the accused who committed the offence, whereas the normal position is that identification evidence is given to prove that it was the accused who committed the offence. That distinction should not make any difference, however. Indeed, it was said that if the girl had said to her mother that it was Sparks who had assaulted her, the mother would not have been able to repeat that statement as evidence of its truth because it would be hearsay. What may be significant about *Sparks* v *R* is that the evidence of the mother could not have been admissible otherwise than as hearsay. Because the girl did not give evidence, her credibility was not in issue.

Had the boy in *Christie* given evidence about the previous identification, all members of the House of Lords would have allowed that evidence. It is not easy to see what difference there is between a witness who says that he himself previously picked out the defendant from a parade, and a police officer or other person who witnessed what happened at the parade and is able to give evidence of it. If evidence of prior identifications falls foul of the hearsay rule, that of itself will not prevent it being given, if it is not put forward as evidence of the truth of the assertion made by the identifier that the person picked out was the offender.

It is arguable that evidence should be allowed in a case like *Christie* to support the credibility of the boy as a witness. It is clear that the longer the time between witnessing an incident and being asked to identify the offender, the less likely it is that the identification will be accurate. To hold an identification parade shortly after the event and ask witnesses to attend, allows a greater chance of accuracy than would be the case if witnesses were given their first opportunity to identify the defendant when he is in the dock months after the event. Whenever it is in issue whether the defendant was the person who committed the offence charged, the accuracy of the evidence saying that it was the defendant is also in issue. Where a witness gives evidence that he is able to identify the defendant as the offender, it is in issue in the case whether that identification is accurate and this can be tested by asking whether the witness has been consistent. It is possible to use evidence of an out-of-court identification to prove the consistency of the witness rather than to prove the truth of what the witness asserted by his act of identification.

The use of identification evidence in this way falls foul of the normal rule against self-serving statements. But, *Christie* seems to be authority that self-serving statements which show that the witness previously identified the accused are admissible to indicate the consistency of the witness. It is made clear in the speeches in *Christie* that evidence of a previous identification may only be given where the witness has identified the accused in the course of his evidence. Viscount Haldane explained the relevance of evidence about the identification parade, as follows:

> 'Its relevancy is to show that the boy was able to identify at the time and to exclude the idea that the identification of the prisoner in the dock was an afterthought or a mistake.'

In other words, evidence about the prior identification is admissible as an exception to the normal rule against self-serving statements.

As was explained briefly in chapter 10, evidence from a witness that he is able to identify the defendant as the offender can be said to involve the giving of an opinion. On this argument, what the witness is really saying is that the person he saw commit the offence has the same facial features, is the same height and weight and so on, as the defendant. Identification evidence is not considered in law to be inadmissible opinion, but is a convenient way of expressing what the witness saw. He could say that the man he saw was six feet tall, had long blond hair, a small nose, a scar on his right cheek, etc. But it is more convenient for him to say that the man he saw had the same appearance as the accused, leaving the jury to draw the conclusion that they are the same person.

No case has fully examined and explained the reasons for the admissibility of evidence about previous identifications. The most comprehensive examination was in *Christie*, but that is authority only for the proposition that the credibility of a witness who identifies the accused in court may be supported by evidence that he has identified him previously. It does not allow evidence of the prior identification unless the identifier gives evidence identifying the accused.

An old case which was not referred to in *Christie*, but is not inconsistent with it, establishes that evidence of previous identifications is admissible in some circumstances where the witness does not expressly identify the accused in court. In *Burke & Kelly* (1847) 2 Cox CC 295 the victim of a robbery attended an identification parade and picked out someone as one of the robbers. When giving evidence he said that he had picked out the correct man but could not remember who it was he picked out. Evidence was allowed from a police officer that it was the defendant Kelly who had been identified at the parade. In effect the witness was in the position of someone who made a contemporaneous note and had no independent recollection of the event in question. Such a witness may read out his note and adopt it as his evidence. Of course the police officer was not in exactly the same position as a contemporaneous note because he may have been mistaken about who the witness identified. Nevertheless, he could be cross-examined about the accuracy of his memory of the identification parade. The evidence of the police officer in *Burke & Kelly* did not go to show consistency in the witness because the witness did not identify the accused from the witness box. However, the result of the case is clearly correct. There was no breach of the hearsay rule because the jury was not being asked to rely on the police officer's repetition of what he was told, but on the witness's evidence that what he told the police officer was correct.

Osbourne and Virtue

The Court of Appeal in *Osbourne and Virtue* [1973] 1 QB 678 dealt with a problem which had not previously been encountered by the appellate courts. Two witnesses who had attended identification parades were called by the Crown. One said in evidence that she did not remember picking anyone out at the parade and the other said that she did pick someone out but that he was not in court. The trial judge allowed evidence from the officer in charge of the parade in which he said who had been picked out by each witness. The Court of Appeal upheld the trial judge and expressed the view that *Christie* held that 'evidence of identification other than identification in the witness box is admissible'.

The evidence in *Osbourne and Virtue* can be criticised on two grounds. First, it is incorrect in stating that the ratio of *Christie* allows evidence of what happened at an out-of-court identification to be given without any limitations. Secondly, the evidence of the police officer was hearsay but the court did not discuss this aspect of it. Perhaps that is not surprising because it appears that it was never suggested in argument that the evidence was hearsay.

The two witnesses who were called did not given evidence against the defendants and there was no question of their credibility being in issue. The first witness, who could not remember picking out anyone, did not come up to proof, but that is no ground for showing her to have said something different on another occasion. If, for example, she had never been able to describe any of the offenders but had given a statement to the police that she saw a blue car drive away from the scene of the crime, her failure to remember this would not justify the reception of her witness statement as evidence that the get-away car was blue, because this would be hearsay. It makes no difference that her previous statement had identified one of the defendants. If she failed to remember, the only purpose of putting in her previous identification was to prove the truth of what she asserted to the officer conducting the parade. The position was even more clearly hearsay in relation to the second witness. She said that the man she picked out was not one of the defendants. To prove that she did pick out a defendant was to give evidence wholly inconsistent with what she had said on oath. Fortunately, *Osbourne and Virtue* is not often followed in practice.

Further grounds of admissibility

A statement identifying someone as the offender may be admissible as a dying declaration, or as part of the res gestae, or as a previous inconsistent statement, provided the conditions for admissibility of evidence under those principles are satisfied.

All cases of dying declarations must involve statements identifying the accused, otherwise the evidence could not be admissible. Many of the cases which have been examined under other chapters in this book deal with evidence of identifications, such as *Buckley, Nye and Loan, Turnbull, Ratten* v *R, Blastland* and *Andrews* in paragraph 4.4 on res gestae; *Thompson, Smith, Straffen* and others in paragraph 7.1 on similar fact evidence.

11.2 Methods of identification

Various methods of conducting tests of identification are provided for in the Codes of Practice issued pursuant to the Police and Criminal Evidence Act 1984. It is outside the scope of this book for them to investigated in any detail, but the basics of Code D are as follows:

'2 IDENTIFICATION BY WITNESSES
(a) Cases where the suspect is known
2.1 In a case which involves disputed identification evidence, and where the identity of the suspect is known to the police, the methods of identification by witnesses which may be used are:
i) a parade;
ii) a group identification;
iii) a video film;
iv) a confrontation.
2.2 The arrangements for, and conduct of, these types of identification shall be the responsibility of an officer in uniform not below the rank of inspector who is not involved with the investigation ("the identification officer"). No officer involved with the investigation of the case against the suspect may take any part in these procedures.
Identification Parade
2.3 In a case which involves disputed identification evidence a parade must be held if the suspect asks for one and it is practicable to hold one. A parade may also be held if the officer in charge of the investigation considers that it would be useful, and the suspect consents.

2.4 A parade need not be held if the identification officer considers that, whether by reason of the unusual appearance of the suspect or for some other reason, it would not be practicable to assemble sufficient people who resembled him to make a parade fair.

2.5 Any parade must be carried out in accordance with Annex A.

Group Identification

2.6 If a suspect refuses or, having agreed, fails to attend an identification parade or the holding of a parade is impracticable, arrangements must if practicable be made to allow the witness an opportunity of seeing him in a group of people.

2.7 A group identification may also be arranged if the officer in charge of the investigation considers, whether because of fear on the part of the witness or for some other reason, that it is, in the circumstances, more satisfactory than a parade.

2.8 The suspect should be asked for his consent to a group identification and advised in accordance with paragraphs 2.15 and 2.16. However, where consent is refused the identification officer has the discretion to proceed with a group identification if it is practicable to do so.

2.9 A group identification should, if practicable, be held in a place other than a police station (for example, in an underground station or a shopping centre). It may be held in a police station if the identification officer considers, whether for security reasons or on other grounds, that it would not be practicable to hold it elsewhere. In either case the group identification should, as far as possible, follow the principles and procedures for a parade as set out in Annex A.

Video Film Identification

2.10 The identification officer may show a witness a video film of a suspect if the investigating officer considers, whether because of the refusal of the suspect to take part in an identification parade or group identification or other reasons, that this would in the circumstances be the most satisfactory course of action.

2.11 The suspect should be asked for his consent to a video identification and advised in accordance with paragraphs 2.15 and 2.16. However, where such consent is refused the identification officer has the discretion to proceed with a video identification if it is practicable to do so.

2.12 A video identification must be carried out in accordance with Annex B.

Confrontation

2.13 If neither a parade nor a video identification nor a group identification procedure is arranged, the suspect may be confronted by the witness. Such a confrontation does not require the suspect's consent, but may not take place unless none of the other procedures are practicable.

2.14 A confrontation must be carried out in accordance with Annex C ...

(b) Cases where the identity of the suspect is not known

2.17 A police officer may take a witness to a particular neighbourhood or place to see whether he can identify the person whom he said he saw on the relevant occasion. Care should be taken however not to direct the witness's attention to any individual.

2.18 A witness must not be shown photographs or photofit, identikit or similar pictures if the identity of the suspect is known to the police and he is available to stand on an identification parade. If the identity of the suspect is not known, the showing of such pictures to a witness must be done in accordance with Annex D ...

3   IDENTIFICATION BY FINGERPRINTS ...

3.1 A person's fingerprints may be taken only with his consent or if paragraph 3.2 applies. If he is at a police station consent must be in writing. In either case the person must be informed of the reason before they are taken and that they will be destroyed as soon as practicable if paragraph 3.4 applies. He must be told that he may witness their destruction if he asks to do so within five days of being cleared or informed that he will not be prosecuted.

3.2 Powers to take fingerprints without consent from any person over the age of ten years are provided by s61 of the Police and Criminal Evidence Act 1984. Reasonable force may be used if necessary ...

4   IDENTIFICATION BY PHOTOGRAPHS ...

4.1 The photograph of a person who has been arrested may be taken at a police station only with his written consent or if paragraph 4.2 applies. In either case he must be informed of the reason for taking it and that the photograph will be destroyed if paragraph 4.4 applies. He must be told that he may witness the destruction of the photograph or be provided with a certificate confirming its destruction if he applies within five days of being cleared or informed that he will not be prosecuted ...

5   IDENTIFICATION BY BODY SAMPLES, SWABS AND IMPRESSIONS ...

5.1 Dental impressions and intimate samples may be taken from a person in police detention only:

i) if an officer of the rank of superintendent or above considers that the offence concerned is a serious arrestable offence; and

ii) if that officer has reasonable grounds to believe that such an impression or sample will tend to confirm or disprove the suspect's involvement in it; and

iii) with the suspect's written consent.

5.2 Before a person is asked to provide an intimate sample he must be warned that a refusal may be treated, in any proceedings against him, as corroborating relevant prosecution evidence.'

A person does not have a statutory right to undergo an identification procedure: see *R* v *Joseph* (1993) The Times 25 May.

The penalty for failing to comply with the many details of the Codes of Practice lies in the discretion of the court to exclude evidence which has been obtained by unfair means. This topic is examined in detail in chapter 9.

One method of identification which is not normally proper is the so-called 'dock identification'. This occurs where a witness who has not previously identified the defendant as the offender is asked when in the witness box whether he sees the offender in court and if so to point him out. A witness who was unsure might be tempted to point out the man in the dock simply because he was there. Despite one or two amusing cases in which the dock officer or one of the solicitors or counsel present was pointed out, it was felt that dock identification was not fair to the accused, so in *Cartwright* (1914) 10 Cr App R 219 the Court of Criminal Appeal held that dock identifications should not normally be allowed. There may be exceptional cases where it is reasonable to ask a witness to make an identification for the first time in court, such as *Caird* [1970] Crim LR 656 where the witness was a police officer who had been knocked unconscious during a riot and had been off duty since that time, and *John* [1973] Crim LR 113 where the defendant denied that he was the offender but refused to go on an identification parade. In these cases the trial judges directed the juries about the need to scrutinise the identification evidence carefully. In the absence of that direction it would have been a wrong to allow the dock identification.

In *R* v *Fergus* [1992] Crim LR 363 the Court of Appeal distinguished recognition from identification. Where the complainant did not know the accused well, it was a question of identification rather than recognition. In such a case an identification parade was desirable and an identification in the dock undesirable.

Evidence of a video tape recording of a robbery and evidence from police officers, who had viewed the video in a police station, of the purported recognition of suspects, is prima facie admissible, subject to the discretion of the judge to exclude it: *R* v *Caldwell* (1993) The Times 8 June. Commenting on such video-based recognition evidence, which was becoming even more prevalent, their Lordships said that some analogy existed between showing videos and showing photographs, as indeed it did between video showing and identification parades. How close the analogy was would depend upon the circumstances. Ordinarily, recognition evidence was quite different from identification evidence. Nevertheless, some at least of the considerations underlying the safeguards built into the regulatory procedures laid down for identification parades and the showing of photographs came into play too with regard to the showing of video tapes.

In *R* v *Jones* (1994) The Times 13 January the Court of Appeal upheld the admission of evidence of identification from a video recording of customers in a public house made 25 days after an attack on the doorman. It was, said the court, equivalent to a street identification or an informal group identification. There had been no element of unfairness.

For other recent identification cases, see *R* v *McCay* [1990] Crim LR 338 (identification parades), *R* v *Constantinou* [1989] Crim LR 571 (photofit pictures) and *R* v *Quinn* [1990] Crim LR 581 (identification by policeman). Although the same rules apply to police officers as to other witnesses in relation to identification evidence, it may be appropriate for the judge to direct the jury that, because of his training and experience, a police officer may have paid greater attention to a person's features and identity: *R* v *Ramsden* [1991] Crim LR 295.

11.3 *R* v *Turnbull*

The guidelines

In 1976 a committee chaired by Lord Devlin reported its findings and recommendations about evidence of identifications. The committee was set up following a number of high-profile cases in which innocent people were convicted on evidence of identification. The principal recommendations of the committee were adopted by the Court of Appeal in the case of *Turnbull* [1977] QB 224 in which a number of appeals were heard together and a court of five judges laid down guidelines which should be followed by trial judges.

Two guidelines were laid down, the first of which is as follows:

'... whenever the case against an accused depends wholly or substantially on the correctness of one or more identifications of the accused which the defence alleges to be mistaken, the judge should warn the jury of the special need for caution before convicting the accused in reliance on the correctness of the identification or identifications. In addition he should instruct them as to the reason for the need for such a warning and should make some reference to the possibility that a mistaken witness can be a convincing one and that a number of such witnesses can all be mistaken. Provided this is done in clear terms the judge need not use any particular form of words.'

This first guideline sets out the basic principle of the law in this area, that identification evidence is inherently suspect and the jury should be told of this because they may not realise it unless they are told by the judge. Everyone can speak of occasions when they have been mistaken for someone else in a shop or in the street. Furthermore, most people are not trained in identification and may not always remember the most distinguishing feature of a person they have seen, or may remember one feature and forget others, so that anyone who shares that feature may be mistaken for the person they have seen.

The second guideline reads:

'... the judge should direct the jury to examine closely the circumstances in which the identification of each witness came to be made. How long did the witness have the accused under observation? At what distance? In what light? Was the observation impeded in any way, as for example by passing traffic or a press of people? Had the witness ever seen the accused before? How often? If only occasionally, had he any special reason for remembering the accused? How long elapsed between the original observation and the subsequent identification to the police? Was there any material discrepancy between the description of the accused given to the police by the witness when first seen by them and his actual appearance? If in any case, whether it is being dealt with summarily or on indictment, the prosecution have reason to believe that there is such material discrepancy they should supply the accused or his legal advisers with particulars of the description the police were first given. In all cases if the accused asks to be given particulars of such descriptions, the prosecution should supply them. Finally he should remind the jury of any specific weaknesses which had appeared in the identification evidence.'

This second guideline is concerned with what the judge should tell the jury. It is detailed, but it will not necessarily be fatal if the judge fails to point out one or more of the items listed in it. As the first guideline says, no particular form of words is necessary. The second guideline reinforces the first by making clear that the jury should examine the evidence of identification very carefully, testing the likelihood of it having been correct when first made and also whether anything has happened during the course of the case which has weakened it.

If the case depends wholly upon identification evidence and the judge feels it is not strong evidence, he should accede to a submission that there is no case to answer. But if there is other evidence connecting the accused to the offence he may be able to allow the case to continue after the close of the prosecution case, but in such circumstances he will have to give the warning mentioned in the guidelines.

The warning

The second guideline details many of the matters which the judge should mention in his summing up, but the main purpose of a '*Turnbull* direction' is to impress upon the jury the special need for caution. The direction which he must give is not a corroboration direction because the technicalities of corroboration do not apply simply because identification is in issue. If the case is one in which corroboration is required as a matter of law or practice, the judge must direct them about corroboration in the normal way and in addition must give the *Turnbull* warning.

Later in the judgment, Lord Widgery said that the judge should point out to the jury those matters which he adjudges are capable of supporting the identification. But, he said, he should make clear that the failure of the accused to give evidence, or the putting forward of a false alibi, are not matters which support the identification evidence because the accused has the right not to give evidence and may have given a false alibi for a number of reasons.

The need for the warning about identification evidence to be clear was stressed in *Keane* (1977) 65 Cr App R 247 in which the appeal was allowed because the judge did not explain the reasons why caution is needed when assessing evidence of identification and did not examine the weaknesses in the identification.

In *R* v *Fergus* (1993) The Times 30 June Steyn LJ said that in a case dependent on visual identification, and particularly where that is the only evidence, *Turnbull* makes it clear that it is incumbent on a trial judge to place before the jury any specific weaknesses which could arguably be said to have been exposed in the evidence and to do so in a coherent manner so that the cumulative impact of the weaknesses is fairly placed before the jury.

In *Reid* v *R* [1989] 3 WLR 771 the Privy Council said that a significant failure to follow the guidelines laid down in *R* v *Turnbull* [1977] QB 224 would cause a conviction to be quashed because it would have resulted in a substantial miscarriage of justice.

Fleeting glimpses

After *Turnbull* a number of cases were decided in which the Court of Appeal seemed to hold that a *Turnbull* direction need only be given where the identification is made by a witness who had only a 'fleeting glimpse' of the offender. In *Turnbull* itself 'fleeting glimpses' cases were said to be the sort of case in which the judge may have to withdraw the matter from the jury after the prosecution's evidence has been completed. But in *Oakwell* [1978] 1 All ER 1223 Lord Widgery CJ said that *Turnbull* was intended primarily to deal with 'fleeting encounters'. In so far as *Oakwell* holds that a *Turnbull* direction should only be given in fleeting glimpse cases, it is directly contrary to what was held in *Turnbull* and is incorrect.

Some difficulty was caused by *Oakwell* such that a court of five judges had to sit in *Weeder* (1980) 71 Cr App R 228, presided over by Lord Widgery's successor Lord Lane, to restate the *Turnbull* rules. It was held in *Weeder* that the importance of fleeting glimpses is that they are likely to be so unreliable that the judge should withdraw the case from the jury. But in all cases where identification is in issue a *Turnbull* direction should be given. The court said that the judge should withdraw the case where the identifying witnesses 'had only the opportunity of a fleeting glance or a longer observation made in difficult conditions, eg the occupants of a bus who observed the incident at night as they drove past'. It was argued in *Weeder* that the evidence of one identification witness should not be capable in law of supporting the evidence of another. This argument was decisively rejected.

In the course of the judgment of the Court of Appeal in *Keane* it was said that *Turnbull* should not be applied inflexibly. Even after the decision in *Weeder*, this caused some judges to fail to give a *Turnbull* direction where the identification evidence seemed strong. In order to ensure that this should not happen in the future, the court took the matter further in *Breslin* (1984) 80 Cr App R 226 and held that in all cases where identification is in issue a *Turnbull* direction should be given, even where there were a number of identification witnesses all of whom had a good view of events.

In *Daley* v *R* [1993] 4 All ER 86 the Privy Council explained that, while a trial judge should not withdraw a case from the jury merely because he considers the prosecution evidence as unworthy of credit, as it is the jury's and not the judge's function to assess the credibility of witnesses, he ought to withdraw the case from the jury if it is based on identification evidence which, even if taken to be honest, is so slender that it is unreliable and therefore not sufficient to found a conviction.

Photographs

While a judge should normally warn the jury of the dangers of relying on photographic evidence, no formula is required and the content of the summing-up has to be governed by the circumstances of the case: *R* v *Dodson* [1984] 1 WLR 971. Indeed, unless there are special factors, the absence of a specific direction will not of itself amount to a misdirection: *R* v *Downey* (1994) The Times 5 April.

12

Real Evidence

12.1 The best evidence rule

12.2 Documents

12.3 Other real evidence

12.1 The best evidence rule

The origin of the rule

The best evidence rule has been described as one of the ghosts of the law of evidence. It is a rule of obscure origin and has been defined in many inconsistent ways. But its ghostliness manifests itself these days by judges referring to it in order to justify the exclusion of evidence, even though it is because of an entirely different rule that the evidence in question is not admissible. It is sometimes said that all exclusionary rules of evidence derive from the basic principle that only the best evidence possible should be called to prove the facts in issue. This, again, is a useful shorthand way to justify exclusionary rules, but it is not right to say that there was ever a time when the law refused to allow anything other than the very best possible evidence. Exclusionary rules developed as the need for them arose, and the fact that many can be justified by saying that they require the best evidence to be called, is coincidental.

It was once said by Lord Hardwicke that 'there is but one general rule of evidence, the best that the nature of the case will allow': *Omychund* v *Barker* (1745) 1 Atk 21. This dictum has both inclusionary and exclusionary aspects – all evidence is admissible if it is the best evidence, and no evidence is allowed unless it is the best evidence. Subsequent cases did not adopt the inclusionary aspect of Lord Hardwicke's formulation, and many which adopted the strict exclusionary aspect were later limited in their effect. Lord Hardwicke's words were accepted in some overseas jurisdictions. South Africa once had a statutory rule in almost identical terms to his dictum, although this was repealed because it was felt to be unfairly restrictive. No English legislation has ever dealt with the best evidence rule and it remains a creature of the common law.

No English case has decided that Lord Hardwicke's rule should be accepted in its entirety. In both civil and criminal courts there are examples of a strict exclusionary rule being applied, but these have all been disapproved. For example, in *Chenie* v *Watson* (1797) Peake Add Cas 123 there was a dispute about the quantity of goods which had been delivered. The court refused to allow oral evidence about the quantity, because the goods themselves could have been brought to court. It is inconceivable that a judge today would rule that oral evidence about the quantity of goods delivered to a buyer is inadmissible; he would leave it to the buyer to decide what evidence to call. But if there was a dispute about quantity he may not feel able to decide on oral evidence alone how much was delivered and in the absence of any other evidence the buyer may lose his claim because he is unable to satisfy the burden of proof. The rule in *Chenie* v *Watson* was relaxed in *Williams* v *East India Co* (1802) 3 East 192 where it was said to be permissible to call evidence of what happened on loading a ship other than by calling the mate who actually supervised the loading. Clearly the mate could give the best evidence about what happened on loading, but that of the officer would be perfectly acceptable provided he did not have to rely on what other people told him. One rule which is properly described as the best evidence rule is that if the court is to be asked to consider a document the original should be produced to the court and evidence should be given to prove that it is the original. In *McDonnell* v *Evans* (1852) 21 LJ CP 141 a witness was shown a letter and was asked whether he had written it in reply to an earlier letter which accused him of fraud. It was held that this question was improper because it attempted to prove the existence and terms of the earlier letter without producing the letter itself to the court.

A similar pattern is seen in criminal cases. In *Smith* (1768) 1 East PC 1000 expert evidence was not allowed about handwriting because the person who it was said had written the document in question was alive and could have been called to say whether or not he wrote it. But in *Francis* (1874) LR 2 CCR 128 the Court for Crown Cases Reserved held that the Crown was entitled to rely on oral evidence about a ring which the defendant allegedly fraudulently described as a diamond ring. It was not necessary to bring the ring into court and Lord Coleridge CJ specifically stated that there is no rule of law requiring a chattel to be produced for the inspection of the jury before oral evidence about it could be given. *Francis* was followed in *Hockin* v *Ahlquist Brothers Ltd* [1944] KB 120 where allegations for breaches of war time restrictions on the amount of cloth which could be used in clothing manufacture were proved by oral evidence of a Board of Trade officer and it was not necessary to produce the jackets, waistcoats and trousers concerned. As in *McDonnell* v *Evans*, criminal courts have long followed the rule that a document may not be put in evidence without the original being proved. For example, in *Regan* (1887) 16 Cox CC it was held that where the words used in a telegram are to be used against the sender of it, the original message which was handed in at the post office should be produced in order to prove the words used.

The limits of Lord Hardwicke's influence are also illustrated by the fact that there has never been an inclusionary rule that the best evidence may always be used. For example, hearsay evidence is generally inadmissible and it is not made admissible by the absence of any better evidence. Children who do not understand the need to tell the truth in court are not rendered competent by the absence of other witnesses. Similar examples can also be used to show that the exclusionary aspect of Lord Hardwicke's rule is limited: hearsay evidence which is admissible under a recognised exception to the hearsay rule is not rendered inadmissible by the fact that direct evidence may also be available; and a child who is competent but whose evidence must be given unsworn is still competent even if other witnesses who can give sworn evidence are available.

The rule today

The present state of the law was stated by Lord Denning MR in *Garton* v *Hunter* [1969] 2 QB 37 in which the question arose as to what value a caravan site had for rating purposes. The Lands Tribunal refused to consider evidence of valuation given by the parties, following a dictum from Scott LJ in *Robinson Brothers (Brewers) Ltd* v *Houghton and Chester-le-Street Assessment Committee* [1937] 2 KB 445 that the rent actually realised by the site was the only permissible evidence of its rateable value. Lord Denning MR said:

> 'It is plain that Scott LJ had in mind the old rule that a party must produce the best evidence that the nature of the case will allow, and that any less good evidence is to be excluded. That old rule has gone by the board long ago. The only remaining instance of it that I know is that if an original document is available in one's hand, one must produce it. One cannot give secondary evidence by producing a copy. Nowadays we do not confine ourselves to the best evidence. We admit all relevant evidence. The goodness or badness of it goes only to weight and not to admissibility.'

The rule was restated in almost identical terms by Ackner LJ in *Kajala* v *Noble* (1982) 75 Cr App R 749, to which reference will be made below. There are, however, still examples of judges referring to the best evidence rule as the reason for rejecting evidence when some other rule should be applied. For example in *Greenaway* v *Homelea Fittings Ltd* [1985] 1 WLR 234, the judge cited the best evidence rule as justifying his refusal of leave to call hearsay evidence. Again, this was a shorthand way of expressing the rule that hearsay is normally inadmissible, but in so far as it suggests that the best evidence rule lies behind the exclusion of hearsay, it is erroneous and should not be followed.

Both Lord Denning and Ackner LJ referred to documents. English law considers any writing to be a document and is not concerned with whether the writing is on paper, parchment or stone: *Daye* [1908] 2 KB 333. There is some authority that tape recordings and films are documents, but they are not treated as documents for the purposes of the best evidence rule: see paragraph 12.3 below.

In *R* v *Governor of Pentonville Prison, ex parte Osman* [1990] 1 WLR 277, Lloyd LJ said that 'although the little-loved best evidence rule has been dying for some time, the recent authorities, including *Kajala* v *Noble* (1982) 75 Cr App R 149, suggest that it is still not quite dead.'

12.2 Documents

Private documents

We are concerned in this chapter with private documents, by which is meant any document which is not a public document. It has already been seen that public documents are admissible as an exception to the hearsay rule. By the nature of most of them copies are used and therefore the rule in *Garton* v *Hunter* and *Kajala* v *Noble* has no application to public documents: Evidence Act 1851 s14. Many private documents are made available to the public, such as newspapers which the plaintiff alleges contain a libel. But many more have only been seen by few eyes before they are used in court. The definition of private documents does not depend upon how many have seen the documents.

The mere fact that a party brings an original document to court is not enough to allow the judge or jury to consider it, because it must be relevant to the case and must not be inadmissible by virtue of any of the other rules considered in this book. Documents may be relevant in many ways. The most common uses of documents in court are three.

First, some documents are the subject matter of the dispute and reference must be made to them to consider the rights of the parties. The classic example of these is contracts. A contract is original evidence of the rights of the parties, and the job of the court is to construe the document to clear up ambiguities, to imply terms if necessary in order to allow the contract to be workable, and to give relief by way of damages or some other remedy where there has been a breach. Similarly in defamation cases the writing about which complaint is made is the very subject matter of the dispute. The newspaper, book or letter in question is not hearsay evidence but is original evidence of what was written, and the court must decide whether the plaintiff has been libelled and if so, how much he should be paid to compensate him for it.

The second use of documents is as hearsay in order to prove the truth of what the document says. We have already seen that in both civil and criminal cases there are limitations on the use of documentary hearsay, although in civil disputes the major limitation is procedural, namely, the need to give notice.

The third use is to show the consistency or inconsistency of a witness. Here the document in question is used in cross-examination and is not adduced as part of the case of the party using it. A party will not put the document before the court until such time as a witness gives evidence which is inconsistent with it. In order to save time it is common practice in civil disputes to prepare a bundle of documents to which reference may be made as and when necessary. They may not be considered by the court until such time as one or other party refers to them, but that does not prevent them being handed up in a bundle at the beginning of the trial. Indeed, if they are agreed by the parties, the judge may refer to them even if no specific reference is made to them in the course of the trial.

Proof of documents

Documents are not accepted as evidence of anything by the court unless there is proof that the piece of paper which is in court is the document relevant to the case. The process of establishing that a particular document is relevant and should be referred to by the judge is known as proving the document. A party may prove a document in three ways. He may call a witness to say that from his own knowledge he can state that the document which is shown to him in the witness box is the one relevant to the court proceedings. Or the party may put the document to his opponent's witness and extract an admission that the document is the relevant one. Or the parties may agree that the document is the one in issue. Which method is used in any case depends upon the circumstances of that case; for example if a party has a document but is unable to call a witness to identify the document, he may hand it to his opponent's witness and ask him to identify it. And if it is common ground between the parties that a particular document is the one in question they may simply agree this fact and hand up the original or a copy to the judge or jury. Which method of proving the document is used in any case depends upon the nature of the document and the position being taken by the parties. A defendant who has no defence on the merits of the case but who wishes to put the plaintiff to proof of his claim may choose not to agree anything and not to give evidence. In such a case the plaintiff will have to call a witness to prove the document, otherwise he will not be able to use it. But if both parties are happy to agree the use of copies, no time will be spend in court proving any of the documents in the case.

The general rule is that a party who wishes to rely on a document must produce the original to court and prove it in one of the ways mentioned above: *McDonnell* v *Evans*. But it is important to analyse the issues in the case in order to work out what is the original document. For example, if it is alleged that a newspaper article libelled the plaintiff, the original document in issue is the article as printed and not what the journalist submitted to the editor, because it may have been altered before publication. Because every publication of a libel is a separate libel, the plaintiff may prove any newspaper which contains the libel, he does not have to prove that every copy of that paper was the same. This example raises another point. The rule in *McDonnell* v *Evans*, that the original must be proved in evidence, does not prevent the plaintiff from proving several imprints of the same paper; although they are referred to in ordinary language as 'copies' of the paper, each is an original example of publication.

It was held in *Slatterie* v *Pooley* (1840) 6 M & W 664 that an admission of the defendant that he had covenanted to indemnify the plaintiff against a debt, was held to relieve the plaintiff from the need to prove the deed in which the defendant made the promise. How far this case can be applied in other situations is open to question. It was said by Parke B that the best evidence rule was not infringed because there can be no better evidence against a party than his admission. But the party must specifically admit both the making and the relevant terms of the contract or other document before his opponent can rely on it, and even then he will only be allowed to rely on those terms which are admitted.

A form of admission is often contained in pleadings. For example, in a landlord and tenant dispute the parties may agree in their pleadings that the tenancy was created by a written contract. In such a case it will not be open to either landlord or tenant to dispute the making of the contract unless they amend their pleadings so as to withdraw the admission. Necessarily where there is a dispute whether the document produced in court is the contract which was signed, neither party can force the judge to accept the document which he hands up, and the judge may hear evidence from all parties: *Boyle* v *Wiseman* (1855) 10 Exch 647. Where there is no dispute about the contract, a copy will be agreed and submitted to the judge.

In the Crown Court, magistrates' courts and county courts witnesses may be summoned to appear and produce a document: Criminal Procedure (Attendance of Witnesses) Act 1965 s2(1); Magistrates' Courts Act 1980 s97; CCR O.20 r.12(1). In the High Court a subpoena duces tecum is issued (RSC O.38 r.14). There is no difference in substance between a witness summons and a subpoena. A witness who is summoned is entitled to be paid witness money, plus reasonable travel expenses, whereas a witness who attends of his own accord does so for nothing. A High Court witness who is subpoenaed is entitled to expenses: see s36(4) of the Supreme Court Act 1981 as amended.

Where the person who has custody of the document is a party, a witness summons or subpoena is not appropriate. There is no procedure in criminal cases by which the defendant may be required to produce any document, although a private prosecutor is in the same position as any other witness and may be served with a witness summons. In civil cases a notice may be served on a party requiring him to produce a document: RSC O.24 r.10, CCR O.20 r.3(4). Such a notice is, not surprisingly, known as a notice to produce. No particular form is prescribed for such a notice, but it must be worded so that it is clear what is meant to be produced. A party who has served a notice to produce does not have to put the document which is produced in evidence, but if he is required to do so by any other party, he must do so: *Senat* v *Senat* [1965] P 172. This rule prevents the speculative serving of notices where the contents of the document are not known. If a notice to produce is not complied with, secondary evidence may be given of the document in question: *Dwyer* v *Collins* (1852) 7 Ex 639. The disclosure of documents on discovery does not dispense with the need for notices to produce because inspection of documents in one's opponent's list of documents does not give those documents any particular evidential effect.

There is a difference in the use which can be made of documents used by a witness to refresh his memory and other documents. Memory refreshing documents may be inspected by the party who is cross-examining the witness without there being any need to show the document to the judge or jury. As we have seen in chapter 1, cross-examination on parts of the document other than those parts from which the memory was refreshed allows the party who called the witness to require the document to be put in evidence. But if cross-examination is restricted to those parts used by the witness, the document does not become evidence unless the cross-examiner wishes. We also saw in that chapter that the note from which memory is refreshed should be the original, although the rules stated below about permissible uses of copies where the absence of the original can be accounted for apply to memory refreshing documents as they do to other documents. Other documents are treated differently. Any document which one party requires another party to deliver up for inspection must be delivered up. But if it is, the party who delivers it may require it to be put in evidence, although he does not have to do so: *Wharam* v *Routledge* (1805) 5 Esp 235. The use to which it may be put once it is in evidence depends upon whether the proceedings are civil or criminal, and the relevant rules are discussed elsewhere in this book.

Two further useful but obscure provisions apply to documentary evidence. The first is that documents which are at least 20 years old 'prove themselves' provided evidence is given that they were produced to court from the custody of someone who might be expected to have possession of them: Evidence Act 1938 s4. These are known as documents which have been produced from 'proper custody', the principle being that the court can draw whatever inference it sees fit from a document which has been in the hands of the sort of person whom one would expect to have it. For example, a receipt for goods which is produced to court by the buyer of those goods can be treated as confirmatory of his oral evidence that he bought them. It is not necessary to call the seller to prove the receipt as being the one which he issued: *Wynne* v *Tyrwhitt* (1821) 4 B & Ald 376. And a letter which is produced to court by the addressee can be received in evidence without there being any need for the signatory to give evidence about it: *Doe d Thomas* v *Benyon* (1840) 12 Ad & El 431. But a general limitation to this rule is that only documents which are over 20 years old and are produced from proper custody prove themselves. The period used to be 30 years but was reduced to 20 by s4 of the Evidence Act 1938. In the county court, however, O.20 r.11(1) extends the rule to all documents, whether or not they are 20 years old; no such special rule applies in the High Court or in the criminal courts.

The second obscure rule is that any document referred to in pleadings may be referred to by the judge without it having to be strictly proved by either plaintiff or defendant. This rule applies not just to contracts but to any document. In *Day* v *William Hill (Park Lane) Ltd* [1949] 1 KB 632 for example, the plaintiff's pleadings referred to a statement of his account with the defendant bookmakers. The Court of Appeal held that the courts were entitled to refer to the statement without it having to be proved. After reference is made to a document in a pleading, many lawyers make clear that they wish to be able to rely on the document without proving it. This is commonly done by adding a sentence saying something like the following: 'The Plaintiff [or Defendant] will refer to the said contract at trial for its full terms and effects.' The decision in *Day* v *William Hill (Park Lane) Ltd* makes clear that this form of pleading is unnecessary because any reference to a document will suffice to allow the court to see it. The use to which the court may put documents referred to in pleadings is limited by the rules of evidence which determine the admissibility of documents, because the pleadings are not themselves evidence, they are simply summaries of the parties' arguments. Which of the three uses summarised above is appropriate depends not upon whether the document is referred to in the pleadings but upon whether it is admissible evidence.

Secondary evidence

Where an original document is not available to the court, there is no absolute rule that the judge or jury may be referred to other evidence which proves its contents. We have already seen that the general rule is that the original must be produced but in some cases this is not required. Apart from those special cases, evidence other than the original may only be used where there is a good reason why production of the original is not made. There are no categories of good reasons, although certain types of case commonly arise, and these are given below. If the reason for not producing the original does not fall within the examples below, that does not mean that other evidence about the document may not be given. Everything depends upon whether the reason for non-production is sufficiently strong.

Failure to comply with a notice to produce, a witness summons or a subpoena duces tecum allows secondary evidence of the document in question to be given. In addition, the failure may itself lead to the court drawing an inference that it was prompted by a fear of the contents of the document being given in evidence. This inference may enhance the weight of the secondary evidence which is called. The party who refuses to produce the document is not entitled to dispute the accuracy of his opponent's secondary evidence by producing the original at trial: *Doe v Hodgson* (1840) 12 Ad & El 135.

When secondary evidence is allowed there is no restriction on the types of secondary evidence which may be called. These days photocopies are the most common type of secondary evidence, but there are no degrees of secondary evidence and the court will not expect the best secondary evidence to be given. Failure to produce a copy or photograph of the document is therefore not fatal. Oral evidence of its contents may be given: *Collins* (1960) 44 Cr App R 170. In *Doe d Gilbert* v *Ross* (1840) 7 M & W 102 the secondary evidence which was given was oral evidence even though copies of the document in question were available. It was held that the court was not restricted to hearing the best secondary evidence and therefore the oral evidence was admissible.

The only distinction between different types of secondary evidence is in the weight they are given. The judge may be less happy to accept oral evidence of the terms of a complex contract than he would be to accept a photocopy. But this is a matter of weight and not admissibility. As has been noted already, the court may feel able to give greater weight to oral evidence where it is called because of a failure to comply with a subpoena, witness summons or notice to admit, although there is no rule of law requiring this.

The most common cases where secondary evidence is given do not arise out of a failure to comply with an order or notice requiring production. They are cases of physical impossibility to produce, inconvenience to produce, reliance on privilege and loss of the original.

No satisfactory authority exists for the proposition that impossibility to produce the original document allows secondary evidence to be given, although dicta in the two cases which follow are sufficient authority for such an obvious rule.

In *Owner* v *Bee Hive Spinning Co Ltd* [1914] 1 KB 105 the original document was a notice attached to a factory wall. The notice could have been taken down and brought to court, but if it had been the owner of the factory would have committed an offence by not displaying the notice. It was not phsically impossible to bring the notice, but it was inconvenient because it would have resulted in the commission of a crime. Similarly in *Mortimer* v *McCallan* (1840) 6 M & W 58 books held by the Bank of England were not produced because it would have caused great public inconvenience; secondary evidence of their contents was therefore admissible.

Privilege was relied upon by a witness in *Mills* v *Oddy* (1834) 6 C & P 728 as a reason for not complying with a subpoena duces tecum. His claim to privilege was perfectly correct, therefore he could not be forced to produce the document to court and secondary evidence of it was allowed. A substantially similar ruling was made in *Nowaz* [1976] 1 WLR 830 where the defendant was charged with making a false statutory declaration to the Pakistani consulate in this country in order to obtain registration as a United Kingdom citizen. On the ground of diplomatic immunity, the Pakistani consul refused to give evidence or produce documents submitted to him by the defendant. This claim to immunity was upheld and in substitution for the original documents a policeman who had seen them was allowed to give oral evidence of their contents. In both of these last two cases the claim to immunity from having to produce the document in court was a proper claim. In *Llanfaethly (Inhabitants)* (1853) 23 LJ MC 33, by contrast, a claim to privilege was incorrectly made. The Court of Queen's Bench refused to allow secondary evidence to be given because the witness who disobeyed the subpoena could have been compelled to give evidence.

Loss of the original will allow secondary evidence to be given provided a reasonable search has been carried out. For example, in *Brewster* v *Sewell* (1820) 3 B & Ald 296 an old insurance policy was the document in question and after a brief search it was given up for lost. Secondary evidence of its contents was admissible, and the Court of King's Bench held that what is a reasonable search depends upon the sort of document concerned – the more important the document to its owner or custodian, the more thorough the search required before secondary evidence will be allowed.

12.3 Other real evidence

Recordings

Audio and video recordings are admissible in evidence provided they do not infringe exclusionary rules. As with all evidence, their admissibility depends upon their relevance. Recordings of interviews of suspects by police officers are frequently used in preference to witnesses reading out notes of the interviews. It is obvious that a tape recording is likely to be more accurate than the notes, because notes do not record everything which is said. We have seen in chapter 6 that the jury are normally entitled to know of what was said in the defendant's interview and it is only right that they receive the most accurate evidence available of what happened in that interview. See also 'Exhibits' below.

The difference between the accuracy of a genuine and complete tape recording of an interview and the reading out of a note of interview is similar to the difference between a video recording of a bank robbery and an eye-witness's evidence of what happened. There are inevitable deficiencies in a note of interview and in a witness's evidence, no matter how honest the note-taker or witness may be. The law recognises the advantage of a live recording of an event over a documentary record of it or a witness's recollection. In *Dodson* [1984] 1 WLR 971 the Court of Appeal held that photographs taken by a camera at a building society were admissible evidence of what actually happened. If the jury was not sure that the robbers shown in the photographs were the defendants they would acquit. But the photographs showed what actually happened and so were admissible.

The leading case in this area is *Kajala* v *Noble* (1982) 75 Cr App R 749 where a copy of a BBC video recording was admitted in evidence against the defendant who was charged with using threatening behaviour. The Queen's Bench Divisional Court held that the copy recording was admissible as real evidence of what happened. It also held that there is no need to produce the original recording to the court, providing there is satisfactory evidence that the copy is genuine, and that it has not been tampered with. There is authority that tape recordings are documents for some purposes of English law. *Grant* v *Southwestern and County Properties Ltd* [1975] Ch 185 holds that a tape recording is a document for the purposes of O.24 of the Rules of the Supreme Court, and must be disclosed on discovery. A year later in *Senior* v *Holdsworth* [1976] QB 23 the Court of Appeal held that film and video recordings were documents for the purposes of O.20 r.8 of the County Court Rules and, therefore, that a subpoena duces tecum could require their production to court. Neither of these cases was cited in *Kajala* v *Noble*, but Ackner LJ said that the best evidence rule only applies to 'written documents in the strict sense of the term, and has no relevance to tapes or films'. Accordingly the *Grant* and *Senior* cases do not undermine the correctness of *Kajala* v *Noble* and *Garton* v *Hunter*.

Grant v *Southwestern and County Properties Ltd* above, was applied in *Derby & Co Ltd* v *Weldon (No 9)* [1991] 2 All ER 901 where Vinelott J held that a computer database which formed part of the business records of a company was, so far as it contained information capable of being retrieved and converted into readable form, a 'document' for the purposes of O.24 and was therefore susceptible to discovery.

Two challenges to the admissibility of a recording may be made. First, it might be argued that the recording is not clear enough to be evidence of anything. Secondly it may be argued that the recording which it is proposed to put before the court is not an accurate copy of the original. Both arguments really amount to the same thing: what must be proved about the accuracy of a recording before it may be used in evidence? *Kajala* v *Noble* holds that a copy of a recording may be used, but says nothing about the need for it to be accurate before it may be admitted at all.

For reasons which are not clear from the authorities a distinction is drawn between recordings of events and the evidence of witnesses to events. There is no doubt that the question whether a witness is accurate in what he says is a question for the jury. His evidence cannot be assessed by the judge first, only allowing it to go before the jury if he is satisfied that the witness is telling the truth. But there is authority that the accuracy of a recording is relevant to its admissibility as well as to its weight as evidence.

Both *Senat* (1968) 52 Cr App R 282 and *Maqsud Ali* [1966] 1 QB 688 hold that an original tape recording of a conversation is admissible, although it was said in the latter case that if the recording is so bad that it was inherently unreliable the trial judge would be entitled to refuse to allow it to go to the jury. The point made was that the trial judge must not allow the jury to waste time considering evidence which is so unclear that it cannot help either prosecution or defence, and this is not a point peculiar to recordings. The position of a very unclear recording is akin to that of a very unsure witness. The judge is entitled to direct the jury not to give the witness's evidence any weight, but he has an advantage with a recording that he is able to hear it first without usurping the function of the jury and may rule that its admission in evidence would not help the jury in its deliberations.

In *Stevenson* [1971] 1 WLR 1 Kilner Brown J held that tape recordings had to be proved to be genuine before they were admissible, but he did not say what standard of proof was required. There are two arguments about the standard of proof of genuineness. On the one hand it is said that normal standard of proof rules should be applied. This would mean that the prosecution in a criminal case would have to prove genuineness beyond reasonable doubt, whereas the defence would be allowed to use any recording unless the Crown proves to the same standard that it is not genuine. And in civil cases the party adducing the recording would have to prove its genuineness on the balance of probabilities. On the other hand it is argued that there need only be prima facie evidence of genuineness, and if any party wishes to say that the recording is not genuine, that is an argument about the weight which should be attached to the evidence and is a question for the tribunal of fact.

Shaw J was invited by counsel in *Robson* [1972] 1 WLR 651 to consider a tape recording and to rule whether, on the balance of probabilities, it was genuine. He did so, but in his ruling expressed the view that where there was prima facie evidence of genuineness, the recording should be left to the jury. This is the same test as was applied in *Maqsud Ali* and amounts to no more than a power in the trial judge to prevent evidence from being called if its probative value is extremely limited.

It can be doubted whether there is good reason for allowing the judge even this limited power where the challenge to evidence is that it has been deliberately fabricated. We have seen in chapter 6 that the Privy Council in *Ajodha* v *The State* [1982] AC 204 held that a defence argument that a confession put forward by the prosecution is the invention of the police is a matter for the jury alone and raises no point of admissibility. The case can be criticised on the ground given in part 1 of chapter 6, that it fails to allow a challenge to admissibility as well as a challenge to genuineness, but the general principle is undoubtedly correct. The trial judge could probably not be criticised for excluding an alleged confession where it is clear even to an amateur lexicographer that the defendant's signature at the foot of the confession is a forgery. But no case has held that he is entitled to do so, and if he must leave the genuineness of the 'confession' to the jury, he should also have to leave the genuineness of an audio or video recording to the jury.

There is no difference between audio tapes, video tapes and photographs in that they may all be recordings of facts – for example, what was said in interview, what happened on a bank robbery, what was said in a conversation. Equally, evidence from a machine or computer is admissible where the machine or computer does no more than record information. For example, photographs of radar recordings were admitted in *The Statue of Liberty* [1968] 1 WLR 739 to prove the positions of two ships at various times before they collided. Similarly the print-out from a computer which performed calculations was admissible in *Wood* (1982) 76 CR App R 23 to prove the chemical composition of metals, and a print-out from a breath testing machine was allowed as evidence of the amount of alcohol in a driver's breath in *Castle* v *Cross* [1984] 1 WLR 1372. There is no distinction between the evidence called in these cases and a tape recording because all that the machines did is to record facts.

If the court sees or hears a genuine recording of an event the judge or jury is being placed in the position of a witness because they actually see what happened. Other people who saw or heard the recording are actually treated as witnesses and may give evidence of what they saw or heard, and this evidence is admissible in the same way that evidence from a true eye-witness is admissible: *Taylor* v *Chief Constable of Cheshire* [1987] 1 WLR 1479.

Where the fact which is recorded is a person's statement, and a party to a case wishes to prove the truth of that statement, the mechanical or computer print-out is hearsay evidence and is subject to the technical rules of s5 the Civil Evidence Act 1968 or s69 of the Police and Criminal Evidence Act 1984. But those complex statutory provisions apply only to hearsay evidence.

Exhibits

In a murder trial the jury may feel aggrieved if they do not have produced before them the knife or cudgel with which the victim was put to death. And in an armed robbery case the gun, balaclava helmets and swag bags add to the fullness of the picture which is painted. But cases where the jury are shown an item involved with crime for anything other than illustrative reasons are rare.

Strictly speaking an item of property may only be exhibited in court if someone is able to give evidence and identify it as the item which he found or saw. But this is just an example of the general rule that no party may put any evidence before the court unless he is able to prove it. As with documents, exhibits can be admitted by agreement. For example, a sketch plan may be drawn to show the lay-out of a pub in which a fight took place. If the drawing is accepted by all parties as accurate, or at least as sufficiently accurate for the purposes of the case, it may be used even if the maker of it does not give evidence.

The purpose of exhibits in criminal cases is to bring the case to life for the jury, and also to allow the jury to assess the strength of the witnesses' evidence. For example, if the defendant is accused of brandishing an iron bar in the course of an affray the jury would be entitled to take the iron bar with them when they retire and see if they can wave it about in the manner alleged. All deliberations in the jury room are secret and no one really knows what use juries make of exhibits, but they are often specifically invited to experiment with the exhibits to see if the prosecution allegations are capable of being true, and it is always likely that they would take up the invitation. Memory refreshing notes which have become exhibits are to be used in very much the same way. The jury should look at the note and ask whether it undermines or supports the credibility of the witness.

There is a difference between memory refreshing notes and other exhibits. The note is not evidence of the truth of its contents and may only be used by the jury in deciding whether the witness whose note it is was consistent and believable: *Virgo* (1978) 67 Cr App R 323. In contrast, an exhibit when examined by the jury will say nothing about the consistency and reliability of the witness, but may say a lot about the truth of the story he has told. To go back to the example of the allegation that the defendant waved an iron bar: if the jury try to wave it in the manner alleged and find this physically impossible, they are not likely to say that undermines the credibility of the prosecution witness. Rather they will say that it shows that the story he told is not true. As was suggested when we examined s1(f) of the Criminal Evidence Act 1898, it may just be a matter of words to distinguish between challenging a witness's evidence by showing him to be unreliable and challenging his evidence by showing the story he tells to be unreliable. But the different uses the jury may make of a memory refreshing note and the iron bar demonstrate that in law such a distinction is recognised.

It has been suggested that the demeanour of a witness when testifying is real evidence from which the jury may draw inferences. Undoubtedly a witness who gives the appearance of being entirely honest is likely to be believed more readily than a witness who is shifty and seems to have no confidence in the story he tells. The jury cannot ignore his demeanour, but it is doubtful whether it is a separate aspect of the case from his oral evidence in the way that a memory refreshing note is separate from the evidence of the witness who relied on it. It is therefore not real evidence but an integral part of his oral evidence.

A tape recording of a police interview with a defendant is primary evidence, which when produced at trial becomes an exhibit and, if the jury wish to hear it rather than to rely on the written transcript, there is no reason why they should not be allowed to do so. However, the jury should be brought back for the tape to be heard in open court (*R* v *Riaz* [1992] Crim LR 366), although they may be allowed to hear it again, in the jury room, if it has been played in open court and there is an agreed transcript of it: *R* v *Tonge* (1993) The Times 16 April.

By virtue of orders made under s60(1) of the Police and Criminal Evidence Act 1984, in specified areas interviews held by police officers at police stations are required to be tape-recorded where a person is suspected, with certain exclusions, of the commission of an indictable offence.

Views

In both civil and criminal cases it is sometimes necessary for the judge or judge and jury to visit the scene of events, sometimes known as the locus in quo. Such visits are called views. A view is similar to an exhibit in many ways because it gives an opportunity for the tribunal of fact to compare what it experiences itself with what the witnesses have said. But views, like many exhibits, are not relevant to credibility, but to the truth of the evidence given. For example, the policeman who says that the defendant waved the iron bar may give evidence that he was standing in a particular place and the defendant in another place when the bar was wielded. If the jury visits the scene and stands where the policeman said he was, they may discover that it is impossible to see the spot where the accused was alleged to be.

Views are not very common and are reserved for cases where the full picture cannot be told by words alone. They are of two types, views with witnesses and views without witnesses. Whether it is necessary for the witnesses to go to the scene with the jury depends entirely upon the reason for the view. If the reason is to enable the jury to have in their minds a general picture of the scene they will be taken to the scene and invited to look around, but their attention will not be drawn to any particular aspect of it. If, on the other hand, the purpose of the view is to enable the witness to explain himself better than he could by words alone or by reference to a sketch plan or photograph, then evidence may be given by the witness during the view. He may, for example, point out where he was standing and the jury may be invited to stand on that spot in order to appreciate what the witness could or could not have seen. Alternatively he may wish to point out where he found something and the jury would bear this in mind when deciding how the item got there in the first place. The range of possible reasons for having a view is enormous and because of this the law does not limit the uses to which views may be put. It does, however, provide that the view is carried out in a manner which is fair and unlikely to be misleading.

For example, in *Tameshwar* v *R* [1957] AC 476 the Privy Council held that the judge must accompany the jury and lawyers on any view. The failure of the judge to do so in *Hunter* [1985] 1 WLR 613 was a good ground of appeal and *Tameshwar* v *R* was followed by the Court of Appeal. *Tameshwar* v *R* also makes clear that there is nothing wrong with witnesses pointing out relevant places or giving demonstrations while on a view but the witness must be on oath and what he says or does must be in the presence of all members of the jury.

Views are permissible in civil actions heard by judge alone as well as in jury trials. RSC O.38 r.8 and CCR O.21 r.6 both specifically state that the judge 'may inspect any place or thing to which any question arises in the proceedings' and that any jury may also attend. Although the Rules say the judge 'may authorise the jury to inspect' it is clear that the jury should accompany the judge on any view because they are the tribunal of fact and the judge is not able to give evidence to them of what he saw.

In *Salsbury* v *Woodland* [1970] 1 QB 324 the trial judge made a private visit to the place where the plaintiff claimed to have been injured by the defendant's negligence. The Court of Appeal said, obiter, that the parties should be notified of the judge's intention to make such a visit and that he ought not to go alone unless all parties consent. The fear of the court was that the place might have changed since the time in issue and it would be unfortunate if the judge drew an erroneous conclusion from what he saw. Undoubtedly there are many criminal cases where individual jury members take it upon themselves to visit the scene of the alleged crime. This would not be a ground for disqualifying them as jurors any more than someone who knew the scene well would be disqualified. The position of magistrates is different. *Parry* v *Boyle* (1986) 83 Cr App R 310 holds that they should only hold a view if the parties are invited to attend – private visits should not take place. *Salsbury* v *Woodland* was applied. The purpose of the decision in *Parry* v *Boyle* is to ensure that the justices do not visit the locus in quo with a view to gathering evidence unless the parties have the opportunity to see what evidence is being gained. But the case does not sit easily with *Ingram* v *Percival* [1969] 1 QB 548 (see Chapter 3) in which it was said that justices should take into account their personal knowledge of whether certain waters in which the defendant had fished were tidal. If they can rely on knowledge of the locality gained in the course of their ordinary lives, why should they not visit the locality privately during the course of the hearing? Had they made a private visit for purposes unconnected with the case the day before the hearing they would be entitled to rely on the knowledge gained.

There is an argument that a view is not real evidence but is simply a means of ensuring that the judge or jury properly understands what witnesses are saying. The authorities, however, are clear in treating views as evidence, so that the court may reach a conclusion from the view which is inconsistent with the oral evidence it has heard. In *Buckingham* v *Daily News Ltd* [1956] 2 QB 534 the plaintiff claimed to have been injured by the negligence of his employer. The trial judge was shown the machine on which the plaintiff worked and formed his own opinion that the evidence of the plaintiff was unreliable. The Court of Appeal held that the judge was entitled to form an opinion about the case from what he saw on the view and that he was also entitled to prefer that opinion to evidence which he heard. The view was evidence as was what was said in the witness box, and it was for the trial judge to decide what evidence he found reliable. A dictum of Denning LJ in *Goold* v *Evans & Co* [1951] 2 TLR 1189 that a view was evidence was accepted as being correct.

Whether the judge or jury is entitled to disbelieve a witness because of what has been seen on a view is a question of fact in each case. Some views are like some exhibits and take place purely in order to give a full picture. For example, in a murder case the knife which was used to kill the deceased may be an exhibit even though the defence accepts that it caused death and merely denies that the defendant was the killer. The picture is fuller if the jury see the knife. But they would not be entitled to entertain doubts about the cause of death by comparing the knife to the evidence they heard of the stab wounds. The cause of death would not be in issue. Similarly, in the same case the jury may be taken to the place of stabbing in order to see where the body was found. The purpose of the view may be simply to illustrate and bring to life the evidence they heard about the killing, but it would not entitle them to draw any conclusions about the cause of death or the identity of the murderer. A view such as that is not really evidence because it does not prove anything. But the vast majority of views are held in order to allow the judge or jury to assess who is telling the truth about what happened. They may reach their own conclusion on the basis of everything they see at the view and hear from the witness box. The view is therefore evidence.

13

Estoppel and Previous Judgments

13.1 Admissibility at common law

13.2 Admitted as evidence of its facts against parties to it

13.3 Section 11 Civil Evidence Act 1968

13.4 Sections 74 and 75 Police and Criminal Evidence Act 1984

13.1 Admissibility at common law

General rule

A previous judgment is inadmissible as evidence of the truth of its contents against strangers to that judgment because it amounts to nothing more than hearsay. It is a statement, tendered for the purpose of proof of the facts contained in it, which was made outside court. Moreover, a previous judgment amounts to nothing more than an opinion by the court and as such is irrelevant. The rule on the admissibility of previous judgments is found in *Hollington* v *Hewthorn* [1943] KB 587. The case involved a collision between two cars. The plaintiff alleged that the collision arose as a result of the negligence of the defendant and wished to put in evidence the fact of the defendant having been convicted of careless driving at the time. Goddard LJ said:

> 'Is (the previous judgment) relevant to an issue (before the court)? ... The record of conviction itself would show no more than that the defendant was convicted for so driving on a certain day ... the conviction is only proof that another court considered that D was guilty of careless driving and no more than (that) ... A judgment obtained by A against B ought not to be evidence against C ... (because) it would be unjust to bind any person who could not be admitted to make a defence or examine a witness, or appeal from a judgment he might think erroneous, and therefore the judgment of the court upon facts found, although evidence against the parties and all claiming under them, are not in general to be used to the prejudice of strangers.'

Some exceptional feature is needed before it will be considered relevant (and therefore admissible) to give evidence of what happened in earlier cases arising out of the same transaction: *Hui Chi-ming* v *R* [1991] 3 All ER 897. In that case the Privy Council held that, at the trial of an accomplice for murder, the judge had rightly excluded evidence of the principal offender's acquittal of murder and conviction of manslaughter. In *Arab Monetary Fund* v *Hashim (No 2)* [1990] 1 All ER 673, an affidavit in support of a Mareva application referred to earlier criminal proceedings and Hoffmann J refused to order the deletion of these references as they were part of the narrative explaining what had happened.

Goddard LJ's words in *Hollington* v *Hewthorn*, above, are true not only of convictions, but also of judgments in civil actions. If given between the same parties they are conclusive but not against anyone else who was not a party. A judgment is however conclusive as against all persons of the existence of the state of things which it actually affects when the existence of that state is a fact in issue. If A sues B alleging that owing to B's negligence he has been held liable to pay a sum to C, the judgment obtained by C is conclusive as to the amount of damages that A has had to pay to C, but it is not evidence that B was negligent: see *Green* v *New River Co* (1792) 4 TR 589. It is clear from this case that the admissibility of a previous judgment as proof of its contents is objected to on the following grounds: first, it amounts to nothing more than opinion; secondly, it is hearsay, and thirdly, if admissible against a party to subsequent proceedings who was a stranger to the original proceedings, he would be bound by it, having had no opportunity himself to construct a defence or examine witnesses or even appeal. Thus the maxim, 'res inter alios acta nocere non debet', applies to prevent such prejudice.

Applying *Hollington* v *Hewthorn*, but stressing that his was not a technical decision based on outdated rules of evidence, in *Land Securities plc* v *Westminster City Council* [1993] 4 All ER 124 Hoffman J held that an arbitrator's award determining the market rent of a property is inadmissible in evidence in another rent review arbitration relating to a comparable property.

Admitted as evidence of effect

These objections are groundless where the judgment is tendered not for the purpose of showing the truth of its contents but to show that it exists as a judgment and the state of things which it actually affects as a judgment.

Thus, there is no objection to the admissibility of a previous judgment where all that is sought to be shown by its admissibility are the formal parts of the judgment.

13.2 Admitted as evidence of its facts against parties to it

Admissibility

Where the party to the present action was also party to the previous action then there is no justification for refusing the admissibility of a previous judgment on the grounds of unfairness to strangers. The application of this principle is seen particularly well in civil cases but it is a matter of some contention as to whether it applies similarly to criminal cases.

Admissibility is justified where the parties to the previous action are parties to the present action or where parties to a present action have a relationship of privity with parties in a previous action. In the latter case the effects of a relationship of privity, for example between an heir and his ancestor or between testator and executor, is to put the subsequent party in the same position as though he himself had been a party to the original proceedings. If previous judgments could not be put in evidence in such cases then the principle of 'res judicata pro veritate accipitur' (a thing adjudicated upon is received as the truth) would have no meaning and parties would be able to re-litigate their issue if dissatisfied with the original decision.

An estoppel arising from a previous judgment will only operate where it is specifically pleaded by the party seeking to rely on it. Otherwise, he will be taken to have waived it: *Vooght* v *Winch* (1819) 2 B & Ald 662.

Cause of action estoppel

It is in fact inaccurate to talk of a previous judgment being admitted in a subsequent case where the parties to both proceedings are identical. In fact the effect of the previous judgment lies in the fact that the parties to a civil action are estopped from re-litigating the same cause of action. This is known as 'estoppel per rem judicatam'.

In *Conqueror* v *Boot* [1928] 2 KB 336, the plaintiff had obtained judgment against a workman for breach of warranty in failing to build a house in a workmanlike manner. He could not then bring a separate claim for breach of warranty in an attempt to claim further loss. The plea of res judicata applied to estop the plaintiff from asserting the subsequent action.

The doctrine of res judicata does not apply in affiliation proceedings: *Hager* v *Osborne* [1992] 2 All ER 494 where Ward J held that paternity cases involving previously inconclusive blood tests could be reopened to take advantage of new DNA genetic fingerprinting methods.

However, the doctrine is applicable in personal injury litigation: *Talbot* v *Berkshire County Council* [1993] 4 All ER 9. In that case Stuart-Smith LJ summed up the position as follows: A was a passenger in a car driven by B which was in a collision caused partly by the fault of B and partly by the fault of C, the local authority responsible for the maintenance of the highway. A and B were both injured. A sued B for damages and B, by his solicitors, issued third party proceedings against C claiming contribution to A's claim, but no claim for B's injuries was made. A joined C as a defendant in the claim. Judgment was given in A's favour against both B and C who were each held partly to blame. Could B subsequently bring a fresh action against C in respect of his injuries? Applying the rule in *Henderson* v *Henderson* (1843) 3 Hare 100, the answer was in the negative and there were not here any special circumstances which took the case outside the general operation of that rule. On the other hand, in *Duchess Theatre Co Ltd* v *Lord* (1993) The Times 9 December Balcombe LJ said that it would be an unwarranted extension of the principle in *Henderson* v *Henderson* to hold that it barred a claim for payment under a guarantee which had not been called in at the date of the original judgment.

Issue estoppel

If the subsequent cause of action is not identical but raises issues already decided upon in the course of the previous judgment, then the parties to the subsequent action are estopped from challenging the previous determination of those issues.

> 'The rule is, that once an issue has been raised and distinctly determined between the parties then as a general rule neither party can be allowed to fight that issue all over again.' – Lord Denning MR in *Fidelis Shipping Co* v *v/o Exportschleb* [1966] 1 QB 630.

The estoppel is known as issue estoppel and it operates to prevent parties to actions asserting, as elements of their case, matters previously asserted and decided upon by the court in a previous case to which they were parties. In *Mills* v *Cooper* [1967] 2 QB 459, Lord Diplock seems to suggest that the previous determination of an issue can be challenged where fresh evidence has become available to do so. While fresh evidence may support an appeal against a previous decision, it is difficult to see how it could permit a party to subsequent proceedings effectively to ignore a previous decision.

In *Sambasivam* v *Public Prosecutor* [1950] AC 458, the Judicial Committee said that the doctrine of res judicata applied equally to civil and criminal cases: a person acquitted cannot be tried again for the same offence, the verdict is binding and conclusive on all subsequent proceedings. In *Hogan* [1974] QB 398, D was convicted of grievous bodily harm with intent, to which he pleaded self defence. When the victim of the attack died he was charged with murder. The court held that he was estopped from denying either the infliction of the grievous bodily harm or the self-defence. Despite this case it is uncertain that issue estoppel has actually survived the decision in *DPP* v *Humphreys* [1967] AC 1, to continue in criminal cases. The House of Lords had there stated most emphatically that the doctrine did not apply to criminal cases.

It is important to note that estoppel per rem judicatem only operates where the parties litigating in both cases are the same, or the parties in the subsequent cases are the privies of those in the previous case. The parties must also be acting in the same capacity in both cases. In *Townsend* v *Bishop* [1939] 1 All ER 805, the plaintiff was driving his father's car when he was in collision with a lorry. He sued the lorry driver for the damage to the car. The defendant successfully raised the plea of contributory negligence, which provided a complete defence at the time, against the plaintiff, who was said to be acting as the agent of his father. The plaintiff subsequently brought an action for personal injuries. He was able to deny that he had been contributorily negligent. He was not estopped from denying the previous finding of contributory negligence because the parties to the two actions were different.

In *McIlkenney* v *Chief Constable of West Midlands Police Force* [1980] 1 QB 283, Lord Denning took a particularly narrow and arguably mistaken view of what was meant by identity of parties. He said that the plaintiffs were estopped from alleging assaults by police officers. This matter had been raised at a previous criminal trial and dispensed with on the voire dire. The civil action was between the Chief Constable of the police force in question and one of the defendants in the criminal action. Lord Denning was clearly mistaken to equate the prosecution with the defendant – the Chief Constable in the civil action and the defendant in the criminal case – with the plaintiffs in the civil action. They could not be treated as identical parties nor was there any privity between them.

The party to the present action will only be estopped from re-litigating or raising issues already determined upon, if he litigates in the same capacity in both actions. If he acts in person in one action, and in a representative capacity in the other, no estoppel will arise. In *Marginson* v *Blackburn Borough Council* [1939] 2 KB 426, Mrs M was killed when a car driven by her in which her husband was a passenger collided with a bus, driven by a council employee. Mr M brought an action for personal injuries. He also sued as personal representative of his wife. A previous action had been brought against Mr M and the council by the owners of the houses damaged in the collision on the basis of their vicarious liability for the accident and for which they were both held to be equally negligent. In the present action Mr M could not deny that his wife was negligent in the claim brought personally by him. However, no estoppel could be made against him in his representative capacity because he was acting in a different capacity from that which he had assumed in the first action.

Not only is it necessary for the parties and their capacities to have been the same, but the issues raised in the subsequent case must be identical to those raised in the previous action; and the previous action must have resulted in a final determination of those issues. The requirement of identity of issues can be viewed in two ways. On the one hand it could be said to require that every single fact and issue raised in the previous case must be identically reproduced in the instant case for an estoppel to arise. For the purpose of determining whether or not there is identity of issues, the judge is able to look at the judgment of the previous case, the arguments of counsel and the pleadings.

In *Re Manly's Will Trust (No 2)* [1976] 1 All ER 673 no estoppel arose regarding the entitlement to certain property of a testator, even though the matter had been determined in previous proceedings as a matter of construction. The present proceedings related to different property, and even though the question of construction was identical, there was no estoppel because the subject-matter of the issue was different.

Such an approach is clearly conducive to proliferation of litigation when it is inflexibly applied. A wider approach was preferred by the court in *Hoystead* v *Commissioner of Taxation* [1926] AC 155, where an estoppel arose on a point of revenue law which had been decided in a previous tax year against the Revenue. The tax commissioner could not raise the same point in a subsequent tax year. This case exemplifies a common-sense approach in that it has regard not to the minutiae of each respective claim in the separate proceedings, but only as to whether the essence or substance of what was previously asserted or adjudicated upon is being re-asserted.

In negligence cases there is a similar conflict of approach. A broad approach as expounded in *Hoystead* would advocate nothing more than substantial similarity of essential issues without identity in peripheral issues. In *Bell* v *Holmes* [1956] 3 All ER 449, Bell sued Holmes for personal injuries incurred by him in a car collision in which Holmes' car collided with his taxi cab. In a previous case both Holmes and Bell had been sued in negligence by a passenger in the car who had sustained injury. Bell was five-sixths liable and Holmes was one-sixth liable. In the present action brought by Bell against Holmes, Bell was estopped from denying that he was five-sixths responsible for the collision.

This broad approach found favour in the case of *Black* v *Mount and Hancock* [1968] SASR 167, where Chamberlain J said.

'The duties of care of each driver owed to the passengers, the breach of those duties, and the extent of their responsibility for the damage, depended on precisely identical facts in each case.'

In *Wall* v *Radford* [1991] 2 All ER 741, following *Bell* v *Holmes*, Popplewell J decided that once liability in a road traffic accident had been apportioned by a passenger suing both drivers, it was not open to one of the drivers relying on the same facts subsequently to argue in her suit against the other driver that that apportionment should be altered. Indeed, his Lordship said that it would have been an affront to justice to have allowed the plaintiff, who had had her liability for the collision already determined, to seek by a separate action to re-litigate it.

In *Randolph* v *Tuck* [1962] 1 QB 175, however, the court were not prepared to adopt the broad approach suggested by, inter alia, *Bell* v *Holmes*. The issues determined in the first case involving a car collision concerned Tuck's liability for the collision, whereas the issue being disputed in the second case was the liability of third parties to the plaintiff, in the same collision. As yet it is unresolved by a higher court which approach is to be followed.

The question of issue estoppel arose in *North West Water Ltd* v *Binnie & Partners* [1990] 3 All ER 547. A water authority (the present plaintiffs) engaged consultant engineers (the present defendants) to design and supervise the construction of a water tunnel and pumping system. After completion of the work an explosion occurred and the victims sued the plaintiffs, the defendants and the contractors. On appeal, it was decided that the defendants were wholly to blame. The plaintiffs now sued the defendants in respect of damages caused to the tunnel system and, by way of defence, the defendants denied negligence. Drake J decided that this defence would be struck out as the issue of negligence had already been determined in the first action. His Lordship said:

'I think that great caution must be exercised before shutting out a party from putting forward his case on the grounds of issue estoppel ... Before doing so the court should be quite satisfied that there is no real or practical difference between the issues to be litigated in the new action and that already decided, and the evidence which may properly be called on those issues in the new action ... in the present case no such real or practical difference does exist ... Even if I am wrong about the limits to issue estoppel and the true limit is in fact the narrower one, that is to say that favoured by Goff LJ in *McIlkenny* v *Chief Constable of West Midlands Police Force* [1980] 1 QB 283 and Lord Diplock on the appeal to the House of Lords ([1982] AC 529), I would still hold that Binnies are in this case caught by issue estoppel. This is because I find that the issues arising in the present action have already been decided and that in practical terms they have been decided between the same parties, the water authority and Binnies.'

Final determination

The previous cause of action and issues contained in it may only give rise to an estoppel where the decision of the previous court was final. The previous action must not have been stayed, withdrawn, dismissed or discontinued.

The finality of the judgment is not affected by the fact of there being an appeal against it, although where the judgment in question has been given by an inferior court then it will operate to create an estoppel only if an appeal is capable of being made against it, even though no appeal is in fact being made. Providing that the judgment is in itself a final determination of the issues, it is irrelevant that it was obtained by default or the hearing upon which it was given was in itself interlocutory: see, eg, *R* v *Governor of Brixton Prison, ex parte Osman (No 1)* [1992] 1 All ER 108 (court's refusal to grant discovery a final decision).

A judgment by consent is a final decision for these purposes because it leaves nothing to be judicially determined or ascertained thereafter in order to render it effective: *Palmer* v *Durnford Ford* [1992] 2 All ER 122; but see *Walpole* v *Partridge & Wilson* [1994] 1 All ER 385.

Estoppel may arise from a decision of commons commissioners (*Crown Estates Commissioners* v *Dorset County Council* [1990] 2 WLR 89) or a planning decision (*Thrasyvoulou* v *Secretary of State for the Environment* [1990] 2 WLR 1), but not if the earlier decision was plainly wrong (*Arnold* v *National Westminster Bank plc* [1991] 3 All ER 41.

Where an action is dismissed solely because the court lacks jurisdiction there is no decision on the matter in dispute estopping an action in a court which does have jurisdiction: *Hines* v *Birkbeck College (No 2)* [1991] 4 All ER 450.

As to when proceedings in England may be barred under the common law principle of former recovery under a foreign judgment, see *Black* v *Yates* [1991] 4 All ER 722.

318 Estoppel and Previous Judgments

13.3 Section 11 Civil Evidence Act 1968

The new rule

Section 11 of the Civil Evidence Act 1968 provides for the statutory admissibility of previous convictions in subsequent civil actions and it has by its wording the effect of shifting the burden of proof from the plaintiff to the defendant. Where the previous conviction is in itself an issue central to the success of the civil case, then the burden of proof shifted to the defendant will be the legal burden.

Where an attempt is made to put a conviction in evidence in civil proceedings, RSC Ord 18 r7(A) must be complied with. This provides:

'(1) If in any action which is to be tried with pleadings any party intends, in reliance on s11 of the Civil Evidence Act 1968 ... to adduce evidence that a person was convicted of an offence by or before a court in the UK or by a court martial, there or elsewhere, he must include in his pleading a statement of intention with particulars of –
a) the conviction and the date thereof;
b) the court or court martial which made the conviction;
c) the issue in the proceedings to which the conviction is relevant.'

A 'subsisting' conviction for the purposes of s11(1) was discussed in *Re Raphael* [1973] 1 WLR 998 and held to exclude an existing conviction which was likely to be quashed on appeal. Goulding J said:

'... Having considered the Act of 1968 it does not seem to me that I can disregard the pending appeal even though the conviction is a subsisting one for the purposes of the Act. Parliament cannot have intended that civil proceeding should be finally disposed of in reliance on a conviction subsequently liable to be quashed.'

If an attempt is made to put in evidence a conviction pending appeal, then the subsequent proceedings would need to be adjourned until after the determination of the appeal, or the proceedings could continue but the plaintiff would be unable to rely on the previous conviction. While the purpose of s11(1) is to admit previous convictions, it will not admit previous acquittals. A previous acquittal is irrelevant for the purposes of the subsequent proceedings.

Shifting the burden

The evidential effect of admission of a previous conviction under s11(1) is found in s11(2). It is clear that s11(2) reverses the burden of proof, and any failure to consider the effect of s11 on the burden will lead to the decision in the case being reversed on appeal: *Wauchope* v *Mordecai* [1970] 1 WLR 317. Given that the burden of proof is reversed, it is not altogether clear what standard of proof is then imposed on the defendant. In the interests of consistency he should bear the burden of disproving the fact on the balance of probabilities. However, there is authority to suggest the existence of a higher standard, that of beyond a reasonable doubt.

The matter was discussed by Lord Denning MR in *Stupple* v *Royal Insurance* [1971] 1 QB 50. He said:

> 'I think that the conviction does not merely shift the burden of proof. It is a weighty piece of evidence of itself ... the weight to be given to a previous conviction is essentially for the judge at the civil trial. Just as he has to evaluate the oral evidence of a witness so he should evaluate the probative force of a conviction: at the end of the civil case the judge must ask himself whether the defendant has succeeded in overthrowing the conviction. If not, the conviction stands and proves the case.'

Lord Denning seems to be suggesting that the effect of adducing a previous conviction is to impose on the defendant a burden of proof which is higher than proof on the balance of probabilities. In this respect his judgment was inconsistent with those of other judges in the same case. Buckley LJ said:

> 'Although the section has made proof of conviction admissible and has given proof of conviction a particular statutory effect under s11(2)(a), it remains, I think, ... true ... that mere proof of conviction proves nothing relevant to the plaintiff's claim, and it cannot be intended to shut out or ... mitigate the effect of any evidence tending to show that the convicted person did not commit the offence ... Proof under this section gives rise to the statutory presumption laid down in s11(2)(a) which, like any other presumption, will give way to evidence establishing the contrary, on the balance of probability, without itself affording any evidential weight to be taken into account in determining whether that onus has been discharged.'

In *Taylor* v *Taylor* [1970] 1 WLR 1148 CA, a wife petitioned for divorce on the grounds of her husband's adultery and admitted evidence of his conviction for incest. The court found that the husband had discharged the burden imposed on him by s11 and gave the decree nisi on the grounds of the wife's adultery. Davies LJ said on appeal that:

> 'Section 11 deals with the effect of convictions and means that the onus of proof of upsetting the previous conviction is on the person who seeks to do so, that is an onus of proof on the balance of probabilities. But, having said that, it nevertheless is obvious that when a man has been convicted by 12 of his fellow countrymen and countrywomen at a criminal trial, the verdict of the jury is a matter which is entitled to very great weight when the convicted person is seeking, in the words of the statute, "to prove the contrary".'

13.4 Sections 74 and 75 Police and Criminal Evidence Act 1984

The background

In 1972, the Criminal Law Revision Committee's 11th Report recommended the abolition of the rule in *Hollington* v *Hewthorn* [1943] KB 587 for criminal proceedings, it having been abolished for civil proceedings by s11 of the Civil Evidence Act 1968. The effect of the rule was that where a person was convicted of a criminal offence, this would be admissible to prove that he had in fact committed the offence, in subsequent criminal proceedings. In *Spinks* [1982] 1 All ER 587 the defendant was convicted of assisting in a stabbing in which he had hidden the weapon.

On a charge of impeding arrest, it was not possible to admit in evidence the confession of the accused who had been convicted of the complete offence, since this was merely hearsay against his co-accused. Nor was it possible to bring in evidence of the conviction because of the rule in *Hollington* v *Hewthorn*. As a result the conviction of the defendant was quashed.

The common law rule in *Hollington* v *Hewthorn* has now been substantially abrogated for criminal proceedings by virtue of ss74 and 75 of the Police and Criminal Evidence Act 1984, giving effect to the recommendations of the Criminal Law Revision Committee and allowing a previous conviction to be used as evidence in subsequent proceedings. It is important to distinguish at this stage between establishing before the court, as a fact, that a person has been convicted of an offence in previous proceedings, and, using the fact of the conviction as evidence in support of the charges against the accused in subsequent proceedings. Whereas ss74 and 75 now allow previous convictions to be used as evidence in subsequent proceedings, it is s73 which provides the method of proving such a conviction.

Previous convictions: sections 74 and 75

Section 74(1) of the Act provides that the fact that a person other than the accused has been convicted of an offence by or before any court in the UK is admissible in evidence for the purpose of proving, where to do so is relevant to any issue in those proceedings, that that person committed that offence, whether or not any other evidence of his having committed that offence is given.

This applies to criminal proceedings as defined by s82(1) of the Act and so includes courts martial and standing civilian courts.

The conviction which is sought to be relied upon must be that of someone other than the accused. This will be admitted to show that that person committed that offence. Thus a conviction for theft by A would be admissible on a subsequent charge of handling by B. On the other hand, the guilty pleas of a defendant's co-accused will not be admitted for the sole purpose of explaining to the jury why the co-accused are not on trial with the defendant: *R* v *Hall* (1993) The Times 5 March. The previous convictions of the accused are generally inadmissible since they are not probative of guilt. However, in circumstances where they become admissible, either because they constitute similar fact evidence or because the accused has lost the protection of s1(f) of the Criminal Evidence Act 1898, their admission will not be prejudiced by the provisions of s74(1) which would apparently allow only for the admission of convictions of others. Section 74(4)(a) specifically preserves the admissibility of any conviction which would be admissible quite apart from s74(1). It is therefore designed to encompass admissibility of previous convictions in the situations outlined above. It would also cover the power of the cross-examiner to question and prove previous convictions under s6 of the Criminal Procedure Act 1865, as an exception to the rule of finality of answers on collateral issues.

Where evidence is admissible under s74(4) that the accused has committed an offence and such evidence is admitted as probative of guilt, then the fact of the conviction will be evidence that he committed the offence: s74(3). Section 74(3) states that he will only be taken to have committed the offence once he is proved to have been convicted, unless the contrary is proved. This presumably means that the accused is subject to the burden of establishing on a balance of probabilities that he did not commit the offence.

If the fact of a conviction before a UK court is to be admitted in evidence to prove that the person convicted actually committed the offence then the conviction must be a subsisting one. Section 75(4) provides that nothing in s74 above shall be construed as rendering admissible in any proceedings evidence of any conviction other than a subsisting one.

This would therefore apparently exclude the admission of convictions which are quashed on appeal or for which there has been a royal pardon. However, this would seem unlikely in the light of *Foster* [1985] QB 115 where the Court of Appeal held that a pardon did not eradicate the conviction itself but only the punishment which would normally result. Where a conviction is deemed to be 'spent' under the Rehabilitiation of Offenders Act 1974, it will still be a subsisting conviction for the purposes of s75(4) since that Act does not apply to criminal proceedings: s7. Details of spent convictions would remain admissible.

A conviction for which the court had given a conditional discharge or imposed a probation order would still be a conviction for the purpose of s74 notwithstanding s13 of the Powers of Criminal Courts Act 1973 which says to the contrary. Section 74 is not affected by the provision of the 1973 Act which would require such a conviction to be disregarded: s75(3)(a). Its admission is mandatory, not at the discretion of the trial judge, although it will have to be shown to be relevant to any issue in the proceedings.

The relevance of a previous conviction may only be apparent where the individual circumstances on which it is based are made known to the court. Section 75(1) allows these facts to be identified by means of either: the contents of any document which is admissible as evidence of the conviction, or the contents of the information, complaint, indictment or charge sheet on which the person in question was convicted.

Either the original or a duly authenticated copy of the document or the relevant part would be admissible under this section: s75(2). Section 75(1) operates without prejudice to other admissible evidence which may be given to the court regarding the facts of the conviction. Presumably then it would be possible to call oral evidence of the facts either instead of, or in addition to, the permitted documentation.

Once the fact of a previous conviction is admitted under s74(1) it will be evidence of the fact that the accused committed the offence unless he proves the contrary on a balance of probabilities: s74(2).

In *R* v *Boysen* [1991] Crim LR 274 the Court of Appeal said that in order to admit evidence of a co-accused's conviction (including plea of guilty) it was necessary to observe the following principles:

1. The conviction must be clearly relevant to an issue in the case.
2. Section 74 of the 1984 Act should be sparingly used.
3. The judge should consider the question of fairness under s78 of the Act and whether the probative value of the conviction outweighs its prejudicial value.
4. The judge must direct the jury clearly as to the issues to which the conviction is not relevant and also why the evidence is before them and to what issue it is directed.

Their Lordships also expressed disapproval of the growing practice of allowing evidence to go before a jury which is irrelevant, inadmissible, prejudicial or unfair simply because it is convenient for the jury to have 'the whole picture'.

In *R* v *Warner* (1993) 96 Cr App R 324 the Court of Appeal decided that a conviction of a third party is admissible in evidence under s74 of the 1984 Act for the purpose of proving, where to do so is relevant to any issue in the proceedings, that the third person had committed a particular offence. In that case the court concluded that the trial judge had been correct in deciding that the character of visitors to the defendants' premises, as demonstrated by their convictions of drug offences, was relevant to provide supporting evidence of the character of the transactions and of the purpose for which the defendants were letting the visitors into their house and, apparently, doing business with them. Accordingly the defendants' appeal against conviction of conspiracy to supply a controlled drug was dismissed, but the court stressed that great care was needed to analyse the issue to which evidence of the convictions was relevant and the purpose for which that evidence was adduced, before the court exercised its powers under s74 of the 1984 Act. See also *R* v *Rothwell* (1993) The Times 27 April where the Court of Appeal stressed that the admission of evidence under s74 is subject to the exercise of the court's discretion under s78(1) of the 1984 Act.

Method of proof

Section 73 repeals s13 of the Evidence Act 1851, s6 of the Criminal Procedure Act 1865 (in part) and s18 of the Prevention of Crime Act 1871: Schedule 7, Part IV, Police and Criminal Evidence Act 1984.

In any proceedings in which the fact of conviction or acquittal is admissible in evidence, it may be proved by production of a certificate of conviction or acquittal relating to the offence and by proof of the fact that the person who is named in the offence is the person whose conviction or acquittal is sought to be proved: s73(1).

This therefore dispenses with the need to call direct oral evidence of the previous conviction from someone with personal knowledge, which could be both costly and protracted. This method is, however, still available since s73(1) operates without prejudice to any other authorised manner of proving conviction or acquittal: s73(4). In particular, these are proof under s9 of the Criminal Justice Act 1967 by means of written statement, a written admission under s10 of that Act, and proof by fingerprints under s39 of the Criminal Justice Act 1948.

Section 73 would be relied upon where:

1. The existence of a previous conviction is relevant to a particular issue before the court, as under s27(3)(b) of the Theft Act 1968.
2. The accused is cross-examined about a previous conviction and he denies it, so that counsel is then entitled to prove it.
3. In any circumstances where the previous conviction of the accused becomes admissible but its accuracy is disputed. It would also assist the court in circumstances where the existence of a previous conviction became relevant on passing sentence.

Section 73(2) stipulates those matters which must be present in a certificate to obtain admissibility. Where there is conviction or acquittal on indictment:

1. It must be signed by the clerk of the court where the conviction or acquittal took place.
2. It must give the substance and effect of the indictment.
3. It must give the substance and effect of the conviction or acquittal: s73(2)(a).

Where there has been conviction or acquittal following summary trial then the following matters must be satisfied: a copy of the conviction or of the dismissal of the information must be signed by the clerk of the court where conviction or acquittal took place and signed by the clerk of the court to which a memorandum of the conviction or acquittal was sent where there has for example been a committal to the Crown Court for sentencing. References in s73(2) to the clerk of the court are to be understood as references to his deputy and anyone else having custody of the court record: s73(3).

There is a presumption to the effect that any duly signed certificate will be one of conviction or acquittal unless the contrary is proved on a balance of probabilities: s73(2). This proof will come from the accused where he is the subject of the certificate. He will be obliged to show that he is not the person to whom the certificate refers, nor was he convicted of the offence in question.

Index